SELF-REGULATION OF LEARNING AND PERFORMANCE
Issues and Educational Applications

SELF-REGULATION OF LEARNING AND PERFORMANCE
Issues and Educational Applications

Edited by

Dale H. Schunk
Purdue University

Barry J. Zimmerman
City University of New York

IEA LAWRENCE ERLBAUM ASSOCIATES, PUBLISHERS
1994   Hillsdale, New Jersey   Hove, UK

Lawrence Erlbaum Associates, Inc., Publishers
365 Broadway
Hillsdale, New Jersey, 07642

Library of Congress Cataloging-in-Publication Data
Self-regulation of learning and performance : issues and educational
  applications / edited by Dale H. Schunk, Barry J. Zimmerman.
      p.   cm.
  Includes bibliographical references and indexes.
  ISBN-0-8058-1334-9 (cloth : acid-free paper). — ISBN
0-8058-1335-7 (pbk. : acid-free paper).
  1. Motivation in education. 2. Academic achievement. 3. Self-
control. I. Schunk, Dale H. II. Zimmerman, Barry J.
  LB1065.S465 1994
  370.15′4—dc20   94-1517
                                                          CIP

Books published by Lawrence Erlbaum Associates are printed on acid-free
paper, and their bindings are chosen for strength and durability.

Printed in the United States of America
10 9 8 7 6 5 4 3

Contents

VI: CONCLUSION

Preface

In recent years educators have moved steadily away from explanations of learning and performance that stress learners' abilities and reinforcement of their responses to environmental stimuli and have become increasingly concerned with students' attempts to manage their achievement efforts through activities that influence the instigation, direction, and persistence of those efforts. These self-regulatory activities have become the focus of much systematic research.

Self-regulation refers to students' self-generated thoughts, feelings, and actions, which are systematically oriented toward attainment of their goals. Research on self-regulation has grown at an exponential pace since the publication of our earlier book, *Self-Regulated Learning and Academic Achievement: Theory, Research, and Practice* (Zimmerman & Schunk, 1989).[1] That volume introduced the topic by bringing together prominent individuals to discuss their unique theoretical perspectives and research on students' self-regulation of their learning, motivation, and achievement.

Despite this surge of research on student self-regulation, there remains considerable confusion over many issues, including what self-regulation is, how it differs from such related constructs as motivation and metacognition, and whether students can be taught self-regulatory skills. This volume addresses these issues and presents the fruits of the first genera-

---

[1] Zimmerman, B. J., & Schunk, D. H. (Eds.). (1989). *Self-regulated learning and academic achievement: Theory, research, and practice.* New York: Springer-Verlag.

tion of research on the topic. The contributors reveal an interesting, uplifting, and at times disturbing picture of how students grapple with the day-to-day problems of achieving in circumstances with inherent limitations and obstacles. The promise for investigating self-regulation is to understand the source of students' capabilities to surmount adversities—the origins of their self-initiated processes designed to improve learning, motivation, and achievement.

A primary contribution of this book is to present a conceptual framework for studying and applying self-regulation in educational contexts. In the first chapter, Zimmerman conceptualizes self-regulation as comprising four dimensions or areas in which students can self-regulate their activities: (a) motives for learning or performing, (b) methods used, (c) performance outcomes or target behaviors, and (d) environmental resources used. To be self-regulated it is not necessary that one exert control over all dimensions; such complete control would be rare in educational settings. Rather, these are four areas in which self-regulation is possible.

In addition to delineating a conceptual framework for self-regulation, this volume has three other objectives:

1. To present the latest theory and research findings on the role of students' self-regulation of their learning and skillful performance.
2. To offer suggestions for future research.
3. To discuss implications of theory and research for education.

Our goals in producing this volume led to several decisions that we felt would increase the book's impact in the field. Although we solicited chapters from individuals actively engaged in self-regulation research, we wanted an integrated series of chapters that surveyed the field, rather than loosely linked chapters summarizing individuals' research programs. To provide this integration we organized the book around the preceding conceptual framework. This framework is of potential value to researchers and practitioners who are confused by the plethora of definitions and purported examples of self-regulation that often do not seem to have much in common. We asked authors to focus on only one of the areas of the conceptual framework, to reduce redundancy between chapters. The authors were also requested to follow a common chapter format: present relevant theoretical ideas, discuss research evidence bearing on these ideas, suggest future research directions, and describe implications for educational practice. In short, we wanted contributors to discuss the current status of their ideas and provide a forward look in terms of research and practice.

The book is subdivided into four major sections: Self-Regulation of Motives, Self-Regulation of Methods, Self-Regulation of Performance

Outcomes, and Self-Regulation of Environmental Resources. There also is an introductory chapter that presents the conceptual framework and a concluding chapter that provides a retrospective overview of research on self-regulation and considers prospects for the future. Chapters in the Overview and Conclusion do not follow the preceding format but rather discuss general issues. The placement of the chapters in one of the sections identifies the chapter's major focus, although the chapters touch on issues from other sections because of the interdependence of the dimensions of self-regulation.

This book is designed to be a resource for educational researchers and practitioners, as well as for graduate students or advanced undergraduates who have a minimal course background in education and psychology. The book is appropriate for courses where self-regulation is covered in some depth—for example, introductory courses in learning, development, and educational psychology, as well as specialty courses in learning, development, cognition, and motivation. It is assumed that students will possess some familiarity with psychological concepts and research methods. The text is written for general audiences and contains minimal discussion of the statistical aspects of research findings.

ACKNOWLEDGMENTS

We want to acknowledge many people for their assistance during the various phases of this project. Our sincere gratitude goes to our contributors. Despite their busy schedules, they worked diligently and made our jobs as editors professionally and personally satisfying. We also express our appreciation to many professional colleagues and students with whom we have worked and discussed issues. In particular, we have benefited from our memberships in two American Educational Research Association Special Interest Groups: Motivation in Education, and Studying and Self-Directed Learning. Hollis Heimbouch, our editor at Lawrence Erlbaum Associates, and Kathy Dolan, her editorial assistant, deserve our thanks for their support and editorial guidance. We express our heartfelt appreciation to Diana Zimmerman and Caryl and Laura Schunk for their encouragement and understanding throughout this effort. Finally, we want to dedicate this book to Albert Bandura, whose guiding influence has provided impetus and direction to the field of self-regulation and has touched our lives in ways that never can be repaid.

Dale H. Schunk
Barry J. Zimmerman

I

Overview

1

Dimensions of Academic Self-Regulation: A Conceptual Framework for Education

Barry J. Zimmerman
City University of New York

Self-education has been discussed for over two centuries as a way to encourage individuals to become educated on their own, primarily by undertaking personal programs of reading. A number of influential American thinkers, such as Benjamin Franklin (*Benjamin Franklin Writings*, 1868/1987) and Thomas Edison (Josephson, 1959), have stressed the value of self-directed reading experiences along with personal efforts to apply this knowledge on their intellectual development. Within the last two decades, researchers have begun to empirically study the role of students' personal attributes and psychological processes underlying their self-regulation of academic learning and performance. The construct of *self-regulation* refers to the degree that individuals are metacognitively, motivationally, and behaviorally active participants in their own learning process (Zimmerman, 1986). The results of these initial investigations have revealed a fascinating but complex picture of the processes through which students become willing and able to assume responsibility for self-regulating their academic achievement. In the chapters that follow, investigators who have contributed prominently to this body of research discuss the results of their own and others' studies.

This introductory chapter sets the stage for those chapters by addressing a number of important issues underlying the scientific investigation of self-regulatory processes. First, I consider the issue of the educational consequences of students' willingness or failure to self-regulate their academic performance, and some key problems involved in operationally defining, describing, and explaining the often subtle phenomenon of self-regulation. Then a conceptual framework involving four dimensions or areas in which students can self-regulate their academic activities is presented and its implications for studying and enhancing self-regulation in educational contexts are considered. Finally, I delineate how each of the subsequent chapters contributes to our understanding of these basic dimensions of students' academic self-regulation.

ACADEMIC FAILURES AND TRIUMPHS: A SELF-REGULATION PERSPECTIVE

As national concern over cause of the low achievement of American students continues to mount, officials at the U.S. Department of Education have begun to look beyond the traditional curriculum for answers—to sources of personal responsibility for learning (Willis, 1992). This change of focus was the result of recent evidence that many American students do not invest much time and effort in their schoolwork. For example, the 1990 National Assessment of Educational Progress report indicated that 71% of the 12th graders studied no more than 1 hour a day and 25% did not study at all.

Yet even within the poorest inner-city schools, there are remarkable examples of academic success in America, such as a core of minority students who manage to succeed despite the odds (Wibrowski, 1992) and recent immigrant refugee children from Southeast Asia (Caplan, Choy, & Whitmore, 1992) who have had to overcome language barriers, gaps in their schooling, economic privation, discrimination, and emotional scars in order to excel. These youngsters were not offspring of highly educated parents, nor did they attend schools endowed with many academic resources. Instead, they succeeded because of their persistence, resourcefulness, and self-reliance. For example, Wibrowski (1992) found that academically successful minority students attending an inner-city high school were willing to work late into the night and to get up early the next morning to finish assignments that were due. In contrast, their less successful classmates preferred to go to bed early and to copy a classmate's work before class or to ask for help from the teacher in class.

In other research, Caplan et al. (1992) showed that immigrant Asian families reserved their evenings for the children to study at the kitchen table, mastering the essential learning methods through repeated performance and assistance from older siblings. In dramatic contrast to the average American student, these immigrant high school students spend more than 3 hours on their homework nightly. They are also distinguished by their commitment to succeed in school and by their strong sense of personal efficacy to achieve this goal. These students' personal attributes—their academic time management, practice, mastery of learning methods, goal-directedness, and a sense of self-efficacy—have been identified as hallmarks of academic self-regulation.

To complement these findings regarding the value of self-regulatory processes to academic success, there is evidence that a major cause of underachievement is the inability of students to self-control themselves effectively (Krouse & Krouse, 1981). Borkowski and Thorpe (this volume) review this body of research indicating that underachievers are more impulsive, have lower academic goals, and are less accurate in assessing their abilities; furthermore, they are more self-critical and less self-efficacious about their performance and tend to give up more easily than achievers. The effect of these self-regulatory deficiencies on underachievers' personality and emotional development appears to be considerable: These students are more anxious, have a lower self-esteem, have a higher need for approval, and are more influenced by extrinsic factors than achievers. Thus, research on academic self-regulation holds the promise of explaining unexpected outcomes at both ends of the achievement spectrum: personal accomplishment in the face of steep odds, as well as underachievement and low self-esteem.

Describing and Explaining Academic Self-Regulation

When used as a descriptive construct, self-regulation is relatively easy to recognize. We have all seen memorable examples of self-regulated students: a Hispanic girl staying after class pleading to practice her word processing "just a little longer"; a suburban boy who is ensconced in the quietude of the vacant school amphitheater trying to memorize his notes before an all-important physics test; the unhappy self-reactions of young Asian girl at her inability to remember the names of the world's oceans for her forthcoming geography test. Research (Zimmerman & Martinez-Pons, 1988) has shown that teachers do not have difficulty in identifying students who are self-regulated by their attributes. These instructors are able to reliably classify their pupils according to such criteria as (a) self-starters who display extraordinary persistence on learning tasks, (b) confident, strategic, and resourceful in overcoming problems, and (c) usually self-reactive to task performance outcomes. There is evidence that students' reports of their self-regulatory activities were consistent with their teachers' judgments of their academic attributes (Zimmerman & Martinez-Pons, 1988). For example, students who were judged to be self-starters reported initiating homework, class assignments, and test preparation without prompting, and continuing their effort until these tasks were completed. Thus, it appears that self-regulatory attributes of students are salient and easily interpreted.

In contrast to such attribute descriptions, researchers have encountered greater difficulty when using self-regulation as an explanatory construct. This involves identifying the key processes that students use to self-regulate their academic performance. An extensive number of self-regulatory processes have been proposed, and many of them, such as cognitive self-monitoring, are both subtle and covert. To complicate the picture even further, many process constructs appear to overlap conceptually, such as metacognition, volition, and planning. In part, this problem stems from researchers' use of different theoretical paradigms to describe and explain their results—theories as diverse as operant, phenomenological, social cognitive, Vygotskian, volitional, attributional, information processing, and constructivist (Zimmerman & Schunk, 1989). Thus, there is a need to identify and describe the key dimensions of academic self-regulation according to an atheoretical conceptual framework in order to integrate and cross-relate empirical outcomes.

**Toward an Operational Definition
of Academic Self-Regulation**

Another concern that has been raised involves the operational criteria that distinguish self-regulatory responses from conventional forms of learning, such as acquisition, transfer, and recall. Frequently, studies are described as measuring self-regulation, yet they seem indistinguishable from prior academic learning studies because the training methods and outcome measures are identical. For example, if one teaches a 4-year-old an elaboration memory strategy, has the youngster become self-regulative? Not if the youngster doesn't use it on his or her own. It is suggested that a defining condition for self-regulation is the availability of choice and control for the subjects: Inferences about students' self-regulatory capability cannot be made if they do not have options available or cannot control an essential dimension of their learning, such as one's method of studying. According to this criterion, the effectiveness of strategy training on students' ability to self-regulate could be tested only if they were given the option of learning or performing it in whatever way they preferred. The purpose of including a self-regulation test phase in one's research design is to make inferences beyond the issue of whether students can use a particular strategy (a learning outcome) to additionally determine whether they see the personal value of it and will self-initiate and self-control its use (a self-regulation outcome).

In contrast to the inclusion of choice and control, traditional learning studies typically preclude most of these self-regulation options. For example, when paired words are presented by a memory drum, the experimenter controls the task environment, the outcome behavior, and, to a large degree, the method of study. Bruner, Goodnow, and Austin (1966) referred to this type of experimental design as a receptive learning paradigm because the subjects' were limited to a passive role. It is suggested that the criterion of personal choice or control is essential to the exercise of self-regulation. It should be noted that schools can also be analyzed in terms of the amount of student choice or control that is permitted.

A DIMENSIONAL ANALYSIS OF ACADEMIC SELF-REGULATION

Although research on academic self-regulation can be distinguished by its unique task conditions, learner attributes, and processes, it also shares some continuities with traditional forms of learning research. Investigators of students' self-regulation must ultimately address the same key scientific questions raised by previous investigators of learning, such as, why or how do students self-regulate? Each of these basic questions is associated with a major psychological dimension of learning, such as motivation and learning methods.

My efforts to analyze and understand these issues has led to the development of the conceptual framework presented in Table 1.1. One purpose of this formulation is to analyze research on academic self-regulation in terms of its common components in order to show their linkages to prior forms of learning. A second purpose is to delineate the task conditions necessary to self-regulate each component, and a third use of the framework is to cross-relate and integrate academic self-regulation findings developed from different theoretical models.

Scientific Questions and Psychological Dimensions

The scientific questions presented in the first column of Table 1.1 are fundamental to understanding all forms of human learning, and each one also pertains to a key psychological dimension of research on academic self-regulation. For example, the question of *why* addresses students' motivation to self-regulate their learning. Phenomenologists (McCombs, 1989) seek to answer this questions by studying students' self-concepts, whereas attributional theorists (Dweck, 1986; Nicholls, 1978) have focused on students' interpretations of personal outcomes in terms of effort or ability. The question of *how* deals with students' methods for self-regulating their learning and performance. Metacognitive theorists (Borkowski, Carr, Rellinger, & Pressley, 1990) approach this question by examining students' use of self-regulated learning strategies, whereas Vygotskian theorists (Rohrkemper, 1989) examine students's self-directed or private speech as the primary method of self-regulation.

TABLE 1.1
Conceptual Analysis of the Dimensions of Academic Self-Regulation

Scientific Questions	Psychological Dimensions	Task Conditions	Self-Regulatory Attributes	Self-Regulatory Processes
Why?	Motive	Choose to participate	Intrinsically or self-motivated	Self-goals, self-efficacy, values, attributions, etc.
How?	Method	Choose method	Planned or automatized	Strategy use, relaxation, etc.
What?	Performance outcomes	Choose performance outcomes	Self-aware of performance outcomes	Self-monitoring, self-judgment, action control, volition, etc.
Where?	Environmental (social)	Control social and physical setting	Environmentally/ socially sensitive and resourceful	Environmental structuring, help seeking, etc.

The question of *what* deals with students' efforts to self-regulate their academic performance outcomes. Volitional theorists (Corno, 1989; Heckhausen, 1991) have pointed out that merely wanting to self-regulate learning is not enough; students must also be able to protect their intentions from distracting or competing intentions. In contrast, metacognitive scholars (Flavell, 1979) have discussed personal control of performance in terms of self-monitoring of cognitive processes during performance. The question of *where* or with whom addresses students' efforts to self-regulate their physical and social environment in order to learn. Constructivist explanations (Paris & Byrnes, 1989) have focused on students constructing supportive environments using their own personal theory of academic tasks, whereas social cognitive theorists have emphasized seeking social models and assistance (Schunk, 1989; Zimmerman, 1989). Thus, a dimensional analysis can facilitate cross-comparison and integration of results from disparate theories of self-regulation.

Essential Task Conditions for Self-Regulation

The third column in Table 1.1 specifies the task conditions necessary for a student to self-regulate the particular psychological dimension in question. By definition, schools or research procedures that externally compel students to participate prevent them from self-regulating their motivation.

To avoid this limitation, researchers have included a separate experimental phase that gave subjects the opportunity to choose to participate or not. For example, Bandura and Schunk (1981) included an additional posttest phase where students were given a choice of solving math problems or engaging in an alternative task. After the experimenter informed the students of their freedom to choose, he left them alone to make their choice. The time spent on the math problems was treated as a measure of the students' intrinsic interest in this task. Bandura and Schunk found their self-regulatory training not only improved students' computational skills, it also enhanced their intrinsic interest in mathematics.

In order for students to self-regulate their method of academic learning, they must be given choice on this psychological dimension as well. For example, Lodico, Ghatala, Levin, Pressley, and Bell (1983) taught elementary school students two strategies for learning paired words—one of which was more effective than the other. After learning both strategies and having an opportunity to self-monitor each one's effectiveness, the students were asked to learn a new list of words using whatever strategy they preferred. By allowing students to choose their preferred learning method, these researchers assessed students' capability to self-regulate this psychological dimension. A significantly greater number of these students than control subjects chose the more effective strategy, confirming they could self-regulate their method of learning.

Another aspect of students' choice of a method of learning involves their use of time. Research on mastery learning (Block, 1971) has shown that individual differences in students' achievement are greatly reduced if they are given an opportunity to work at their own pace. Children's self-regulation of their problem-solving time was studied by Zimmerman and Ringle (1981). These researchers were interested in the effect of an adult model's length of effort and self-expressed confidence on the youngsters' persistence during problem solving. After watching the model unsuccessfully try to solve the puzzle during either a long or short effort and express either confidence or pessimism regarding possible solution, the students were told they had unlimited time to solve a different puzzle. Both the model's problem-solving time and expressed confidence significantly affected the students' persistence on a similar puzzle, as well as on a transfer task. Clearly, how the model self-controlled his problem-solving time, both positively and negatively, had an impact on the students' personal regulation of their solution time.

In order for students to self-regulate their academic performance, they must be given choice over their performance outcomes. This form of self-regulation involves more than a willingness or motivation to participate; it involves self-monitoring and self-modulating selected outcomes of one's performance. If students cannot monitor their behavioral outcomes because feedback is prevented or deliberately biased, their self-regulation will be impaired. Both of these methods have been used in traditional learning studies to obtain "pure" measures of external learning influences.

This flexibility in selecting performance outcomes is especially important to becoming self-educated because virtually all academic learning skills are multifaceted in the sense that they involve many parts that must be coordinated together. For example, children learning to add numbers must not only memorize the sum of all combinations of single digits, they must learn to write the answers in the right column, they must learn to carry, and so forth. In order for them to learn on their own, they must be able to focus on a part of their skill that is deficient and monitor its effectiveness while they attempt to improve it. Once it is learned sufficiently, the children must shift their attention to another part of the task until mastery is achieved.

Typically, when students are asked to self-record selected outcomes of their behavior, associated aspects of their performance will immediately begin to change in the direction of their implicit goals—an effect that has been labeled *reactivity* (Mace & Kratochwill, 1988). Reactivity is controlled in conventional learning studies by preventing subjects from choosing their behavioral outcomes or by denying them access to interpretable feedback. It is suggested that students must be able to select and control their response outcomes in order to measure self-regulatory performance. For example, a study by Harris (1986) revealed that the part of a response a learner chooses to self-record directly influences the type of self-regulation that occurs.

Question 4 pertains to students' opportunity to choose or control their physical and social environment in order to self-regulate their academic functioning. Typically, these environmental conditions are carefully controlled in traditional learning research by holding the physical setting constant and denying access to social confederates. If students are given the opportunity to selectively access information of their own choosing, there is evidence that their performance is enhanced. For example, Risemberg (1993) studied student self-regulation of their writing. College students were asked to write a essay comparing Martin Luther King and Malcolm X by computer. These subjects were provided with a menu of resources including access to texts about each man, as well as to two "model" essays. They could view any of the text sources whenever they wished and could use the computer to revise their prose at any point during the episode. Risemberg found that students' accessing the two model essays during a prewriting planning phase was significantly correlated with the quality of their essays. Clearly, allowing students to choose or control their learning environments enabled them to self-regulate this important psychological dimension.

Self-Regulatory Attributes

Two distinctive paths were followed in investigating the topic of academic self-regulation: Some researchers sought to identify students who were self-regulated and learn more about their distinctive personal attributes. A second path that was chosen involved teaching theoretically derived processes that were hypothesized to enhance students' self-regulation of learning and performance. Significant progress has been made following both of these paths.

Turning first to self-regulatory attributes that have been identified, there is evidence that these students are more intrinsically motivated or more self-motivated. The term *intrinsic* has been used to describe the willingness of self-regulated students to continue to practice or study in the absence of direct external control by parents and teachers. For example, Zimmerman and Martinez-Pons (1988) found students who reported using self-regulated learning strategies were significantly more likely to volunteer for special projects and to bring into class relevant information that was not included in assigned readings. Social cognitive theorists (Zimmerman, 1985; Zimmerman, Bandura, & Martinez-Pons, 1992) prefer the term *self-motivated* to intrinsic motivation because the latter is often assumed to imply that the motivation is derived from the task, whereas the former assumes that students' continuing motivation is derived from their self-efficacy perceptions and use of self-regulatory processes during learning such as goal setting.

A second attribute of self-regulated students is their reliance on a planned or an automatized method of learning. Planned approaches have often been described in terms of learning strategies, which Weinstein and Mayer (1986) grouped into two major classes: strategies associated with product or outcome goals, and strategies associated with process goals such as monitoring or controlling affect. The latter strategies are by definition *self-regulatory*. Zimmerman and Martinez-Pons (1986) found that students in an advanced track in high school used significantly more self-regulation strategies than regular students, including goal setting and planning, organizing and transforming, rehearsing and memorizing, record keeping and self-monitoring, and giving self-consequences. Furthermore, there is evidence that self-regulative strategies predicted students' academic performance better than cognitive strategies (Pintrich & De Groot, 1990). It would appear that students require more than task-oriented strategies: They need learning strategies that focus on self-regulatory processes.

As students achieve a high level of academic mastery, their cognitive functioning becomes automatized (Schneider & Shiffrin, 1977), a self-regu-latory state often described as spontaneous and freed from strategic control of conscious processes. However, information-processing researchers such as Carver and Scheier (1981) concluded that cognitive monitoring of learning does not cease under conditions of automatization but rather shifts to a different hierarchical level. For example, after learning to read for comprehension, students shift from cognitively monitoring text at a word level to larger units of meaning such as a sentence or phrase. However, they remain cognitively attuned to any signs of misunderstanding during reading, and when any occur, they strategically revert to a word level of text processing.

Furthermore, elite athletes often use cognitive strategies to prepare themselves to function at an automated level, a state that has been often labeled as being "in the zone" (Garfield, 1984). For example, competitive skiers often strategically rehearse going through each slalom gate imagistically before making a actual run and strategically concentrate on remaining relaxed during their run. Thus, it can be argued that automatization of performance can be facilitated through specific strategic planning and practice—by shifting monitoring from specific response components to more generic features of performance.

Students' self-regulation of their academic performance is closely linked to their heightened *self-awareness* of covert and overt outcomes of their behavioral functioning. For example, self-regulated students were significantly more likely than nonself-regulated students to know how well they did on a test before it was graded by their teacher (Zimmerman & Martinez-Pons, 1988). This awareness may be due to self-regulated learners' greater proclivity to keep records on many aspects of their academic performance, including the results of self-testing on class lecture notes and readings (Zimmerman & Martinez-Pons, 1990). There is also evidence that self-regulated students perceive greater self-efficacy for concentrating in the face of distractions than regular students (Zimmerman, Bandura, & Martinez-Pons, 1992).

The importance of the role of self-awareness in the ability to regulate one's performance was revealed in a study by Hunter-Blanks, Ghatala, Pressley, and Levin (1988). These researchers studied the role of adults' monitoring their learning of two types of factual sentences that appeared to be alike semantically but actually varied in level of cognitive difficulty. Virtually none of the students were aware of the differences in difficulty before attempting to learn the sentences, but many of them became cognizant of the differences during the study. Students who displayed low levels of accuracy in evaluating their performance of each of the sentences failed to learn how to classify the sentences according to their difficulty and displayed poorer overall learning. It appears that the accuracy of one's self-monitoring directly influences one's capability to self-regulate performance outcomes.

Finally, self-regulated students are distinguished by their sensitivity to and resourcefulness in terms of the effects of the social and physical environment on their learning. These learners are significantly more likely to organize or restructure their place of study than regular learners, and they also more likely to seek social assistance than regular students (Zimmerman & Martinez-Pons, 1986, 1988). Critics might contend that help seeking represents dependency, not self-regulation. Newman (this volume) notes, however, that the type of help seeking displayed by self-regulated students differs from mere dependency by its form: It is selective in scope and directed to a person who is known to be capable. In this sense, seeking information from social sources is not different from seeking it from written sources.

Self-Regulatory Processes

The second path in research on self-regulation has involved teaching theoretically derived processes hypothesized to enhance students' self-regulation of learning and performance. A primary source of students' intrinsic or self-motivation is their academic goals, sense of self-efficacy, and values (Meece, this volume; Schunk, 1990; Wigfield, this volume). For example, Zimmerman, Bandura, and Martinez-Pons (1992) studied the role of academic grade goals and perceptions of academic efficacy in predicting student achievement in social studies at the end of a semester. These two measures, which were given at the outset of the semester, predicted 31% of the variance in the final grades.

Students' motivation to self-regulate learning is also related to their attributional processes (Borkowski & Thorpe, this volume). Youngsters who attribute any lack in goal progress to low ability are unlikely to feel self-efficacious or motivated to continue. However, providing feedback to students that improvement is contingent on perseverance can instill confidence that they have the ability to succeed eventually and can enhance motivation to persist (Andrews & Debus, 1989). Schunk (1982) demonstrated that providing effort feedback for successes supports students' sense of goal progress, sustains their motivation, and increases efficacy for further learning.

Turning next to the psychological dimension of method, there is a considerable body of evidence that teaching students to use self-regulatory or metacognitive strategies can improve the effectiveness of their learning methods. Research has shown that strategy training that includes metacognitive components prepares students to know when and where to use it. For example, Borkowski, Weyhing, and Carr (1988) studied the effects of summarization strategy training on reading comprehension. Learning-disabled students who were taught the reading strategy along with attributional statements regarding its effectiveness not only showed reliable gains in reading comprehension from pre- to posttesting, but they also surpassed control group students on an inferential subtest of the Stanford Reading Test. Clearly, strategy training that incorporated metacognitive components improved not only the students' acquisition of a reading comprehension strategy but also their transfer to a unfamiliar reading task. A model of students' strategic and metacognitive knowledge called the Good Strategy User model (Pressley, Borkowski, & Schneider, 1987) is discussed by Brown and Pressley (this volume).

The strategies of time planning and time management have been widely discussed as a key method of self-regulation. Weinstein describes an instructional procedure for teaching students to manage the study time more effectively (Zimmerman, Greenberg, & Weinstein, this volume). She asked college students in an academic skills course to keep a detailed log on their use of time for 1 week. These records revealed vast amounts of wasted time, an outcome that shocked many of her students. Subsequently, they were instructed to use this record to plan their future use of study time, and Weinstein found they greatly improved their time management scores during her course. Interestingly, the students' grade-point average in other courses during that semester improved substantially from prior semesters. It appears that time planning and management training does help students to better self-regulate their use of study time.

Relatively little research on automatized functioning has focused on academic learning tasks. Desensitization and relaxation training have been used to assist test-anxious students to relax and disengage ruminative cognitions about their test performance, which are two features of automatization. For example, Mann (1972) presented a videotape of a test-anxious student who practiced relaxing as he was asked to imagine various testing situations by a therapist. This vicarious training procedure was effective not only in reducing observers' test anxiety but also in raising their test scores. Thus, it appears that mere exposure to a modeled relaxation strategy can assist students to rid themselves of intrusive fears during test taking. In the field of sports psychology, imagery strategy training has been used to prepare elite athletes for competition such as ski races, ice skating events, and weight lifting. The relaxed but alert state that allows one to perform in an automatized way typically requires extensive practice in order to sustain it between competitive performances (Garfield, 1984).

Regarding the psychological dimension of performance outcomes, a number of researchers have sought to increase students' self-awareness and behavioral control by teaching them to self-record or to cognitively self-monitor. For example, Ghatala, Levin, Foorman, and Pressley (1989) told students to study a passage until they felt they could answer all questions on posttest. The data revealed that these youngsters had much difficulty monitoring their learning: Unless they were given external feedback, they greatly understudied the passage. Ghatala et al. found that poor cognitive monitoring was due to the multiple-choice nature of the posttest and that accurate monitoring did occur when they studied for a recall test.

The latter outcome is consistent with social cognitive (Bandura, 1986; Schunk, 1989; Zimmerman, 1989) analysis of self-regulation, which distinguishes self-judgment from self-observation and self-reaction processes. The multiple-choice criterion proved to be more ambiguous than the recall criterion for self-judging learning and self-responding with further studying. Self-judgment refers to the comparison of that performance to a standard, whereas self-observation involves self-directed attention, and self-reaction refers to one's cognitive, affective, and behavioral reactions to self-judgments.

Volition theorists (Corno, this volume; Heckhausen, 1991; Kuhl, 1985) focus on "protecting one's intention to learn" from distractions or competing intentions as key to remaining self-aware and in control of one's performance. Volitional processes that learners use to self-control their actions once they have embarked on a learning task are distinguished from the motivational processes that learners use to decide upon and plan for one's learning ahead of time. Heckhausen (1991) and Corno (1993) described the barrier between the motivation and volitional action-control processes metaphorically in terms of Caesar's "Rubicon" (river of no return). This distinction is recognized in the conceptual framework in Table 1.1 by the placement of action control and volition within the psychological dimension of performance.

Turning finally to the environmental dimension of self-regulation, there is evidence that learning to self-select exemplary models to observe can be an effective way to learn. For example, Benjamin Franklin described in his *Autobiography* (*Benjamin Franklin Writings*, 1868/1987) how he mastered the art of formal writing through modeling. When he came upon a written passage that was especially well written, he would try to emulate it. First, he would make brief notes about each sentence in the passage, and then he would attempt to rewrite it from his notes. Finally, he would compare his version with the original and correct his deficiencies. He credited this literary modeling procedure with improving not only his writing but also his memory and his "arrangement of thoughts." Within the last two decades, videotaped instructional models have become a major industry based on demonstrating how to learn a wide variety of personal and professional skills, such as writing, exercise, and even self-relaxation. By combining video with computer technology, learners can achieve even greater self-regulation because computer programming can allow learners to choose their own level of instructional support from a menu (Henderson & Cunningham, this volume).

ORGANIZATION OF THE BOOK

Subsequent chapters of this volume summarize research on key self-regulatory processes related to each of the scientific questions in the conceptual framework. Chapters 2–5 deal with self-regulatory processes that primarily impact students' intrinsic or self-motivation.

Meece discusses the role of two types of goal orientation on self-regulation: learning and performance goals. Students with a learning goal orientation seek to enhance their competence or understanding, whereas students with performance-oriented goals are primarily concerned with gaining favorable judgments of others. Meece reports evidence that learning-oriented youths use self-regulated learning strategies significantly more frequently than performance-oriented youths. The former students are also more likely than the latter to choose challenging tasks that allow them to learn new skills and to attribute their outcomes to their strategic efforts.

Borkowski and Thorpe consider the role of deficiencies in student self-regulation that can lead to significant underachievement involving a sizable discrepancy between students' ability and their academic achievement. Typically, underachievement has been attributed to academic skill deficits of students. Borkowski and Thorpe provide evidence that motivational and behavioral factors are equally important. In terms of their motivation, underachievers lack a sense of self-efficacy and self-esteem, and they have notable problems self-controlling their behavior. These researchers suggest that in order for remedial programs to reverse underachievement, they should encourage children to metacognitively integrate their self-regulation, affect, and motivation.

Schunk focuses on the role of self-efficacy beliefs and outcome attributions on students' academic self-regulation. He summarizes research indicating that encouraging students to attribute their academic outcomes to effort raised students' perceptions of self-efficacy and achievement. Furthermore, student perceptions of self-efficacy influence their choice of activities, their effort, and their persistence in learning.

According to Wigfield, students' perceptions of value of a skill influence their willingness to self-regulate. Academic values refer to desired modes and outcomes of personal endeavor, such as competence, ambitions, a sense of accomplishment, and responsibility. If an academic skill is not valued, students will not be motivated to self-regulate their academic functioning. Wigfield discusses longitudinal data indicating that students' values about mathematics predicted their decision to enroll in advanced senior level courses in this subject area. Thus, the students' academic values had a long-term impact on their academic choices, a key indicator of intrinsic or self-motivation.

Chapters 6, 7, and 8 deal with self-regulatory processes that influence students' choice and use of strategic methods to self-regulate learning and performance. Garcia and Pintrich discuss the need for an integrated account of student cognition and motivation in order to explain students' self-regulation in classroom settings. In their model of strategic regulation, these authors draw a distinction between self-regulative knowledge, strategies, and outcome behavior. Self-regulative knowledge about academic tasks and oneself are theorized to underlie students' choice of regulative strategies and their implementation during performance. Garcia and Pintrich describe how these elements are integrated cognitively in a student's self-schema, which is an individually constructed, dynamic, and flexibly organized form of knowledge about oneself.

Brown and Pressley focus on teaching of reading strategies in classroom contexts. Strategy use becomes self-regulated when students use learning strategies in conjunction with metacognitive knowledge and self-efficacy. This includes knowledge of when and where particular strategies are effective and self-beliefs about one's competence to use them. These researchers caution against teaching single strategies in narrow contexts and recommend instead the use of broader methods of strategic training in field settings. From their research, Brown and Pressley recommend a transactional strategy teaching program that involves long-term modeling and explanation (thinking aloud) by both the teacher and student during the course of regular reading activities.

Zimmerman, Greenberg, and Weinstein survey research on academic study time and focus on the role of key self-regulatory processes such as time planning and management. Students' planning, goal setting, and self-monitoring of their use of time during studying are found to be significantly related to their academic achievement. This research reveals that students' perceptions of self-efficacy for managing their study time are especially important. Finally, these authors describe the results of a program designed to teach time planning and management to college students

Chapters 9 and 10 are devoted to self-regulatory processes that students use to self-regulate their academic performance outcomes. Graham and Harris describe a multistage instructional program for teaching writing that includes self-monitoring. After a writing strategy is modeled, students develop their own personal self-statements to guide their writing. As the students and teacher practice writing and verbalizing collaboratively, self-recording and self-assessment are encouraged. Once the writing strategy is mastered, the self-recording and self-assessment procedures are faded out. Graham and Harris report evidence that students continued to self-monitor the effectiveness of their written performance outcomes.

Corno discusses a volitional approach for self-regulating academic performance that is designed to assist students to protect their intentions to accomplish goals from competing intentions and other distractions. These include action-control processes to manage perceptions of the difficulty of the task or the distractiveness of the learning environment, and volitional strategies for controlling one's emotions, sustaining one's attention, and managing one's cognitive and situational resources. Finally, Corno discusses three bodies of evidence regarding the influence of volitional processes on academic performance: action-control studies, goal-related cognition investigations, and volitional styles research.

Chapters 11 and 12 are devoted to self-regulatory processes that students use to self-regulate their academic social and physical environment. Henderson and Cunningham discuss how social and physical contexts can be created to facilitate self-regulation from a Vygotskian perspective. According to this theory, self-regulation is seen as a linguistically guided process in which regulation-through-commands of others shifts developmentally to self-regulation involving the use of goal-oriented monitoring, appraisal, and coping. Henderson and Cunningham discuss the implications of this theory for the development of classroom environments and computerized instructional programs with interactive videodisks.

Newman focuses on academic help seeking as a self-regulated learning strategy. Although it is often assumed that poor achievers rely on others, he suggests that elementary school children who do not understand lessons don't usually ask for help, and he cites evidence indicating that these youngsters perceive high social costs for help seeking, such as appearing dumb. In contrast, research reveals that students with greater self-confidence to seek academic assistance are higher achievers. Newman also discusses developmental and personal factors that influence students' adaptive help seeking and the design of classroom environments that facilitate this form of self-regulation.

In the final chapter, the state of research on academic self-regulation and its application in instructional contexts is discussed retrospectively, and prospects for future investigation are considered.

CONCLUSION

Although research on academic self-regulation is at an early stage of development, it has already provided insight into key processes that are used by achieving students to overcome personal and environmental obstacles to their academic success. Conversely, other results indicate that these same self-regulatory processes are not utilized by underachieving students. As a topic of study, students' self-regulation has attracted researchers from diverse theoretical traditions; however, interpretation of the outcomes of their studies has often been difficult because of varying definitions of constructs and processes. This chapter seeks to clarify these matters by providing an operational definition of self-regulation that is multidimensional in form and by identifying the main scientific questions that underlie a complete account of this important personal capability. Finally, a common conceptual framework is offered for classifying and cross-relating self-regulation findings in the chapters that follow.

ACKNOWLEDGMENT

I would like to thank Dale H. Schunk and my wife Diana for their helpful comments on an earlier draft of this chapter.

REFERENCES

Andrews, G. R., & Debus, R. L. (1978). Persistence and the causal perception of failure: Modifying cognitive attributions. *Journal of Educational Psychology, 70*, 154–166.

Bandura, A. (1986). *Social foundations of thought and action: A social cognitive theory.* Englewood Cliffs, NJ: Prentice-Hall.

Bandura, A., & Schunk, D. H. (1981). Cultivating competence, self-efficacy, and intrinsic interest through proximal self-motivation. *Journal of Personality and Social Psychology, 41*, 586–598.

Benjamin Franklin Writings. (1987). New York: Literary Classics of the United States. (Original *Autobiography* published in 1868)

Block, J. H. (Ed.). (1971). *Mastery learning* New York: Holt, Rinehart & Winston.

Borkowski, J. G., Carr, M., Rellinger, E., & Pressley, M. (1990). Self-regulated cognition: Interdependence of metacognition, attributions, and self-esteem. In B. Jones & L. Idol (Eds.), *Dimensions of thinking and cognitive instruction* (Vol. 1, pp. 53–92). Hillsdale, NJ: Lawrence Erlbaum Associates.

Borkowski, J. P., Weyhing, R. S., & Carr, M. (1988). Effects of attributional retraining on strategy-based reading comprehension in learning disabled students. *Journal of Educational Psychology, 41*, 586–598.

Bruner, J., Goodnow, J. J., & Austin, G. A. (1956). *A study of thinking.* New York: Wiley.

Caplan, N., Choy, M. H., & Whitmore, J. K. (1992, February). Indochinese Refugee families and academic achievement. *Scientific American*, 37–42.

Carver, C. S., & Scheier, M. F. (1981). *Attention and self-regulation: A control theory approach to human behavior.* New York: Springer.

Corno, L. (1989). Self-regulated learning: A volitional analysis. In B. J. Zimmerman & D. H. Schunk (Eds.), *Self-regulated learning and academic achievement: Theory, research, and practice* (pp. 111–141). New York: Springer-Verlag.

Corno, L. (1993). The best laid plans: Modern conceptions of volition and educational research. *Educational Researcher, 22*, 14–22.

Dweck, C. S. (1988). Motivational processes affecting learning. *American Psychologist, 41,* 1040–1048.

Flavell, J. (1979). Metacognition and cognitive monitoring: A new era in cognitive-developmental inquiry. *American Psychologist, 34,* 906–911.

Garfield, H. Z. (1984). *Peak performance.* New York: Warner Books.

Ghatala, E. S., Levin, J. R., Foorman, B. R., & Pressley, M. (1989). Improving children's regulation of their reading PREP time. *Contemporary Educational Psychology, 14,* 49–66.

Harris, K. R. (1986). Self-monitoring of attentional behavior versus self-monitoring of productivity: Effects of on-task behavior and academic response rate among learning disabled children. *Journal of Applied Behavior Analysis, 48,* 417–423.

Heckhausen, H. (1991). *Motivation and action* (P. K. Leppmann, Trans.). Berlin: Springer-Verlag.

Hunter-Blanks, P., Ghatala, E. S., Pressley, M., & Levin, J. R. (1988). Comparison of monitoring during study and during testing on a sentence-learning task. *Journal of Educational Psychology, 80,* 279–283.

Krouse, J. H., & Krouse, H. J. (1981). Toward a multimodal theory of academic achievement. *Educational Psychologist, 16,* 151–164.

Kuhl, J. (1985). Volitional mediators of cognitive-behavior consistency: Self-regulatory processes and action versus state orientation. In J. Kuhl & J. Beckman (Eds.), *Action control* (pp. 101–128). New York: Springer-Verlag.

Josephson, M. (1959). *Edison: A biography.* New York: McGraw-Hill.

Lodico, M. G., Ghatala, E. S., Levin, J. R., Pressley, M., & Bell, J. A. (1983). The effects of strategy-monitoring training on children's selection of effective memory strategies. *Journal of Experimental Child Psychology, 35,* 263–277.

Mace, F. C., & Kratochwill, T. R. (1988). Self-monitoring: Applications and issues. In J. Witt, S. Elliott, & F. Gresham (Eds.), *Handbook of behavior therapy in education* (pp. 489–502). New York: Pergamon.

Mann, J. (1972). Vicarious desensitization of test anxiety through observation of videotaped treatment. *Journal of Counseling Psychology, 19,* 1–7.

McCombs, B. L. (1989). Self-regulated learning and academic achievement: A phenomenological view (pp. 51–82). In B. J. Zimmerman & D. H. Schunk (Eds.), *Self-regulated learning and academic achievement: Theory, research, and practice* (pp. 51–82). New York: Springer.

Nicholls, J. G. (1978). The development of the concepts of effort and ability, perception of academic attainment, and the understanding that difficult tasks require more ability. *Child Development, 49,* 800–814.

Paris, S. G., & Byrnes, J. P. (1989). The constructivist approach to self-regulation and learning in the classroom. In B. J. Zimmerman & D. H. Schunk (Eds.), *Self-regulated learning and academic achievement: Theory, research, and practice* (pp. 169–200). New York: Springer-Verlag.

Pintrich, P. R., & De Groot, E. V. (1990). Motivational and self-regulated learning components of classroom academic performance. *Journal of Educational Psychology, 82,* 33–40.

Pressley, M., Borkowski, J. P., & Schneider, W. (1987). Cognitive strategies: Good strategy users coordinate metacognition and knowledge. In R. Vasta & G. Whitehurst (Eds.), *Annals of child development* (Vol. 5, pp. 89–129). Greenwich, CT: JAI Press.

Risemberg, R. (1993). *Self-regulated strategies of organizing and information seeking when writing expository text from sources.* Unpublished doctoral dissertation, Graduate School of the City University of New York.

Rohrkemper, M. M. (1989). Self-regulated learning and academic achievement: A Vygotskian view. In B. J. Zimmerman & D. H. Schunk (Eds.), *Self-regulated learning and academic achievement: Theory, research, and practice* (pp. 143–167). New York: Springer-Verlag.

Schneider, W., & Shiffren, R. M. (1977). Controlled and automatic human information processing: I. Detection, search, and attention. *Psychological Bulletin, 84*, 1–66.

Schunk, D. H. (1982). The effects of effort attribution feedback on children's perceived self-efficacy and achievement. *Journal of Educational Psychology, 74*, 548–556.

Schunk, D. H. (1989). Social cognitive theory and self-regulated learning. In B. J. Zimmerman & D. H. Schunk (Eds.), *Self-regulated learning and academic achievement: Theory, research, and practice* (pp. 83–110). New York: Springer-Verlag.

Schunk, D. H. (1990). Goal setting and self-efficacy during self-regulated learning. *Educational Psychologist, 25*, 71–86.

Weinstein, C. E., & Mayer, R. E. (1986). The teaching of learning strategies. In M. C. Wittrock (Ed.), *Handbook of research on teaching* (pp. 315–327). New York: Macmillan.

Wibrowski, C. R. (1992). *Self-regulated learning processes among inner city students.* Unpublished doctoral dissertation, Graduate School City University of New York.

Willis, S. (1992). Why don't students work harder? *ASCD Update, 34*(4), 1–8.

Zimmerman, B. J. (1985). The development of "intrinsic" motivation: A social learning analysis. *Annals of Child Development, 2*, 117–160.

Zimmerman, B. J. (1986). Development of self-regulated learning: Which are the key subprocesses? *Contemporary Educational Psychology, 16*, 307–313.

Zimmerman, B. J. (1989). A social cognitive view of self-regulated academic learning. *Journal of Educational Psychology, 81*, 329–339.

Zimmerman, B. J., Bandura, A., & Martinez-Pons, M. (1992). Self-motivation for academic attainment: The role of self-efficacy beliefs and personal goal setting. *American Educational Research Journal, 29*, 663–676.

Zimmerman, B. J., & Martinez-Pons, M. (1986). Development of a structured interview for assessing student use of self regulated learning strategies. *American Educational Research Journal, 23*, 614–628.

Zimmerman, B. J., & Martinez-Pons, M. (1988). Construct validation of a strategy model of student self-regulated learning. *Journal of Educational Psychology, 80*, 284–290.

Zimmerman, B. J., & Martinez-Pons, M. (1990). Student differences in self-regulated learning: Relating grade, sex, and giftedness to self-efficacy and strategy use. *Journal of Educational Psychology, 82*, 51–59.

Zimmerman, B. J., & Ringle, J. (1981). Effects of model persistence and statements of confidence on children's efficacy and problem solving. *Journal of Educational Psychology, 73*, 485–493.

Zimmerman, B. J., & Schunk, D. H. (Eds.). (1989). *Self-regulated learning and academic achievement: Theory, research, and practice.* New York: Springer-Verlag.

II

Self-Regulation of Motives

2

The Role of Motivation in Self-Regulated Learning

Judith L. Meece
University of North Carolina-Chapel Hill

Most educators and researchers would agree that learning involves the active process of integrating and organizing information, constructing meaning, and monitoring comprehension. For even the most capable students, high levels of effort, concentration, and persistence are needed in order to develop a sound understanding of a subject matter. What motivates students to allocate time and mental effort to learning tasks? How can educators create the motivational conditions that facilitate self-regulatory learning processes in the classroom?

Recent analyses of achievement-related behavior have indicated that students pursue different achievement goals in learning situations (Dweck & Elliot, 1983; Maehr & Nicholls, 1980; Nicholls, 1984; Nicholls, Patashnick, & Nolen, 1985). Some students seek to increase their competencies, whereas others seek to demonstrate high ability. Research has further shown that the priority given to one achievement goal versus the other influences how students subsequently interpret, approach, and respond to achievement activities (Ames, 1992a, 1992b; Dweck & Leggett, 1988; Elliot & Dweck, 1988; Nicholls, 1984). Therefore, according to achievement goal research, students influence their learning by adopting achievement goals that optimize self-regulatory processes.

This chapter examines self-regulated learning in the context of achievement goal theory. It begins with a brief overview of achievement goal research and applications of this research to classroom learning. In subsequent sections, I present findings from my own research on individual and classroom differences in students' achievement goal orientations. The chapter concludes with implications for future research and educational practice.

OVERVIEW OF ACHIEVEMENT GOAL THEORY

Goal conceptions of motivation focus on the purposes of students' achievement behavior. This research maintains that the distinguishing feature of achievement behavior is that "its goal is competence or perceptions of competence" (Nicholls, 1984, p. 328). Achievement goals are thus defined by whether the anticipated or desired outcome guiding the individual's behavior involves increasing or demonstrating competence. Consistent with other cognitive mediation models of motivation (expectancy value, self-efficacy, attribution), achievement goal theory emphasizes the active role of the individual in choosing, structuring, and interpreting his or her achievement experiences. According to Dweck and Leggett (1988), the achievement goals individuals pursue "create the framework within which they interpret and react to events" (p. 256).

Research has primarily focused on two types of achievement goals. Individuals who pursue what are known as learning-oriented (Dweck & Elliot, 1983) or task-oriented (Nicholls, 1984) goals seek to improve their level of competence or understanding. Learning is valued as an end in itself. Subjective feelings of pride, success, and accomplishment are derived from achieving a sense of mastery or developing one's competence based on self-referenced standards. In contrast, individuals who pursue performance-oriented (Dweck & Elliot, 1983) or ego-oriented (Nicholls, 1984) goals seek to demonstrate high ability or to gain favorable judgments of their abilities in relation to the efforts and performances of others. These individuals generally use norm-referenced standards to judge the adequacy of their performance. A sense of accomplishment is derived from doing well with little effort, doing better than others, or meeting some other normatively defined standard of success.

What orients students toward these different goals? Most theoretical perspectives on motivation discuss the critical influence of ability perceptions on achievement patterns. Reviews of this research indicate that individuals who develop and maintain positive perceptions of their abilities report higher performance expectations, greater control over learning, and greater interest in learning for intrinsic reasons (Covington, 1992; Eccles et al., 1983; Harter & Connell, 1984).

Ability perceptions also guide the selection of achievement goals. However, this research emphasizes differences in the conceptions of ability individuals use to judge their competence. Individuals are more likely to adopt a learning or task orientation when they believe that they can improve their ability by investing greater effort (Dweck & Bempechet, 1983; Dweck & Leggett, 1988; Nicholls & Miller, 1984). Dweck and Bempechet (1983) reported that individuals who have this *incremental* conception of ability prefer tasks that are hard, new, and challenging so "they can learn from them." For these individuals, feelings of competence are maximized by high effort.

Individuals who adopt performance or ego goals are more likely to view their abilities as stable traits that can be judged in relation to others (Dweck & Leggett, 1988; Nicholls & Miller, 1984). These individuals tend to use a differentiated conception of ability, in which higher effort implies lower ability given equal outcomes (Jagacinski & Nicholls, 1984). By late childhood, most individuals have acquired these different conceptions of ability (Dweck & Leggett, 1988; Nicholls & Miller, 1984). Ego-oriented individuals are distinguished by (a) their preoccupation with ability and (b) the degree to which they view high ability as essential to success (Nicholls, 1989).

Research has shown that socialization experiences in the home help to shape students' ability conceptions and achievement goals. In a study that examined mothers' beliefs about the role of effort and ability in school learning, Ames and Archer (1987) found that mothers differed in the relative priority they attached to different achievement goals. About 60% of the mothers expressed a belief pattern that was consistent with a mastery (learning) goal pattern, whereas 40% judged "getting good grades" and "doing better than others" as more important achievement goals for their children. These maternal belief patterns were also associated with different task selections, preferences for normative evaluation, and causal attribution patterns. The overall findings suggest that mothers may influence their children's achievement goal orientations through the types of activities they encourage, how they define success, and the information they use to judge their children's performance outcomes.

In addition to socialization experiences at home, the child's learning environment at school can also elicit different goal orientations. Learning situations that emphasize self-improvement (Ames & Archer, 1988; Butler, 1987; Graham & Golan, 1991), discovery of new information (Jagacinski & Nicholls, 1984), and the usefulness of learning material (Elliot & Dweck, 1988) can induce task or learning goal states. Under these conditions, high effort attributions result in high perceived competence. By contrast, learning conditions that raise concerns about one's ability, such as interpersonal competition (Ames, 1984; Graham & Golan, 1991), tests of intellectual skills (Jagacinski & Nicholls, 1984; Stipek & Kowalski, 1989), and public learning situations that involve normative evaluations (Elliot & Dweck, 1988), can elicit ego or performance goals. In these cases, low effort attributions increase perceptions of ability, particularly if the individual outperforms others who exhibit high effort.

Theoretical Links to Self-Efficacy Research

Self-efficacy research has examined the influence of goal setting on students' achievement behavior (Schunk, 1991a). The conceptions of goals used in this research are analogous to task or learning goals, because judgments of competence are generally tied to perceptions of progress, effort expended, amount of work completed, and other task-specific performance standards. This research (Schunk, 1991a, 1991b) suggests that enhanced feelings of competence and interest occur when goals are attainable within a short period of time (proximal) and framed in terms of discrete actions (specific).

Achievement Goals and Self-Regulatory Processes

Self-regulated learning refers to the processes by which students exercise control over their thinking, affect, and behavior as they acquire knowledge and skills (Zimmerman, 1989). Research has identified several specific patterns that are "set in motion" by different achievement goals (Elliot & Dweck, 1988, p. 11).

Achievement goals influence students' task persistence and problem-solving efforts, especially for children who lack confidence in their abilities (Elliot & Dweck, 1988; Stipek & Kowalski, 1989). Under performance-oriented conditions, children with low perceived ability express negative affect toward their learning abilities and show a marked deterioration in their problem-solving efforts when they begin to experience failure. This pattern is not evident for children with high perceived ability in the performance-oriented condition or for children in the learning-oriented condition, regardless of perceived ability.

Ames and Archer (1988) reported comparable findings in a study that examined the influence of the classroom goal structure on junior high school students' strategy use and attribution patterns. The results showed that the perceived mastery goal orientation of the classroom related positively to students' reported use of effective learning strategies, attributions to effort, and feelings toward the class. These patterns were not observed in the classes where high ability and grades, outperforming others, and normative evaluation were the salient classroom norms.

Additionally, research has demonstrated relations between students' achievement goals and activity choices (Nicholls, 1984). In the Elliot and Dweck (1988) study mentioned earlier, children in the learning condition were more likely to choose challenging tasks that would allow them to learn new skills, whereas performance-oriented children were more likely to choose tasks that would allow them to demonstrate competence, even though they might not learn anything new. Similarly, Ames and Archer (1988) reported positive relations between the mastery orientation of the classroom and students' preferences for challenging activities.

Finally, achievement goals can affect how students study and what they remember. Several recent studies (Graham & Golan, 1991; Nolen, 1988; Nolen & Haladyna, 1990a; Pintrich & Garcia, 1991) indicate that learning-oriented students tend to use deep processing strategies that enhance conceptual understanding and require cognitive effort, such as integrating information or monitoring comprehension. By contrast, ego-oriented goal patterns have been associated with short-term and surface-level processing strategies, such as memorizing and rehearsing strategies. Not surprisingly, students operating under ego-involved conditions show poor recall of information when the task requires deeper levels of information processing (Benware & Deci, 1984; Graham & Golan, 1991).

A CLASSROOM STUDY OF INDIVIDUAL
AND CONTEXTUAL INFLUENCES
ON STUDENTS' GOAL ORIENTATIONS

Over the past several years, I have examined individual and situational influences on students' goal orientations in the classroom. This section presents and discusses findings from this research. The first study examines sources of individual differences in students' goal orientations and strategy-use patterns. A follow-up study illustrates what is gained from analysis procedures that examine students' patterns of responses across goal measures. The last study examines the influence of the classroom environment on students' goals and use of self-regulated learning strategies.

Attitudinal and Cognitive Correlates
of Students' Achievement Goal Patterns

An initial study (Meece, Blumenfeld, & Hoyle, 1988) examined relations between achievement goals and other motivation variables, including ability perceptions, intrinsic motivation, and subject matter attitudes. These variables were conceptualized as individual differences that could predispose students to adopt a particular goal orientation (Dweck & Elliot, 1983). This study also examined the relative influence of students' achievement goals on different measures of strategy use in the classroom.

The data for these studies were gathered during the 1985–1986 school year as part of an investigation of students' motivation in science. The sample consisted of 100 fifth graders and 175 sixth graders from 10 science classes taught by 5 teachers. Students attended schools located in predominantly White, middle- to upper middle-class suburban neighborhoods in southeastern Michigan.

At the beginning of the project, students completed a set of surveys (see Meece et al., 1988). The Perceived Competence subscale consists of seven items to assess students' perceptions concerning how well they understand their schoolwork, how easy it is for them to figure out class assignments, how smart they feel, and how well they are doing in school (Harter, 1982). The Science Ability subscale includes eight items that ask students to rate their general ability in science, to rate their ability in relation to other students and subjects, and to rate how well they perform on specific tasks in science (experiments, tests, remembering facts, etc.). The Intrinsic Motivation subscale consists of 18 items to assess the degree to which students manifest an intrinsic interest in learning, view themselves as curious, and show a preference for challenging and independent work (Harter, 1981). The Science Attitudes scale, developed for the National Assessment of Educational Programs (Hueffle, Rakov, & Welch, 1983), contains 12 items to assess the enjoyment and usefulness of science.

During the second half of the year, students completed a group-administered questionnaire after six different lessons that varied with regard to length, difficulty, format, and structure (whole class, small group, etc.). The student questionnaire assessed three types of goals. *Task-mastery* goals represent a desire to learn something new, master a task, or improve one's competence, whereas *ego-social* goals represent a desire to demonstrate high ability, outperform others, or please the teacher. The third category, *work-avoidant* goals, represents a form of avoidance motivation that is found in classroom settings. The questionnaire also assessed students' use of self-regulated learning strategies (*active engagement*), as well as their use of strategies to minimize effort (*superficial engagement*). Examples of scale items are shown in Table 2.1.

Because we had assessed students' goal and strategy-use patterns in relation to six different learning tasks, it was possible to assess the consistency of students' responses across situations. We assumed that students' goal and strategy-use ratings would vary depending on the nature of the learning task. However, contrary to expectations, we found a fairly high degree of stability in students' ratings. Stability coefficients ranged from .87 to .91. Values of this magnitude generally imply traitlike characteristics (Mischel & Peake, 1982), but it is equally possible that the overall structure of the classroom may explain the high degree of consistency in students' goal and strategy-use ratings. The influence of the classroom environment is discussed in a later section.

TABLE 2.1
Examples of Scale Items

Task-mastery orientation
  I wanted to find out something new.
  I wanted to learn as much as possible.
Ego-social orientation
  I wanted others to think I was smart.
  It was important to do better than the other students.
Work-avoidant orientation
  I wanted to do things as easily as possible.
  I wanted to do as little work as possible.
Active engagement
  I went back over the things I didn't understand.
  I tried to figure out how today's work fit with what I had learned before in science.
Superficial engagement
  I skipped the hard parts.
  I guessed so I could finish quickly.

Note. The goal items were rated on a 4-point scale ranging from *Not very true* to *Very true*. The engagement items were rated on a 3-point scale, from *Not at all like me* to *A lot like me*. Information about scale construction and validation appears in Meece, Blumenfeld, and Hoyle (1988).

Table 2.2 presents the intercorrelations among the individual difference, goal, and strategy-use measures. For these analyses, we computed a mean score for goal and engagement measures by aggregating students' responses across the six lessons. The results of the correlational analysis showed that students' goal and strategy-use ratings are strongly related. Students who are high on task-mastery goals report a fairly high level of engagement in science activities as indicated by their reported use of self-regulated learning strategies (focusing attention, monitoring comprehension, organizing information). Conversely, students who rate their ego-social or work-avoidant goals as strong in science report a greater use of effort-minimizing strategies, such as guessing at solutions, copying answers, and so forth.

Subsequent analyses focused on individual differences in students' achievement goals. Table 2.2 shows that students' task-mastery goals relate positively to individual differences in general and science-related ability perceptions, intrinsic motivation to learn, and attitudes toward science. Ego-social and work-avoidant goals are each related negatively to these measures.

This study also employed analysis methods to examine the relative influence of general measures of motivation and task-specific goal ratings on students' reported use of self-regulated learning strategies. The results showed that students' scores on the Active Engagement scale were most

TABLE 2.2

Intercorrelations Among Goals, Attitudinal, and Cognitive Engagement Measures

	1	2	3	4	5	6	7	8	9
1. Task-mastery goals	—								
2. Social-ego goals	.13	—							
3. Work-avoidant goals	-.50**	.29**	—						
4. Perceived competence	.23**	-.15*	-.22**	—					
5. Perceived science ability	.27**	.22**	-.14*	.62**	—				
6. Intrinsic motivation	.46**	-.20*	-.40**	.63**	.46**	—			
7. Science attitudes	.48**	-.14	-.35**	.39**	.58**	.56**	—		
8. Active engagement	.70**	.21*	-.39**	.16*	.22**	.21*	.31**	—	
9. Superficial engagement	-.43**	-.33**	.71**	-.26**	-.21**	-.42**	-.33**	-.34**	—
10. Standardized achievement	.03	-.19*	-.21**	.42**	.42**	.29**	.24**	.04	-.28**

Note. $N = 256$. *$p < .05$. **$p < .01$.

directly related to their mastery and ego goal ratings. These variables had a comparatively stronger influence on students' use of self-regulated strategies in the classroom than did measures of perceived ability, intrinsic motivation, and subject matter attitudes. It was interesting that neither the student's achievement level nor sex aided in the prediction of goal orientations. The lack of significant direct effects for these variables is consistent with cognitive theories of motivation that emphasize the importance of interpretative processes and personal beliefs rather than fixed student characteristics (Eccles et al., 1983).

Single or Multiple Goals?

Much of the research on students' achievement goals has used a single-variable approach. The strength of each goal is assessed, but goal ratings are then individually related to other attitudinal and behavioral measures. Such an approach does not assess the possibility that more than one goal may be simultaneously operative. To explore this question, Meece and Holt (1993) examined how different goals combine within individuals to influence self-regulated learning patterns in the classroom. We reanalyzed data from the Meece et al. (1988) study to identify students with similar profiles of scores across goal measures. The cluster profiles appear in Fig. 2.1. The first cluster represents 33% of the students (n = 85), who have significantly higher task-mastery goals than do

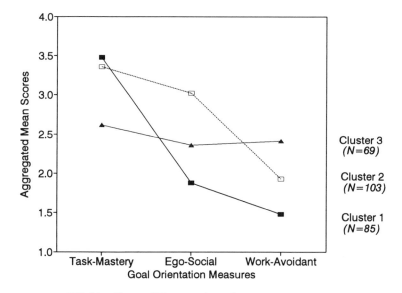

FIG. 2.1. Cluster differences in goal orientation measures.

students in the other two clusters. They also show a differentiated pattern, in which their mastery goals were strong relative to ego-social and work-avoidant goals. Cluster 2 is the largest cluster, representing nearly 40% of the sample (n = 103). Students in this group place an equally strong emphasis on task-mastery and social-ego goals, but they are more ego-oriented than students in the other clusters. Twenty-seven percent of the students (n = 69) show a relatively flat profile, but members of this group report greater work-avoidance than the other two clusters.

To further describe the clusters, we examined group differences in the self-perception and attitude variables examined in the Meece et al. (1988) study. The analyses identified significant cluster differences in students' ability perceptions, intrinsic motivation, and science attitudes. Cluster 1 students (high mastery) have the most positive ability perceptions and attitudes toward learning. Interestingly, Cluster 2 students (combined mastery-ego) have significantly higher scores than Cluster 3 students (low mastery-ego) on the intrinsic motivation and science attitude measures, but these two groups do not differ in terms of their perceived abilities.

The results also revealed interesting cluster differences in students' self-reports of strategy use. Cluster 1 students report a relatively high level of active engagement in learning activities and the lowest level of superficial engagement. Cluster 3 students show the opposite pattern. They report the lowest level of active engagement and the highest use of effort-minimizing strategies.

The strategy-use patterns of students in Cluster 2 are most noteworthy, because they report relatively high use of both active learning and effort-minimizing strategies. One explanation for this finding is that the strategy selections of these students are likely to vary across different types of learning activities. Students who are high on both mastery and ego goals may report greater cognitive engagement in activities when they are confident of doing well and of avoiding negative ability judgments, but less involvement when the learning activity is challenging, competitive, and/or public, because social comparisons and negative ability judgments are possible (Meece & Holt, 1993).

This reanalysis of students' goal patterns indicated that variations in students' self-reports of strategy use are explained by mean differences in the strength of individual goals and by the patterning of these goals within individuals. Two of the groups show different patterns of strategy use, even though there is no significant difference in the absolute strength of their mastery goals. The findings support other research suggesting that a mastery focus may have its strongest influence in the absence of competing goals or motives (Pintrich & Garcia, 1991; Spence & Helmreich, 1983).

TABLE 2.3
Descriptive Statistics on Validation and Achievement by Cluster

Measures	Cluster 1 High Mastery			Cluster 2 Mastery-Ego			Cluster 3 Low Mastery-Ego		
	n	*M*	*SD*	*n*	*M*	*SD*	*n*	*M*	*SD*
Perceived competence	83	3.12	.59	98	2.81	.66	68	2.66	.63
Perceived science ability	83	2.24	.37	98	2.08	.38	68	1.99	.34
Intrinsic motivation	83	3.14	.44	98	2.82	.52	68	2.58	.49
Science attitudes	83	4.11	.51	98	3.72	.53	68	3.43	.63
Active engagement	85	2.38	.31	103	2.38	.29	69	1.96	.31
Superficial engagement	85	1.20	.18	103	1.39	.30	69	1.60	.29

Note. Fluctuations in sample size across measures are due to missing data.

Classroom Differences in Students' Achievement Goals and Strategy-Use Patterns

A number of studies have clearly demonstrated that students show high levels of self-regulated learning and task engagement when they are oriented toward learning or mastery goals. Only a few studies, however, have examined the influence of the classroom environment on students' goal and strategy-use patterns (Ames & Archer, 1988; Nolen & Haladyna, 1990b). In a recent qualitative study, my colleagues and I (Meece, 1991; Meece, Blumenfeld, & Puro, 1989), analyzed observational records from the 10 classrooms that participated in the Meece et al. (1988) study. Trained observers collected detailed observation records on 15 science lessons in each class. Lesson transcripts included information on (a) lesson presentations, (b) teacher and student questioning patterns, (c) feedback patterns, (d) grouping arrangements, (e) evaluation practices, and (f) motivational strategies. We then analyzed lesson transcripts to identify patterns that may potentially explain classroom differences in students' goal and strategy-use patterns.

For analysis purposes, we grouped teachers according to their students' task-mastery scores. Two fifth-grade teachers formed the high mastery group, because their students had the highest average score on the task-mastery scale (group mean = 3.40, based on a 4-point scale). Over half of the students who were classified as high mastery (cluster 1) in the Meece and Holt (1993) study were from these classes. Two sixth-grade classes formed the low mastery group, because these classes reported the lowest level of mastery orientation (mean score = 2.99). A disproportionate number (76%) of the students who showed the low mastery-ego pattern were from these classes.

What type of classroom environment is more likely to elicit the high mastery pattern? As previously described (Meece, 1991), the high mastery teachers used an instructional approach that promoted meaningful learning. They expected students to understand, to apply, and to make sense of what they were learning. To facilitate participation, the teachers modified lessons to increase their personal relevance, provided opportunities for peer collaboration and cooperation, and emphasized the intrinsic value of the learning material. Grades and other extrinsic incentives were rarely used to motivate students in the high mastery classes.

There were some interesting differences in students' strategy-use patterns between the two high mastery teachers. One of the high mastery teacher's classes reported greater active engagement in learning activities than did the second teacher's classes. The first teacher presented coherent lessons that proceeded in small steps and that allowed students to see the connections between ideas. She also regularly monitored students' comprehension of the lesson and held students individually accountable for what they were learning. In contrast, the other high mastery teacher tended to summarize and connect ideas for the students. He did not monitor students' understanding of ideas or experimental procedures throughout the lesson. When students experienced confusion or difficulty, this teacher was more likely to provide the answer than to help students figure it out. Thus, although both of the high mastery teachers generated interest in the learning material, one of the teachers did not provide adequate instructional support or hold students accountable for understanding the learning material as consistently as the other. These differences could explain variations in students' cognitive engagement patterns between the two high mastery teachers (see also Blumenfeld, Puro, & Mergendoller, 1992).

In the low mastery classes, learning activities emphasized the memorization and recall of isolated facts and information. Students had limited opportunities to actively construct meaning, to view themselves as sources of knowledge, and to apply what they were learning to new situations. The low mastery teachers made very little effort to adapt lessons to the students' ability levels and interests. Also, compared with the high mastery classes, there were fewer opportunities for peer collaboration and self-directed learning. Most significantly, grades and evaluation were a salient feature of the low mastery classes.

One sixth-grade teacher's classes did not fit either the high or low mastery-oriented pattern. Over half of this teacher's students were high on both mastery and ego goals, but they reported relatively high levels of active engagement in lessons. Interestingly, this teacher's instructional practices resembled some of those used by one of the high mastery teachers. She modeled difficult procedures, helped students break complex tasks into smaller units, and guided students' independent problem-solving efforts. However, evaluation was an implicit feature of many lessons in this teacher's classes, and it was sometimes used to control students' behavior and productivity (see Meece, 1991).

The patterns uncovered by this qualitative study are consistent with several theoretical reviews (Ames, 1992a, 1992b; Corno & Rohrkemper, 1985; Marshall, 1990; Nicholls, 1989; Ryan, Connell, & Deci, 1985). Teachers can promote and sustain a goal orientation that facilitates learning and achievement by (a) stressing the importance of conceptual understanding, (b) minimizing social comparisons among students, (c) providing opportunities for peer collaboration, and (d) enabling students to make decisions and choices. However, the lack of adequate instructional support and guidance can subvert these efforts. One of the high mastery teachers was particularly skilled at involving all students in the learning activities, supporting their independent problem-solving efforts, and conveying the inherent value of the learning material. This teacher had the lowest number of students who displayed the low mastery-ego goal pattern and who reported the highest use of self-regulated learning strategies.

ISSUES FOR FUTURE RESEARCH

The research reviewed in this chapter has shown that the achievement goals students pursue in classroom settings have important implications for self-regulated learning processes. Numerous studies involving different age groups, subject areas, and academic tasks indicate that children benefit the most from their learning when they focus on mastery and learning. Relations between achievement goals and behavior that were originally established in laboratory settings have now been confirmed by classroom research (Ames & Archer, 1988; Meece et al., 1988; Nolen, 1988; Nolen & Haladyna, 1990a).

The measures of achievement goals and self-regulated learning used in the Meece et al. (1988) study were specific to science. Although the domain specificity of these measures may increase their predictive validity (Assor & Connell, 1992), it is not clear how well the findings will generalize to other subject areas. A related question concerns the continuity of students' goal and strategy-use patterns over time. Research is needed to examine the longitudinal stability of these patterns. If students' goal and strategy-use patterns show a high degree of continuity across time, when do these stable patterns emerge? What might give coherence to students' motivation and learning patterns over time? Answers to these questions will involve longitudinal research designs, preferably ones that also include a variety of achievement domains.

The nonlinear analysis procedures used in the Meece and Holt (1993) study revealed patterns that were not apparent in previous correlational and experimental studies. The results challenge some implicit assumptions of achievement goal research. For example, it is generally assumed that the integration of task and ego orientations will enhance academic performance, because it should increase the flexibility of students to perform effectively across a range of learning settings (Dweck & Leggett, 1988). The Meece and Holt (1993) study suggests that this hypothesis may need further testing. Additionally, the findings revealed that a large number of students are relatively low or high on both task-mastery and ego goals. These patterns have not been previously established in samples of elementary school children. Further research using pattern analysis methods seems warranted on the basis of these findings.

The classroom interaction patterns that differentiated the high and low mastery classes in the Meece (1991) study also need further examination. This qualitative investigation did not formally test the effects of classroom variables on students' goal patterns, and it was based on a small number of teachers who were highly experienced. Different patterns of achievement goals may occur in classes taught by less experienced teachers. In addition, students were not randomly assigned to classrooms. It is therefore possible that the differences identified in students' goal and strategy-use patterns reflect preexisting conditions rather than classroom effects.

Finally, additional research is needed to examine how individual children respond to different classroom goal structures. Experimental studies (Dweck & Elliot, 1988; Stipek & Kowalski, 1989), suggest that students with low abilities or low perceived competence may benefit the most from mastery goal structures. Interactions between student characteristics and different goal structures have not been systematically examined in classroom studies (see also Ames, 1992a).

EDUCATIONAL IMPLICATIONS

The research discussed in this chapter offers a number of suggestions for how teachers can enhance students' motivation to engage in self-regulatory processes. Most classroom interventions have focused on enhancing students' ability perceptions by modifying attributions, by training learning strategies, or by helping students to set challenging but achievable goals. Although these efforts may have short-term benefits for students who have motivational problems or skill deficits, they are likely to have a limited impact unless teachers can create a classroom environment that supports a mastery orientation toward learning.

Classroom studies have noted the strong emphasis on memorization and rote-level learning, even at the upper grade levels (Eccles & Midgley, 1989). Instructional practices that involve the simple transmission and recall of facts are not conducive to the development of mastery goals and self-regulated learning. In the high mastery classes described earlier, the teachers used an instructional approach that promoted meaningful learning and conceptual understanding. One of the high mastery teachers "presses" for understanding in the following example:

T: What happens to the population if 80 of the 100 skunks are trapped (points to graph on board)? What happens to the population of the other things in the pond?

S: Less snapping turtles are eaten.

T: Yes, what does that mean?

S: More ducks being eaten.

T: Ok, if fewer skunks, fewer turtle eggs eaten, what happens to the turtles?

S: Goes up.

T: What happens to the ducks?

S: Fewer skunks means more snapping turtles and they eat more ducks, their population drops. The snapping turtles continue to grow—no more ducks.

T: Class, do you agree?

In this activity, students had to use their existing knowledge to make predictions and evaluations. The teacher added new information as the lesson progressed to probe the depth of students' understanding. The questioning patterns used by this teacher not only elicit higher order thinking, but also convey to students that they are expected to understand, apply, and make sense of what they are learning.

Teachers can also encourage students to engage in self-regulatory processes by providing opportunities for students to initiate and to direct their own learning. In most classrooms, students exercise limited control over the pace of lessons, the materials used, and how to complete assignments. To give students more responsibility for their own learning, teachers might allow students to develop questions for class discussions, to design class projects, to choose learning partners, or to decide the order they want to complete their work. Ryan, Connell, and Deci (1985) proposed that the availability of choice and some degree of student control can enhance feelings of autonomy and self-determination. These conditions are likely to result in higher levels of self-regulated learning, because students are less likely to believe that their learning is controlled by others (Grolnick & Ryan, 1987).

Teachers can help students maintain a mastery focus by supporting students' independent learning efforts. The challenge for teachers is to provide support that students are not yet able to provide for themselves, and then to withdraw that support as they become more knowledgeable or skilled in a particular area. Farnham-Diggory (1990) referred to this teaching strategy as "scaffolding and fading." In the classrooms described earlier, teachers supported students' learning by helping students set goals, by providing memory cues, by modeling difficult procedures, and by problem solving with students when they had difficulty. These strategies are consistent with an apprenticeship model of learning, in which teachers help students acquire knowledge and skills by appropriately structuring learning activities and by working alongside students as coparticipants and facilitators (Farnham-Diggory, 1990; Tharp & Gallimore, 1988).

Normative and public forms of evaluation can elicit an ego goal orientation and reduce students' interest in learning, even if the student receives positive feedback (Butler, 1987). Students are more likely to adopt a mastery orientation that supports self-regulated learning when teachers reward self-improvement, provide students with opportunities to improve their grades, use a variety of evaluation methods, and avoid comparing students' work (Ames, 1992b). Some of these evaluation practices were observed in the high mastery classes described in the previous section. In contrast, tests were fairly frequent in the low mastery classes, and students were routinely reminded that they would need to know the learning material for an upcoming test.

Finally, students benefit from opportunities to work with their peers in the classroom. Peers function as important teachers and models, and learning is enhanced when low-ability students are paired with more capable peers (Carter & Jones, in press; Schunk, 1991a). Motivation research suggests that cooperative learning activities can also have a positive influence on students' ability perceptions and mastery goal orientations (Ames, 1984; Nicholls, 1989). By contrast, learning structures that encourage competition among students can lower ability perceptions, increase social comparisons between students, and elicit self-derogatory thought processes that impede learning (Ames, 1984; Stipek & Daniels, 1988).

It is clear that any effort to change the classroom environment will need to be comprehensive in its approach. Ames (1992a, 1992b) offered one of the most comprehensive approaches to classroom change. Consistent with the suggestions outlined above, this intervention program stressed the importance of providing learning activities that are meaningful and relevant, providing opportunities for student choice and decision-making, rewarding and recognizing personal improvement, and reducing emphasis on social competition and comparisons. Initial results indicated that as teachers implement strategies consistent with the change program, their classes became more mastery focused (Ames, 1990). The results were especially positive for low-achieving students (Powell, Ames, & Maehr, 1990).

Most studies to date have focused on the classroom. Maehr and Midgley (1991) pointed out how teachers' efforts to enhance students' motivation to learn can be subverted by schoolwide policies and practices that rank students according to ability, require strict adherence to textbook guidelines, and limit opportunities for self-governance. To create more long-term effects in students' motivation patterns, changes may need to occur at both the classroom and school level.

CONCLUSIONS

This chapter has focused on how students regulate their learning processes by the type of achievement goals they pursue in learning situations. Considerable research indicates that students benefit the most from learning situations when they focus on mastering the task at hand rather than competing with others for grades and teacher approval. Although socialization experiences in the home help to shape students' motivational patterns, intervention efforts focused on the classroom environment have been relatively successful in enhancing the quality of students' motivation and learning. However, much remains to be done with regards to preparing teachers to implement the changes suggested by this research. Efforts to modify students' academic motivation and achievement behavior in the classroom will require fundamental changes in how learning is currently defined and assessed in schools (Covington, 1992; Marshall, 1992; Nicholls, 1989).

ACKNOWLEDGMENTS

The research described in this chapter was supported by a grant (MDR-8550437) from the National Science Foundation to Phyllis Blumenfeld and Judith Meece. The opinions expressed are the author's own, although I gratefully acknowledge the contributions of Phyllis Blumenfeld and Pam Puro. Special thanks are also extended to Dale Schunk and Barry Zimmerman for their helpful comments on an earlier draft.

REFERENCES

Ames, C. (1984). Achievement attributions and self-instructions under competitive and individualistic goal structures. *Journal of Educational Psychology, 76*, 478–487.

Ames, C. (1990, April). *Achievement goals and classroom structure: Developing a learning orientation.* Paper presented at the annual meeting of the American Educational Research Association, Boston.

Ames, C. (1992a). Classrooms: Goals, structures, and student motivation. *Journal of Educational Psychology, 84*, 261–271.

Ames, C. (1992b). Achievement goals and the classroom climate. In D. H. Schunk & J. L. Meece (Eds.), *Student perceptions in the classroom* (pp. 327–348). Hillsdale, NJ: Lawrence Erlbaum Associates.

Ames, C., & Archer, J. (1987). Mothers' beliefs about the role of ability and effort in school learning. *Journal of Educational Psychology, 79*, 409–414.

Ames, C., & Archer, J. (1988). Achievement goals in the classroom: Student learning strategies and motivation processes. *Journal of Educational Psychology, 80*, 260–267.

Assor, A., & Connell, J. (1992). The validity of students' self-reports as measures of performance affecting self-appraisals. In D. Schunk & J. Meece (Eds.), *Student perceptions in the classroom* (pp. 25–50). Hillsdale, NJ: Lawrence Erlbaum Associates.

Benware, C., & Deci, E. (1984). Quality of learning with an active versus passive motivational set. *American Educational Research Journal, 21*, 755–765.

Blumenfeld, P. C., Puro, P., & Mergendoller, J. (1992). Translating motivation into thoughtfulness. In H. Marshall (Ed.), *Redefining student learning: Roots of educational change* (pp. 207–240). Norwood, NJ: Ablex.

Butler, R. (1987). Task-involving and ego-involving properties of evaluation. Effects of different feedback conditions on motivational perceptions, interest and performance. *Journal of Educational Psychology, 79*, 474–482.

Carter, G., & Jones, G. (in press). The relationship between ability-paired interactions and the development of fifth graders' concepts of balance. *Journal of Research on Science Teaching.*

Corno, L., & Rohrkemper, M. (1985). The intrinsic motivation to learn in classrooms. In C. Ames & R. Ames (Eds.), *Research on motivation in education: The classroom milieu* (Vol. 2, pp. 53–84). New York: Academic Press.

Covington, M. (1992). *Making the grade: A self-worth perspective on motivation and school reform.* New York: Cambridge University Press.

Dweck, C. S., & Bempechet, J. (1983). Children's theories of intelligence: Consequences for learning. In S. Paris, G. Olson, & H. Stevenson (Eds.), *Learning and motivation in the classroom* (pp. 239–258). Hillsdale, NJ: Lawrence Erlbaum Associates.

Dweck, C. S., & Elliot, E. S. (1983). Achievement motivation. In P. H. Mussen (Series Ed.) & E. M. Hetherington (Vol. Ed.), *Handbook of child psychology: Vol. 4. Socialization, personality, and social development* (pp. 643–691). New York: Wiley.

Dweck, C. S., & Leggett, E. L. (1988). A social-cognitive approach to motivation and personality. *Psychological Review, 95*, 256–273.

Eccles (Parsons), J. S., Adler, T., Futterman, R., Goff, S., Kaczala, C., Meece, J., & Midgley, C. (1983). Expectancies, values, and academic behavior. In J. Spence (Ed.), *Achievement and achievement motives* (pp. 75–146). San Francisco: W. H. Freeman.

Eccles, J., & Midgley, C. (1989). Stage/environment fit: Developmentally appropriate classrooms for early adolescents. In C. Ames & R. Ames (Eds.), *Research on motivation in education: The classroom milieu* (Vol. 2, pp. 249–286). New York: Academic Press.

Elliot, E., & Dweck, C. (1988). Goals: An approach to motivation and achievement. *Journal of Personality and Social Psychology, 54,* 5–12.

Farnham-Diggory, S. (1990). *Schooling.* Cambridge, MA: Harvard University Press.

Graham, S., & Golan, S. (1991). Motivational influences on cognitive: Task involvement, ego involvement, and depth of information processing. *Journal of Educational Psychology, 83,* 187–196.

Grolnick, W. S., & Ryan, R. M. (1987). Autonomy support in education: Creating the facilitating environment. In N. Hasting & J. Schwieso (Eds.), *New directions in educational psychology: Behavior and motivation* (pp. 213–232). London: Falmer Press.

Harter, S. (1981). A new self-report scale of intrinsic versus extrinsic orientation in the classroom: Motivation and informational components. *Developmental Psychology, 17,* 300–312.

Harter, S. (1982). The Perceived Competence Scale for children. *Child Development, 53,* 87–97.

Harter, S., & Connell, R. (1984). A model of children's achievement and related self-perceptions of competence, control, and motivational orientation. In J. Nicholls (Ed.), *Advances in motivation and achievement* (Vol. 3, pp. 219–250). New York: JAI Press.

Hueffle, S., Rakow, S., & Welch, W. W. (1983). *Images of science: A summary of results from the 1981–82 National Assessment of Science.* Minneapolis: University of Minnesota, Minnesota Research and Evaluation Center.

Jagacinski, C. M., & Nicholls, J. G. (1984). Conceptions of ability and related affects in task involvement and ego involvement. *Journal of Educational Psychology, 76,* 909–919.

Maehr, M., & Midgley, C. (1991). Enhancing student motivation: A schoolwide approach. *Educational Psychologist, 26,* 399–428.

Maehr, M., & Nicholls, J. G. (1980). Culture and achievement motivation: A second look. In W. Warren (Eds.), *Studies in cross-cultural psychology* (pp. 221–267). New York: Academic Press.

Marshall, H. (1990). Beyond the workplace metaphor: Toward conceptualizing the classroom as a learning setting. *Theory into Practice, 29,* 94–101.

Marshall, H. (1992). Seeing, redefining, and supporting student learning. In H. Marshall (Ed.), *Redefining student learning: Roots of educational change* (pp. 1–32). Norwood, NJ: Ablex.

Meece, J. L. (1991). The classroom context and students' motivational goals. In M. Maehr & P. Pintrich (Eds.), *Advances in motivation and achievement* (Vol. 7, pp. 261–286). Greenwich, CT: JAI Press.

Meece, J., Blumenfeld, P. C., & Hoyle, R. (1988). Students' goal orientations and cognitive engagement in classroom activities. *Journal of Educational Psychology, 80,* 514–523.

Meece, J., Blumenfeld, P. C., & Puro, P. (1989). A motivational analysis of elementary science learning environments. In M. Matyas, K. Tobin, & B. Fraser (Eds.), *Looking into windows: Qualitative research in science education* (pp. 13–23). Washington, DC: American Association for the Advancement of Science.

Meece, J., & Holt, K. (1993). Variations in students' goal patterns. *Journal of Educational Psychology, 85,* 582–590.

Mischel, W., & Peake, P. (1982). Beyond deja vu: In search of cross-situational consistency. *Psychological Review, 89,* 730–755.

Nicholls, J. G. (1984). Achievement motivation: Conception of ability, subjective experience, task choice, and performance. *Psychological Review, 91,* 328–346.

Nicholls, J. G. (1989). *The competitive ethos and democratic education.* Cambridge, MA: Harvard University Press.

Nicholls, J. G., & Miller, A. (1984). Development and its discontents: The differentiation of the concept of ability. In J. Nicholls (Ed.), *Advances in motivation and achievement* (Vol. 3, pp. 185–218). New York: JAI Press.

Nicholls, J. G., Patashnick, M., & Nolen, S. (1985). Adolescents' theories of education. *Journal of Educational Psychology, 77,* 683–692.

Nolen, S. B. (1988). Reasons for studying: Motivational orientations and study strategies. *Cognition and Instruction, 5,* 269–287.

Nolen, S. B., & Haladyna, T. M. (1990a). Motivation and studying in high school science. *Journal of Research on Science Teaching, 27,* 115–126.

Nolen, S. B., & Haladyna, T. M. (1990b). Personal and environmental influences on students' beliefs about effective study strategies. *Contemporary Educational Psychology, 15,* 116–130.

Pintrich, P. R., & Garcia, T. (1991). Student goal orientation and self-regulation in the college classroom. In M. L. Maehr & P. R. Pintrich (Eds.), *Advances in motivation and achievement* (Vol. 7, pp. 371–402). Greenwich, CT: JAI Press.

Powell, B., Ames, C., & Maehr, M. L. (1990, April). *Achievement goals and student motivation in learning disabled and at-risk children.* Paper presented at the annual meeting of the American Educational Research Association, Boston.

Ryan, R., Connell, J. P., & Deci, E. (1985). A motivational analysis of self-determination and self-regulation in education. In C. Ames & R. Ames (Eds.), *Research on motivation in education: The classroom milieu* (Vol. 2, pp. 1–51). New York: Academic Press.

Schunk, D. (1991a). Goal setting and self-evaluation: A social cognitive perspective on self-regulation. In P. Pintrich & M. Maehr (Eds.), *Advances in motivation and achievement* (Vol. 7, pp. 85–114). Greenwich, CT: JAI Press.

Schunk, D. (1991b). Self-efficacy and academic motivation. *Educational Psychologist, 26,* 207–232.

Spence, J., & Helmreich, R. (1983). Achievement-related motives and behaviors. In J. Spence (Ed.), *Achievement and achievement motives: Psychological and sociological approaches* (pp. 7–74). San Francisco: W. H. Freeman.

Stipek, D. J., & Daniels, D. H. (1988). Declining perceptions of competence: A consequence of changes in the child or in the educational environment? *Journal of Educational Psychology, 80,* 352–356.

Stipek, D. J., & Kowalski, P. (1989). Learned helplessness in task-orienting versus performance-orienting testing conditions. *Journal of Educational Psychology, 81,* 384–391.

Tharp, R., & Gallimore, R. (1988). *Rousing minds to life.* New York: Cambridge University Press.

Zimmerman, B. (1989). A social cognitive view of self-regulated academic learning. *Educational Psychology, 81,* 329–339.

3

Self-Regulation and Motivation: A Life-Span Perspective on Underachievement

John G. Borkowski
Pamela K. Thorpe
University of Notre Dame

Although underachievement characterizes the life stories of millions of people in our society, its scientific framework rests on shaky grounds. It is difficult to find unambiguous evidence on the central issues surrounding this phenomenon (cf. Thorndike, 1963): Who are underachievers? What are their salient characteristics? When, and by whom, are they first identified? Are there different etiologies underlying underachievement. Does early underachievement generally result in lifelong underachievement? Is the phenomenon reversible at any point during the life span?

These complex and important questions form the background for this chapter. We argue that educators and psychologists need to devote greater energies and resources to addressing the critical issues that surround the ever increasing problem of underachievement, especially as it is occurring in North America. More specifically, we propose that an understanding of the phenomenon of underachievement can be found in the failure to integrate self-regulation and affect and is attributable, at least in part, to insensitivities, unresponsiveness, or unrealistic demands placed by parents on very young children as they struggle to develop cognitively and emotionally.

UNDERACHIEVEMENT: DEFINITIONS
AND ORIGINS

Although the extant literature reveals that researchers as well as educators do not agree as to who is and who is not an underachiever, most would probably hold that underachievement consists of a discrepancy between predicted and actual levels of academic performance. An underachiever, therefore, is a student who performs more poorly in school than would be expected based on his or her ability (McCall, in press; McCall, Evahn, & Kratzer, 1992).

Empirical and Theoretical Views of Underachievement

Empirical Definitions. Operational definitions of underachievement have varied greatly, with the result that students who are identified as underachievers by one researcher are not necessarily identified as underachievers by the next. Some use measures of ability (such as IQ test scores), tests of mental aptitude, or achievement tests, in combination with measures of academic performance (such as grades or grade-point averages), to calculate difference scores. From this perspective, a sizeable discrepancy between ability and achievement would indicate that a student is underachieving. Other researchers, instead of adopting a difference score approach, use regression analysis to identify under-achievers. Essentially, achievement scores are regressed on an ability measure; then the deviation of each student's score is obtained from the regression line. Students who have large negative deviations (e.g., the bottom 15%) are classified as underachievers. This method, using statistical analyses to identify underachievers as "errors" from the regression line, leaves researchers pondering whether such an approach is suitable for identifying underachievers, given that there are few psychological criteria available for deciding about previous cutoff points. Discussion of alternative methods of identification, as well as the strengths and weaknesses of each approach, can be found in McCall et al. (1992).

Conceptual Definitions. There are multiple theoretical views of underachievement. The literature of the 1960s was dominated by a focus on gifted underachievers, a small portion of the population of under-achieving students. Definitions of underachievement in this special population highlighted superior mental ability—that is, underachieve-ment was viewed as the discrepancy between exceptional potential ability and average achievement. More recently, concerns about low achievement among more typical students, regardless of potential or ability, have dictated the concerns of both the educational and research communities.

A long-standing distinction involves *situational* versus *chronic* underachievement (Covington, 1992; McCall et al., 1992). Situational underachievement is tied to temporary, environmental conditions. That is, students may decline in academic performance due to a dislike of a particular teacher, or a disruption in family life such as divorce or death in the immediate family. Chronic underachievement refers to students who achieve less than their ability would indicate over prolonged periods of time without a clearly identifiable precipitating event. There is, however, no clear length of time that serves to differentiate situational from chronic underachievers.

Another categorization of underachievement that is used in the literature distinguishes *general* from *specific* underachievers (Whitmore, 1980). Underachievement can occur in a particular school subject, such as geometry; in an academic domain, such as mathematics; or in a more general and pervasive sense, such as in mathematics, history, science, and reading. Underachievement in a school subject is believed due to temporary motivational factors, and is usually remediable. Consistent underachievement in a single academic domain occurs relatively infrequently, and because its cause(s) can often be identified, its treatment is more promising. It is the case of general underachievement, where students do not perform up to their ability levels in several subject areas, that is most troublesome, because of its frequency and intractibility. Not surprisingly, it is this aspect of underachievement that has received the most attention among educational researchers.

For the purposes of this review, we do not include a discussion of "gifted" underachievers, nor learning-disabled children who have specific disabilities and identifiable physiological etiologies. It is possible, however, that much of what we propose has relevance to understanding these classifications of learning impairments. Instead, we focus on children who have no identifiable neurological involvement impacting a variety of information-processing skills across several academic domains.

Multiple Perspectives on Underachievement

Environmental Correlates of Underachievement. Various approaches have been used to examine environmental influences on academic underachievement. For example, Broman, Bien, and Shaughnessy (1985) analyzed a sample of 35,000 children who were tested at 7 years of age. They initially identified about 1,000 students who had normal intelligence but who showed substandard academic performance, and they compared this group with 6,000 children who had normal school performance. Broman et al. (1985) concluded that the factors surrounding underachievement existed not in the biomedical histories of the children but rather in the environments in which they lived.

The major characteristics found to be related to underachievement are lower socioeconomic status (Broderick & Sewell, 1985), higher birth order (Sutton-Smith, 1982), larger family size (Nuttall, Nuttall, Polit, & Hunter, 1976), and gender (Bar-Tal, 1978), with boys being more likely to be so classified than girls. Although these correlates of underachievement can help researchers to identify children who may be at risk for underachievement, they do not form a theoretical basis for understanding the nature and consequences of prolonged, general academic underachievement.

Academic Skills, Personality, and Self-Control. Krouse and Krouse (1981) constructed a multidimensional theory of underachievement that emphasized a complex interplay among academic skill deficits (Briggs, Tosi, & Moreley, 1971), personality dysfunctions (Shaw & Black, 1960), and deficiencies in self-control (Thoreson & Mahoney, 1974).

Because skill deficits have been seen as antecedents to poor academic performance, programs in reading effectiveness and study skills have been designed in the hopes of remediating specific skill deficits and raising students' academic performance (Haslam & Brown, 1968). Despite good intentions, however, the effectiveness of such training programs was limited (Fremouw & Freindler, 1978). Hence, Krouse and Krouse (1981) concluded that other factors, such as personality and affective characteristics, should be taken into account if training programs for underachievers are to be maximally effective.

Personality characteristics found to impact underachievement are anxiety (Sepie & Keeling, 1978), fear of failure (Simons & Bibb, 1974), impulsiveness (McKenzie, 1964), self-assurance (Davids, 1966), and a high need for approval (Heck, 1972). In addition, research on self-concept and underachievement has established a link between underachievement and perceived versus actual academic abilities (Bailey, 1971). Kanoy, Johnson, and Kanoy (1980) also showed that achievers had higher self-concepts than underachievers. Related research on the specific characteristics of self-concept found that achievers had higher occupational goals than underachievers (Jhaj & Grewal, 1983).

With respect to personal belief and reward systems, Haywood (1968) reported that overachievers were motivated by factors intrinsic to an academic task, whereas underachievers were more likely to be motivated by extrinsic factors. Claes and Salame (1975) also found that underachievers were less accurate in assessing their abilities and more self-critical than academic achievers. In addition, students who felt efficacious about mastering academic tasks tended to persist in the face of learning difficulties, expend greater effort toward attaining academic goals, and strive for higher levels of academic performance. By contrast, underachievers, who were generally less efficacious about mastering academic tasks, tended to give up in difficult learning situations, expended less effort toward attaining academic goals (setting lower goals than academic achievers), and aspired to minimal levels of academic performance (Covington, 1992; Schunk, 1989).

A more extensive review of the literature on personality characteristics and underachievement can be found in Mandel and Marcus (1988) and Covington (1992). In general, the existing literature provides a broad perspective on the importance of personal beliefs and self-worth evaluations, together with their accompanying affective components, on determining academic achievements.

Krouse and Krouse's (1981) model of underachievement has a final component which includes students' deficits in self-control. A critical finding is that academic underachievement usually occurs when a student is unable to manage his or her own behavior (Thoreson & Mahoney, 1974). In response, treatment programs have been designed to remediate self-control deficits, emphasizing self-monitoring, self-reinforcement, and stimulus control. In summary, Krouse and Krouse's (1981) model contains cognitive, motivational, and behavioral characteristics of underachievement. These three components—and their developmental interrelationships—are explored in the next section in terms of a more precise model of metacognitive development that has as its cornerstone the self-regulation of skills and strategies.

A METACOGNITIVE MODEL OF UNDERACHIEVEMENT: THE INTEGRATION OF REGULATION, AFFECT, AND MOTIVATION

Characteristics of Ideal Students: Good Information Processors

In order to understand the mechanisms underlying underachievement, a description of a child who is a "good information processor" is an appropriate starting point. Although few teachers have actually discovered a child who actually mirrors our hypothetical conceptualization of a good information processor (Borkowski, Carr, Rellinger, & Pressley, 1990; Pressley, Borkowski, & Schneider, 1990), a broad-based metacognitive perspective serves as a "lofty objective" to strive for in understanding and facilitating children's learning. The unique aspect of the good information processor model is the successful integration of the main components of the metacognitive system, including cognitive, motivational, personal, and situational characteristics. Borkowski and Muthukrishna (1992) listed 10 major characteristics that seem essential for achieving this integration (see Table 3.1). Most of these components are developed initially by early home experiences and then reshaped by later classroom experiences. The child who is a good information processor, and who achieves at his or her expected level of academic performance, has developed many of the characteristics listed in Table 3.1.

Although it is possible that underachieving students are deficient in all of the essential defining attributes of good information processing, we believe that it is the incomplete or inadequate integration of self-regulation (Point 3), with strong motivational beliefs about the power and importance of self-efficacy (Points 5 and 6), that is at the heart of underachievement. This failure of integrated metacognitive development often occurs in a context where "hoped-for" future selves (Point 8) are absent or unrealistic. Interestingly, several different developmental patterns might lead to the same level and type of underachievement in early adolescence but perhaps with differential long-term consequences. It is to these causes and consequences surrounding the breakdown of the integration of regulation and motivation in underachieving students that we orient the remainder of this chapter.

Metacognition: A Model of Strategy-Based Learning

Because good information processors are flexible, adaptive learners, it is not surprising that the centerpiece of metacognitive theory is strategy selection, monitoring, and revision. From a developmental perspective, specific strategies are essential for effective learning and successful problem solving, in large part because they provide the context for developing higher level planning and executive skills as well as the basis for forming attributional beliefs and enhancing a positive sense of self-efficacy.

TABLE 3.1
Characteristics of Good Information Processing

1. Knows a large number of learning strategies.
2. Understands when, where, and why these strategies are important.
3. Selects and monitors strategies wisely, and is extremely reflective and planful.
4. Adheres to an incremental view regarding the growth of mind.
5. Believes in the importance of carefully deployed effort.
6. Is intrinsically motivated, task-oriented, and has mastery goals.
7. Does not fear failure—in fact, realizes that failure is essential for success; hence, is not anxious about tests but sees them as learning opportunities.
8. Has concrete, multiple images of possibles selves, both hoped-for and feared selves in the near and distant future.
9. Knows a great deal about many topics and has rapid access to that knowledge.
10. Has a history of being supported in all of these characteristics by parents, schools, and society at large.

Attributional Beliefs and Self-Regulation. Most of the research supporting an interactive view of metacognition has focused on attributional and executive processes as they jointly influence strategy use (Borkowski et al., 1990). Perhaps the strongest evidence comes from a study by Reid and Borkowski (1987) on the combined effects of attributional beliefs and self-control in producing multiple instances of strategy use with learning disabled and hyperactive children.

The intervention program in the Reid and Borkowski (1987) study contained three components: detailed information about two specific strategies, self-control procedures useful in implementing these strategies (i.e., executive processing), and a recognition of the importance of effort and personal causality in producing successful performance. In the self-control condition, the instructor modeled self-verbalization procedures for the child (e.g., "look to see how the problem might be solved"; "stop and think before responding"). Self-control procedures were taught in the context of specific strategy training that focused on the use of interrogative-associative mediators appropriate for a paired associate task and a clustering-rehearsal strategy for use on a sort–recall readiness task. The interaction of the three metacognitive components seems to play an essential role in the generalization and maintenance of strategic behavior, which failed to occur to the same extent in conditions that did not integrate regulatory and motivational processes. We believe that the emphasis on strategy-based effort in the Reid and Borkowski (1987) study set in motion a reciprocal chain of events between strategic behaviors, executive or self-control processes, and positive beliefs about the importance of effort. The net result was that children who, for the most part, were not spontaneous strategy users at the study's outset, used "low-level" strategies with greater flexibility and persistence following self-regulatory and attributional training.

The results of the Reid and Borkowski (1987) study led to the development of a more complex metacognitive model (Borkowski et al., 1990). This stage of model development, which can be seen in Fig. 3.1, emphasized the integration of executive processes and attributional beliefs: As connections among regulation and motivation are formed, a fully integrated metacognitive system emerges. When this system functions properly, motivation drives cognition and, in turn, cognitive actions serve to strengthen motivational beliefs. Furthermore, the most important activity in achieving this reciprocity is not so much strategy-based performance per se but rather decisions to be strategic and remain strategic in the face of problem-solving challenges.

Another important, although underresearched, aspect of metacognitive theory is the linkage between self-regulation and long-term personal goals (Day, Borkowski, Dietmeyer, Howsepian, & Saenz, 1992). Because the

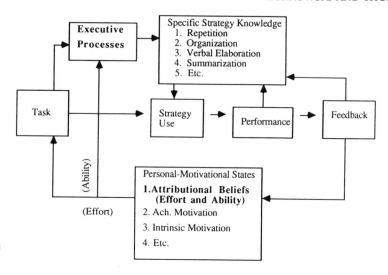

FIG. 3.1. A metacognitive model showing the interrelationships among executive processing, attributional beliefs, and strategy use.

importance of long-term goals and the development of self-regulation has not been extensively discussed in the extant literature, some reflections on the nature and functioning of possible selves are in order.

The Concept of Possible Selves. Markus and Nurius (1986) referred to visions of oneself in the future as "possible selves." More recently, Day et al. (1992) argued that academically relevant possible selves can affect a student's behavior along several dimensions. Positive visions of the future for a young adolescent (such as "me as a lawyer or as a paramedic") give meaning to school subjects related to those visions ("I study English so I can learn to communicate" or "I study science so that I can realize my goal to become a physician"). The important point is that academic tasks with personal meaning are those that students strive to complete with high achievement. It is no wonder that their level of intrinsic motivation often becomes elevated (Nicholls, 1984).

When school subjects are personally relevant, students are more likely to espouse learning goals—desiring to increase their mental competence—over performance goals (Dweck, 1986). They seek favorable judgments about their competence from themselves as well as from others. Indeed, students who strive to increase their intellectual competence persist in their problem-solving efforts even after receiving negative evaluative feedback. Thus, feedback, positive or negative, is more likely to influence students who are invested in mastering a topic rather than solving a problem.

Possible Selves and Self-Regulation. An essential aspect of self-regulation is its goal directedness (Zimmerman & Schunk, 1989). Possible selves represent goals, and once a child envisions a future goal, he or she has taken the first step in actualizing or developing self-regulatory processes. Possible selves facilitate another component of self-regulation—self-monitoring. Envisioning a future self allows a child to evaluate progress and to judge the distance from a desired goal. This realization of progress becomes the basis for self-reinforcement, whereas the recognition of failure and stagnation can lead a child to reevaluate, and perhaps alter, the strategies used to reach the desired goal. The processes of self-reinforcement and strategy modification are also integral to the emergence of other forms of self-regulation.

In short, we hypothesize that the concept of possible selves is integral to the development and functioning of self-regulation and planfulness, both in terms of fostering opportunities for executive decisions and, later, by providing long-range sources of motivation for their utilization. This hypothesized linkage between future goals and the operation of executive processing has clear and important educational consequences, especially if self-regulation is the defining characteristic of successful students (Pressley et al., 1990): If students have not developed, or are not committed to, academically supportive short- and long-term personal goals, self-regulation of their study behaviors becomes problematic.

Metacognition and Underachievement: A General Model

Given the developmental context we have established for the simultaneous emergence of regulation, motivation, and affect, there are several possible scenarios that might characterize metacognitive development in underachievement students. In this section we focus on dysfunctional metacognitive processes that are typically observed during the middle school years. In later sections we present several hypotheses that would argue for different developmental patterns that eventually yield somewhat similar behaviors during the early adolescent years. Finally, we suggest differential behavioral outcomes during the adult years based on the nature of the causal variables that underlie early types of underachievement.

A Componential Analysis of Underachievement. Figure 3.2 presents a recent model of metacognition (Borkowski & Muthukrishna, 1992) that we believe has relevance for understanding underachievement. The dashed lines in the model indicated four potential problems in the linkages among major components of metacognition that may lead to underachievement:

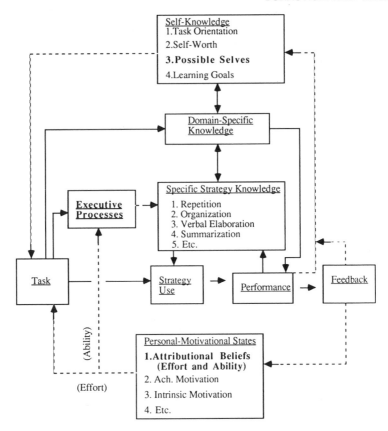

FIG. 3.2. A complete model of metacognition, showing the relationship among executive processing, attributional beliefs, possible selves, and strategy use. After Borkowski and Muthukrishna (1992). Adapted by permission.

1. Most importantly, there is disassociation in the way feedback about the causes of successful and unsuccessful performance becomes linked to positive attributional beliefs. That is, underachieving students typically fail to develop appropriate connections among successful, strategy-based actions, beliefs about the importance of appropriately deployed effort, and the corresponding belief that actually ability is "enhanced" by strategy-governed achievements.

2. Deficiencies in the attributional belief system have important consequences for whether executive processes are fully developed and/or successfully deployed on future occasions. Both effort and ability attributions are hypothesized to energize executive processing by prompt-

ing students to approach tasks with confidence, to analyze tasks deliberately, to select reasonable strategic approaches, and to monitor progress with diligence. These aspects of self-regulation seem less likely to develop in underachieving students because they are neither promoted nor maintained by a mature attributional belief system.

3. It is not surprising that we predict less planfulness, greater impulsivity, and less persistence among underachieving students. That is, the essential link in the entire metacognitive system—the association between executive processing and strategy-based actions—is generally weak and underdeveloped.

4. Over time, unacceptably low levels of performance negatively impact the emergence of the self system. One important consequence may be a failure to create multiple visions of oneself in various future states (e.g., "me as a successful graduate in accounting from the University of Kansas"; "me as a successful husband, father, and CPA"; etc.).

The failure to develop multiple, positive possible selves in early childhood may create a condition in which there is little long-term motivation for pursuing current and complex problem solving activities (Day et al., 1992). That is, the absence of vivid, dynamic, and functional possible selves may inhibit the emergence of executive processing, especially on challenging, demand situations (i.e., a failure to aspire to a college career may not only restrict the choice of college preparatory courses but produce less reflective, deliberate decision-making activities in many academically related areas). Hence, an immature developmental connection between the emerging self and executive systems likely prolongs or exacerbates academic difficulties for underachieving students.

When viewed from this perspective, underachievement is primarily the result of insufficient maturity in the development of the executive or regulatory system. This deficiency in the regulation of cognitive activities arises from a history of negative experiences that also handicap the development of motivational (i.e., attributional beliefs) and personal (e.g., possible selves) states. In turn, continued failures due to inadequate cognitive self-regulation prolong motivational, emotional, and interpersonal problems. If this perspective is plausible, it would not be surprising to find that underachievement is a life-long affliction. In support of these developmental possibilities, we first review the literature that seems relevant to our theory of underachievement. Then we offer several life-span perspectives on the causes and consequences of school-based underachievement that flow from the proposed model.

Evidence on Metacognition and Underachievement

Empirical Support. Perhaps the best single review of this literature is the recent life-span treatment of underachievement by McCall et al. (1992). The extant literature, however, does not address the issue of whether executive processing and attributional beliefs fail to become integrated in underachieving students. The intention here is to review three examples of recent research—based on correlational, manipulative, and case study designs—that provide preliminary evidence for our proposed metacognitive model of underachievement.

A Correlational Approach. Carr, Borkowski, and Maxwell (1991) assessed the functioning of attributional beliefs as they influenced the reading performance of normally achieving and underachieving students. The selection of 110 underachievers was based on a four-step process:

1. Third-, fourth-, and fifth-grade teachers were asked to nominate children who were currently receiving C or D grades and yet who appeared capable of working at a higher level of performance. It should be added that none of the nominated children were participating in special classes.

2. Next, children were given two tests of ability—the Slossen IQ and the Peabody Picture Vocabulary tests. Averaged ability scores were transformed to z-scores using national norms.

3. Reading grades were then averaged over two semesters, and individual grades were transformed to z-scores using reading distributions from the local school system.

4. Finally, each child's z-score for reading was subtracted from his or her z-score for intelligence. Children with difference scores of .5 or above were designated as underachievers. Approximately one-half of the children originally nominated by the teachers were eventually classified as underachievers.

Teachers also nominated achievers through the same process. Achievers were children who were currently receiving C or B grades and appeared to be working at their grade level. These children were given the same ability tests as the underachievers. One hundred and ten children, with transformed difference scores between .49 and −.49, were considered normal achievers. We believe this approach is a more precise way to select underachievers than approaches used in previous research (see

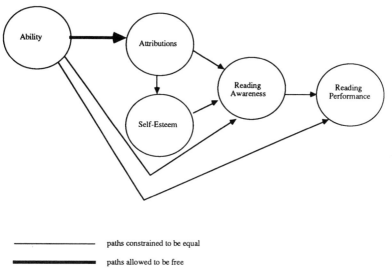

paths constrained to be equal

paths allowed to be free

FIG. 3.3. Hypothesized model of ability, attributions, and reading performance. After Carr, Borkowski, and Maxwell (1991). Adapted by permission.

earlier sections) in that it yields a specific underachievement (or achievement) score for each student.

Both groups were given a battery of tests assessing the five constructs that are depicted in Fig. 3.3. An analysis of mean differences revealed that achievers, in contrast to underachievers, had higher self-esteem, a stronger belief in the utility of effort, enhanced reading awareness, better academic performance, and were more intrinsically motivated. Based on structural equation modeling techniques, it was shown that intellectual ability facilitated reading performance as well as the development of reading awareness for both achievers and underachievers. Performance was also mediated by attributions, self-esteem, and reading awareness.

Interestingly, it was the connection between ability and attributional beliefs that distinguished the two groups. The attributional beliefs of achievers seem to develop in tandem with their ability; that is, achievers credited themselves, at least to some extent, for their prior successful performance. In contrast, underachievers failed to associate their abilities with the appropriate expenditure of effort; that is, they did not take credit for their intellectual performance. The failure to make this essential connection may have retarded the development of the underachiever's metacognitive system. In short, the acquisition of appropriate attributional belief patterns most likely augments the development and integration of other components in the metacognitive system of achievers, especially regulating processes.

The Manipulative Approach. Carr and Borkowski (1989) developed an intervention program testing the hypothesis that strategy-plus-attribution training would be maximally effective in producing changes in reading performance. The assumption was based on the belief that underachievers do not so much lack knowledge of reading strategies, but rather a realistic understanding that strategic behavior in tandem with effort results in reading achievements. This "misunderstanding" was hypothesized to be a major underlying source of underachievement.

Fifty-two underachieving students were randomly assigned to one of three conditions. In a strategy-plus-attribution condition, underachieving students were given direct instructional training in reading comprehension strategies and attributional training. Children were taught the steps to each strategy (e.g., first read the entire paragraph and make sure you understand what you read). For the strategy-plus-attribution group, at each step of the strategy, the instructor reinforced the need for effort in the form of attentiveness to the strategy. The instructor then suggested that reading and searching for meaning required considerable effort but that this extra effort was necessary for successful recall. Attributional beliefs were the focus of the training program for two reasons: Changes in attributional beliefs were thought to affect self-esteem in the long run and reading awareness in the short run. Each of three strategies (topic sentence, summarization, and questioning) was trained over two 30-minute sessions, for a total of six training sessions. Children in the strategy-only condition received strategy training through direct instruction without attributional training. The control group received the same tasks as the treatment groups, but without strategy training.

The addition of the attributional component to the training program produced significant gains in strategy use, recall performance, reading grades, and attributional beliefs. Not only did the strategy-plus-attribution condition promote the maintenance of the trained strategies, it facilitated generalization of the strategies. It should be pointed out that no type of training increased self-esteem. Longer, or more intense, instructions, which would produce extensive generalized use of the strategy in classroom contexts, may be necessary to alter self-esteem. Hence, the results of the Carr and Borkowski (1989) study suggested that strategy-based interventions should explicitly include motivational components aimed at modifying attributional beliefs.

Several major conclusions about the processes that distinguish achievement and underachievement can be drawn from the results of the two studies just described. In contrast to much of the earlier work on underachievement, this research brings together many of the major variables—including the affective, motivational, and cognitive processes suggested by Krouse and Krouse (1981)—that have hitherto been studied in isolation. The structural equations modeling approach sheds new light on the relationships among affective, motivational, and metacognitive processes in both achievers and underachievers. The results of the modeling technique suggested that a primary difference between underachievers and achievers was the connection between extant ability and attributional beliefs: Attributional beliefs appeared to drive or energize other components of metacognition (such as reading awareness and perhaps self-esteem). As a result, the entire system suffers when children fail to develop appropriate attributional beliefs in concert with their intellectual and/or academic achievements. Finally, the training study suggested that underachieving children need to be instructed not only in specific strategies but also in accompanying effort-related beliefs and metacognitive knowledge, in order for that knowledge to be translated into successful reading performance.

The Case Study Approach. With respect to the general model of underachievement proposed earlier, the research reviewed thus far suggests the potential importance of the attributional belief system in developing strategies and skills. But what about the two other metacognitive components we have implicated as causal factors in underachievement: self regulation and possible selves? We turn to the extensive clinical work of Harvey Mandel to find insights about these metacognitive components.

Mandel, Marcus, and Mandel (1992) studied the emergence of various types of underachievers who display different symptoms and etiologies. The importance of regulatory processes and possible selves can be seen in the symptoms that Mandel et al. (1992) have found in a class of underachievers without mental disorders and of average intellectual capacity, referred to as nonachievement syndrome (NAS) students.

With respect to problems in self regulatory or executive processes, underachieving students with NAS showed a failure to plan ahead (even though they expressed good intentions to succeed); displayed inaccurate self-appraisal and monitoring (frequently overestimating performance); and were easily distracted in the face of academic challenges. With respect to the phenomenon of possible selves, NAS students showed a clear lack of introspection about setting and fulfilling future goals even though they were reasonably content with their current level of performance (e.g., displaying little anxiety or mood swings). In short, the clinical insights and case study approach of Mandel et al. (1992) provide initial support for deficiencies in executive processing and the formation of possible selves in at least one type of underachieving students.

A LIFE-SPAN PERSPECTIVE ON
UNDERACHIEVEMENT

It is important, for both scientific and practical reasons, to understand both the causes and the consequences of underachievement. From a theoretical perspective, we know little about the origins of self-regulated behaviors, especially how environmental factors influence the dysfunctional development of regulation (cf. Zimmerman & Schunk, 1989). From an educational perspective, such theoretically relevant information is essential for knowing when, where, and how to intervene. For instance, the time when underachievement is first "diagnosed"—usually during the late elementary or middle school years—may be too late for effective remediation. That is, the failure to integrate cognition and motivation, which presumably has already occurred, may be resilient to significant alteration.

We argue that it is important to understand the developmental sequelae that underlie underachievement and, furthermore, to isolate precisely how academically related underachievement may have major consequences for interpersonal and career adjustment problems across the entire life span, as is implied by the research of McCall et al. (1992). In the next sections, we trace the potential origins of self-regulation in two classes of underachievers; discuss adult consequences associated with early achievement; and speculate about self-regulation, self-efficacy, and aging.

Origins of Self-Regulation and Implications
for Underachievement

As Mandel and colleagues have argued, there is considerable clinical evidence suggesting that underachievement develops under different sets of conditions and has distinct symptomatologies. One type of underachievement discussed earlier, the NAS student, appears rather late in development and may be more treatable through educational intervention in the home and in the school than other types of underachievement. With the NAS type of underachievement, parents seem to show a pattern of ineffectiveness and inconsistency in confronting their child on a number of home and school tasks. They frequently try to minimize conflicts with their child in setting expectations because they fear (in an extremely vague sense) what unintended consequences the increased tension may trigger. They tend to "own" their child's problems and are fearful of the natural consequences of poor effort (Mandel et al., 1992). In short, the NAS student never learns to accept the responsibility which is rightfully his or her own and to develop the sense of efficacy and higher order executive skills necessary to meet cognitive-academic responsibilities.

Another form of underachievement—the conduct disordered (CD) underachievers—seemingly develops much earlier and may prove more resistant to remediation. Its early roots likely reside in the emotional consequences of insecure attachment. This source and the timing of its developmental onset seem essential for designing educational-therapeutic programs. That is, the nature of early mother–infant interactions may set the stage for life-long underachievement.

Colin (1991) summarized the attachment literature, showing the probably causes and consequences of insecure attachment between 10 and 18 months. Relatedly, Crittenden (1992) showed the continuity between early insecurity and the emergence of *coercive* and *defended* patterns of insecure attachment at around ages 3–4. We hypothesized that the developmental processes associated with the coercive pattern may characterize the CD underachiever and serve as precursors for later dysfunctional metacognitive development.

In support of these ideas about CD underachievers, Moss (1992) found that interpersonal regulation is consolidated in secure dyads by the beginning of the second year of life, whereas greater mother–child mutual attention is directed to insecure children. More specifically, insecure children showed more management of their mother's behavior and were less likely to comply with her orienting attempts. In addition, there was a greater likelihood that mothers and infants in the insecure classification would respond to each others' disapproval with negative gestures or comments, suggesting the emergence of a cycle of negative reciprocity.

In a more recent study, Moss, Gosselin, Parrot, and Dubeau (1993) found striking evidence that mothers of secure preschoolers combined verbal instructions about problem solving with progressive empowerment in problem regulation. In contrast, mothers of insecure preschoolers tended to teach less sophisticated planning and regulatory skills. These data suggest an important linkage between attachment security and the development of cognitive self-regulation.

In a similar vein, Borkowski et al. (1992) recently examined the concurrent relationships among the security of an infant's attachment, the occurrence of attentional flexibility (as reflected in the type and quality of toy play), and subsequent intellectual development at age 3. It was expected that differences in attentional flexibility between securely and anxiously attached infants would be particularly pronounced during the two reunion episodes of the Strange Situation paradigm. For secure infants, the caregiver's return should be anticipated and expected; once reunited, such infants should be free to return their attention to exploring their environment. In contrast, anxiously attached infants should experience stress both during and following separations; hence, they might be expected to experience cognitive confusion upon the caregiver's return. This emotional confusion was expected to impede cognitive flexibility as the child explored his or her immediate environment.

The hypothesis was tested with a sample of 59 first-time adolescent mothers and their infants. Infants were videotaped in the Strange Situation when they were approximately 12 months of age. Interestingly, the correlation between security of attachment and attentional flexibility during the first reunion episode was significant (r = .27). It should be noted that this outcome occurred in the presence of attenuated ranges for each variable. Additionally, the measure of attentional flexibility correlated significantly with Bayley mental development at 1 year (r = .45), Stanford-Binet IQ at 3 years (r = .47), and receptive language (PPVT-R) at 3 years (r = .48; for the baseline period only). Although these preliminary analyses are only suggestive of early reciprocal linkages between the flexibility of attention and attachment, as well as their subsequent ties with later cognitive-intellectual development, they do provide an intriguing framework for broadening our views about the potential causes of underachievement. Specifically, in stressful situations (such as the Strange Situation paradigm), infants with anxious attachments may be compelled to direct their attention to emotional relationships rather than to exploring, and learning from, important aspects of their environments, steps essential for achieving cognitive regulation.

Although yet to be substantiated, the implications of this hypothesis for understanding delays in cognitive development are straightforward: Contingent social interactions tend to direct an infant's attention to critical aspects of environmental stimulation, whereas noncontingent interactions reduce attention to such events. Simultaneously, consistent and contingent responses to an infant's needs and verbalization also contribute to the quality of attachment relationships. Although contingent responsivity itself provides explanations for both anxious attachment and the regulation of attention, we believe the emergence of insecure attachment further interferes with attentional flexibility, inhibiting the development of critical self-regulatory skills that are at the heart of metacognition. Thus, early insecurity might lead to defects in metacognition, especially in terms of self-regulatory processing, thus setting the stage for the development of the CD underachiever.

THE UNDERACHIEVER AS AN ADULT

Vocational Implications of Academic Underachievement

McCall et al. (1992), in their study of underachievement, analyzed data gathered from 6,720 juniors and seniors in high school during 1965–1966 and again 13 years later. McCall et al. (1992) used the data from both periods to analyze the association between early underachievement and its adult consequences. These researchers sought to answer such questions as (a) is underachievement distinguishable from low grades for later educational and occupational achievement, and (2) which types of underachievers (if any) overcome poor performance in high school and subsequently reach their educational and occupational potentials (as predicted by ability measures)?

With respect to planning for the future, McCall et al. (1992) found that high school underachievers thought less about their future careers and preferred less demanding academic courses, especially math and science coursework, than students who had the same mental ability and were academic achievers. Underachievers had lower educational and vocational goals as well as lower perceptions of their current and future academic abilities. In addition, underachievers had lower status and lower paying jobs than achievers with the same mental ability. No differences were found between underachievers and those students who had the same grade-point average (GPA) but lower intellectual ability.

Underachievers also tended to complete fewer years of college education than achievers with the same ability. Underachieving males were twice as likely to attend a vocational or technical school and only half as likely to attend a college or university. Those who did attend a college or university were twice as likely to drop out and only half as likely to graduate. Fifty-seven percent of female underachievers were more likely to enroll in a technical or vocational school and were only 42% as likely to attend a college or university. They were much more likely to drop out of college than female students with the same mental ability. Most importantly, all underachievers were less likely to complete college than achievers with the same high school grades but with lesser abilities.

Thirteen years after graduation, underachievers tended to display more job instability when compared with achievers who had the same mental abilities. Furthermore, underachievers were 50% more likely to divorce during the 13-year period following high school than students with the same GPAs but lesser abilities. Finally, academic underachievers were less likely to complete 4 years of college, were more likely to have lower paying and less status jobs, as well as more job instability, and were more likely to divorce than students who had the same grades but lesser academic ability. McCall et al. (1992) concluded that underachievers lacked persistence in facing challenges and adversities in their educational, vocational, and personal adult lives.

Persisting Problems of Underachievement and Possible Selves

Possible Selves and Self-Schemas. Possible selves guide individuals in their selection and persistence of actions in educational and occupational activities (Markus & Wurf, 1987). The development of possible selves is enhanced by the quality of attributions made for the abilities that a person possesses (Graham, 1991; Platt, 1988; Taylor & Boggiano, 1987; Weiner, 1986). These attributions need to be both internal (in particular, ability attributions) and stable in order to create a possible self. This type of attribution implies personal responsibility for one's actions (Markus, 1983), and further denotes the necessity of regulating one's own behavior. Markus, Cross, and Wurf (1990) maintained that effort attributions inhibit the construction of a self-schema of ability in specific domains. We believe, however, that the combination of ability and effort attributions will also lead to the construction of self-schemas, and thus the formation of possible selves. An absence of these schemas diminishes the universe of "vocational" possible selves which individuals may choose from. Possible selves, when present, become potential options people see for themselves, and they contain the expectations of success that people have for realizing that possible selves (Cantor, Markus, Niedentha, & Nurius, 1986).

In short, we hypothesize that self-regulatory and motivational processes are intimately intertwined. Motivational habits, such as causal attributions and representations of possible selves, persist into adulthood and play vital roles in occupational goals which students establish for themselves. From a developmental perspective, Markus, Cross, and Wurf (1990) have emphasized that self-schemas are generated by a student's experience in a given domain. These domain-specific schemas include information about ability that, in turn, provides direction from childhood to adulthood on how to use their skills and talents in vocational settings. Furthermore, the use of skills requires planning and execution—processes that we hypothesize are deficient in adult underachievers.

Possible Selves and Self-Efficacy. Studies of self-efficacy provide supporting evidence for the role of possible selves in the construction of career goals. Students' efficacious beliefs will influence their choice of career aspirations, will guide how much effort they will put forth to realize those aspirations, and will determine how long they will choose to persevere during periods of setbacks (Bandura, 1991). In addition, students with strong self-efficacy beliefs will tend to achieve more favorable academic outcomes (Brown, Lent, & Larkin, 1989). Furthermore, a meta-analysis of self-efficacy and academic outcomes suggested that efficacy effects are particularly facilitative for low-achieving students (Multon, Brown, & Lent, 1991), that is, underachieving students.

The relationships among efficacy, academic achievement, and possible selves have been examined with young adults. For instance, Lent, Lopez, and Bieschke (1991) and Betz and Hackett (1983) explored the sources of mathematics self-efficacy and its relationship to science-based career choices in college-aged students. Lent, Brown, and Larkin (1986) reported that efficacy beliefs about the ability to complete various science and engineering coursework predicted subsequent performance in these courses for college undergraduates. In addition, self-efficacy differences were found to predict persistence in technical/scientific college majors (Brown, Lent, & Larkin, 1989), academic accomplishment for migrant or seasonal farmworking high school students (Bores-Rangel, Church, Szendre, & Reeves, 1991), rejection by women of occupations dominated by men (Betz & Hackett, 1981; Church, Teresa, Rosebrook, & Szendre, 1992), and perceived career options of American Indian, Hispanic, and White rural high school students (Lauver & Jones, 1991).

Possible Selves and Goals. Markus and Ruvolo (1989) conceptualized possible selves as personalized representations of goals. They strongly emphasized that though motivated behavior depends on one's attributions, the referent of those attributions that endures is the possible self. What this implies is that possible selves developed during childhood become the lasting or durable goals throughout adulthood and into old age. Attributions that helped to create the possible selves, being both internal and stable, contribute strongly to the formation of possible selves for the duration of one's occupational career. If the possible self incorporates achievement behavior in adolescence, then this achievement orientation should continue in adult vocational domains.

If, however, the possible self is an enduring representation of underachieving goals and expectations, then the underachievement in the educational arena can be expected to continue into the vocational setting. Research on vocational behavior illustrates the importance of possible selves in the workplace. For example, Roberson, Houston, and Diddams (1989) examined work outcomes through a content analysis of the worker's goals. Generally, goals of successful workers contained a mixture of possible selves for employee's ongoing performance, for the development of skills related to professional development, as well as for the building of autonomy-independence in fulfilling those goals.

In conclusion, the metacognitive model of Borkowski and Muthu-krishna (1992) postulated that attributional patterns and representations of possible selves in childhood will continue into adulthood. Additionally, the regulatory processes that are underdeveloped in educational settings will serve to constrain the likelihood of reaching satisfactory achievement in vocational settings. Essential self-monitoring and decision-making processes will continue to be lacking and may well become even more deficient. The underachieving adult may not be aware of what can be accomplished by forming alternative goals (possible selves) and changing causal attributions. Even if the adult underachiever desires to change and upgrade his or her career aspirations, the abilities to create appropriate strategies, together with the necessary motivation to implement and sustain the use of those strategies, may be lacking (Latham & Locke, 1991; Locke, 1991). From this perspective, it becomes apparent why McCall et al. (1992) found that underachievers in school settings tended to remain underachievers throughout their vocational careers.

Aging and Underachievement

Intellect and Efficacy. Individuals who have high efficacy beliefs appear to have motivational patterns, self-regulatory capacities, and possible selves that will engender lasting achievement in educational settings as well as in vocational careers. Low efficacy beliefs lead to academic underachievement, resulting in motivational patterns, self-regulatory capacities, and possible selves that will reproduce the products of underachievement in the workforce. Because these characteristics do not change upon retirement, it is interesting to explore the consequences of underachievement in the aging adult.

Recent research has examined older adults' beliefs and attitudes about their cognitive and intellectual abilities and what happens to those abilities in concert with the aging process (Cornelius & Caspi, 1987; Lachman, 1986). Many older individuals who are aging "normally" believe that their intellectual performance will decline with age. Consequently, they will likely experience the effects of underachievement as they "unnecessarily" set lower personal and intellectual goals for themselves, thus restricting opportunities for self-regulated activities. But what happens to the person with a life-long history of underachievement? We expect these problems will be exacerbated as the underachieving adult grows old.

Possible Selves. Ryff (1991) studied possible selves in adulthood and old age. She examined several dimensions of psychological well-being (including autonomy in controlling one's activities and general purpose in living) and their relationships to possible selves. Ryff (1991) found that older adults did not differ in their past and future assessments of autonomy; in contrast, younger adults anticipated greater autonomy to develop as they increased in age. Furthermore, older men believed that they had experienced a recent decline in their purpose in life. In addition, older adults, both men and women, believed that they would experience a further decrement in their purpose for living as they continued along the aging process. Ryff's study, much like similar studies on aging and intellectual efficacy, seems to be related to changes in the dimensions of possible selves as adults entered old age. Once again, it is a "normal" type of underachievement that may occur with regularity during the later stages of life.

Underachievement in Older Adults. The developmental perspective contained in the metacognitive model of Borkowski and Muthukrishna (1992) provides a potential framework for determining when "underachieving" behaviors and beliefs have distinct onsets in old age versus when they are simply a continuation of behaviors developed early during childhood. The implications for the underachiever as an older adult are not promising: A lifetime of poor motivational patterns and deficient self-regulatory skills leaves the older underachiever lacking the ability to successfully address the multiple problems typically found in the aging population, such as managing insufficient funds, making the necessary decisions to manage health-care needs, and developing auxiliary support systems. We believe that the lack of coordination between "will and skill" cultivated throughout their lifetimes will continue to haunt the older underachievers.

RESEARCH AND EDUCATIONAL IMPLICATIONS

When viewed from a life-span perspective, it is clear that early prevention programs represent the best approach for treating the problems of underachievement. Although it is possible to design remediation programs that address the integration of cognition, affect, and motivation in adolescent underachievers, a more efficacious approach is to develop at-risk profiles for young students in kindergarten and the early elementary school years and then to institute special pull-out programs as early as possible.

Diagnoses and Intervention

Although research has not advanced to the point of identifying the exact nature and scope of an at-risk test battery of underachievement, the shape of such an assessment instrument might be driven by the theory of metacognition we have proposed. Clearly, the measurement of attributional beliefs and domain-specific beliefs about self-efficacy would occupy a preeminent role. This is because dysfunctional beliefs are almost always linked with underachievement—irrespective of etiology—and because beliefs likely precede the emergence of self-regulatory mechanisms.

At this stage of metacognitive theory development, we are encountering problems in operationalizing regulatory processes and developing widely accepted and reliable measures of self-regulation. Although it would be desirable to have available an arsenal of tasks that would, in unique ways, assess the concept of executive processing, it is unlikely that such a battery of tests will soon be developed. Hence, a focus on the assessment of beliefs is both practical and theoretically sound. A second diagnostic focus would pinpoint the emergence of possible selves—both short-term ("me as a successful second grader") and long-term ("me as a successful school psychologist"), because we have argued that is a major developmental problem for underachievers.

After establishing the reliability as well as the concurrent, construct, and predictive validity of a test battery that featured beliefs about efficacy and visions of possible selves, research might turn to the design and analysis of various types of intervention programs. The intervention effort might well involve the integrated training of study strategies; executive processes necessary to implement and monitor those strategies; positive beliefs about the importance of strategy-based effort and the growth of mental competence; and the emergence of hoped-for, sought-after visions of future selves. Such programs might be imbedded in pull-out or whole-classroom contexts and would contrast integrated training with a detailed analyses of individual metacognitive components, as well as the order and timing of their delivery within the curriculum.

Suggestions about the development of self-regulation and self-efficacy are available in the literature to build on in designing intervention programs (Bandura, 1991). Less guidance is available on how to introduce formal instructions about the creation of possible selves into the educational curriculum. However, Day et al. (1992) developed a training program with the intention of elaborating the contents of students' hopes and fears, especially as they relate to academic and occupational achievements. The basic aim was to enhance young students' awareness of the variety of jobs that they eventually might hold as adults and to emphasize that the completion of middle school and graduation from high school are essential steps for assuring multiple vocational career options. An attempt was also made to enhance students' self-efficacy by inculcating the belief that each student can realize his or her personal goals, but only through the expenditure of personal effort.

A metaphor, the "Possible-Me Tree," made concrete the idea that visions of oneself develop over time and that there are multiple facets to our lives. Thus, the four branches of the Possible-Me Tree were designed to represent four important areas of life: family and friends, free time, school, and work. In addition, the Possible-Me Tree had leaves of two colors (green and red) that represented students' hopes (e.g., securing a well-paying job, driving a fancy car) and fears (e.g., unemployment, a high school dropout).

Day et al. (1992) attempted to make vivid both hopes and fears and to clarify the steps necessary to achieve them so as to motivate students to work toward lofty goals and to continually revise and update these goals. The training program was delivered in a give-and-take interactive format, with artwork serving as the central medium. The Possible-Me Tree metaphor was introduced and described; then students created their own Possible-Me Trees.

Major topics of discussion included:

1. Different people have different definitions of success.
2. Activities students enjoy can become occupations they choose.
3. Education is needed to obtain many jobs that students desire.
4. Individuals in different jobs (both desirable and undesirable occupations) spend their work and free time in a variety of ways.
5. Obstacles (e.g., unfair teachers, negative peer pressure) are inevitable as students try to achieve success.

Throughout the lessons the Possible-Me Tree was referred to repeatedly, and students added leaves (both red and green) to indicate new visions of their future selves.

The major results suggested that relative to a no-intervention control group, children who participated in the intervention endorsed more positive possibilities for their future (e.g., "Do you ever think you will be successful in the future?") and rejected more negative possibilities (e.g., "Do you ever think you will be absent from school often in the future?"). In addition, trained subjects rated specific occupations (e.g., judge, physician) as significantly more likely for them in the future (Day et al., 1992). These results suggested that specific activities can take place in the classroom that contribute to the formation of possible selves, providing an additional rationale (and motivation) for developing and utilizing executive processes and study skills.

General Conclusions About Underachievement

In summary, we believe that the life-long afflictions associated with early underachievement might be lessened by an early focus on three essential metacognitive components: executive processes, beliefs about personal control, and hoped-for future goals. This orientation should begin early, perhaps in preschool or Head Start programs. It is an academic question whether or not an explicit focus on the teaching of these components will prove equally beneficial, or even more beneficial, for average-achieving and gifted students than for underachieving students. The main point is, however, that by focusing on underachievement we address the least understood disability facing the current generation of school-age children. Although future research might well address various kinds of underachievement at their respective points of origin, it may prove more practical to treat the disability of underachievement immediately before it surfaces in academic settings, perhaps as early as the first or second grade as reading skills emerge and become perfected. As McCall (in press) cogently argued: The problems of underachievement do not disappear with age, and their ramifications are so pervasive that a national research priority should be given to the identification and treatment of a legion of misunderstood and misclassified students—academic underachievers. We suggest that metacognitive theory can play a constructive role in guiding these preventive and remedial efforts.

REFERENCES

Bailey, R. C. (1971). Self-concept differences in low and high achieving students. *Journal of Clinical Psychology, 27*(2), 188–191.

Bandura, A. (1991). Social cognitive theory of self-regulation. *Organizational Behavior and Human Decision Processes, 50,* 248–287.

Bar-Tal, D. (1978). Attributional analysis of achievement related behavior. *Review of Educational Research, 48,* 259–271.

Betz, N. E., & Hackett, B. (1983). The relationship of mathematics self-efficacy expectations to the selection of science-based college majors. *Journal of Vocational Behavior, 23,* 329–345.

Betz, N. E., & Hackett, B. (1991). The relationship of career-related self-efficacy expectations to perceived career options in college women and men. *Journal of Counseling Psychology, 28,* 399–410.

Bores-Rangel, E., Church, A. T., Szendre, D., & Reeves, C. (1991). Self-efficacy in relation to occupational consideration and academic performance in high school equivalency students. *Journal of Counseling Psychology, 37,* 407–418.

Borkowski, J. G., Carr, M., Rellinger, E., & Pressley, M. (1990). Self-regulated cognition: Interdependence of metacognition, attributions, and self-esteem. In B. Jones & L. Idol (Eds.), *Dimensions of thinking and cognitive instruction* (Vol. 1, pp. 53–92). Hillsdale, NJ: Lawrence Erlbaum Associates.

Borkowski, J. G., & Muthukrishna, N. (1992). Moving metacognition into the classroom: "Working models" and effective strategy teaching. In M. Pressley, K. R. Harris, & J. T. Guthrie (Eds.), *Promoting academic literacy: Cognitive research and instructional innovation* (pp. 477–501). Orlando, FL: Academic Press.

Borkowski, J. G., Whitman, T. L., Wurtz-Passino, A., Rellinger, E., Sommer, K., Keogh, D., & Weed, K. (1992). Unraveling the "New Morbidity": Adolescent parenting and developmental delays. In N. Bray (Ed.), *International review of research in mental retardation* (Vol. 18, pp. 159–196). San Diego: Academic Press.

Briggs, R. D., Tosi, D. J., & Morely, R. M. (1971). Study habit modification and its effect on academic performance: A behavioral approach. *Journal of Educational Research, 64,* 110–115.

Broderick, P. C., & Sewell, T. E. (1985). Attribution for success and failure in children of different social class. *Journal of Social Psychology, 5,* 591–599.

Broman, S., Bien, E., & Shaughnessy, P. (1985). *Low achieving children: The first seven years.* Hillsdale, NJ: Lawrence Erlbaum Associates.

Brown, S. D., Lent, R. W., & Larkin, K. C. (1989). Self-efficacy as a moderator of scholastic aptitude-academic performance relationships. *Journal of Vocational Behavior, 35,* 64–75.

Cantor, N., Markus, H., Niedenthal, P., & Nurius, P. (1986). On motivation and the self-concept. In R. M. Sorrentino & E. T. Higgins (Eds.), *Handbook of motivation and cognition: Foundations of social behavior* (pp. 96–121). New York: Guilford Press.

Carr, M., & Borkowski, J. G. (1989). Culture and the development of the metacognitive system. *Zeitschrift fur Pedagogische Psychologie, 3,* 219–228.

Carr, M., Borkowski, J. G., & Maxwell, S. E. (1991). Motivational components of underachievement. *Developmental Psychology, 27,* 108–118.

Church, A. T., Teresa, M. S., Rosebrook, R., & Szendre, D. (1992). Self-efficacy for careers and occupational consideration in minority high school equivalency students. *Journal of Counseling Psychology, 39,* 498–508.

Claes, M., & Salame, R. (1975). Motivation toward accomplishment and the self-evaluation of performances in relation to school achievement. *Canadian Journal of Behavioral Science, 7*(4), 397–410.

Colin, V. L. (1991). *Human attachment: What we know now.* Report prepared under contract HHS-100-90-00 for the Office of Planning and Evaluation, Department of Health and Human Services, Washington, DC.

Cornelius, S. W., & Caspi, A. (1987). Every day problem solving in adulthood and old age. *Psychology and Aging, 2,* 144–153.

Covington, M. V. (1992). *Making the grade: A self-worth perspective on motivation and school reform.* New York: Cambridge University Press.

Crittenden, P. M. (1992). Quality of attachment during the preschool years. *Development and Psychopathology, 4,* 209–241.

Davids, A. (1966). Psychological characteristics of high school male and female potential scientists in comparison with academic underachievers. *Psychology in the Schools, 3*(1), 79–87.

Day, J. D., Borkowski, J. G., Dietmeyer, D. L., Howsepian, B. A., & Saenz, D. S. (1992). Possible selves and academic achievement. In L. T. Winegar & J. Valsinar (Eds.), *Children's development within social context* (Vol. 2, pp. 181–202). Hillsdale, NJ: Lawrence Erlbaum Associates.

Dweck, C. S. (1986). Motivational processes affecting learning. *American Psychologist, 41,* 1040–1048.

Fremouw, W. J., & Freindler, E. L. (1978). Peer versus professional models for study skills training. *Journal of Counseling Psychology, 25,* 576–580.

Graham, S. (1991). A review of attribution theory in achievement contexts. *Educational Psychology Review, 3*(1), 5–39.

Haslam, W. L., & Brown, W. F. (1968). Effectiveness of study skills instruction for high school sophomores. *Journal of Educational Psychology, 59,* 223–226.

Haywood, H. C. (1968). Motivational orientation of overachieving and underachieving elementary school children. *American Journal of Mental Deficiency, 72,* 667.

Heck, R. A. (1972). Need for approval and its relationship to under, expected and over achievement. *Dissertation Abstracts International, 32*(7-A), 3688.

Jhaj, D. S., & Grewal, J. S. (1983). Occupational aspirations of the achievers and underachievers in mathematics. *Asian Journal of Psychology and Education, 11,* 36–39.

Kanoy, R. C., Johnson, B. W., & Kanoy, K. W. (1980). Locus of control and self-concept in achieving and underachieving bright elementary students. *Psychology in the Schools, 17,* 395–399.

Krouse, J. H., & Krouse, H. J. (1981). Toward a multimodal theory of academic underachievement. *Educational Psychologist, 16,* 151–164.

Lachman, M. E. (1986). Personal control in later life: Stability, change, and cognitive correlates. In M. M. Baltes, & P. B. Baltes (Eds.), *The psychology of control and aging* (pp. 207–236). Hillsdale, NJ: Lawrence Erlbaum Associates.

Latham, G. P., & Locke, E. A. (1991). Self regulation through goal setting. *Organizational Behavior and Human Decision Processes, 50,* 212–247.

Lauver, P. J., & Jones, R. M. (1991). Factors associated with perceived career options in American Indian, White, and Hispanic rural high school students. *Journal of Counseling Psychology, 38,* 159–166.

Lent, R. W., Brown, S. D., & Larkin, K. C. (1986). Self-efficacy in the prediction of academic performance and perceived career options. *Journal of Counseling Psychology, 33,* 265–269.

Lent, R. W., Lopez, F. G., & Bieschke, K. J. (1991). Mathematics self-efficacy: Sources and relation to science-based career choice. *Journal of Counseling Psychology, 38,* 424–430.

Locke, E. A. (1991). The motivation sequence, the motivation hub, and the motivation core. *Organizational Behavior and Human Decision Processes, 50,* 288–299.

Mandel, H. P., & Marcus, S. I. (1988). *The psychology of underachievement.* New York: Wiley.

Mandel, H. P., Marcus, S. I., & Mandel, D. E. (1992). *Helping the non-achievement syndrome student.* Toronto: Institute on Achievement and Motivation.

Markus, H. (1983). Self-knowledge: An expanded view. *Journal of Personality, 51,* 543–565.

Markus, H., Cross, S., & Wurf, E. (1990). The role of the self-system in competence. In R. J. Sternberg & J. Kolligian (Eds.), *Competence considered* (pp. 205–225). New Haven, CT: Yale University Press.

Markus, H., & Nurius, P. (1986). Possible selves. *American Psychologist, 41,* 954–969.

Markus, H., & Ruvolo, A. (1989). Possible selves: Personalized representations of goals. In L. A. Pervin (Ed.), *Goal concepts in personality and social psychology* (pp. 211–242). Hillsdale, NJ: Lawrence Erlbaum Associates.

Markus, H., & Wurf, E. (1987). The dynamic self-concept: A social psychological perspective. In M. R. Rosenzweig & L. W. Porter (Eds.), *Annual review of psychology* (Vol. 38, pp. 299–337). Palo Alto, CA: Annual Reviews.

McCall, R. (in press). Academic underachievers. *Current Directions in Psychological Science.*

McCall, R. B., Evahn, C., & Kratzer, L. (1992). *High school underachievers.* Newbury Park, CA: Sage.

McKenzie, J. D. (1964). The dynamics of deviant achievement. *Personnel & Guidance Journal, 42,* 683–686.

Moss, E. (1992). The socioaffective context of joint cognitive activity. In L. T. Winegar & J. Valsiner (Eds.), *Children's development in social context* (Vol. 2, pp. 117–154). Hillsdale, NJ: Lawrence Erlbaum Associates.

Moss, E., Gosselin, C., Parent, S., & Dubeau, D. (1993, March). *Does attachment influence shared metacognitive experiences?* Paper presented at the annual meetings of the Society for Research in Child Development, New Orleans.

Multon, K. D., Brown, D. S., & Lent, R. W. (1991). Relation of self-efficacy beliefs to academic outcomes: A meta-analytic investigation. *Journal of Counseling Psychology, 38,* 30–38.

Nicholls, J. G. (1984). Achievement motivation: Concepts of ability, subjective experience, task choice, and performance. *Psychological Review, 91,* 328–346.

Nuttall, E. V., Nuttall, R. L., Polit, D., & Hunter, J. B. (1976). Effects of family size, birth order, sibling separation and crowding on the achievement of boys and girls. *American Educational Research Journal, 13,* 217–223.

Platt, C. W. (1988). Effects of causal attributions for success on first-term college performance: A covariance structure model. *Journal of Educational Psychology, 80,* 569–578.

Pressley, M., Borkowski, J. G., & Schneider, W. (1990). Good information processing: What it is and how education can promote it. *International Journal of Educational Research, 2,* 857–867.

Reid, M. K., & Borkowski, J. G. (1987). Causal attributions of hyperactive children: Implications for training strategies and self-control. *Journal of Educational Psychology, 79,* 296–307.

Roberson, L., Houston, J. M., & Diddams, M. (1989). Identifying valued work outcomes through a content analysis of personal goals. *Journal of Vocational Behavior, 35,* 30–45.

Ryff, C. D. (1991). Possible selves in adulthood and old age: A tale of shifting horizons. *Psychology and Aging, 6,* 286–295.

Schunk, D. H. (1989). Self-efficacy and cognitive skill learning. In C. Ames & R. Ames (Eds.), *Research on motivation in education: Goals and cognitions* (Vol. 3, pp. 13–44). San Diego, CA: Academic Press.

Sepie, A. C., & Keeling, B. (1978). The relationship between types of anxiety and underachievement in mathematics. *Journal of Educational Research, 72,* 15–19.

Shaw, M. D., & Black, M. D. (1960). The reaction to frustration of bright high school underachievers. *California Journal of Educational Research, 11,* 120–124.

Simons, R. H., & Bibb, J. (1974). Achievement motivation, test anxiety, and underachievement in the elementary school. *Journal of Educational Research, 67,* 366–369.

Sutton-Smith, B. (1982). Birth order and sibling status effects. In M. E. Lamb & B. Sutton-Smith (Eds.), *Sibling relationships: Their nature and significance across the lifespan* (pp. 203–247). Hillsdale, NJ: Lawrence Erlbaum Associates.

Taylor, J., & Boggiano, A. K. (1987). The effects of task-specific self-schemata on attributions for success and failure. *Journal of Research in Personality, 21,* 375–388.

Thoreson, C. E., & Mahoney, M. J. (1974). *Behavioral self-control.* New York: Holt, Rinehart, & Winston.

Thorndike, R. L. (1963). *The concepts of over and under achievement.* New York: Teachers College Press.

Weiner, B. (1986). *An attributional theory of motivation and emotion.* New York: Springer-Verlag.

Whitmore, J. R. (1980). *Giftedness, conflict, and underachievement.* Boston: Allyn & Bacon.

Zimmerman, B. J., & Schunk, D. H. (Eds.). (1989). *Self-regulated learning and academic achievement: Theory, research, and practice.* New York: Springer-Verlag.

4

Self-Regulation of Self-Efficacy and Attributions in Academic Settings

Dale H. Schunk
Purdue University

Self-regulation refers to the process whereby students activate and sustain cognitions, behaviors, and affects that are systematically oriented toward the attainment of goals (Zimmerman, 1989, 1990). Self-regulation includes such activities as attending to and concentrating on instruction; organizing, coding, and rehearsing information to be remembered; establishing a productive work environment and using resources effectively; holding positive beliefs about one's capabilities, the value of learning, the factors influencing learning, and the anticipated outcomes of actions; and experiencing pride and satisfaction with one's efforts (Schunk, 1989).

Effective self-regulation requires that students have goals and the motivation to attain them (Bandura, 1986; Zimmerman, 1989). Students must regulate not only their actions but also their underlying motives—their achievement-related cognitions, beliefs, intentions, and affects. This view of self-regulation fits well with the notion that, rather than being passive recipients of information, students are mentally active during learning and exert a large degree of control over attainment of their goals (Pintrich & Schrauben, 1992).

This chapter focuses on the self-regulation of two types of motives: self-efficacy and attributions. *Self-efficacy* refers to personal beliefs about one's capabilities to learn or perform skills at designated levels (Bandura, 1986). *Attributions* are beliefs concerning the causes of outcomes (Weiner, 1979). Research substantiates the idea that self-regulation depends on students feeling efficacious about performing well and forming attributions that sustain learning efforts (Schunk, 1989; Zimmerman & Martinez-Pons, 1992).

I initially present a theoretical overview of self-regulation based on Bandura's (1986) social cognitive theory. Within this framework I describe the operation of self-efficacy and attributions. A discussion of research bearing on the these processes follows, and I offer suggestions for future research. The chapter concludes with implications of the theory and research for educational practice.

THEORETICAL BACKGROUND

Social Cognitive Theory of Self-Regulation

Social cognitive theory views self-regulation as comprising three processes: self-observation, self-judgment, and self-reaction (Bandura, 1986; Kanfer & Gaelick, 1986). At the start of learning activities students have such goals as acquiring skills and knowledge, finishing work, and making good grades. During the activities students observe, judge, and react to their perceptions of goal progress (Fig. 4.1).

Self-Observation. Self-observation is deliberate attention to aspects of one's behavior (Bandura, 1986). Learners cannot regulate their actions until they know what they do. Behaviors can be assessed on such dimensions as quantity, quality, rate, and originality. Behavioral assessment helps to gauge goal progress (Schunk, 1989). Self-observation also can

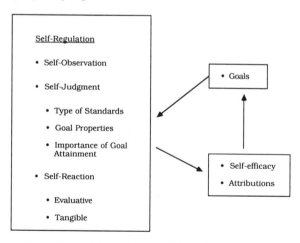

FIG. 4.1. Social cognitive model of self-regulation.

motivate. Students with poor study habits often are surprised to learn they waste much study time on nonacademic concerns. Such knowledge can motivate students to improve their studying.

Self-observation is aided with self-recording, where behavioral instances are recorded along with such features as time, place, and duration of occurrence (Mace, Belfiore, & Shea, 1989). Without recording, observations may not reflect behaviors accurately, due to selective memory. Regardless of whether self-observations are recorded, two important self-observation criteria are regularity and proximity (Bandura, 1986). *Regularity* is observing behavior frequently instead of sporadically. Nonregular observation yields misleading results. *Proximity* means that behavior is observed close in time to its occurrence rather than long afterward. One records behavior when it occurs, rather than waiting until later to reconstruct events.

Self-Judgment. Self-observation is necessary but insufficient for sustained self-regulation. A second process is self-judgment, which refers to comparing present performance with one's goal. Self-judgments are affected by the type of standards employed, goal properties, and the importance of goal attainment.

Goals may be cast as absolute or normative standards. Absolute standards are fixed: Students whose goal is to read 15 book pages in 1 hour gauge their progress against this absolute standard. Many grading systems are based on absolute standards (e.g., A = 93–100, B = 85–92). Normative standards are based on performances of others and often are acquired by observing models (Bandura, 1986). Social comparison of one's performances with those of others helps one evaluate the appropriateness of behavior. Social comparison becomes more likely when absolute standards do not exist or are unclear (Festinger, 1954).

Standards inform and motivate. Comparing one's performance with standards is informative of goal progress. Students who complete 3 pages in 10 minutes realize they are ahead of schedule and should accomplish their goal. The belief that one is making progress enhances self-efficacy and sustains motivation.

Important goal properties are specificity, proximity, and level of difficulty (Bandura, 1988; Locke & Latham, 1990). Goals incorporating specific performance standards are more likely to enhance learning and activate self-evaluations than general goals (e.g., "Do your best"). Specific goals specify the amount of effort required for success and boost self-efficacy because progress is easy to gauge.

Proximal (close-at-hand) goals result in greater motivation than distant goals. It is easier to gauge progress toward a short-term goal, and the perception of progress raises self-efficacy. Proximal goals are especially influential with young children who do not represent distant outcomes in thought.

Goal difficulty—the level of task proficiency required as assessed against a standard—influences learners' efforts. Assuming requisite skills, individuals expend greater effort to attain difficult goals than when standards are lower. Learners initially may doubt whether they can attain difficult goals, but working toward them builds self-efficacy.

Self-judgments are affected by the importance of goal attainment. When students care little about how well they perform, they may not assess their performance or expend effort to improve (Bandura, 1986). Progress judgments are made for valued goals.

Self-Reaction. Self-reactions to goal progress may be evaluative or tangible (Bandura, 1986). Evaluative reactions involve students' beliefs about their progress. The belief that one is making progress, along with the anticipated satisfaction of goal accomplishment, enhances self-efficacy and sustains motivation. Negative evaluations will not decrease motivation if individuals believe they are capable of improving (e.g., through enhanced effort or better use of strategies; Schunk, 1989). Motivation is not enhanced if students believe they lack the ability to succeed and that more effort or better strategy use will not help.

Students sometimes react in a tangible fashion to academic progress by buying something they want or taking a night off from studying. Anticipated consequences of behavior rather than the consequences themselves boost motivation (Bandura, 1986). Rewards enhance self-efficacy when they are tied to students' accomplishments—for example, when students receive free time based on their mastery of skills. Self-efficacy is validated as students work on the task and note progress, and the actual reward further validates efficacy because it symbolizes greater competence (Schunk, 1989).

Interaction of Processes. These self-regulatory processes interact with one another. As students observe aspects of their behavior, they judge them against standards and react positively or negatively. Their evaluations and reactions set the stage for additional observations of the same behaviors or others. These processes also interact with the environment (Zimmerman, 1989). Students who judge their learning progress as inadequate may react by asking for teacher assistance. In turn, teachers may teach students a more efficient strategy, which students then use to foster learning. That environmental factors can help develop self-regulation is important, because educators increasingly are advocating teaching students self-regulatory strategies (Schunk, 1989; Zimmerman, 1990).

Self-Efficacy Theory

Self-efficacy is hypothesized to influence choice of activities, effort expended, and persistence (Bandura, 1986). Compared with students who doubt their learning capabilities, those with high self-efficacy for accomplishing a task participate more readily, work harder, and persist longer when they encounter difficulties.

Learners acquire information to appraise their self-efficacy from their performance accomplishments, vicarious (observational) experiences, forms of persuasion, and physiological reactions. Students' own performances offer reliable guides for assessing self-efficacy. Success generally raises efficacy and failure lowers it, although a strong sense of efficacy is unlikely to be affected by an occasional setback (Schunk, 1989).

Students acquire efficacy information by socially comparing their performances with those of others. Similar others offer the best basis for comparison (Schunk, 1989). Students who observe similar peers perform a task are apt to believe that they, too, are capable of accomplishing it. Information acquired vicariously typically has a weaker effect on self-efficacy than performance-based information because the former can be outweighed by subsequent failures.

Learners often receive from teachers and parents persuasive information that they are capable of performing a task (e.g., "You can do this"). Positive persuasive feedback enhances self-efficacy, but this increase will be temporary if subsequent efforts turn out poorly. Students also acquire efficacy information from physiological reactions (e.g., sweating, heart rate). Symptoms signaling anxiety may convey that one lacks skills; students who believe they are reacting in less agitated fashion feel more capable of performing well.

Information acquired from these sources does not influence self-efficacy automatically but rather is cognitively appraised (Bandura, 1986). Learners weigh and combine the contributions of such factors as perceptions of their ability, task difficulty, amount of effort expended, amount and type of assistance received from others, perceived similarity to models, and persuader credibility (Schunk, 1989).

Self-efficacy is not the only influence on achievement behavior. High self-efficacy will not produce competent performances when requisite knowledge and skills are lacking. Outcome expectations, or beliefs concerning the probable outcomes of actions, are important because students engage in activities they believe will result in positive outcomes. Perceived value refers to the importance students attach to learning or what use they will make of what they learn. Assuming that students possess adequate skills, believe that positive outcomes will result, and value what they are learning, self-efficacy is hypothesized to influence the choice and direction of much achievement behavior.

Attribution Theory

Historical Views. Attribution theory originated with Heider's (1958) *naive analysis of action*, which examines how ordinary people view the causes of important events. Heider believed that people attribute causes to internal (*effective personal force*) and external (*effective environmental force*) factors. The personal force is subdivided into *power* and *motivation*. Power refers to abilities; motivation (trying) denotes intention and exertion. Collectively, power and environment constitute the *can* factor, which combined with the *try* factor explains outcomes. One's power (or ability) is relative to the environment. Assuming that ability is sufficient to conquer environmental forces, then trying (effort) affects outcomes.

Kelley (1967; Kelley & Michela, 1980) believed that attributions represent a process where individuals decide on the explanation that best fits the observed phenomenon. When there are several possible reasons why an event occurs, people decide which is the most probable. Rules guide the process of forming attributions. *Covariation* means that when an event occurs repeatedly across time, individuals determine which potential causes consistently accompany that event. For example, assume that a student fails five straight quizzes. On three of the five occasions the student felt ill, but on all five occasions the student studied very little. The more likely cause is lack of studying rather than illness, because the former covaries with the outcome consistently.

Discounting means that a given factor will be eliminated as a cause if other likely causes are present. If the preceding student receives an A on the sixth quiz, he or she is apt to discount high ability as the cause if there are other probable causes (e.g., easy quiz). *Augmentation* refers to the increased likelihood of making an internal attribution for an outcome when powerful environmental conditions are present that inhibit the outcome. If the instructor tells students what to study for the seventh quiz and the problem student still fails the quiz, he or she may attribute the failure to a personal quality (low ability, lack of motivation, poor studying) because a strong environmental force (teacher's help) was working against failure.

Weiner's Theory. Guided by Heider's work, Weiner (1979; Weiner et al., 1971) developed an attributional theory of achievement behavior and postulated that students attribute their successes and failures to such factors as ability, effort, task difficulty, and luck (among others). These factors are given general weights, and for any given outcome one or two factors will be perceived as primarily responsible. Thus, a student who receives an A on a science test might attribute it largely to ability ("I'm good in science") and effort ("I studied hard for the test").

Causes can be represented along three dimensions: *internal* or *external* to the individual, relatively *stable* or *unstable* over time, and *controllable* or *uncontrollable* by the individual. Effort is generally viewed as internal, unstable, and controllable; ability is generally viewed as internal, stable, and uncontrollable. People use situational cues to form attributions. Salient ability cues are success attained easily or early in the course of learning, as well as many successes. Effort cues are physical exertion, expending mental effort, or persisting for a long time. Task difficulty cues include task features (e.g., number and length of words in a reading passage) and social norms (how other students do). Random outcomes signal luck; success or failure occurs regardless of what one does.

Attributions affect students' expectations, motivation, and emotions (Weiner, 1979). Stability influences expectancy of success. Assuming that task conditions remain much the same, success ascribed to stable causes (high ability, low task difficulty) results in higher expectations of success than attributions to unstable causes (immediate effort, luck). Locus influences affective reactions. Learners experience greater pride (shame) after succeeding (failing) when outcomes are attributed to internal causes rather than to external ones. Controllability has diverse effects. Feelings of control increase one's choice of academic tasks, effort, persistence, and achievement (Bandura, 1986). The perception of little control over academic outcomes negatively affects expectations, motivation, and emotions (Licht & Kistner, 1986).

Self-Regulation of Self-Efficacy and Attributions

Effective self-regulation depends on holding an optimal sense of self-efficacy for learning during task engagement (Bandura, 1986; Bouffard-Bouchard, Parent, & Larivee, 1991; Zimmerman, 1989). As students work on a task they compare their performances to their goals. Self-evaluations of progress enhance self-efficacy and keep students motivated to improve.

Although low self-efficacy is detrimental, effective self-regulation does not require that self-efficacy be extremely high. Salomon (1984) found that lower self-efficacy led to greater mental effort and better learning than when self-efficacy was higher. Assuming that learners feel efficacious enough to surmount difficulties, harboring some doubt about whether one will succeed may mobilize effort and effective use of strategies better than will feeling overly confident.

Effective self-regulation depends on students making attributions that enhance self-efficacy and motivation. Attributions enter into self-regulation during the self-judgment and self-reaction stages when students compare and evaluate their performances (Schunk, 1989). Whether goal progress is deemed acceptable depends on its attribution. Students who attribute success to factors over which they have little control (e.g., luck, task ease) may hold low self-efficacy if they believe they cannot succeed on their own. If they believe they lack ability to perform well, they may judge learning progress as deficient and be unmotivated to work harder. Conversely, students who attribute success to ability, effort, and effective use of strategies, should experience higher self-efficacy and remain motivated to work productively.

RESEARCH EVIDENCE

In this section I review research that investigates self-efficacy and attributional processes in cognitive achievement settings. Much of this research was not primarily directed toward exploring how students self-regulate attributions and self-efficacy but rather examined the influences on and effects of these processes. Initially I discuss research addressing the influences on self-efficacy and attributional processes, after which I review evidence on their relation to achievement outcomes. This review is selective rather than exhaustive. Interested readers should consult additional sources (Bandura, 1986; Karoly & Kanfer, 1982; Zimmerman & Schunk, 1989).

Influences on Self-Efficacy and Attributions

Much of the research investigating influences on self-efficacy and attributions comes from studies in which investigators attempt to modify learners' attributions and achievement outcomes by providing feedback linking their successes or failures with one or more attributions. Although there is evidence that attributional feedback changes students' attributions (Andrews & Debus, 1978; Carr & Borkowski, 1989; Dweck, 1975), many studies did not assess self-efficacy. There also are studies in which attributions were not assessed but which show that attributional feedback influences students' self-efficacy (Schunk, 1982; Schunk & Gunn, 1985).

A series of studies demonstrates that attributional feedback affects students' attributions and self-efficacy (Schunk, 1983, 1984; Schunk & Cox, 1986; Schunk & Rice, 1986). Schunk (1983) provided children deficient in subtraction skills with instruction and self-directed problem solving over sessions. Children were assigned to one of four feedback conditions: ability, effort, ability plus effort, none. During the problem solving, ability-feedback children periodically received verbal feedback linking their successful problem solving with ability (e.g., "You're good at this"), effort-feedback subjects received effort statements ("You've been working hard"), ability-plus-effort students received both forms of feedback, and no-feedback students did not receive attributional feedback. Self-efficacy and subtraction skill were assessed following the last instructional session. Children also judged the amount of effort they expended during the sessions, which, although not a pure attributional measure, reflects the extent that children believed their successes were due to effort.

Ability feedback promoted self-efficacy and skill more than did the other three conditions; the effort and ability-plus-effort conditions outperformed the no-feedback group. The three treatment conditions solved more problems during self-directed practice (a measure of motivation) than did the no-feedback condition. The effort and ability-plus-effort conditions judged effort expenditure greater than the ability group, who judged effort higher than the no-feedback condition.

These findings support the point that the same degree of success attained with less effort strengthens self-efficacy more than when greater effort is required (Bandura, 1986). Ability-plus-effort subjects may have discounted ability information in favor of effort; they may have wondered how good they were if they had to work hard to succeed. By the third grade most children use inverse compensation in judging ability from effort information (i.e., more effort required to succeed implies lower ability; Surber, 1980).

Schunk (1984) conducted two experiments to determine how the sequence of attributional feedback influences achievement outcomes. Children with low subtraction skills received instruction and self-directed practice over sessions. One group (ability–ability) periodically received ability feedback for their successes, a second group (effort–effort) received effort feedback, in a third condition (ability–effort) ability feedback was given during the first half of the instructional program and effort feedback during the second half, and for a fourth condition (effort–ability) this sequence was reversed. Self-efficacy, skill, and attributions for problem-solving progress during the instructional sessions were assessed following the last session.

In both experiments, children who initially received ability feedback (ability–ability and ability–effort conditions) demonstrated higher self-efficacy and skill than those initially receiving effort feedback (effort–ability and effort–effort conditions). Subjects initially given ability feedback also placed greater emphasis on ability attributions than did subjects who initially received effort feedback. Early successes constitute a prominent cue for forming ability attributions. Telling students that ability is responsible for their successes supports these perceptions. Ability attributions for successes enhance self-efficacy. Effort–ability students may have discounted ability feedback; they may have wondered how competent they were because their prior successes were attributed to effort. Although effort feedback raises self-efficacy and promotes skill development (Schunk, 1982), its overall effects are weaker than when successes are attributed to ability.

Working with children with learning disabilities, Schunk and Cox (1986) provided subtraction instruction with self-directed practice; children received effort feedback during the first half of the instructional program, effort feedback during the second half, or no effort feedback. Effort feedback enhanced self-efficacy, skill, and self-directed problem solving (motivation) more than no effort feedback. Effort feedback also led to higher effort attributions than no feedback; students who received effort feedback during the first half of the instructional program judged effort as a more important cause of success than subjects who received feedback during the second half.

Telling students that effort is responsible for their successes likely was credible to these students, who had encountered prior difficulties learning mathematical skills. Effort feedback conveys that students can continue to improve by working hard, which raises self-efficacy and motivation. Schunk and Cox postulated that first-half effort feedback would be more effective than second-half feedback because by discontinuing effort feedback students might believe they were expending less effort to succeed and feel more efficacious; however, the two effort feedback conditions did not differ. Students' learning disabilities may have forced them to expend effort to succeed throughout the instructional program, so later effort feedback also seemed credible.

Schunk and Rice (1986) gave children with reading deficiencies instruction and practice in identifying important ideas. One group (ability–ability) periodically received ability feedback for their successful comprehension, a second group (effort–effort) received effort feedback, a third group (ability–effort) was given ability feedback during the first half of the instructional program and effort feedback during the second half, and for a fourth condition (effort–ability) this sequence was reversed. Although practice time was not self-directed but rather under the direction of a teacher, self-regulatory processes were involved because children were taught a comprehension strategy and were largely on their own during the instructional sessions to apply it.

The four conditions did not differ in comprehension skill, but ability–ability and effort–ability students judged self-efficacy higher on completion of instruction than did students in the other two conditions. Children who received ability feedback during the second half of the instructional program placed greater emphasis on ability as a cause of success than children who received effort feedback during the second half. Ability–effort students made higher effort attributions than ability–ability children.

It is difficult to reconcile these findings showing benefits of later ability feedback with those of Schunk (1984) who found that early ability feedback was better. These studies differed in type of subjects, content, and number and format of instructional sessions. Schunk and Rice's subjects were children who had severe reading problems and experienced much school failure. It is possible that the early ability feedback had less impact because they discounted it due to their history of failure but that after continued successes over sessions they were more likely to adopt the ability information. These studies should be replicated over longer time periods—Schunk (1984) used 4 instructional sessions and Schunk and Rice (1986) employed 15—to determine whether attributional feedback effects differ depending on the time students receive feedback.

Relich, Debus, and Walker (1986) explored attributional feedback effects during instruction on long division. Subjects were children identified as learned helpless based on their attributions of failure to low ability and their devaluation of the role of effort. Some subjects were exposed to modeled demonstrations of division operations, whereas others reviewed an instructional booklet. Within each of these treatments, half of the subjects received attributional feedback stressing effort and ability for success and failure (e.g., "That's incorrect; I know you have the ability but you just have to try harder"). All students participated in self-directed practice over sessions. Self-efficacy, division skill, and attributions were assessed before and after instruction. A control condition received only the assessments.

Compared with the control condition, the conditions that received attributional feedback demonstrated higher self-efficacy and skill than did the treatments not given attributional feedback. Attributional feedback treatments displayed less learned helplessness following training compared with the control and nonfeedback conditions (i.e., less attribution of failure to low ability and greater emphasis on effort as a cause of success and failure). Unlike the previous studies by Schunk and his colleagues, this study provided attributional feedback for success and failure, which helps substantiate the link between attributional feedback and self-efficacy.

There also are research studies in which attributional feedback was not provided but that investigated the operation of self-efficacy and attributions during self-regulation. Butkowsky and Willows (1980) assessed good, average, and poor readers' initial expectancies for success (analogous to self-efficacy) for solving anagrams, after which subjects attempted to solve anagrams and were given a line-drawing task. Success and failure were manipulated. Following the tests, children made attributions for their performances and again judged expectancies for success. Good and average readers held higher initial expectancies for success and persisted longer on the tasks than poor readers, and good readers judged expectancies higher than average readers. Poor readers were more likely to attribute failure to internal and stable causes (e.g., low ability) and less likely to attribute success to ability. Relative to good and average readers, poor readers showed a greater decrement in expectancy of success following failure.

Collins (1982) measured fifth-graders' self-efficacy for solving mathematical word problems and mathematical ability. Students were classified as high, average, or low ability; within each level students were categorized as high or low in self-efficacy. Students then were given word problems to solve (some of which were unsolvable) and the opportunity to rework any problems they missed. Self-regulatory processes came into play during the problem solving because students decided for how long and in what fashion to work on problems.

High self-efficacy students solved more problems correctly than low-efficacy students. In the low and average ability groups, high-efficacy students spent more time working the unsolvable problems than low-efficacy students; this relationship was reversed in the high ability group. Regardless of ability group, high-efficacy students chose to rework more problems they missed than low-efficacy students. Low-efficacy students reported lower ratings for their ability relative to that of peers than did high-efficacy students. High-efficacy students were more likely than low-efficacy students to attribute failure to low effort.

In the Salomon (1984) study mentioned earlier, children assessed attributions for success and failure in learning from printed materials and from television and judged self-efficacy for learning different content from print and from TV. They then either watched a silent film or read the comparable narrative text, judged the amount of mental effort they expended in attempting to learn the content, and took an achievement test.

Children judged self-efficacy for learning from TV higher than learning from print. They attributed success in learning from print more to internal factors (ability, effort) and success in learning from TV to external causes. For failure, they gave external attributions (task difficulty) for print and internal attributions for TV. Compared with TV subjects, print children scored higher on the achievement test and judged mental effort higher. That a lower sense of self-efficacy can enhance effort, self-regulation, and achievement is important, but it is imperative that students feel they are capable of learning. When self-efficacy is too low, students will not be motivated to learn. An adequate level of self-efficacy is needed to sustain motivation and self-regulation.

Relation of Self-Efficacy and Attributions to Achievement Outcomes

Correlation/Regression Analyses. Research has examined the relation of self-efficacy and attributions to each other and to achievement outcomes. Studies have consistently obtained a significant and positive correlation between perceived self-efficacy and skillful performance (Relich et al., 1986; Schunk, 1983, 1984; Schunk & Cox, 1986; Schunk & Gunn, 1986; Schunk & Rice, 1986). Salomon (1984) found that self-efficacy correlated positively with skill among subjects who studied print but negatively among those who watched TV.

Most studies also have obtained positive correlations between ability attributions and self-efficacy (Schunk, 1984; Schunk & Cox, 1986; Schunk & Gunn, 1986; Schunk & Rice, 1986). Schunk and Cox (1986) found a positive relation between effort attributions for success and self-efficacy. Self-efficacy also correlates positively with attributions of success to task ease and negatively with luck attributions (Schunk & Gunn, 1986). Relich et al. (1986) found that their learned helplessness index (which emphasized effort as a cause of outcomes and deemphasized ability as a cause of failure) correlated positively with self-efficacy and achievement. In Salomon's (1984) study, subjects' judgments of mental effort during learning correlated positively with self-efficacy among print subjects and negatively among TV subjects.

Research shows that achievement correlates positively with attributions to ability (Schunk, 1984; Schunk & Cox, 1986; Schunk & Gunn, 1986), effort (Schunk & Cox, 1986; Schunk & Gunn, 1986), and task ease (Schunk & Gunn, 1986). Schunk (1984) found a negative correlation between achievement and luck attributions. Schunk and Cox (1986) obtained a positive correlation between ability and effort attributions for success.

Schunk and Gunn (1986) used multiple regression to determine the percent of variance in achievement outcomes accounted for by various predictors. Children received instruction in long division and engaged in self-directed practice. During part of the problem solving children verbalized aloud. Verbalizations were categorized as reflecting effective or ineffective task strategies, depending on whether they would lead to a correct answer. Attributions for successful problem solving were assessed, along with self-efficacy and skill. Ability and luck attributions accounted for significant increments in the explained variability of self-efficacy (the luck effect was in a negative direction). For division skill, self-efficacy and use of effective task strategies accounted for significant increments in variability.

Predictive Utility. Research also has tested causal models. Relich et al. (1986) explored the effects of attributional feedback on attributions, self-efficacy, and achievement; the effects of attributions on self-efficacy and achievement; and the influence of self-efficacy on achievement. Attributional feedback had a significant direct effect on attributions, self-efficacy, and achievement; attributions influenced self-efficacy; and self-efficacy had a direct effect on achievement. Thus, feedback affected achievement directly and indirectly through its effects on attributions and self-efficacy. The effect of attributions on achievement was weak, which suggests that attributions affect achievement indirectly through self-efficacy.

Schunk and Gunn (1986) hypothesized that use of effective task strategies would affect attributions, self-efficacy, and skill; attributions were predicted to influence self-efficacy and skill; and self-efficacy was expected to affect skill. The largest direct influence on changes in children's division skill was due to use of effective strategies; skill also was heavily influenced by self-efficacy and effort attributions. The strongest influence on self-efficacy was ability attributions for success, which suggests that instructional variables affect self-efficacy in part through the intervening influence of attributions.

SUGGESTIONS FOR FUTURE RESEARCH

Research supports the point that self-efficacy and attributions are important self-regulatory processes that affect achievement outcomes. At the same time, we know very little about the self-regulation of attributions and self-efficacy in academic contexts. Most research studies have not explored how students self-regulate attributions and self-efficacy but rather have examined the causes and consequences of these processes. We need replication of studies with different student populations and academic content. Some areas especially deserving of research attention are summarized next.

Operation of Self-Regulatory Processes

One research need is to investigate how attributions and efficacy interact with other beliefs and self-regulatory processes during academic engagement. Self-regulated learners are active behaviorally, cognitively, and affectively (Zimmerman, 1989). They organize and transform information, rehearse information to be remembered, and use memory aids. Investigating how self-efficacy and attributions interact with these strategies would provide insight into learning processes and have implications for teaching.

As an example of a research focus, we know that effective self-regulation depends on students having goals and evaluating their goal progress during task engagement. Performance self-judgments are affected by goal properties: proximity, specificity, difficulty level. Goal effects also may depend on whether the goal denotes a learning or performance outcome (Ames, 1992; Meece, 1991). A *learning goal* refers to what knowledge and skills students are to acquire; a *performance goal* denotes what task students are to complete. Goal-setting research typically has focused on such goals as rate or quantity of performance, but educators increasingly are advocating that greater emphasis be placed on learning processes (e.g., strategies; Borkowski, Carr, Rellinger, & Pressley, 1990).

Learning and performance goals may exert different effects on self-regulatory activities even when the goals are similar in goal properties (Schunk & Swartz, 1993a, 1993b). A learning goal focuses students' attention on processes and strategies that help them acquire knowledge and skills. Students who adopt a learning goal are apt to experience a sense of self-efficacy for skill improvement and engage in activities they believe enhance learning (e.g., expend effort, persist, use effective strategies). As they work and perceive improvement, they may attribute it to such factors as effort, ability, and strategy use. Perceived learning progress also raises self-efficacy and enhances self-regulation over time.

In contrast, a performance goal focuses students' attention on completing the task. Such a goal may not highlight the importance of the processes and strategies underlying task completion or result in a sense of self-efficacy for learning. During task engagement, students may compare their work with that of their peers instead of with their prior performances. For students who experience difficulties, these social comparisons result in low perceptions of ability (Ames, 1992). Although performance goals may motivate students over short periods or on easier tasks, an overall lower sense of self-efficacy and possibly dysfunctional attributions will not sustain self-regulation.

Research testing these ideas has yielded mixed evidence (Elliott & Dweck, 1988; Meece, Blumenfeld, & Hoyle, 1988). Elliott and Dweck provided children with goals (learning or performance) and ability assessments (high or low). Children receiving learning goals chose challenging tasks and displayed effort and persistence regardless of ability assessment. Children with performance goals who perceived ability as high selected challenging performance tasks that allowed them to appear competent; those perceiving ability as low selected easier tasks allowing them to avoid judgments of incompetence. Meece et al. assessed children's goal orientations, perceived competence, intrinsic motivation, and cognitive engagement patterns during science lessons. Orientations were task mastery (understand material and learn as much as possible), ego/social (please others), and work-avoidant (minimize effort and do as little as possible). Students emphasizing task-mastery (learning) goals reported more active cognitive engagement characterized by self-regulatory activities (e.g., review material not understood, relate current to prior material). Higher motivation to learn was associated with greater emphasis on goals stressing learning and understanding.

Research has not investigated how goal orientations, attributions, and self-efficacy interact during learning and change as students acquire skills. Such research might be aided with think-aloud protocols, where students verbalize aloud as they work on a task and their verbalizations are classified according to the type of self-regulatory process they reflect.

Developmental Changes

Developmental factors should influence how learners regulate self-efficacy and attributions during learning (Paris & Newman, 1990). For example, children perceive effort as the prime cause of outcomes, but around the age of 9 a distinct conception of ability begins to emerge (Nicholls, 1978). Ability attributions become increasingly important with development, whereas effort attributions decline in importance. This suggests that young children's self-regulation is heavily dependent on perceptions of effort, which seems to conflict with the earlier point that as skills develop self-efficacy is influenced more by perceptions of ability than of effort. That issue requires empirical investigation.

There are also developmental changes in children's conceptions of ability. Children below about the age of 6 years typically hold an incremental view: Ability is roughly synonymous with learning, and children believe that greater effort leads to higher ability (Nicholls, 1983). Ability is judged relative to previous performance, and feelings of efficacy result when performance is improved. With development, children may develop an entity perspective: Ability as an independent entity with an upper limit, and effort increases skill only up to that limit. Students determine their ability levels by comparing their performances to those of others. Improving one's performance will not raise efficacy unless students believe that others cannot perform as well with the same effort.

This research suggests that effective self-regulation requires changes in efficacy and attributional beliefs with development. There also is the question of which views of ability and effort best sustain self-regulation over time among adults who presumably could hold either view. Research might investigate how different tasks affect conceptions of ability. Speed tasks might engender an entity view; tasks that require effort for success (e.g., long-term projects) may foster an incremental perspective. Finally, there is a need for cross-cultural research exploring developmental changes in conceptions of ability, because most of the extant research has been conducted in Western cultures.

Longitudinal Studies

More longitudinal research would be valuable because self-efficacy and attributions might undergo changes over time. Many academic activities are long term in nature: building a science fair project, writing a lengthy term paper or article, conducting an experiment over several days. In the early stages of learning, students may not feel skillful but stay on-task as long as they believe they can learn. Effort attributions are highly credible (Schunk, 1989). As skills develop, learners should be able to work on tasks with less effort and, depending on developmental level, ability attributions may become more credible.

Self-efficacy researchers typically have employed quantitative methods using between-conditions comparisons in short-term studies. Long-term studies may require alternative forms of data collection (case studies, ethnographies). Although such studies might include fewer subjects, they would yield rich data. Self-efficacy assessment might be broadened from reliance on numerical scales to include qualitative indexes. Subjects could describe how confident they feel about performing tasks. Statements also could be scored for degree of efficacy with a procedure similar to the content analysis of verbatim explanations (CAVE) technique (Schulman, Castellon, & Seligman, 1989). This technique is used to score individuals' verbal and written statements for attributional style. Each statement receives three ratings. Ratings are made on a 7-point scale along three dimensions: external (1) versus internal (7), unstable (1) versus stable (7), specific (1) versus global (7). Some examples are "I did well on the test because I studied hard" (rating of 7 on the internal scale), "I'm not doing well in school because I'm such a lazy person" (7 on the stable scale), and "I got a speeding ticket; I guess the cop had to fill his quota for the day" (1 on the specific scale).

Think-aloud protocols are useful for exploring the operation of self-regulatory processes. Schunk and Gunn (1986) found that children verbalize task strategies and achievement beliefs while working on cognitive tasks. Use of think-aloud probes at various times during a longitudinal study could show how changes in self-efficacy and attributions relate to task performance.

Strategy Use in the Classroom

Self-regulation research examining the effects of attributions on self-efficacy in learning settings is needed. To date, most work examining acquisition of attributions and self-efficacy has been conducted outside of classrooms. In many studies students make judgments about hypothetical situations (Graham, 1991). These studies are informative but do not address how the complexities of classrooms affect self-regulation.

Research is also needed on the effectiveness of classroom methods to train students to effectively regulate self-efficacy and attributions during cognitive skill learning. Research using teachers, textbooks, and computers is desirable. Researchers should work directly with teachers to evaluate the effectiveness of methods. Teachers may need to be trained to administer treatments that are designed to influence self-regulation. Once trained, teachers can become active research collaborators.

Conducting research in classrooms will require broadening our attributional focus. Attributional research has focused on ability and effort attributions. Although there are theoretical and practical reasons for this, it does not reflect the emphasis of self-regulation on effective use of strategies (Zimmerman, 1989, 1990). Schunk and Gunn (1986) found that 94% of students' verbalizations represented application of strategic steps oriented toward problem solving. We need research examining the interface of strategy attributions and self-efficacy during skill learning. Given that teachers teach strategies and that strategy use is controllable by students, strategy attributions are apt to facilitate self-efficacy, motivation, and learning (Borkowski, Weyhing, & Carr, 1988; Zimmerman & Martinez-Pons, 1992).

IMPLICATIONS FOR CLASSROOM PRACTICE

In this section I demonstrate how some principles discussed in this chapter can be applied in classrooms to enhance self-regulation of self-efficacy and attributions. I focus on the domain of writing, which lends itself well to self-regulation (Graham & Harris, this volume). Contemporary theories view writing as a problem-solving process that reflects goal-directed behaviors (Flower & Hayes, 1981). Writers generate goals and alter them as they compose. Effective self-regulation requires that writers feel efficacious about attaining their goals and make attributions that enhance motivation.

Carl Swartz and I (Schunk & Swartz, 1993a, 1993b) conducted research that explored the effects of learning goals and progress feedback on children's self-efficacy, use of writing strategies, and writing skill. The context was instruction on writing paragraphs. Most of our subjects were of average ability, although we did one project with gifted students. Many students held low perceptions of self-efficacy for writing skills at the outset. Following a pretest we assigned subjects to experimental conditions and gave them 45-minute instructional sessions over 20 days. The instruction covered four types of paragraphs: descriptive, informative, narrative story, narrative descriptive. Five days were devoted to each type of paragraph. Children assigned to the same experimental condition met in small groups with a teacher from outside the school.

The procedure during the five sessions devoted to each type of paragraph was identical. At the start of the first session the teacher gave the goal instructions appropriate for children's experimental assignment, after which he or she presented this writing strategy: What do I have to do? (1) Choose a topic to write about. (2) Write down ideas about the topic. (3) Pick the main idea. (4) Plan the paragraph. (5) Write down the main idea and the other sentences.

The first 10 minutes were devoted to *modeled demonstration* in which the teacher verbalized the strategy's steps and applied them to sample topics and paragraphs. Children were taught to construct a web consisting of a box in the center and lines emanating from it. The teacher put the main idea in the box and the other ideas at the ends of the lines. To show organization, the teacher ordered the ideas starting at the top and working around the box. Students then received *guided practice* (15 minutes); they applied the steps under the guidance of the teacher. The last 20 minutes were devoted to *independent practice*; students worked alone while the teacher monitored their work. The daily content coverage was as follows: Session 1—Strategy Steps 1, 2, 3; Session 2—Strategy Step 4; Session 3—Strategy Step 5; Session 4—review entire strategy; Session 5—review entire strategy without the modeled demonstration. Children worked on two or three paragraph topics per session.

There were four experimental conditions: process (learning) goal, process goal plus progress feedback, product (performance) goal, and general goal (instructional control). To children assigned to the process goal and the process goal plus progress feedback conditions the teacher said at the beginning of each session, "While you're working it helps to keep in mind what you're trying to do. You'll be trying to learn how to use these steps to write a (type of) paragraph." Children assigned to the product goal condition were told at the start of each session, "While you're working it helps to keep in mind what you're trying to do. You'll be trying to write a (type of) paragraph." These latter instructions controlled for the effects of goal properties included in the process goal treatment. General goal students were told, "While you're working, try to do your best." This condition controlled for the effects of receiving writing instruction, practice, and goal instructions, included in the other conditions.

Each child assigned to the process goal plus progress feedback condition received feedback three or four times during each session, which conveyed that children were making progress toward their goal of learning to use the strategy to write paragraphs. Teachers delivered feedback to individual children with such statements as, "You're learning to use the steps," and, "You're doing well because you followed the steps in order." Teachers provided feedback contingent on children using the strategy properly to ensure that feedback was credible. This feedback conveyed strategy attributions because it linked children's writing successes with use of the strategy's steps.

Strategy use, self-efficacy, and writing skills were assessed following the instruction. We did not measure attributions, so treatment effects on attributions are unknown. In general we found that the process goal plus feedback condition was the most effective and that there also were some benefits of providing students with a process goal alone. In the first study (Schunk & Swartz, 1993a), process goal plus feedback students judged self-efficacy higher than the product goal and general goal conditions, and process goal children judged self-efficacy higher than general goal students. General goal students demonstrated the lowest skill, and the process goal and process goal plus feedback conditions demonstrated higher skill than the product goal condition.

In a second study (Schunk & Swartz, 1993a), process goal plus feedback students judged self-efficacy higher than general goal students and demonstrated higher skill than general goal and product goal students; process goal children scored higher on skill than general goal students. Process goal plus feedback children reported and demonstrated the highest strategy use during test sessions. We also found that gains were maintained 6 weeks after completion of instruction. Self-efficacy, strategy use, and skill were positively correlated.

In the project with gifted students (Schunk & Swartz, 1993b) we found that process goals and progress feedback led to higher self-efficacy and skill than product goals; process goals by themselves promoted skill better than product goals. Process goal plus feedback students judged strategy use higher than children in the other conditions. The benefits of process goals plus feedback maintained themselves over a 6-week maintenance period. This study also assessed the effects of treatments on students' goal orientations. Process goal plus feedback students scored higher than product goal students on task orientation (emphasis on learning goals) and significantly lower on ego orientation (emphasis on performance goals) compared with process and product goal students. Task orientation correlated positively with self-efficacy, skill, and strategy use.

This procedure could be modified to further enhance students' self-regulatory activities. We used teachers to model the writing strategy. Within this context, models could provide attributional and efficacy information. The progress feedback stressed strategy attributions, which also could be verbalized and exemplified by the models with such statements as "I was able to write this paragraph because I applied the strategy's steps" and, "I'm not doing well because I'm not really trying to apply the strategy's steps properly."

Models also can enhance learners' self-efficacy. Theory and research show that observing similar others improving their skills can raise observers' self-efficacy for skill improvement. Peer models can serve as a vicarious source of efficacy information. Teachers could select students to write paragraphs and verbalize aloud their thoughts while others observed.

The type of feedback provided could be broadened to include effort and ability information. Effort feedback is credible during skill acquisition (e.g., "You're getting better because you're trying to do well"). Effort feedback ("You need to work harder") will not be beneficial when students already are working hard and lack the skills to perform better with greater effort. As skills develop, teachers might introduce ability feedback (e.g., "That's good, you're really becoming a good writer"). Feedback also can be provided by peers. Peer conferences are commonly employed during writing instruction, in which students read each other's writing and provide feedback on strong points and areas requiring revision (DiPardo & Freedman, 1988). Peers can be taught to provide feedback on ways that students' writing has improved and to link improvement with attributions to effort, strategy use, and ability.

Students' self-observations and self-evaluations of their writing are critical components of self-regulation (Bandura, 1986; Zimmerman, 1990), and can be incorporated into regular writing instruction. Self-observation and self-evaluation of one's work can involve counting the number of sentences one has written, determining whether one has written a sentence on each idea generated, deciding whether the story has a beginning and an end, and judging whether ideas are presented in a sensible order. Graham and Harris (1989) note that these techniques by themselves do not always produce gains in student writing but are more effective when combined with other self-regulation procedures. They describe an intervention in which students set goals for the number and type of vocabulary items to include in stories, and after each writing period students gauged their performance and evaluated their success in meeting their goals. Sawyer, Graham, and Harris (1992) describe an intervention using self-observation and self-evaluation in which students counted the number of story grammar elements they used, graphed the number, and compared it to the goal.

CONCLUSION

Self-efficacy and attributions are important self-regulatory processes during academic activities. Drawing on the social cognitive perspectives of Bandura (1986) and Zimmerman (1989), I have integrated self-efficacy and attributions into a social cognitive framework and discussed how these processes might operate while students are engaged with academic material.

A focus on self-regulation in education has occurred recently, and we need much more research before we can offer solid ideas for educational practice. Nonetheless, I believe there is sufficient evidence on ways that we can enhance students' self-regulatory activities and I believe we are justified in doing so. The future undoubtedly holds many exciting developments in this area, and my hope is that this chapter will serve to stimulate research and applications of procedures designed to influence self-regulation of attributions and self-efficacy.

ACKNOWLEDGMENT

I wish to thank Barry J. Zimmerman for his comments on an earlier version of this chapter.

REFERENCES

Ames, C. (1992). Classrooms: Goals, structures, and student motivation. *Journal of Educational Psychology, 84,* 261–271.
Andrews, G. R., & Debus, R. L. (1978). Persistence and the causal perception of failure: Modifying cognitive attributions. *Journal of Educational Psychology, 70,* 154–166.
Bandura, A. (1986). *Social foundations of thought and action: A social cognitive theory.* Englewood Cliffs, NJ: Prentice-Hall.
Bandura, A. (1988). Self-regulation of motivation and action through goal systems. In V. Hamilton, G. H. Bower, & N. H. Frijda (Eds.), *Cognitive perspectives on emotion and motivation* (pp. 37–61). Dordrecht, The Netherlands: Kluwer Academic Publishers.
Borkowski, J. G., Carr, M., Rellinger, E., & Pressley, M. (1990). Self-regulated cognition: Interdependence of metacognition, attributions, and self-esteem. In B. F. Jones & L. Idol (Eds.), *Dimensions of thinking and cognitive instruction* (pp. 53–92). Hillsdale, NJ: Lawrence Erlbaum Associates.

Borkowski, J. G., Weyhing, R. S., & Carr, M. (1988). Effects of attributional retraining on strategy-based reading comprehension of learning-disabled students. *Journal of Educational Psychology, 80,* 46–53.

Bouffard-Bouchard, T., Parent, S., & Larivee, S. (1991). Influence of self-efficacy on self-regulation and performance among junior and senior high-school age students. *International Journal of Behavioral Development, 14,* 153–164.

Butkowsky, I. S., & Willows, D. M. (1980). Cognitive-motivational characteristics of children varying in reading ability: Evidence for learned helplessness in poor readers. *Journal of Educational Psychology, 72,* 408–422.

Carr, M., & Borkowski, J. G. (1989). Attributional training and the generalization of reading strategies with underachieving children. *Learning and Individual Differences, 1,* 327–341.

Collins, J. (1982, March). *Self-efficacy and ability in achievement behavior.* Paper presented at the meeting of the American Educational Research Association, New York.

DiPardo, A., & Freedman, S. W. (1988). Peer response groups in the writing classroom: Theoretical foundations and new directions. *Review of Educational Research, 58,* 119–149.

Dweck, C. S. (1975). The role of expectations and attributions in the alleviation of learned helplessness. *Journal of Personality and Social Psychology, 31,* 674–685.

Elliott, E. S., & Dweck, C. S. (1988). Goals: An approach to motivation and achievement. *Journal of Personality and Social Psychology, 54,* 5–12.

Festinger, L. (1954). A theory of social comparison processes. *Human Relations, 7,* 117–140.

Flower, L., & Hayes, J. R. (1981). A cognitive process theory of writing. *College Composition and Communication, 32,* 365–387.

Graham, S. (1991). A review of attribution theory in achievement contexts. *Educational Psychology Review, 3,* 5–39.

Graham, S., & Harris, K. R. (1989). Cognitive training: Implications for written language. In J. R. Hughes & R. J. Hall (Eds.), *Cognitive-behavioral psychology in the schools: A comprehensive handbook* (pp. 247–279). New York: Guilford Press.

Heider, F. (1958). *The psychology of interpersonal relations.* New York: Wiley.

Kanfer, F. H., & Gaelick, L. (1986). Self-management methods. In F. H. Kanfer & A. P. Goldstein (Eds.), *Helping people change: A textbook of methods* (3rd ed., pp. 283–345). New York: Pergamon Press.

Karoly, P., & Kanfer, F. H. (1982). *Self-management and behavior change: From theory to practice.* New York: Pergamon Press.

Kelley, H. H. (1967). Attribution theory in social psychology. In D. Levine (Ed.), *Nebraska symposium on motivation* (Vol. 15, pp. 192–238). Lincoln, NE: University of Nebraska Press.

Kelley, H. H., & Michela, J. (1980). Attribution theory and research. *Annual Review of Psychology, 31,* 457–501.

Licht, B. G., & Kistner, J. A. (1986). Motivational problems of learning-disabled children: Individual differences and their implications for treatment. In J. K. Torgesen & B. W. L. Wong (Eds.), *Psychological and educational perspectives on learning disabilities* (pp. 225–255). Orlando, FL: Academic Press.

Locke, E. A., & Latham, G. P. (1990). *A theory of goal setting and task performance.* Englewood Cliffs, NJ: Prentice-Hall.

Mace, F. C., Belfiore, P. J., & Shea, M. C. (1989). Operant theory and research on self-regulation. In B. J. Zimmerman & D. H. Schunk (Eds.), *Self-regulated learning and academic achievement: Theory, research, and practice* (pp. 27–50). New York: Springer-Verlag.

Meece, J. L. (1991). The classroom context and students' motivational goals. In M. L. Maehr & P. R. Pintrich (Eds.), *Advances in motivation and achievement* (Vol. 7, pp. 261–285). Greenwich, CT: JAI Press.

Meece, J. L., Blumenfeld, P. C., & Hoyle, R. H. (1988). Students' goal orientations and cognitive engagement in classroom activities. *Journal of Educational Psychology, 80,* 514–523.

Nicholls, J. G. (1978). The development of the concepts of effort and ability, perception of academic attainment, and the understanding that difficult tasks require more ability. *Child Development, 49,* 800–814.

Nicholls, J. G. (1983). Conceptions of ability and achievement motivation: A theory and its implications for education. In S. G. Paris, G. M. Olson, & H. W. Stevenson (Eds.), *Learning and motivation in the classroom* (pp. 211–237). Hillsdale, NJ: Lawrence Erlbaum Associates.

Paris, S. G., & Newman, R. S. (1990). Developmental aspects of self-regulated learning. *Educational Psychologist, 25,* 87–102.

Pintrich, P. R., & Schrauben, B. (1992). Students' motivational beliefs and their cognitive engagement in classroom academic tasks. In D. H. Schunk & J. L. Meece (Eds.), *Student perceptions in the classroom* (pp. 149–183). Hillsdale, NJ: Lawrence Erlbaum Associates.

Relich, J. D., Debus, R. L., & Walker, R. (1986). The mediating role of attribution and self-efficacy variables for treatment effects on achievement outcomes. *Contemporary Educational Psychology, 11,* 195–216.

Salomon, G. (1984). Television is "easy" and print is "tough": The differential investment of mental effort in learning as a function of perceptions and attributions. *Journal of Educational Psychology, 76,* 647–658.

Sawyer, R. J., Graham, S., & Harris, K. R. (1992). Direct teaching, strategy instruction, and strategy instruction with explicit self-regulation: Effects on the composition skills and self-efficacy of students with learning disabilities. *Journal of Educational Psychology, 84,* 340–352.

Schulman, P., Castellon, C., & Seligman, M. E. P. (1989). Assessing explanatory style: The content analysis of verbatim explanations and the Attributional Style Questionnaire. *Behaviour Research and Therapy, 27,* 505–512.

Schunk, D. H. (1982). Effects of effort attributional feedback on children's perceived self-efficacy and achievement. *Journal of Educational Psychology, 74,* 548–556.

Schunk, D. H. (1983). Ability versus effort attributional feedback: Differential effects on self-efficacy and achievement. *Journal of Educational Psychology, 75,* 848–856.

Schunk, D. H. (1984). Sequential attributional feedback and children's achievement behaviors. *Journal of Educational Psychology, 76,* 1159–1169.

Schunk, D. H. (1989). Social cognitive theory and self-regulated learning. In B. J. Zimmerman & D. H. Schunk, *Self-regulated learning and academic achievement: Theory, research, and practice* (pp. 83–110). New York: Springer-Verlag.

Schunk, D. H., & Cox, P. D. (1986). Strategy training and attributional feedback with learning disabled students. *Journal of Educational Psychology, 78,* 201–209.

Schunk, D. H., & Gunn, T. P. (1985). Modeled importance of task strategies and achievement beliefs: Effects on self-efficacy and skill development. *Journal of Early Adolescence, 5,* 247–258.

Schunk, D. H., & Gunn, T. P. (1986). Self-efficacy and skill development: Influence of task strategies and attributions. *Journal of Educational Research, 79,* 238–244.

Schunk, D. H., & Rice, J. M. (1986). Extended attributional feedback: Sequence effects during remedial reading instruction. *Journal of Early Adolescence, 6,* 55–66.

Schunk, D. H., & Swartz, C. W. (1993a). Goals and progress feedback: Effects on self-efficacy and writing achievement. *Contemporary Educational Psychology, 18,* 337–354.

Schunk D. H., & Swartz, C. W. (1993b). Writing strategy instruction with gifted students: Effects of goals and feedback on self-efficacy and skills. *Roeper Review, 15,* 225–230.

Surber, C. F. (1980). The development of reversible operations in judgments of ability, effort, and performance. *Child Development, 51,* 1018–1029.

Weiner, B. (1979). A theory of motivation for some classroom experiences. *Journal of Educational Psychology, 71,* 3–25.

Weiner, B., Frieze, I., Kukla, A., Reed, L., Rest, S., & Rosenbaum, R. M. (1971). Perceiving the causes of success and failure. In E. E. Jones, D. E. Kanouse, H. H. Kelley, R. E. Nisbett, S. Valins, & B. Weiner (Eds.), *Attribution: Perceiving the causes of behavior* (pp. 95–120). Morristown, NJ: General Learning Press.

Zimmerman, B. J. (1989). A social cognitive view of self-regulated academic learning. *Journal of Educational Psychology, 81,* 329–339.

Zimmerman, B. J. (1990). Self-regulating academic learning and achievement: The emergence of a social cognitive perspective. *Educational Psychology Review, 2,* 173–201.

Zimmerman, B. J., & Martinez-Pons, M. (1992). Perceptions of efficacy and strategy use in the self-regulation of learning. In D. H. Schunk & J. L. Meece (Eds.), *Student perceptions in the classroom* (pp. 185–207). Hillsdale, NJ: Lawrence Erlbaum Associates.

Zimmerman, B. J., & Schunk, D. H. (1989). *Self-regulated learning and academic achievement: Theory, research, and practice.* New York: Springer-Verlag.

5

The Role of Children's Achievement Values in the Self-Regulation of Their Learning Outcomes

Allan Wigfield
University of Maryland

Children's ability to regulate their own learning is a phenomenon that is of great interest to many educators, and a topic that many researchers currently are investigating. Zimmerman (1989a) defined self-regulation as follows: "Students can be described as self-regulated to the degree that they are metacognitively, motivationally and behaviorally active participants in their own learning processes" (p. 4). As Zimmerman (1989a, this volume), Schunk (1991a), and others have discussed, students who are self-regulated are more likely to use effective learning strategies, be meaningfully engaged in their own learning, and attain their academic goals. Thus, helping students become self-regulated learners is an important educational task. Yet many students do not become self-regulated learners, and these (and other) students do not attain their educational goals, or may not even have important goals for their education. One reason this can occur is that some students do not value learning. A recent "Calvin and Hobbes" cartoon illustrates this problem. Calvin tells Hobbes that to do his history assignment he needs to break it into small parts, and take it one step at a time; thus, he knows how to regulate his studying. However, at the end of the strip he tosses the book away because he doesn't care about doing the assignment!

In this chapter I review research on children's valuing of achievement, and how their achievement values help regulate various outcomes of their learning. Much of the research I review comes from a research program on the development and socialization of children's achievement values that Jacquelynne Eccles, I, and our colleagues have been conducting over the last few years. We broadly defined achievement values as the incentives or purposes individuals have for succeeding on a given task. I discuss how children's valuing of achievement tasks relates to the ways they regulate their choices of which achievement activities to pursue, and their performance on different academic tasks and in different school subjects. I also consider how children's valuing of achievement relates to more specific processes associated with self-regulated learning, including the use of appropriate cognitive learning strategies, degree of effort they are willing to expend, and degree of persistence. In essence, I argue that children's achievement values are a crucial motivational mediator of their self-regulation. When students value a particular task they will be more likely to continue to engage in it, expend more effort on it, and do better on it. I begin with a brief overview of research on motivation and self-regulation, and then turn to a more detailed discussion of our conception of children's achievement values. I then discuss how children's achievement values help regulate their learning outcomes.

STUDENT MOTIVATION AND SELF-REGULATION: AN OVERVIEW

Researchers interested in students' motivation have argued that motivation is crucial to students' use of self-regulated learning strategies and to their school achievement (e.g., Eccles et al., 1983; Garcia & Pintrich, this volume; Pintrich & DeGroot, 1990; Wigfield, in press). As Pintrich and DeGroot (1990) put it, "knowledge of cognitive and metacognitive strategies is usually not enough to promote student achievement; students also must be motivated to use the strategies" (p. 33). We and other researchers have assessed different motivational constructs that relate to how students regulate their achievement outcomes. One of these constructs is children's beliefs about their ability. Ability beliefs are children's evaluations of their competence in different areas, and researchers have examined these beliefs in several different activity domains, such as academics, sports, social, and other domains. As discussed in more detail later, these beliefs have been shown to predict children's performance in different achievement domains (see Eccles et al., 1983; Meece, Wigfield, & Eccles, 1990). Some sample items from our measures of children's ability beliefs are shown in Table 5.1.

A construct closely related to children's ability beliefs is their expectancies for success. However, expectancies refer more to children's sense of how well they will do on an upcoming task, instead of their general belief of how good they are at the task (see Stipek, 1984). Like ability beliefs, individuals' expectancies for success relate strongly to their performance on different tasks (e.g., Eccles, 1984a, 1984b; Meece et al., 1990), and Table 5.1 presents items we have used to measure children's expectancies for success. The construct of self-efficacy proposed by Bandura (1977; see also Schunk, 1991a) also deals with individuals' expectancies. Bandura (1977) proposed that individuals' efficacy expectations for different achievement tasks are a major determinant of activity choice, willingness to expend effort, and persistence. In work with school-aged children, Schunk and his colleagues (see Schunk, 1991a, 1991b, this volume, for reviews) clearly demonstrated that students' sense of efficacy relates to their academic performance (see also Zimmerman, Bandura, & Martinez-Pons, 1992). They also showed that training students both to be more efficacious and to believe they are more efficacious improves children's achievement in different subject areas such as math and reading.

TABLE 5.1
Sample Items Assessing Children's Ability Beliefs, Expectancies
for Success, and Achievement Values

Ability Belief Items
  1. How good at math are you?
  2. If you were to order all the students in your math class from the worst to the best in math, where would you put yourself?
Expectancies for Success
  3. Compared to other students, how well do you expect to do in math this year?
  4. How well do you think you will do in your math course this year?
Perceived Task Value Items
  Intrinsic Interest Value
  5. In general, I find working on math assignments (*very boring, very interesting*).
  6. How much do you like doing math?
  Attainment Value/Importance
  7. For me, being good in math is (*not at all important, very important*).
  8. Compared to your other activities, how important is it to you to be good at math?
  Utility Value/Usefulness
  9. In general, how useful is what you learn in math?
  10. Compared to your other activities, how useful is what you learn in math?
  Cost of Success
  11. How much does the amount of time you spend on math keep you from doing other things you would like to do?

Note. Mathematics items are used for illustrative purposes; similar items were asked for other achievement activities. Items were answered on 1 to 7 scales; some of the end points of the scales are shown in parentheses.

During the 1980s researchers examined in more detail motivational constructs that have more to do with the question "Do I want to succeed on this task?" rather than focusing solely on ability and efficacy-related beliefs. Answering the question "Do I want to succeed?" affirmatively is critical to self-regulation; even if individuals believe they are competent and efficacious at a task and know what to do to succeed, they may not engage in it if they have no compelling purpose for doing so. Children's and adolescents' valuing of achievement is one major construct related to the question of "Do I want to succeed?" Achievement values were an important part of seminal early theoretical work on achievement motivation such as Atkinson's (1957) expectancy-value model of achievement motivation. In general, however, researchers have paid less attention to individuals' achievement values than they have to individuals' ability-related achievement beliefs (see Wigfield & Eccles, 1992, for more detailed discussion).

DEFINING ACHIEVEMENT VALUES

In his theory of achievement motivation, Atkinson (1957) stated that expectancies (or probabilities) of success and incentive value are two important situational determinants of resultant achievement motivation. He defined incentive value as the relative attractiveness of succeeding on a given achievement task. Although he defined incentive value as a separate construct, through algebraic manipulation of the terms in his equation for achievement motivation Atkinson reduced incentive value to the inverse of the probability of success. Hence much of the empirical work done by Atkinson and his colleagues focused on how different levels of probabilities for success influenced individuals' choice of achievement tasks (see Atkinson & Feather, 1966, for a review). Thus, even in this expectancy-value model, values were relatively neglected empirically (see Wigfield & Eccles, 1992, for further discussion).

Feather (1982, 1992) expanded on Atkinson's definition of achievement values. He described values as core beliefs about what the individual should or should not do (see also Rokeach, 1973). He argued that values emerge from society's rules as well as the individual's psychological needs, and are basic to the individual's sense of self. Feather also believes values are one class of motives that guide individuals' behaviors in different settings (see Feather, 1992). Individuals with different values will regard different goal objects as more or less attractive, so their motivation to attain those goal objects will be based (at least in part) on their values. As an expectancy-value theorist, Feather also argued that the likelihood of attaining the goal also will influence behavior; a valued goal may not be approached if the expectancy for achieving that goal is very low.

Eccles' and Wigfield's Work: Components of Achievement-Related Values

Eccles and her colleagues proposed a model of achievement choice that posits individuals' expectancies and values as the primary determinants of achievement performance and choice (Eccles, 1984a, 1984b; Eccles et al., 1983). Eccles and her colleagues based their expectancy and value constructs in part on Atkinson's (1957) expectancy-value model. This model is broader than Atkinson's, however, in that it includes a variety of achievement-related beliefs and socialization influences that impact individuals' expectancies and values, and performance and choice. The model has provided the conceptual framework for studies concerned with individuals' decisions about their involvement in different activities, with adolescents' decisions about whether or not to continue taking mathematics a primary focus. Thus, research based on the model concerns children's self-regulation of two broad achievement outcomes, performance and choice.

The portion of the Eccles et al. (1983) model most relevant to the issue of how children's achievement values regulate their learning outcomes is presented in Fig. 5.1. As can be seen in the figure, children's and adolescents' expectancies and values are assumed to have the most direct effects on their performance, persistence, and choice of achievement tasks. To couch this in terms of self-regulation, children's expectancies and values are posited to influence how students regulate their levels of performance, degree of persistence, and choice of whether or not to continue a given activity. I discuss these processes more fully later. Expectancies and values themselves are influenced by children's task-specific beliefs, which Eccles et al. (1983) defined as beliefs about ability and perceptions of the difficulty of different tasks, and their goals and self-schemata. In this model, *goals* are defined as the broad purposes children have for learning or doing different activities, and include such things as career plans, and conformity to gender-role appropriate behaviors (other researchers' definition of achievement goals are discussed later). These variables are in turn influenced by children's interpretations of their own previous performance, and their understanding of socializers' reactions to their performance. Due to space limitations I do not discuss socialization influences in this chapter; see Wigfield and Eccles (1992) for discussion of the socialization of children's achievement values.[1]

---

[1]Another very important application of the model has been to understand sex differences in achievement choices; in particular, why girls are less likely to continue taking mathematics classes and choose math and science majors in college. Due to space limitations I do not discuss in this chapter the work on sex differences in achievement values and choice; see Eccles (1984a, 1984b), Eccles et al. (1983), Wigfield (in press), and Wigfield and Eccles (1992) for reviews of this work.

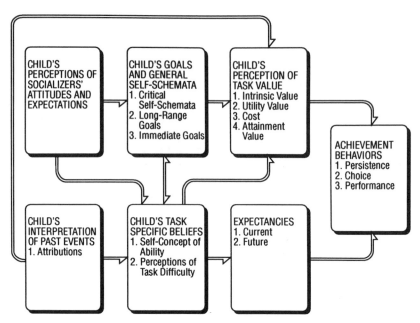

FIG. 5.1.   Eccles et al. expectancy-value model of achievement choice. From Eccles et al. (1983). Adapted by permission.

One of the major contributions of this model is the broader definition of achievement task values that Eccles and her colleagues provided. In defining different aspects of achievement values, Eccles et al. (1983) expanded on earlier work on achievement values (e.g., Atkinson, 1957; Battle, 1965, 1966), and research on intrinsic and extrinsic motivation (e.g., Deci & Ryan, 1985; Harter, 1981). Eccles et al. (1983) defined four aspects of achievement task values: attainment value, intrinsic value, utility value, and cost. Like Battle (1965, 1966), Eccles et al. defined attainment value as the importance of doing well on the task. The posited that tasks will have higher attainment value to the extent that they allow the individual to confirm salient aspects of their self-schemata, such as masculinity or femininity, or competence in different domains. To illustrate generally, if a child views the student role as a central part of her sense of self, then achievement tasks in school will take on greater importance. More specifically, if mathematics success is salient to the individual, then math classes may have the highest attainment value for the individual. Thus the importance of a given task should have strong consequences for students' engagement in the task. The attainment value component of the model relates most directly to the broader perspective on values discussed by Feather (1982, 1992) in that the importance individuals attach to a given task relates to the broader, core values they have about themselves. Sample items we have used to measure the importance students attach to mathematics are presented in Table 5.1.

Intrinsic or interest value is the enjoyment the individual gets from performing the activity, or the subjective interest the individual has in the subject; sample items are presented in Table 5.1. Eccles et al. (1983) argued that when a task has high interest value, the individual will be intrinsically motivated to do the task. Thus, interest value relates to the construct of intrinsic motivation as defined by Deci and his colleagues (e.g., Deci & Ryan, 1985) and by Harter (1981). When individuals do tasks that they intrinsically value, their engagement with and performance on the tasks often improve (e.g., Schiefele, 1992; this work is discussed in more detail later). Also, when children are intrinsically motivated for a given activity they have more positive competence beliefs for the activity as well (see Harter, 1981).

Utility value is how the task relates to future goals, such as career or social goals (see Table 5.1 for sample items). The individual may pursue some tasks because they are important for future goals, even if he or she is not that interested in the task for its own sake. For instance, students often take classes that they do not particularly enjoy but that they need to take to pursue their real interests, such as taking several years of foreign language to meet college entrance requirements. Or, individuals may take classes or do tasks be with their friends; here the utility value would be social in nature. This component captures more "extrinsic" reasons for engaging in a task, such as doing a task not for its own sake but to reach some desired end state (see Deci & Ryan, 1985, and Harter, 1981, for further discussion of extrinsic motivation).

Recently, Eccles and Wigfield (in press) examined whether these three components of achievement task values could be empirically distinguished. They did confirmatory factor analyses of 5th- through 12th-grade students responses to items measuring each of these constructs. The factor models clearly indicated that three-factor models positing separate factors for importance, interest, and utility value provided the best fit to the data. These results give empirical support to the theoretical distinctions between different components of achievement values defined by Eccles et al. (1983).

Finally, Eccles and her colleagues also discussed the "cost" of engaging in different tasks (Eccles et al., 1983). They conceptualized cost in terms of all the negative aspects of engaging in the task. These include anticipated negative emotional states (e.g., performance anxiety and fear of both failure and success) as well as the amount of effort that will be necessary to succeed at the task (see Table 5.1 for a sample item). Cost of engaging in different tasks has not received as much empirical attention as the other value components, but it likely has important implications for students' self-regulation of their learning outcomes, particularly the amount of effort students may be willing to put forth. If a task costs too much effort, perhaps the student will decide not to do it.

RESEARCH ON ACHIEVEMENT VALUES
AND SELF-REGULATION

Relation of Children's Achievement Values
to Their Performance and Choice

Referring back to Fig. 5.1, Eccles et al. (1983) posited that students' expectancies for success and achievement values predicted their regulation of three important achievement outcomes: students' performance, their persistence in math, and their choices about whether or not to continue taking math courses. In two longitudinal studies done with early adolescents and adolescents, we have assessed the links of students' ability-expectancy beliefs and values to their performance and choice. The studies included approximately 1,600 students in 5th through 12th grades. The students completed questionnaires once a year over a 2-year period. The questionnaires contained items assessing their ability beliefs, expectancies for success, achievement values for both math and English, and intentions to continue taking more math courses (see Eccles et al., 1983; Wigfield, Eccles, Mac Iver, Reuman, & Midgley, 1991, for more detailed discussion of the questionnaires, and Table 5.1 for sample items). Students' grades in math and English were obtained from school records, as were their enrollment decisions about whether to keep taking math.

For the purposes of this chapter, two main results from these studies are most relevant. First, in our work and others' work, the relations between children's achievement values, expectancies for success, and beliefs about their ability are positive (e.g., Battle, 1966; Eccles et al., 1983; Eccles & Wigfield, in press; see Wigfield & Eccles, 1992, for a more complete review). Most of these studies have been done in real-world settings and concern achievement values and expectancies for academic subjects such as mathematics and English. In related work, studies of studies of children's intrinsic motivation and competence beliefs show that those two constructs are positively related (Harter, 1981). Thus, children value tasks on which they do well. An important implication of these results is that to foster students' regulation of their learning, they must be successful on the achievement tasks that they value.

Second, a major finding from these studies is that even when level of previous performance is controlled for, students' expectancies for success strongly predict their performance in mathematics and English. Students' achievement task values predict both intentions and actual decisions to keep taking mathematics and English (Eccles, 1984a, 1984b; Eccles et al., 1983; Meece et al., 1990). To provide some more details about these findings, using path analysis Eccles (1984b) showed that 5th- through 12th-grade students' expectancies for success predicted subsequent performance in math more strongly than did their achievement values, and more strongly than did their previous performance. Students' valuing of math predicted their intentions to keep taking math more strongly than did their expectancies for success. Eccles (1984a) showed that 8th-through 10th-grade students' valuing of math strongly predicted their actual decisions to continue taking math later in their high school careers, whereas their ability beliefs in math did not predict enrollment decisions.

Meece et al. (1990) assessed how 7th- through 9th-grade students' ability beliefs and performance in math Year 1 predicted their achievement beliefs and performance a year later. The Year 2 beliefs included in their analyses were expectancies for success, perceived importance of math, math anxiety, and intentions to continue taking more math. Meece et al. found that Year 1 ability beliefs positively predicted Year 2 expectancies for success and importance attached to math, and negatively predicted math anxiety. Year 2 importance ratings predicted the students' intentions to continue taking math more strongly than did their expectancies for success in math. Students' expectancies for success predicted subsequent math performance more strongly than did the importance of math. Math anxiety did not directly predict either math performance or intentions to continue taking math. The only direct link of Year 1 performance was to Year 2 performance; however, that path coefficient was not as strong as the one from Year 2 expectancies for success to Year 2 performance.

We also have found that the predictive links of students' achievement values to their intentions to keep taking math vary across age. Wigfield and Eccles (1989) found that 7th- through 9th-grade students' interest in math most strongly predicted their intentions to keep taking math. Both interest in math and its utility value predicted 10th- through 12th-grade students' intentions to keep taking math. These findings demonstrate the importance of distinguishing different components of task value, because those components have different predictive links to intentions in younger and older students.

Recently, Wigfield (1992) explored how students' ability beliefs and achievement values predicted their performance in math and continued enrollment in math over an 8-year period. Students first completed questionnaires, and then their grades and enrollment decisions were gathered each subsequent year until the youngest students graduated from high school 8 years later. Path analyses assessing the links of ability beliefs, achievement values, performance, and enrollment were done separately for three age groups of students: 5th through 7th graders, 8th and 9th graders, and 10th through 12th graders. Results indicated that for the youngest and oldest groups, ability beliefs in math significantly predicted grades in 12th-grade mathematics courses (this path approached significance in the middle group). For the course enrollment decisions, in all three age groups students' math ability beliefs significantly predicted whether students were enrolled in math at 12th grade. For the oldest group, students' valuing of math also significantly predicted their course enrollment decisions. These results show the long-term impact of these beliefs on students' performance and choice, two important aspects of self-regulation.

Implications for Students' Regulation of Their Performance and Choice

These results show the predictive power of adolescents' ability-related beliefs and achievement values on how students regulate their performance in mathematics, and their choices of whether to continue taking math. Students' expectancies for success and their valuing of math predict grades and enrollment decisions as long as 8 years after the self-perception variables were assessed. The results provide important support for the Eccles et al. (1983) model of achievement choice. To date we have looked primarily at how children's achievement values regulate rather general learning outcomes like course grades and course enrollment decisions. More micro-level analyses of how children's achievement values help regulate these outcomes should now be pursued. Students' valuing of those specific activities could relate to such self-regulated processes as self-observation, judgment, and goal setting. For instance, students who value math likely study for math tests more diligently and effectively. They also should be more likely to set important goals for their mathematics performance, and to continue to pursue those goals even if they encounter difficulty in reaching them. They should be more attuned to their level of performance, and should adjust it if necessary. Students who do not value math very much would be less likely to do any of these things.

Although we can talk about children's overall valuing of different tasks, it is clear in our work that values are made up of different components (Eccles & Wigfield, in press), and that these components predict achievement outcomes in different ways for younger and older students (Wigfield & Eccles, 1989). Given these separate components of children's values, it is important to consider whether or not those component are in sync with one another, because this synchrony could influence how children regulate their achievement outcomes. For instance, some children may find certain tasks important for different reasons, but not be at all interested in doing them, whereas other children may see those tasks as both important and interesting. Indeed, we have found that many children do believe math is important but say it is not very interesting (Wigfield et al., 1991). Generally, children whose values are in synchrony may be more positively motivated to regulate their learning about a particular kind of academic task, whereas those whose values are out of synchrony may be less likely to do so. The differences between these groups should be most apparent in effort, persistence, and strategy use. Both groups may set the goal of achieving a certain level of math proficiency by taking a certain set of courses. As first the assignments in a particular course and then the courses themselves become more difficult, students viewing math as both interesting and important should be more likely to persist, even if they are having difficulty. They may see failures as learning opportunities, and may continue trying even after failure, using more sophisticated learning strategies in their further attempts to learn the material. Children lacking interest in math may give up more quickly, and may decide it is not so important after all. They may decide to put effort into other activities, as the costs of math may be too much for them. Similar examples could be traced for students seeing math as useful and interesting, as compared to those simply viewing it as useful. Researchers have not yet assessed many of these specific links between achievement values and different aspects of self-regulated learning. One area that researchers have addressed is how students' achievement values regulate their reported strategy use; that work is considered next.

Achievement Values, Cognitive Strategy Use, and Levels of Learning

Students' valuing of achievement tasks has been found to relate to their use of different cognitive strategies, their perceived self-regulation, and to their performance on different achievement tasks. The research of Pintrich and his colleagues focused on these relations in both junior high school students and college students (see Garcia & Pintrich, this volume; Pintrich, 1989; Pintrich & DeGroot, 1990). In their studies, students completed the Motivated Strategies for Learning Questionnaire, a questionnaire that assesses students' perceived self-efficacy, achievement values, cognitive strategy use, self-regulation of their learning, and test anxiety. The values measure is a composite measure that taps the interest, importance, and usefulness dimensions of task values that Eccles et al. (1983) defined. Pintrich and his colleagues also obtained different kinds of performance indicators, from grades on classroom assignments and classroom tests to semester grades in college courses. They found that students' perceived self-efficacy and values relate positively to their reported use of cognitive strategies and self-regulation. The relations between achievement values, strategy use, and self-regulation are stronger than those between self-efficacy, strategy use, and self-regulation. As in our work, they found that expectancies relate more strongly to performance than do achievement values. However, in their regression analyses predicting performance from the motivational variables, strategy use, and perceived self-regulation, they found that it is the cognitive strategy and self-regulation scales that directly predict performance; the effects of self-efficacy and values on performance appear to be mediated through the other measures. Pintrich and DeGroot argued that students' self-efficacy may facilitate their cognitive engagement, and their achievement values relate to their choices about whether to become engaged, but their use of cognitive strategies and self-regulation relates more directly to performance. Although these proposed linkages need to be tested longitudinally, these results provide fascinating evidence for the ways motivation and cognition can work together to facilitate (or impede) performance on different school tasks.

Pokay and Blumenfeld (1990) reported somewhat similar results in a longitudinal study of how students' expectancies, values, and cognitive strategy use related to performance in high school geometry, in a group of high school students who had all taken algebra the previous year. Early in the school year they assessed students' prior math (algebra) ability concepts, valuing of algebra, and expectancies for success in geometry. Next they measured cognitive strategy use, and effort management during geometry instruction. At a third time of measurement they assessed the same cognitive and effort management variables, but measured ability beliefs and valuing of geometry. They also obtained grades on geometry tests as performance measures. Pokay and Blumenfeld used path analytic techniques to assess relations among the motivational, cognitive strategy, and performance variables at different time points. As in Pintrich and DeGroot's (1990) study, students' valuing of math had only indirect effects on geometry test performance; the cognitive strategy and effort management variables, along with previous performance, had direct effects on performance. In the model for performance early in the semester, students' geometry expectancies for success directly related to their performance on an early geometry test. Later in the semester students' beliefs about their geometry ability also directly predicted test performance; in fact, this variable was the strongest predictor of performance. Thus in this work students' values influenced whether or not they used different cognitive strategies, rather than influencing performance directly. However, in contrast to Pintrich and

DeGroot's findings, ability-related beliefs did relate directly to students' performance.

In Pintrich and DeGroot's (1990) study and Pokay and Blumenfeld's (1990) study, composite measures of students' achievement values were used, so we do not know which of the different components of achievement values we have defined might relate most strongly to either cognitive strategy use or self-regulation. Other researchers have studied how one particular aspect of achievement values, students' interest in what they are doing, affects their reading comprehension and their regulation of learning strategies. Schiefele (1992) assessed how college students' interest in text materials influenced their comprehension, when the students' prior knowledge of the materials and general intelligence were controlled. He found that college students who were interested in the text materials used in the study processed those materials more deeply and used more elaborate learning strategies while reading than did students less interested in the materials. Shirey and Reynolds (1988) found that adults actually read sentences they find interesting more quickly than those they find less interesting, and recalled more about the interesting materials. Working with children, Renninger (1992) found in studies of Grade 5 and 6 students that their interest in the materials read enhanced their comprehension, even of materials that were quite difficult for the children (although there were some gender differences in these patterns). And Anderson (1982) found that children paid more attention (as measured by duration of reading time) to interesting than to less interesting materials. Overall, these results indicate that students' interest in the material relates quite clearly to several important aspects of self-regulation, including the use of effective learning strategies, level of attention, and actual comprehension of reading materials. Thus, these researchers have identified more micro-level ways in which children's valuing of achievement tasks influences the regulation of their learning outcomes.

Achievement Values and Volition

One other important connection between achievement values and self-regulation should be mentioned. Kuhl (1985, 1987) discussed how many motivational theorists have discarded volitional, or willful, processes, and instead assumed that motivation directs action. Kuhl argued that this view is simplistic, and posited instead that motivational processes only lead to action. Once the individual engages in action, volitional processes take over and determine whether or not the intention is fulfilled (see also Corno, 1989, 1993; Zimmerman, 1989b). Ajzen (1985), in his modification of the theory of reasoned action, also discussed how one's plans or goals sometimes are not carried through, even if the plans remain in place. To solve this conceptual problem, Kuhl proposed that we need to understand better how individuals control (or don't control) the actions they undertake. He proposed several different strategies individuals can use to help them carry through their plans: selective attention, encoding control, emotional control, motivational control, environmental control, and parsimony of information processing.

Although a detailed discussion of these strategies is beyond the scope of this chapter, Kuhl's distinction between motivation and volition has important implications for how expectancy-value theorists consider how students' expectancies and values regulate their achievement outcomes and relate to their engagement in different tasks. For instance, students' relative valuing of different activities may relate to their engagement in the strategies of action control Kuhl proposes. When students are interested in a task, they likely will attend to it better, use more efficient information processing strategies, and be more in control of their encoding. Similarly, when they are doing tasks they value, students may be more in control of their emotions so that setbacks would not throw them off track as much, and their motivation would be focused on continuing involvement with the task. As discussed earlier, these relations between students' valuing of different tasks and their volitional control may be most likely when they view the task as interesting, useful, and important, rather than when they see a task as (for example) important but not interesting.

SUGGESTIONS FOR FUTURE RESEARCH

Some suggestions for future research already have been made. One is the need to learn more about microlevel relations between children's valuing of different activities and the regulation of their learning on those tasks. We now know a good deal about relations between students' achievement values and their enrollment decisions, particularly in mathematics. However, less is known about the more everyday operation of students' values in regulating their learning on specific tasks within different subjects like math, English, or social studies. Better understanding those everyday links would give us a much clearer picture of why some students disengage from a particular subject, and others continue to be engaged.

Another area for future research on values and self-regulation is to look more closely at links between children's achievement values and their achievement goals. During the 1980s researchers extensively examined children's achievement goals, which (like achievement values) is a construct that refers to the purposes children have for achievement (e.g., Ames, 1992b; Dweck & Leggett, 1988; Nicholls, 1984, 1990; Nicholls, Cheung, Lauer, & Patashnick, 1989). The kinds of goals these researchers have addressed are different from the career plans kinds of goals included in Eccles et al. (1983) expectancy-value model. Ames, Dweck, Nicholls, and their colleagues focused instead on children's and adolescents' goals for success in achievement situations, and discussed two major kinds of achievement goals. One kind concerns doing achievement tasks in order to learn and build skills; this kind of goal is called *mastery* by Ames and her colleagues, *learning* by Dweck and her colleagues, and *task involved* by Nicholls and his colleagues. The other kind of goal concerns doing achievement tasks to demonstrate one's ability, or to outperform others; this is called *performance* by Ames and by Dweck, and *ego involved* by Nicholls.

Clearly these goals are different than those described by Eccles and her colleagues in their model. However, achievement values and these kinds of goals are similar in certain respects. Both constructs have to do with the purposes children have for school learning. From an achievement values perspective, a student can do a task because she is interested in it, or because it is useful to her. From a goals perspective, a student can do a task because he wants to learn it, or to outperform his classmates. Children's values and goals both likely influence their choice of achievement tasks. When a student is interested in a task, she may persist longer even if the task gets difficult; the same is true if the student has a learning goal for the task. If the goal is to outperform others, or the task is valued for a more utilitarian reason, the student may give up more quickly when difficulties arise (see Ames, 1992b; Dweck & Leggett, 1988). Yet there are differences between the constructs as well. As described by Nicholls and Dweck, the achievement goal patterns sometimes appear to be broad orientations to learning that influence students' approaches to many different achievement tasks. In contrast, as defined and assessed in our work, achievement values are domain-specific beliefs about particular achievement tasks, and so can vary greatly both across individuals and across achievement tasks. An important issue for future research is to consider how these constructs are related, in order to determine if the goals and expectancy-value perspectives can be integrated more fully (see Wigfield, in press, for further discussion).

Nicholls and his colleagues (e.g., Nicholls et al., 1989; Nicholls, Cobb, Yackel, Wood, & Wheatley, 1990) developed scales to measure task and ego goals. Items on the task goals scales include "I work hard all the time" and "I find a new way to solve a problem." Items on the ego orientation scale include "I finish before my friends" and "I know more than the others." It would be interesting for researchers to administer these scales along with our scales measuring achievement values to groups of children, to determine how similar or different these constructs are. Factor analyses could be done on the complete set of items, and relations among the constructs could be assessed. These sorts of analyses would provide an empirical indication of similarities and differences across these constructs; for instance, do certain of the goals and values items form single factors, or are the constructs distinct? Including measures of the kinds of broader goals Eccles et al. (1983) discussed would allow for the assessment of links between broader and more specific goals, and their relations to achievement values. Such work would provide greater theoretical clarity in this area.

In the self-regulation literature, researchers (e.g., Schunk, 1991a; Zimmerman et al., 1992) have discussed more specific kinds of goals students set for achievement tasks, rather than focusing on the broader goal orientations discussed by Ames, Dweck, and Nicholls. How do learners decide on specific goals for individual learning tasks? Schunk (1991a) reviewed his and others' work showing that the following aspects of goal setting are crucial for understanding students' effort and task engagement: goal specificity, challenge, and proximity. Children having clear, specific goals develop higher self-efficacy and perform better than do children with more general goals, such as the instruction to "work hard." Children appear to enjoy challenging goals rather than goals that are too easy. They also become more motivated when goals are "in sight" or proximal, rather than when the goals seem to be a long way off (this last point may be particularly true for low-achieving children). From the perspective of this chapter, we could consider how children's valuing of different tasks may influence their goal setting. At the broadest level, children finding a particular achievement task interesting, important, or useful may be more likely to set specific, challenging goals for their performance on that and related tasks. Those finding little value for a task may not have such positive goals; indeed, their goal may be to avoid the task. Children valuing tasks in different ways may also set different kinds of goals. For children interested in a task, challenging goals may be most salient. They enjoy the task, and taking their performance to another level may increase that enjoyment. They also may be less concerned about outcomes and more focused on improvement, so challenge would be a key goal. This argument mirrors the points Nicholls, Dweck, and Ames make about the implications of having a mastery or performance focus on learning.

Children doing a task for more utilitarian purposes may not want to be as challenged as those simply interested in the task. If a task is too challenging, such children may begin to question its utility, and try to find other tasks that could meet their utilitarian needs in a less challenging way. The salience of proximal or distal goals also may vary depending on a task's utility. Children hoping to be doctors may take math and science courses in high school to reach that distal goal; the more proximal goal of doing well in those particular classes actually may be a less important motivation than the more distal career goal.

These different scenarios could be tested by measuring children's valuing of different tasks that they are doing, and then assessing the kinds of goals they have for those tasks and which of those goals seem most motivating. Longitudinal studies of this kind would be most valuable; there still are too few studies of how children's self-regulation and motivation change over time, and of the complex relations of self-regulation and motivation at different points in development. In this section I have argued that children's achievement values may influence the goals they have; it also is quite possible that their goals influence their achievement values! Certainly by the middle elementary school grades, relations in these two sets of constructs likely are reciprocal. Longitudinal studies are needed to try to untangle the causal sequences in these relations.

EDUCATIONAL IMPLICATIONS

Increasing Children's Valuing of Different Tasks

One important educational implication of the work reviewed in this chapter is that we need to find ways to enhance children's valuing of the important educational tasks they face, so that they will be more likely to regulate their learning in positive ways. Much has been written about how teachers can foster students' engagement by presenting material in different and innovative ways (e.g., see Brophy, 1987). However, observation studies of classroom instruction show that teachers rarely stress why what they are teaching has value for children (Brophy, 1983). In looking at how teachers presented new tasks to children in elementary school, Brophy found that they very rarely said that the tasks would be enjoyable, and made few attempts to relate the tasks to students' daily lives. Instead, they were more likely to state that children would be tested on the material, and even that they may not like the tasks! Certainly these kinds of introductions to new school tasks would not foster children's valuing of those tasks.

Indeed, results of studies looking at changes in the mean level of children's values generally show that children value academic tasks less as they get older (see Eccles & Midgley, 1989). In our work with 5th- through 12th-grade students, we have found both age-related and domain differences in students' achievement values (Eccles et al., 1983; Wigfield, 1984). In both these studies younger students valued math more highly than did older students, whereas exactly the opposite pattern occurred for English. Eccles et al. (1989) and Wigfield et al. (1991) looked at how the transition to junior high influenced children's valuing of different activities. They found that children's ratings of both the importance of math and English and their liking of these school subjects decreased across the transition from elementary to junior high school. In math, students' importance ratings continued to decline across seventh grade, whereas their ratings of the importance of English recovered somewhat. Also, students valued nonacademic activities like sports and social activities much more than the academic activities.

In a study of the early development of children's achievement values, Eccles, Wigfield, Harold, and Blumenfeld (1993) assessed children's valuing of different activities (math, reading, computers, music, and sports) in first, second, and fourth grade children. Across age there were no differences in the value attached to math, although at all grades math was not valued very highly. Children's valuing of reading, music, and computer activities decreased across grade, whereas valuing of sports increased. In related work on children's intrinsic motivation (or interest value in the context of this chapter) Harter (1981) assessed different components of intrinsic motivation in third through ninth grade students. She found that older children's preference for challenge, curiosity/interest, and independent mastery were much lower than those of the younger children. Harter concluded that children's intrinsic motivation is stifled in important ways during the school years (see Eccles & Midgley, 1989, for further discussion).

As a whole, these findings suggest that many children come to devalue some academic activities, especially after students reach junior high and especially for mathematics. It is particularly striking that Eccles et al. (1983) and Wigfield (1984) found that older high school students see math as being less useful than did the younger children, since the older students in the sample were those who continued to take college-preparatory mathematics courses. Even among this more select and reasonably high-performing group, math loses its value. Students who elect to discontinue taking math likely have even lower math achievement values. Such findings have important implications for how students regulate their learning. As they value different achievement tasks less, it seems very likely that they would persist at them less, be less likely to use efficient cognitive strategies as they do the tasks, and exert less effort. Such changes in self-regulation certainly would decrease students' overall level of performance.

In explaining these changes in students' ability beliefs and achievement values, researchers have suggested that they are due to a combination of changes in individuals' processing of the evaluative information they receive, and changes in school and classroom environmental factors. In terms of changes in processing of evaluative feedback, researchers have found that children become both more accurate and more pessimistic in their ability beliefs over the school years (see Stipek & Mac Iver, 1989, for a review). The growing realization that they are doing poorly in certain school subjects may lead some students to devalue those activities, as a way to maintain a positive sense of general self-worth (see Harter, 1985). Harter found that students whose competence beliefs about an activity are in sync with their beliefs about the importance of that activity report higher general self-worth than students whose competence and importance beliefs are not in sync. For example, students who believe math is very important but do not think they are very able in math will have a lower sense of their general self-worth. Thus when students' ability beliefs about a given task become more negative, it is likely they will come to devalue the task as well.

Along with these more organismic psychological factors, however, are factors in the school and classroom environments that could lessen students' valuing of different tasks. Brophy's (1983) work suggests that teachers do not often stress the value of different academic tasks. Further, as children move through school there are important changes in school environments that can impact students' valuing of different school subjects and school in general; these changes are most dramatic when children move from elementary into middle-grades schools (see Eccles & Midgley, 1989; Eccles, Wigfield, Midgley et al., 1993; Simmons & Blyth, 1987). Briefly, the most problematic of these changes include the move to a larger, more bureaucratic, and controlling environment experienced by many students as they move into middle grades school; the shift to more stringent, normative-based grading standards from criterion-based grading standards; more controlling and less trusting relations between teachers and students; and a lowering of teachers' sense of efficacy (see Eccles & Midgley, 1989, and Eccles, Wigfield, Midgley et al., 1993, for more detailed discussion). Eccles and Midgley have argued that such changes create a developmental mismatch between students and their school environments. As they get older children desire more independence and autonomy and control over the tasks that they do. Yet traditional middle-grades schools often do just the opposite.

Reports like the *Turning Points* report of the Carnegie Council on Adolescent Development (1989) made many important suggestions for changing the organization of middle schools to avoid the kinds of problems just discussed in order to help students better adjust to the transition from elementary to middle-grades school. These suggestions include the use of more cooperative grouping in middle school; creating "schools in a school" to create smaller, more manageable learning environments; and trying to establish more positive relations between teachers and students. Many middle-grades schools now are responding to these reports and adopting many of the suggested school environmental and organizational changes. It will be very informative to see if the observed declines in children's valuing of different school subjects attenuates as a result of some of these changes and, as a result, more students regulate their learning in positive ways during the middle school years. A complete review of the literature on schooling's effects on motivation and self-regulation is beyond the scope of this chapter; interested readers should consult Eccles and Midgley (1989), Eccles, Wigfield, Midgley et al. (1993), and Maehr and Midgley (1991) for discussion of how changes in the school environment may explain the negative changes in achievement motivation and values just discussed.

As important as these broad changes in school environment and organization may be in explaining the decreases in children's valuing of different achievement tasks, it also is crucial to consider how specific teacher–student interactions regarding different academic tasks can foster or inhibit children's valuing of those tasks. Researchers such as Ames (1992a) and Brophy (1987) who are interested in fostering positive motivation in the classroom have discussed a variety of ways teachers can maximize student motivation: varying the ways in which materials are presented, presenting information enthusiastically, allowing students more choice in how they do different assignments, helping students establish realistic goals, and recognizing students' effort and improvement rather than focusing on students' ability, to name a few. Ames developed intervention programs to help teachers maximize students' motivation in these ways. In the context of this chapter, these sorts of strategies should foster students' interest in learning different school subjects. Teachers' attempts to make material more meaningful and related to students' everyday lives would seem to be essential for fostering children's sense of the importance and usefulness of different tasks. As children's valuing of different tasks increases, so should their use of strategies to regulate their learning in positive ways; thus these changes should have an impact both on students' values and on their self-regulation.

Turning these relations around, it also seems likely that as students learn more about how to regulate their learning, and become more successful at doing so, their valuing of those tasks at which they are successful will increase as well. As noted earlier, in our work and that of others, children's sense of competence for a given achievement task relates positively to their valuing of that task. Although determining the causal sequence in this relationship would be difficult, it seems most plausible that the relations between children's valuing of different tasks and their regulation of their learning likely become reciprocal as children proceed through school. As children become better at regulating their learning, they should value learning tasks more; as their valuing of the tasks increases, they should become even more proficient at regulating their learning. Exploring these relations more fully remains an important task for research; there still are few studies that have measured both children's valuing of different tasks and their use of different strategies to regulate their learning.

Of course, even when teachers use the strategies outlined earlier to engage their students in learning, there still will be individual differences across students in their willingness to engage in different tasks. Despite teachers' best efforts, some students will continue to dislike math, or social studies, and so it seems unlikely that they will become efficient self-regulated learners in those areas. Again, this illustrates the point that children's valuing of different academic tasks may be an important precursor of their willingness to devote the time and energy needed to become proficient at that task. Researchers need to explore these individual differences more fully. From an educational perspective, we also need to find ways to maximize students' regulation of their learning in the areas that they find most interesting, or useful, to them, so that they continue to be engaged in school learning.

In conclusion, during the last decade we have begun to understand better the nature of children's valuing of different academic subjects, and how those values relate to their regulation of broad achievement outcomes such as overall performance, and choice of whether or not to continue taking a particular subject. During the 1990s we can build on this work by looking more closely at how children's valuing of different tasks relates to their regulation of their day-to-day learning activities. We also need to explore more completely how contextual factors in different school and classroom environments influence both students' valuing of different achievement tasks, and their regulation of their learning outcomes on those tasks.

ACKNOWLEDGMENTS

I would like to thank the students, teachers, and principals who participated in our studies described in this chapter. I would also like to thank my colleagues Jacquelynne S. Eccles, Harriet Feldlaufer, Rena Harold, Janis Jacobs, Douglas Mac Iver, Carol Midgley, and David Reuman for their collaboration on the studies described in this chapter. Our research was made possible by grants from the National Institute of

Child Health and Human Development (HD31724 and HD17553) and the National Science Foundation (BNS-8510504).

REFERENCES

Ajzen, I. (1985). From intentions to action: A theory of planned behavior: In J. Kuhl & J. Beckman (Eds.), *Action control: From cognition to behavior* (pp. 11–39). Heidelberg: Springer-Verlag.

Ames, C. (1992a). Achievement goals and the classroom climate. In D. H. Schunk & J. L. Meece (Eds.), *Student perceptions in the classroom* (pp. 327–348). Hillsdale, NJ: Lawrence Erlbaum Associates.

Ames, C. (1992b). Classrooms: Goals, structures, and student motivation. *Journal of Educational Psychology, 84,* 261–271.

Anderson, R. C. (1982). Allocation of attention during reading. In A. Flammer & W. Kintsch (Eds.), *Discourse processing* (pp. 292–305). New York: North-Holland.

Atkinson, J. W. (1957). Motivational determinants of risk taking behavior. *Psychological Review, 64,* 359–372.

Atkinson, J. W., & Feather, N. T. (1966). Review and appraisal. In J. W. Atkinson & N. T. Feather (Eds.), *A theory of achievement motivation* (pp. 327–370). New York: Wiley.

Bandura, A. (1977). Self-efficacy: Toward a unifying theory of behavioral change. *Psychological Review, 84,* 191–215.

Battle, E. (1965). Motivational determinants of academic task persistence. *Journal of Personality and Social Psychology, 2,* 209–218.

Battle, E. (1966). Motivational determinants of academic competence. *Journal of Personality and Social Psychology, 4,* 534–642.

Brophy, J. (1983). Fostering student learning and motivation in the elementary school classroom. In S. Paris, G. Olson, & H. Stevenson (Eds.), *Learning and motivation in the classroom* (pp. 283–305). Hillsdale, NJ: Lawrence Erlbaum Associates.

Brophy, J. (1987). Socializing student motivation to learn. In M. L. Maehr & D. Kleiber (Eds.), *Advances in motivation and achievement* (Vol. 5, pp. 181–210). Greenwich, CT: JAI Press.

Carnegie Council on Adolescent Development. (1989). *Turning points: Preparing American youth for the 21st century.* New York: Carnegie Corporation.

Corno, L. (1989). Self-regulated learning: A volitional analysis. In B. J. Zimmerman & D. H. Schunk (Eds.), *Self-regulated learning and academic achievement: Theory, research, and practice* (pp. 111–141). New York: Springer-Verlag.

Corno, L. (1993). The best-laid plans: Modern conceptions of volition and educational research. *Educational Researcher, 22,* 14–22.

Deci, E. L., & Ryan, R. M. (1985). *Intrinsic motivation and self-determination in human behavior.* New York: Plenum.

Dweck, C. S., & Leggett, E. L. (1988). A social-cognitive approach to motivation and personality. *Psychological Review, 95,* 256–273.

Eccles, J. S. (1984a). Sex differences in achievement patterns. In T. Sonderegger (Ed.), *Nebraska Symposium on Motivation* (Vol. 32, pp. 97–132). Lincoln, NE: University of Nebraska Press.

Eccles (Parsons), J. S. (1984b). Sex differences in mathematics participation. In M. Steinkamp & M. L. Maehr (Eds.), *Advances in motivation and achievement* (Vol. 2, pp. 93–137). Greenwich, CT: JAI Press.

Eccles, J., Adler, T. F., Futterman, R., Goff, S. B., Kaczala, C. M., Meece, J., & Midgley, C. (1983). Expectancies, values and academic behaviors. In J. T. Spence (Ed.), *Achievement and achievement motives* (pp. 75–146). San Francisco: W. H. Freeman.

Eccles, J. S., & Midgley, C. (1989). Stage-environment fit: Developmentally appropriate classrooms for young adolescents. In C. Ames & R. Ames (Eds.), *Research on motivation in education* (Vol. 3, pp. 139–186). San Diego, CA: Academic Press.

Eccles, J. S., & Wigfield, A. (in press). In the mind of the achiever: The structure of adolescents' academic achievement related-beliefs and self-perceptions. *Personality and Social Psychology Bulletin.*

Eccles, J. S., Wigfield, A., Flanagan, C., Miller, C., Reuman, D., & Yee, D. (1989). Self-concepts, domain values, and self-esteem: Relations and changes at early adolescence. *Journal of Personality, 57,* 283–310.

Eccles, J. S., Wigfield, A., Harold, R., & Blumenfeld, P. (1993). Age and gender differences in children's achievement self-perceptions during the elementary school years. *Child Development, 64,* 830–847.

Eccles, J. S., Wigfield, A., Midgley, C., Reuman, D., Mac Iver, D., & Feldlaufer, H. (1993). Are traditional middle grades schools undermining the academic motivation of early adolescents? *Elementary School Journal, 93,* 553–574.

Feather, N. T. (1982). Expectancy-value approaches: Present status and future directions. In N. T. Feather (Ed.), *Expectations and actions: Expectancy-value models in psychology* (pp. 395–420). Hillsdale, NJ: Lawrence Erlbaum Associates.

Feather, N. T. (1992). Values, valences, expectations, and actions. *Journal of Social Issues, 48,* 109–124.

Harter, S. (1981). A model of intrinsic mastery motivation in children: Individual differences and developmental change. In W. A. Collins (Ed.), *Minnesota symposia on child psychology* (Vol. 14, pp. 215–255). Hillsdale, NJ: Lawrence Erlbaum Associates.

Harter, S. (1985). Competence as a dimension of self-evaluation: Toward a comprehensive model of self-worth. In R. Leahy (Ed.), *The development of the self* (pp. 55–121). New York: Academic Press.

Kuhl, J. (1985). Volitional mediators of cognition-behavior consistency: Self-regulatory processes and action versus state orientation. In J. Kuhl & J. Beckman (Eds.), *Action control: From cognition to behavior* (pp. 101–128). Berlin: Springer-Verlag.

Kuhl, J. (1987). Action control: The maintenance of motivational states. In F. Halisch & J. Kuhl (Eds.), *Motivation, intention, and volition* (pp. 279–307). Berlin: Springer-Verlag.

Maehr, M. L., & Midgley, C. (1991). Enhancing student motivation: A schoolwide approach. *Educational Psychologist, 26,* 399–427.

Meece, J. L., Wigfield, A., & Eccles, J. S. (1990). Predictors of math anxiety and its consequences for young adolescents' course enrollment intentions and performances in mathematics. *Journal of Educational Psychology, 82,* 60–70.

Nicholls, J. G. (1984). Achievement motivation: Conceptions of ability, subjective experience, task choice, and performance. *Psychological Review, 91,* 328–346.

Nicholls, J. G. (1990). What is ability and why are we mindful of it? A developmental perspective. In R. J. Sternberg & J. Kolligan (Eds.), *Competence considered* (pp. 11–40). New Haven, CT: Yale University Press.

Nicholls, J. G., Cheung, P., Lauer, J., & Patashnick, M. (1989). Individual differences in academic motivation: Perceived ability, goals, beliefs, and values. *Learning and Individual Differences, 1,* 63–84.

Nicholls, J. G., Cobb, P., Yackel, E., Wood, T., & Wheatley, G. (1990). Students' theories about mathematics and their mathematical knowledge: Multiple dimensions of assessment. In G. Kulm (Ed.), *Assessing higher order thinking in mathematics* (pp. 11–40). Washington, DC: American Association for the Advancement of Science.

Pintrich, P. R. (1989). The dynamic interplay of student motivation and cognition in the college classroom. In M. Maehr & C. Ames (Eds.), *Advances in motivation and achievement* (Vol. 6, pp. 117–160). Greenwich, CT: JAI Press.

Pintrich, P. R., & DeGroot, E. (1990). Motivational and self-regulated learning components of classroom academic performance. *Journal of Educational Psychology, 82,* 33–40.

Pokay, P., & Blumenfeld, P. C. (1990). Predicting achievement early and late in the semester: The role of motivation and use of learning strategies. *Journal of Educational Psychology, 82,* 41–50.

Renninger, K. (1992). Individual interest and development: Implications for theory and practice. In K. A. Renninger, S. Hidi, & A. Krapp (Eds.), *The role of interest in learning and development* (pp. 361–396). Hillsdale, NJ: Lawrence Erlbaum Associates.

Rokeach, M. (1973). *The nature of human values.* New York: The Free Press.

Schiefele, U. (1992). Topic interest and levels of text comprehension. In K. A. Renninger, S. Hidi, & A. Krapp (Eds.), *The role of interest in learning and development* (pp. 151–182). Hillsdale, NJ: Lawrence Erlbaum Associates.

Schunk, D. H. (1991a). Goal setting and self-evaluation: A social cognitive perspective on self-regulation. In M. L. Maehr & P. R. Pintrich (Eds.), *Advances in motivation and achievement* (Vol. 7, pp. 85–113). Greenwich, CT: JAI Press.

Schunk, D. H. (1991b). Self-efficacy and academic motivation. *Educational Psychologist, 26,* 233–262.

Shirey, L. L., & Reynolds, R. E. (1988). Effect of interest on attention and learning. *Journal of Educational Psychology, 80,* 159–166.

Simmons, R. G., & Blyth, D. A. (1987). *Moving into adolescence: The impact of pubertal change and school context.* Hawthorne, NY: Aldine de Gruyler.

Stipek, D. J. (1984). Young children's performance expectations: Logical analysis or wishful thinking? In J. G. Nicholls (Ed.), *The development of achievement motivation* (pp. 33–56). Greenwich, CT: JAI Press.

Stipek, D. J., & Mac Iver, D. (1989). Developmental change in children's assessment of intellectual competence. *Child Development, 60,* 521–538.

Wigfield, A. (1984, April). *Relations between ability perceptions, other achievement-related beliefs, and school performance.* Paper presented at the annual meeting of the American Educational Research Association, New Orleans.

Wigfield, A. (1992, March). *Long-term predictors of adolescents' performance and choice in high school mathematics.* Paper presented at the biennial meeting of the Society for Research on Adolescence, Washington, DC.

Wigfield, A. (in press). Why do I have to learn this? Adolescents' valuing of school. In M. L. Maehr & P. R. Pintrich (Eds.), *Advances in motivation and achievement* (Vol. 8). Greenwich, CT: JAI Press.

Wigfield, A., & Eccles, J. S. (1989, April). *Relations of expectancies and values to students' math grades and intentions.* Paper presented at the annual meeting of the American Educational Research Association, San Francisco.

Wigfield, A., & Eccles, J. S. (1992). The development of achievement task values: A theoretical analysis. *Developmental Review, 12,* 265–310.

Wigfield, A., Eccles, J., Mac Iver, D., Reuman, D., & Midgley, C. (1991). Transitions at early adolescence: Changes in children's domain-specific self-perceptions and general self-esteem across the transition to junior high school. *Developmental Psychology, 27,* 552–565.

Zimmerman, B. J. (1989a). A social cognitive view of self-regulated learning. *Journal of Educational Psychology, 81,* 329–339.

Zimmerman, B. J. (1989b). Models of self-regulated and academic achievement. In B. J. Zimmerman & D. H. Schunk (Eds.), *Self-regulated learning and academic achievement: Theory, research, and practice* (pp. 1–25). New York: Springer-Verlag.

Zimmerman, B. J., Bandura, A., & Martinez-Pons, M. (1992). Self-motivation for academic attainment: The role of self-efficacy beliefs and personal goal setting. *American Educational Research Journal, 29,* 663–676.

III

Self-Regulation of Methods

6

Regulating Motivation and Cognition in the Classroom: The Role of Self-Schemas and Self-Regulatory Strategies

Teresa Garcia
The University of Texas at Austin

Paul R. Pintrich
The University of Michigan

Research on student cognition has demonstrated that students' prior knowledge and use of cognitive and self-regulatory strategies play a very important role in their actual learning from academic tasks (Alexander & Judy, 1988; Pintrich, Cross, Kozma, & McKeachie, 1986; Weinstein & Mayer, 1986). At the same time, motivational models have shown that students' motivational beliefs about the self-efficacy and attributions for learning, their goals and the value they place on learning, and their affective reactions to academic tasks are related to choice of academic tasks, level of engagement, and persistence (Eccles, 1983; Schunk, 1991; Weiner, 1986). Traditionally, these cognitive and motivational models have not been integrated; the paradigms have developed separately and have pursued different research agendas. Motivational models provide insight into questions about the "whys" of student choice, level of activity and effort, and persistence at classroom academic tasks, whereas cognitive models provide descriptions of "how" students come to understand and master these tasks through the use of various cognitive resources (e.g., prior knowledge, others such as adults and peers) and tools (e.g., cognitive and regulatory learning strategies). Accordingly, neither motivational or cognitive models alone can fully describe the various aspects of student academic learning, yet the two types of models are complementary due to the respective strengths and weaknesses of motivational and cognitive models. It is especially important to examine the motivation–cognition interface in the classroom context, where both motivational and cognitive factors operate simultaneously (e.g., Ames, 1992; Graham & Golan, 1991; Pintrich & Schrauben, 1992).

This chapter presents a model that explicitly attempts to integrate both motivational and cognitive components and describe how these components can serve to regulate motivation, cognition, and learning in the classroom. We offer two suggestions: First, we propose that self-schemas may be used to bridge motivational and cognitive models of learning, and second, that students regulate their learning not only by use of cognitive and metacognitive strategies, but also by motivational strategies. By using self-schemas to integrate both motivational and cognitive components, we gain a richer understanding of the role of the self in self-regulated learning (McCombs, 1989). By adding motivational strategies to our discussions of how students regulate their learning, we can begin to address how students' affective concerns may also play a role in self-regulated learning.

CONCEPTUAL FRAMEWORK
AND RESEARCH FINDINGS

Table 6.1 displays the general framework. There are two general domains, motivational and cognitive, which are related to different types of outcomes (e.g., quantity vs. quality of effort), although in the classroom these domains are obviously intertwined. Nevertheless, it is possible to make distinctions between the two domains in terms of their relevant components. Within each of these two domains, there are two general organizing constructs, knowledge/beliefs and strategies. Knowledge refers to students' declarative knowledge about the actual content of the tasks, their knowledge and beliefs about classroom tasks and the classroom context, as well as their knowledge about themselves (Alexander, Schallert, & Hare, 1991). In the cognitive domain, conceptual knowledge is the traditional cognitive domain that includes students' mental models and naive conceptions or misconceptions about the actual content and the discipline (Alexander & Judy, 1988; Schommer, 1990). Besides this conceptual knowledge, students have metacognitive knowledge of tasks and classrooms, which includes knowledge about the cognitive requirements of different classroom tasks, as well as knowledge about different types of strategies that can be used for these tasks (Doyle, 1983; Flavell, 1979). In the motivational domain, declarative knowledge about tasks and classrooms includes students' goals or orientation to learning for tasks as well as their beliefs about task difficulty. These beliefs also my include their knowledge and beliefs about the classroom norms (e.g., Blumenfeld, Pintrich, & Hamilton, 1987). Knowledge about the self includes students' self-schemas, which comprise their beliefs about themselves (Markus & Nurius, 1986). Note that although both Cell 1 and Cell 2 refer to beliefs and knowledge, Cell 1 can be characterized as "hot" cognitions (e.g., goals and self-schemas), whereas Cell 2 can be characterized as "cold" cognitions (e.g., content and disciplinary knowledge).

TABLE 6.1
Motivational and Cognitive Components of Knowledge, Beliefs,
Strategies, and Outcomes

	Motivational Components	*Cognitive Components*
Knowledge and beliefs	Cell 1 Beliefs about task/class • goal orientation • personal interest • classroom norms	Cell 2 Conceptual knowledge • content knowledge • disciplinary knowledge
	Self-schemas • affect • temporal sign • efficacy • value/centrality	Metacognitive knowledge • regarding tasks • regarding strategies
Strategies used for regulation	Cell 3 Motivational strategies • self-handicapping • defensive pessimism • self-affirmation • attributional style	Cell 4 Cognitive learning strategies • rehearsal • elaboration • organization
		Regulatory learning strategies • goal-setting • planning • monitoring • self-testing

Outcomes	Cell 5
	Quantity of effort
	• amount of effort
	Self-Schema Activation/
	   Restructuring
	Choice
	Persistence
		Cell 6
		Quality of effort
		• deeper processing
		Knowledge Activation/
		   Restructuring
		Academic Performance

Besides knowledge, students use a variety of cognitive, motivational, and self-regulatory strategies to accomplish classroom academic tasks (see Table 6.1). We use the term strategy in a relatively global fashion to refer to various cognitive processes and behaviors that students employ to accomplish their self-set goals or the goals implied by the academic task (Weinstein & Mayer, 1986). These strategies can be conscious and under the control of the learner (Garner & Alexander, 1989; Paris, Lipson, & Wixson, 1983), but they also may be performed automatically without much conscious awareness due to practice and habitual use (Schneider & Pressley, 1989). Research on cognition has shown that there are many different memory and learning strategies (e.g., rehearsal, elaboration, and organizational) students may use to do various academic tasks (Pintrich,

1989; Pintrich & Schrauben, 1992; Schneider & Pressley, 1989; Weinstein & Mayer, 1986). In addition, there are metacognitive control and self-regulatory learning strategies students can use to improve their learning such as planning and monitoring (cf. Corno, 1986; Pintrich & De Groot, 1990; Zimmerman & Martinez-Pons, 1986).

Paralleling the work on cognitive strategies, research on social cognition and personality has focused on various motivational strategies that students may use to accomplish their social and personal goals. For example, Cantor and Kihlstrom (1987) suggested that individuals adopt different procedures, rules, or strategies for dealing with various life tasks that guide and shape their motivation, cognition, and behavior. These strategies can be used to control effort, motivation, and affect, as suggested by Kuhl (1992). Strategies used to regulate motivational beliefs and effort include: (a) self-handicapping, the withholding of effort to maintain self-worth (Berglas, 1985; Covington, 1992); (b) defensive pessimism, which involves harnessing anxiety and self-doubt to increase effort (Norem & Cantor, 1986); (c) self-affirmation, a process whereby self-worth is protected by reassessing the value of different domains (Steele, 1988; Steele & Liu, 1983); and (d) attributional style, making adaptive or nonadaptive attributions for performance (Peterson & Seligman, 1984; Peterson et al., 1982).

In terms of this simple framework, research on cognition and learning has addressed the linkages between Cells 2 and 6 and Cells 4 and 6 in Table 6.1 (cf. Alexander et al., 1991; Pintrich et al., 1986; Weinstein & Mayer, 1986). In addition, there has been research on the linkages between Cells 1 and 4, specifically in terms of the linkages between students' goals and interest and their cognitive strategy use (e.g., Ames, 1992; Pintrich & Schrauben, 1992; Schiefele, 1991). Finally, there is a great deal of motivational research that has established the links between Cells 1 and 5 (e.g., Ames, 1992; Schunk, 1991; Weiner, 1986). Although we assume that there are important reciprocal relations between all six cells displayed in Table 6.1 and that there is a need for more research on the relations between some of the other cells (e.g., between Cells 1 and 2), in this chapter we concentrate on the linkages between Cell 1 (motivational knowledge and beliefs) and Cells 3 and 4 (strategies used to regulate motivation and cognition). In addition, because there has been research on the role of students' goals and interest on their regulation of motivation and cognition in classrooms (and other chapters in this volume address this issue, e.g., Meece), we concentrate on the relations between students' self-schemas and their regulation of motivation and cognition. The literature on self-schemas and self-regulation from social cognition and social psychology has examined some of these relations, but it has not really addressed the application of these constructs to academic learning in classroom settings. Accordingly, in this chapter we apply the constructs of self-schemas and motivational strategies to the issue of self-regulation of academic learning in the classroom. We begin with a discussion of self-schemas, then move to how self-schemas may be related to motivational, cognitive, and regulatory learning strategies. The chapter concludes with sections on directions for future research and implications for instruction.

Motivational Beliefs and Knowledge: The Structure and Role of Self-Schemas

Within the category of motivational beliefs and knowledge, there are two general constructs, beliefs about tasks and classrooms and self-schemas (Cell 1 in Table 6.1). Students' beliefs about the tasks they confront in classrooms and their general goal orientation to the classroom can have a major influence on students' engagement in learning, their motivation, and their performance (Ames, 1992). In addition, students' interest in the content of the tasks can influence their cognition and use of learning strategies (Renninger, 1992; Schiefele, 1991). Finally, although there is very little research on their links to performance or self-regulated learning, students' endorsement of classroom norms may also be an important belief that shapes students' response to the culture of the classroom (cf. Bereiter, 1990; Blumenfeld et al., 1987). However, in this chapter, we concentrate on students' beliefs about themselves.

Besides beliefs about tasks and classrooms, individuals have declarative knowledge about themselves. The notion of a self-schema from the social psychology literature maps the idea of internal cognitive structures and knowledge about objects onto the self and self-knowledge. Markus and her colleagues define *self-schemas* as "the cognitive manifestation of enduring goals, aspirations, motives, fears, and threats" (Markus & Nurius, 1986, p. 954), which incorporate cognitions and affective evaluations of agency, volition, and ability (Markus & Nurius, 1986; Markus & Wurf, 1987). Self-schemas are conceptions of ourselves in different situations such as what we are like or want to be like in a math classroom, in a science classroom, on the tennis court, with friends, with another person on a date, or with strangers at a party. Self-schema theory highlights the idea that it is individuals' personal construal of themselves and the situation that mediates their behavior (Cantor & Kihlstrom, 1987; Markus & Nurius, 1986; McCombs, 1989). Markus rejects the formulation of the self-concept as a monolithic, fixed structure, instead proposing that the self-concept can be seen as a constellation of multiple self-schemas, only a few of which are activated at any one point in time. That is, the conceptions of the self active at a particular instance can be seen as a "working self-concept" or an "on-line self-concept," paralleling cognitive theories of memory that include notions of working memory and content knowledge that are active in working memory (Markus & Nurius, 1986; Markus & Wurf, 1987). As organized cognitive structures, self-schemas may be characterized by four dimensions: an *affective* dimension (we have positive and negative self-conceptions); a *temporal* dimension (our experiences result in conceptions of past, present, and future (possible) selves); an *efficacy* dimension (beliefs about what we can do to become or avoid particular self-conceptions); and a *value* dimension (tapping into the importance or centrality of the self-schema to the individual).

The *affective* dimension refers to the idea that we may have positive and negative self-conceptions that we may want to approach or avoid, thereby providing a motivational "force" mechanism lacking in the traditional self-concept literature. Both positive and negative self-schemas can be active simultaneously in the working self-concept; because each self-schema is tied to some particular affective value, the individual's global affective state is a function of the positive and negative self-schemas activated at that time. Therefore, the ratio of positive and negative schemas activated in the working self-concept and their affective power to motivate individuals allow us to incorporate affect into our motivational models as a central component, not just as an outcome of prior cognitions (Markus & Nurius, 1986).

Markus and her colleagues also propose that the self in memory is represented not only as present self-schemas, but also as possible selves (Markus & Nurius, 1986; Markus & Wurf, 1987). The *temporal* dimension helps distinguish between selves that we once were and could again become, selves that we are now, and selves we have never been or are not now, but that we could possibly become in the future. In probabilistic terms, this temporal sign characterizes selves where $p = 1.0$ and selves where $p < 1.0$ but > 0. The temporal dimension represents a way to incorporate a developmental perspective on our self-conceptions by allowing for the existence of past, present, and possible selves that can influence our actions.

The *efficacy* dimension refers to beliefs about what we can do to become or avoid particular self-conceptions and includes perceptions of instrumentality and control. These perceptions of efficacy and control operate in the same manner as predicted by efficacy (Bandura, 1982; Schunk, 1991) and self-determination theory (Deci & Ryan, 1985); however, by incorporating them into a self-schema model, they are now part of a larger network of self-related beliefs that can be situation specific but can also have some intraindividual consistency over time and situations.

The *value* dimension taps into the importance of centrality of the self-schema, incorporating notions of attainment value beliefs from expectancy-value motivational models (cf. Eccles, 1983; Feather, 1982). There may be self-schemas that are more central to our self-conceptions and that are chronically accessible in many different situations. For example, a generally good student may be much more likely to activate an academic self-schema when confronted with a learning task in contrast to a student who sees herself as more of an athlete and interprets different tasks and situations in terms of her athletic abilities. Although there is an almost infinite number of self-schemas that an individual can hold in long-term memory, the value dimension provides a mechanism to ensure that some are more important to us than others, addressing why some self-schemas are consistently activated in working memory (cf. "core" conceptions of the self; James, 1890). The self-schemas that are more central to our core conceptions of ourselves are also more likely to generate a self-protective focus if threatened with negative feedback, in contrast to those self-schemas that are less central or less valued to us.

There are several advantages of the self-schema construct for our theories of self-regulation. First, self-schemas are a means of putting the self in the foreground of "self-regulated learning." McCombs (1989) argued for a phenomenological approach to self-regulated learning, one that emphasizes personal construal and meaningfulness. She charged that educational psychologists doing work in self-regulated learning have narrowly focused on the regulation aspect and have largely ignored the self aspect. In the same vein, Borkowski and his colleagues (Borkowski, Carr, Rellinger, & Pressley, 1990) contended that researchers should pay greater attention to the self, because beliefs and affective evaluations about the self are what provide the incentives for self-regulatory behaviors.

Second, this structural perspective allows for the situational specificity of motivational beliefs (i.e., different beliefs may be activated depending on the features of context), while at the same time proposing some overarching structure that can represent past experience and provide some intraindividual continuity across situations. By applying the self-schema construct to classroom academic learning, we can highlight how different classroom tasks, activities, and processes can activate different self-schemas, reflecting recent work in educational psychology that has stressed the idea of *modules* that include a variety of cognitive and motivational components which are situation-specific but show some intraindividual continuity (e.g., Bereiter, 1990).

Third, self-schemas, as organized knowledge structures, are a means for networking multiple motivational beliefs at a higher level. That is, if goals are a form of knowledge, then self-schemas as organized knowledge structures provide the conceptual means for linking multiple goals. For example, the intrinsic goal of mastering a subject and the extrinsic goal of getting a good grade may be encompassed in the self-schema of oneself as a good student. There is a growing body of research that testifies to the multiplicity of goals individuals possess and can pursue simultaneously (e.g., Cantor & Fleeson, 1991; Markus & Nurius, 1986; Pintrich & Garcia, 1991; Wentzel, 1989). However, these multiple goals may not always be actively pursued on all tasks. The notion of differential activation of self-schemas allows for several goals to be active at a particular instance, while other goals lie dormant.

Finally, although the relations between motivation and strategy use have been examined (Pintrich & Schrauben, 1992), there has been no clear unifying construct that affords a bridge between the two: Self-schemas may provide us with that bridge. Neisser (1976) contended that a schema, as a cognitive framework, can be seen "not only as the plan but the executor of the plan. It is a pattern *of* action as well as a pattern *for* action" (p. 56). That is, if we postulate that individuals have beliefs about what they can *be* and what they can *do*, then there must exist some mechanisms, procedures, and strategies that guide and regulate their behavior according to those beliefs. Beliefs about the likelihood of attaining a possible self and of the ability to effect that possible self serve as general patterns of action and for action (cf. general strategy knowledge, Borkowski et al., 1990; action vs. state orientations, Kuhl, 1992). It may be that when certain self-schemas are activated, specific motivational and cognitive strategies such as defensive pessimism, self-handicapping, elaboration, and rehearsal are tools in the individual's repertoire that can be implemented during the course of action.

Methods of Self-Regulation: The Role of Motivational, Cognitive, and Regulatory Learning Strategies

As discussed earlier, self-schemas are viewed as cognitive organizations of our self-beliefs; incorporated within these cognitive organizations are general plans of action for enacting these selves. The reasoning behind this formulation is that if individuals have particular self-conceptions, then they must have some implicit notions of how they became that way (past selves) or how they may stay that way (present selves) or how to become that way (future selves). The idea of probability, the likelihood of attaining or maintaining a particular self-conception—"I can be this"—underlies self-regulatory behavior. In other words, we regulate our behavior to become positive possible selves, and to maintain positive present selves; we work to avoid becoming negative possible selves, and strive to change negative present selves (an average, psychologically "healthy" individual is assumed in this chapter). This anticipatory or aversively driven striving is more or less effective, depending on the strategies implemented toward those desired or avoided end-states. The following section is addressed toward individuals' attempts at achieving positive selves and avoiding negative selves through the use of various motivational, cognitive, and metacognitive strategies (see Table 6.1, Cells 3 and 4).

Motivational Strategies

Motivational strategies are affectively laden processes that are related to the individual's self-schemas and goals (see Table 6.1). Although some researchers may consider these strategies as personality traits or styles, we use the term *strategy* to denote that these coping strategies are learned and that there is always the possibility that individuals can actively change their strategies as a function of both personal and contextual factors and that they can always learn new strategies. At the same time, these motivational strategies are not just transitory affective states; it is assumed that there is some intraindividual consistency over time and tasks (cf. Norem & Cantor, 1986). The motivational strategies that are used to help regulate motivation through maintenance of positive self-worth and influence the amount of effort expended include self-handicapping (Berglas, 1985; Covington, 1992) and defensive pessimism (Norem & Cantor, 1986). They also can include self-affirmation (Steele, 1988) and attributional style (e.g., Peterson et al., 1982), strategies that regulate different motivational beliefs such as attributions, self-efficacy, and value.

Self-Handicapping. The essence of self-handicapping is the creation of obstacles to success in order to maintain self-worth and positive self-schemas. Self-handicappers have fragile self-schemas of themselves as competent, and self-handicapping is a coping strategy designed to protect one's self-esteem when that tenuous self-schema is threatened (Berglas, 1985). Covington and his colleagues (Covington, 1992; Covington & Beery, 1976) proposed that individuals are motivated to maximize their self-worth, and they documented how effort is a "double-edged sword" for students. That is, the expenditure of effort has positive or negative consequences for self-worth, depending on the performance resulting from those efforts (cf. Baumeister & Scher, 1988; Berglas, 1985). The highest ability evaluations result from success coupled with low effort, and the lowest ability evaluations result from failure coupled with high effort. Deliberately exerting low effort ("underachieving") is a form of self-handicapping. If maintaining self-worth is more important than the actual performance itself, self-handicapping by exerting low effort is a win–win situation. Self-handicapping maximizes ability interpretations, for success following little effort implies high ability, and failure following little effort can be attributed to low effort; thus, either outcome of low effort serves to protect the individual's sense of self-worth and can maintain fragile self-schemas.

Other possible self-handicapping scenarios include taking on too many projects and "spreading oneself too thin" and waiting until the last moment to write a term paper or to study for an exam (procrastination; see Covington, 1992). The important aspect of self-handicapping to note is that self-handicapping is anticipatory. An evaluative situation is somewhere in the future, and the individual is working to construct circumstances that may serve as plausible alternative reasons for a possible failure outcome. Self-handicapping is a priori preparation for a possible failure, not post hoc, reactive rationalizing for an actual failure outcome.

The self-handicapping strategy has clear implications for self-regulated learning in terms of the cognitive and regulatory strategies in Cell 4 of Table 6.1. If students differ in the degree of self-regulated learning they show, the low quality and quantity of effort they demonstrate may not only be due to lack of knowledge about appropriate, effective strategies, but may be driven by this self-protective motivational strategy. Self-handicapping may be related to less use of cognitive and regulatory strategies and overall poor achievement outcomes, but it is very adaptive in terms of affective outcomes. Given that individuals are hedonistically inclined to maximize positive affect (in this case, self-worth stemming from the maintenance of positive self-schemas), self-handicapping may be a strategy in which one engages when negative self-schemas (e.g., "I'm a failure at X") are activated in the working self-concept. Consequently, instead of working harder and engaging in high levels of self-regulated learning to avoid becoming those negative selves, the individual instead engages in activities designed to make failure attributable to events or circumstances and not to (or at least less to) one's own ability and efforts. If the student who has failure schemas activated does an emotional cost–benefit analysis, self-handicapping proves to be a strategy with a very high affective payoff, albeit one that may have great costs in terms of use of learning strategies and actual learning.

Defensive Pessimism. Related to self-handicapping is the strategy of defensive pessimism. Whereas self-handicapping is an anticipatory strategy involving low, or last-minute effort and may be due to the activation of negative self-schemas, defensive pessimism is an anticipatory strategy involving high effort due to the activation of negative self-schemas. Norem and Cantor (1986) defined defensive pessimism as "setting unrealistically low expectations . . . in an attempt to harness anxiety . . . in order to prepare . . . for potential failure and to motivate oneself to work hard in order to avoid that failure" (pp. 1208–1209). Accordingly, a student may activate a negative self-schema due to an evaluative situation ("I'm going to fail this exam because I'm not good at math") and then in trying to avoid this negative self-schema actually exert more effort in studying for the exam.

Defensive pessimists are characterized by their protestations of how poorly prepared they are and/or of how difficult a task (exam, course, etc.) is; although the anxiety and low expectations expressed are genuine, these individuals are also characterized by high levels of effort and histories of above-average performance. The anxiety expressed is used to drive effort, and that effort usually pays off in better performance. These individuals can be thought of as being driven by negative "failure" self-schemas, perhaps arising from being in highly competitive environments that make salient differences in ability (many defensive pessimists can be identified in academia). The defensive pessimism strategy is a clear example of anxiety-arousing negative self-schemas driving defensive efforts to avoid attaining those negative self-conceptions.

With regard to self-regulated learning, defensive pessimists are likely to show levels of effort and learning strategy use that are on par with individuals with very positive academic self-schemas. In this case, it is interesting to note that high levels of self-regulated learning need not always be driven by perceptions of high self-efficacy and competence, as it is often depicted (e.g., Pintrich & De Groot, 1990; Schunk, 1989; Zimmerman, 1990); self-regulated learning may also arise from concerns about lack of efficacy and lack of competence.

Self-Affirmation. Another strategy for regulating motivation that serves to maintain self-worth is self-affirmation. For example, Steele and his colleagues (Steele, 1988; Steele & Liu, 1983) discussed the psychology of self-affirmation, where they argued that individuals engage in a hedonistic cognitive search when self-esteem is threatened. If an individual experiences a negative evaluation of the self in some particular, valued domain (the value dimension), a self-affirmative process is initiated, and the individual will seek to affirm a positive global evaluation of the self by activating positive conceptions of the self (those in other, equally valued domains). Negative affect will result if one has no other schemas from which to seek positive evaluations of the self. For example, a student may feel dissatisfied with the quality and progress of his academic work (thus threatening his conceptions of himself as intelligent and productive). To avoid feeling depressed, he seeks to affirm his esteem by spending time with his significant other as playing squash and winning (thus affirming other important positive self-schemas of himself as loved or himself as active and athletic). It is important to note that, in contrast to self-handicapping and defensive pessimism, which are anticipatory strategies, self-affirmation is a reactive strategy to failure events and negative selves.

The switching of values to protect self-worth also has been suggested as a possible cause of minority students' low achievement. It has been noted that minority students often maintain relatively high efficacy perceptions for academics (e.g., Hare, 1985; Rosenberg & Simmons, 1972) but still do not do well in school. Steele (1992) proposed that the general self-affirmation process leads many minority students to "disidentify" with the values of school, rejecting the idea that one should want to succeed and do well in school, which can then lead to lower levels of effort. Fordham and Ogbu (1986) suggested that if African-American students identify too closely with the values of school and enact the various motivational (trying hard) and cognitive (using deeper processing strategies to study effectively) strategies, they are seen as "acting White" and can be rejected by their peer group. Although there is a great need for more research on this topic with larger representative samples of minority students, it may be that self-schemas play an important role. African-American students may want to avoid the self-schema of a "good student" because it represents an internalization of "acting white" that is at odds with their self-schema for "being an African American." It is the content of these self-schemas and the individual's personal construal of the positive or negative valence of the content that would predict future behavior. Accordingly, some minority students may be able to adopt the "good student" self-schema without feeling any negative affect or conflict with other aspects of their self-schemas.

In any event, self-affirmation and disidentification would be predicted to be linked to self-regulated learning through the lessened use of cognitive and regulatory learning strategies. If students do not value academic achievement and success, then they will be much less likely to take the additional time that is needed to engage in some of the deeper processing cognitive strategies such as elaboration or organization. In addition, they would be less likely to engage in various planning, monitoring, or regulating strategies that are important for learning (Pintrich & Schrauben, 1992).

Attributional Style. Another motivational coping strategy that helps to control motivation through the adoption of certain types of beliefs is attributional style. Attributions are defined as causal explanations for outcomes, experiences, events. The fundamental assumption of attribution theory is that the individual seeks to understand the world—that attributions are responses reflecting attempts to make sense of the environment. These attempts to identify causal relationships provide information to the individual about certain circumstances, and the data gleaned from the causal search result in schemas, modifying or confirming old or creating new schemas of the self, others, and situations (see Neisser, 1976; Weiner, 1986). Self-schemas and expectations are then used to determine appropriate behavioral responses to future events and in this manner help in goal attainment. We define attributional style as a mode of responding to events that develops as a result of multiple experiences with those events, and that attributional style reflects particular, well-defined self-schemas. Note that self-handicapping and defensive pessimism are anticipatory motivational strategies that may result from a particular attributional history; attributional style and the attributions made according to that habitual mode comprise a reactive motivational strategy.

Given that the potential number of different attributions one may make is infinite, researchers have attempted to identify dimensions on which causal explanations lie. Peterson et al. (1982) proposed three causal dimensions: locus, stability, and globality. Weiner (1986) added controllability as another possible dimension. *Locus* refers to whether the cause is seen as internal to the person or external, outside the person; *stability* refers to the static nature of the cause, whether it is transient or chronic; *globality* relates to the omnipresence of the cause, whether it is delimited to particular situations or pervasive to many; and finally, *controllability* refers to the degree of control the individual has over the cause. Locus appears to be more closely related to self-esteem and affective reactions such as shame, guilt, and pride; stability, globality, and controllability are more directly tied to expectancies, one's hopefulness or resignation about the future (Peterson & Seligman, 1984; Weiner, 1986).

Research has shown that different types of attributions are related to different affective and behavioral outcomes (Weiner, 1986). For example, an attribution of lack of effort (whose normative dimensions are internal, unstable, situation-specific, controllable) to a failure outcome is related to a more positive affective response, higher expectancies, and increased future levels of persistence than an attribution to low ability (whose normative dimensions are internal, stable, global, uncontrollable), which is related to depressive affect, lower expectancies, and decreased future levels of persistence (Dweck & Leggett, 1988; Elliott & Dweck, 1988; Peterson et al., 1982). There have been many applications of the basic attributional model to classroom learning and motivation, but one of the most interesting is the role of attributions in self-regulated learning.

In terms of the link between attributional style and self-regulated learning, attributions have been presented as being an integral part of the metacognitive system (Borkowski et al., 1990). Borkowski et al. argued that attributions to effort are crucial in promoting strategy use and generalization because motivational factors such as attributions "play a key role in subsequent 'spontaneous' strategy use by providing incentives necessary for deploying strategies, especially on challenging transfer tasks" (p. 58). Borkowski et al. contended that attributions to effort as opposed to ability enhance metacognitive development "because children must first believe in the utility of their strategy-related effort before they will apply those efforts in situations that demand strategic behavior" (p. 64). Accordingly, if students believe that their learning is under their control and they can enact certain behaviors that will result in better performance, they will be more likely to use those cognitive tools. We turn now to a discussion of those cognitive resources and tools and their potential links to self-schemas.

Cognitive and Regulatory Learning Strategies

Cell 4 in Table 6.1 provides a list of various cognitive and regulatory strategies that individuals might use to improve their academic learning. These strategies are the various tools and methods that individuals may use to regulate their learning. Although the links between these strategies and actual performance are fairly well established, the links between these strategies and self-schemas have not been discussed much and have been researched even less. Accordingly, we provide some potential hypotheses and directions for future research on self-schemas and cognitive and regulatory learning strategies.

Cognitive Learning Strategies. In terms of cognitive learning strategies, we have followed the work of Weinstein and Mayer (1986) and identified rehearsal, elaboration, and organizational strategies as important cognitive strategies that are related to academic performance in the classroom (McKeachie, Pintrich, & Lin, 1985; Pintrich, 1989; Pintrich & De Groot, 1990). These strategies can be applied to simple memory tasks (recall of information, words, lists, etc.) or more complex tasks that require comprehension of the information (understanding a piece of text or a lecture), not just recall (Weinstein & Mayer, 1986).

Students do confront classroom tasks that call for the memorization of facts, names of places, foreign words, and so forth. There are a number of different strategies available that students might use for these basic memory tasks, including rehearsal, clustering, imagery, and use of mnemonic techniques (see Schneider & Pressley, 1989; Weinstein & Mayer, 1986). Rehearsal strategies involve the reciting of items to be learned or the saying of words aloud as one reads a piece of text. Highlighting or underlining text in a rather passive and unreflective manner also can be more like a rehearsal strategy than an elaborative strategy. These rehearsal strategies are assumed to help the student attend to and select important information from lists or texts and keep this information active in working memory.

Memory strategies are helpful for many classroom tasks when students are only asked to remember certain information. However, there are many classroom tasks that require more than just recall of information. In fact, it may be a more important educational goal that students come to understand the material they are learning at a relatively deep, conceptual level. Research on strategy use and information processing suggest that students will gain a deeper level of comprehension when they use elaboration and organizational strategies in contrast to simple rehearsal strategies (Entwistle & Marton, 1984). Rehearsal strategies do not seem to be very effective in helping the student incorporate the new information into existing schemas in long-term memory (McKeachie et al., 1985; Weinstein & Mayer, 1986). Cognitive strategies such as elaboration and organization seem to be much more useful for integrating and connecting new information with previous knowledge.

Elaborative strategies include paraphrasing or summarizing the material to be learned, creating analogies, generative note-taking (where the student actually reorganizes and connects ideas in their notes in contrast to passive, linear note-taking), explaining the ideas in the material to be learned to someone else, and question asking and answering (Weinstein & Mayer, 1986). The other general type of deeper processing strategy, organizational, includes behaviors such as selecting the main idea from text, outlining the text or material to be learned, and the use of a variety of specific techniques for selecting and organizing the ideas in the material (e.g., sketching a network or map of the important ideas, identifying the prose or expository structures of texts; see Weinstein & Mayer, 1986). All these strategies have been shown to result in a deeper understanding of the material to be learned in contrast to rehearsal strategies. For example, Swing and Peterson (1988) found that fifth graders' self-reports of using elaborative and integrative strategies in math classes (retrieving prior knowledge of definitions, linking new information with prior knowledge by recalling previous instruction, comparing words or definitions) were correlated with actual math performance, even when prior math ability was partialed out.

It should be noted that knowledge of these cognitive strategies (Cell 2) may be different from actual use (Cell 4). Some students may know about these strategies but not use them at all, or when formally trained to use the strategies, fail to transfer them to domains outside the experimental training context. Knowledge of these different strategies may be necessary for actual strategy use, but it may not be sufficient (cf. Schneider & Pressley, 1989). Students may have to be motivated to actually use this knowledge. Accordingly, it may be that knowledge about cognitive strategies (Cell 2) is not related to motivational belief components (Cell 1), but actual use of strategies is related to student motivation.

For example, in terms of self-schemas, students that have a self-schema of a "good strategy user" (Pressley, 1986) may be more likely to use the appropriate cognitive learning strategies. In this way of conceptualizing the link between self-beliefs and cognitive strategy use, it is not enough for researchers to describe a good strategy user and for teachers to teach about good strategy use; the individual student also must construct the self-schema of a good strategy user for herself. This would involve the student having a self-schema of herself as a good strategy user in terms of the four dimensions of a self-schema. In other words, she would have a present and possible self as a good strategy user (e.g., seeing herself as using the cognitive strategies) and would see this as a positive self-schema to enact (e.g., working hard and studying well is not "nerdy" or "acting White"). In addition, she would believe that she could enact this self-schema for a variety of tasks (the efficacy dimension) and also would value this self-schema as an important aspect of her school behavior (the value dimension). As Schneider and Pressley (1989) suggested, the good strategy user model "represents a hypothetical memorizing superperson" (p. 122); and we propose that if one has a self-schema that matches this description, then one will be more likely to use and enact those strategies and behaviors that fit the description. Of course, there is a need for empirical research on this link, but it is an interesting avenue for future research.

Metacognitive and Self-Regulatory Strategies. Besides cognitive strategies, students' metacognitive knowledge and use of metacognitive strategies can have an important influence upon their achievement. There are two general aspects of metacognition, knowledge about cognition (Cell 2) and self-regulation of cognition (Cell 4; Brown, Bransford, Ferrara, & Campione, 1983; Flavell, 1979). Some of the theoretical and empirical confusion over the status of metacognition as a psychological construct has been fostered by the confounding of issues of metacognitive knowledge and awareness with metacognitive control and self-regulation (Brown et al., 1983). Paris and Winograd (1990) recently suggested that metacognition be limited to students' knowledge about person, task, and strategy variables, with the inclusion of motivational beliefs such as self-efficacy or self-perceptions of competence as aspects of metacognition. Self-regulation would then refer to students' monitoring, controlling, and regulating their own cognitive activities and actual behavior.

This distinction between metacognitive knowledge and self-regulation seems to be useful and appropriate. However, in our social cognitive model of motivation and cognitive engagement, metacognitive knowledge does not include motivational constructs such as self-efficacy. We consider metacognitive knowledge as more "static" knowledge about strategy and task variables (Cell 2) and self-beliefs about efficacy and competence (Cell 1) to be more "dynamic" motivational constructs that influence students' choice, effort, level of involvement, and persistence. Metacognitive knowledge about strategy and task variables can influence level of involvement (e.g., if you don't know about elaboration strategies, then you may not use them to become more deeply engaged in learning), but this type of metacognitive knowledge probably does not influence choice, effort, or persistence directly, in contrast to motivational beliefs such as self-efficacy that do influence these behaviors.

Most models of metacognitive control or self-regulating strategies include three general types of strategies—planning, monitoring, and regulating (cf. Corno, 1986; Zimmerman & Martinez-Pons, 1986)—and our model is no different (see Pintrich, 1989; Pintrich & De Groot, 1990; Pintrich & Garcia, 1991; Pintrich, Smith, Garcia, & McKeachie, in press). Although these three types of strategies are highly related and, at least in our data (e.g., Pintrich, 1989; Pintrich et al., in press), seem to be highly correlated empirically, they can be discussed separately.

Planning activities that have been investigated in various studies of students' learning include setting goals for studying, skimming a text before reading, generating questions before reading a text, and doing a task analysis of the problem. These activities seem to help the learner plan their use of cognitive strategies and also seem to activate or prime relevant aspects of prior knowledge, making the organization and comprehension of the material much easier. Learners that report using these types of planning activities seem to perform better on a variety of academic tasks in comparison to students who do not use these strategies (McKeachie et al., 1985; Pressley, 1986).

Monitoring one's thinking and academic behavior seems to be an essential aspect of metacognition. Weinstein and Mayer (1986) see all metacognitive activities as partly the monitoring of comprehension. Monitoring activities include tracking of attention while reading a text or listening to a lecture, self-testing through the use of questions about the text material to check for understanding, monitoring comprehension of a lecture, and the use of test-taking strategies (i.e., monitoring speed and adjusting to time available) in an exam situation. These various monitoring strategies alert the learner to breakdowns in attention or comprehension that can then be subjected to repair through the use of regulating strategies.

Regulation strategies are closely tied to monitoring strategies. For example, as learners ask themselves questions as they read in order to monitor their comprehension, and then go back and reread a portion of the text, this rereading is a regulatory strategy. Another type of self-regulatory strategy for reading occurs when a student slows the pace of reading when confronted with more difficult or less familiar text. Of course, reviewing any aspect of course material (e.g., lecture notes, texts, lab material, previous exams and papers, etc.) that one does not remember or understand that well while studying for an exam reflects a general self-regulatory strategy. During a test, skipping questions and returning to them later is another strategy that students can use to regulate their behavior during an exam. All these strategies are assumed to improve learning by helping students correct their studying behavior and repair deficits in their understanding.

The final aspect in our model of learning and self-regulatory strategies, resource management strategies, concerns strategies that students use to manage their environment, such as their time, their study environment, and others including teachers and peers (cf. Corno, 1986; Zimmerman & Martinez-Pons, 1986). In line with a general adaptive approach to learning, we assume that these resource management strategies help students adapt to their environment as well as change the environment to fit their goals and needs. The resource management strategies that we have focused on in our research include time and study environment and help-seeking.

Students' management of their time and the actual place they choose to study are not cognitive or metacognitive strategies that may have a direct influence on eventual learning, but they are general strategies that can help or hinder the students' efforts at completing the academic task. In the same fashion, students that know when, how, and from whom to seek help (see Newman, this volume) should be more likely to be successful than those students who do not seek help appropriately. These resource management strategies may be linked to self-schemas. For example, a student that holds a "good student" self-schema may be less likely to feel threatened by asking for help from the teacher or peers. At the same time, other students that hold a "poor student" self-schemas could seek help quite often. However, this difference in self-schemas should be related to the quality of help seeking such that the first student seeks help to learn and master the material, whereas the second student may be seeking help in a more dependent manner that only focuses on completion of the task, not actual learning.

FUTURE DIRECTIONS FOR RESEARCH
AND IMPLICATIONS FOR INSTRUCTION

The general framework we have described in this chapter represents a synthesis of a number of different research programs including our own. Some of these programs have been based in classroom settings, and others have developed in the context of social and personality psychology and have not been explicitly concerned with academic learning. Accordingly, the first direction for future research is to examine the full model in the context of classrooms and academic learning tasks. Although there is some empirical evidence that self-schemas are related to motivational strategies and there seem to be good logical and theoretical rationales for the proposed links between self-schemas and cognitive and self-regulatory strategies, there is a need for actual empirical research on these links. We have begun to collect some data on these relations in junior high classrooms and do find that positive self-schemas and defensive pessimism are positively related to the use of cognitive and self-regulatory strategies and that negative self-schemas are related to the use of the self-handicapping and defensive pessimism motivational strategies (Garcia & Pintrich, 1993). Nevertheless, there is a need for more research on the full model, including the role of conceptual knowledge (Cell 2 in Table 6.1) and its link to self-schemas and motivational strategies, an area that no one has addressed as far as we know.

A second direction for future research is to examine the developmental progression of self-schemas and motivational and cognitive strategies within individuals over time. Although there has been some cross-sectional research on the development of self-schemas and self-concept (e.g., Cross & Markus, 1991; Marsh, 1990), there is still a need for longitudinal studies of intraindividual change in self-schemas. The cross-sectional studies do provide a description of general patterns of change in self-schemas over the life course (e.g., hierarchical structure in middle childhood and early adolescence vs. multifaceted, but nonhierarchical in later adolescence; see Wigfield & Karpathian, 1991), but they do not address issues regarding stability and change of self-schemas within individuals as they move through different contexts. In this sense, we are advocating a move away from general models of universal developmental change to a focus on differential, intraindividual trajectories of self-schema development (see Asendorpf & Valsiner, 1992; Kindermann & Skinner, 1992). In the same fashion, previous research on college students' motivational strategies (e.g., Norem & Cantor, 1986) has not examined the ontogenesis of these strategies. There is a need for research that investigates how different individuals come to learn about and adopt these strategies in different situations. Although there is some research on the intraindividual development of the use of cognitive strategies (see Schneider & Pressley, 1989), there also is a need for more longitudinal research on the development of cognitive and self-regulatory strategy use from a differential perspective (Asendorpf & Valsiner, 1992). This research that focuses on intraindividual development not only would provide us with better descriptions of the development of self-schemas and strategies, but also would provide insights into the nature of the relations between motivation and cognition.

As part of this developmental agenda for future research, we need to determine the range of applicability of the model in terms of both children's age and contexts. Much of the research on self-schemas and motivational strategies has been done with college-age students or adults, and it is not clear how applicable some of the constructs are to young children's lives and capabilities. We would surmise that some of the motivational strategies that involve rather complicated cognitive and metacognitive processes would not be feasible for early elementary school age children because they may lack some of the cognitive capabilities. In addition, they might not have very many or well-elaborated self-schemas or the capability to coordinate multiple schemas and strategies. Of course, this is an empirical question that needs to be examined in both cross-sectional and longitudinal research. At the same time, we need to examine the contextual sensitivity of the model. It may be that it is not that young children do not have the capabilities, but rather that the school contexts they experience do not afford them the opportunity to develop and use different self-schemas and strategies. For example, school tasks in different academic domains may be similar enough (e.g., worksheets) that students do not have to develop very differentiated self-schemas or cognitive strategies to perform the tasks. In addition, there may be less actual choice or control over tasks in the classroom environment, thereby affording less opportunity to exercise different motivational strategies, in contrast to the college environment where students have much more freedom to adopt different motivational and cognitive strategies. Finally, there is a need for research on how changes in contexts interact with changes in self-schemas and strategy use (cf. Kindermann & Skinner, 1992). How do students coordinate schemas and strategy use across contexts when the contexts differ (e.g., math vs. social studies) or change over time (elementary vs. junior high; high school vs. college)? For example, do students adapt their self-schemas and strategies to changes in the nature of the discipline, the tasks, and the method of instruction in math in contrast to social studies? More importantly, when students make major transitions in school contexts (Eccles et al., 1993), how do these changes relate to changes in self-schemas and strategies? This research will provide us with better insights into the nature of the contextual–individual interaction and represents a more ecologically valid perspective on the development of motivation and cognition.

Another direction for future research is the examination of gender and ethnic differences in self-schemas and motivational strategies. In our previous research we have found very few gender differences in the use of cognitive and self-regulatory strategies, but we have found differences in efficacy and goal orientation beliefs (Pintrich & Garcia, 1991). In addition, there is some evidence (Norem & Cantor, 1986) that females are more likely to use the motivational strategy of defensive pessimism. Although the work of Steele and Ogbu has not explicitly used the framework proposed here, their results and general theoretical writings suggest that there may be differences by ethnicity in minority students' self-schemas and their use of various motivational strategies. However, there has not been enough careful empirical research on these issues (see Graham, 1992), and certainly more is needed that grows out of a well-grounded psychological perspective that examines not only group differences but also within-group individual differences.

Moving beyond these future directions for research, the general conceptual framework does have some implications for instruction, albeit direct applications await actual empirical research. First, the model and our previous research (Pintrich & De Groot, 1990; Pintrich & Garcia, 1991) highlight the importance of considering both motivational and cognitive components. The model sketched in Table 6.1 lists four domains (Cells 1–4) that could be units in any training course to improve student learning (e.g., McKeachie et al., 1985; Weinstein & Underwood, 1984). A training course could include presenting information about all four cells and then using various instructional strategies to help students become aware of their own knowledge/beliefs and strategies in both the motivational and cognitive domains. For example, regarding content knowledge (Cell 2), students should be aware of the influence of prior knowledge on their learning and then introduced to techniques that can help them develop their content knowledge (e.g., concept mapping). In the same way, instructors might help students become aware of their own self-schemas and motivational beliefs (Cell 1) through the use of various self-report questionnaires (e.g., the MSLQ; Pintrich et al., in press). Besides these two knowledge domains, it would be important to make students aware of the different types of motivational strategies they may use besides the traditional instruction in the different types of cognitive strategies available for use (Cells 3 and 4). Instruction could include teaching students about the different types of motivational strategies (self-handicapping, defensive pessimism, self-affirmation, attributional style) and the cognitive and self-regulatory strategies through the use of case studies and vignettes about students who use these strategies and the implications these strategies have for their learning. In addition, part of the instruction could include "self-diagnosis" of the students' own motivational and cognitive strategies through the use of various self-report instruments, not unlike the current use of the LASSI (Weinstein, Zimmerman, & Palmer, 1988) or the MSLQ (Pintrich et al., in press) to provide feedback to students on their cognitive strategies. Finally, following this instruction that focuses on awareness and knowledge of the different motivational and cognitive strategies, instruction could involve teaching about the conditions under which these motivational and cognitive strategies may or may not be appropriate—that is, the conditional knowledge about appropriate strategy use (Paris et al., 1983).

Moving beyond a consideration of specific training courses, a second general instructional implication is that teachers should be aware of the role beliefs and strategies may play in student learning and how their classrooms may influence these motivational and cognitive components. Again, paralleling the work on students' prior conceptual knowledge that suggests teachers should try to understand the various conceptions and misconceptions that students have for the content of instruction, teachers might want to be apprised of the various self-schemas that students bring to these same tasks. In a collaborative research project with a team of researchers from the University of Michigan and a group of middle school teachers, we have shared some data on students' self-schemas (the classroom means on efficacy, interest, value) and the teachers have reported that they find it useful. Of course, it is difficult for teachers to deal with all the individual differences that could be represented in students' self-schemas; hence, we do not provide individual students' scores. We suggest that in much the same way the conceptual change literature suggests teachers use general patterns in students' misconceptions to guide instruction, teachers could use general patterns in students' self-schemas to guide their use of various motivational and instructional techniques.

For example, if teachers begin to see that many of their students do not have positive possible selves for their content area (low efficacy, interest, value), there may be some changes they can make in their instruction as suggested by various motivational theories. If the dimension of the possible self that seems particularly low across many students is self-efficacy, then various strategies suggested by Schunk (1991) may be used at the classroom level. These could include feedback that is contingent on actual academic performance, development of tasks and activities that are within the range of students' capabilities, and the provision of mastery models through direct modeling by the teacher (as in reciprocal teaching) or the use of collaborative student groups where coping models may be presented to the students. In contrast, if the value dimension of the possible self seems low, then various extrinsic and intrinsic instructional strategies to increase students' value and interest beliefs may be used (see Brophy, 1987; Malone & Lepper, 1987). These could include giving students somewhat more choice and control over how tasks are done, as well as attempts to make the content area more interesting and relevant to students through the use of more authentic activities that attempt to connect the content with real-world examples or students' prior knowledge. These suggestions are not new to our model; they can be derived from goal theory (Ames, 1992), expectancy-value theory (Brophy, 1987; Eccles et al., 1993), and self-determination theory (Deci & Ryan, 1985). At the same time, as Blumenfeld, Mergendoller, and Puro (1992) pointed out, there are teachers who make tasks and instruction interesting and motivating but do not cognitively engage the students at a deep level. Accordingly, our model emphasizes the importance of considering both cognitive and motivational components; hence, teachers cannot ignore cognitive considerations when attempting to motivate students.

In summary, the model we have outlined in this chapter provides a framework for the integration of motivation and cognition in the context of academic learning. The model proposes that students' knowledge and beliefs about themselves and their classrooms are organized, represented, and operate in a fashion that is isomorphic with current cognitive models of content and disciplinary knowledge. In addition, the model suggests that, just as there are cognitive learning strategies that operate in conjunction with students' content knowledge to influence learning, there are motivational strategies that operate in conjunction with students' motivational beliefs and self-schemas to influence motivated behavior such as choice, effort, and persistence. Moreover, these motivational beliefs and strategies may influence the activation and use of various cognitive and self-regulatory learning strategies. Finally, the model suggests promising avenues for future research on the relations between motivation and cognition by attempting to integrate within one general framework the core constructs of current models of self-regulated learning: knowledge, beliefs, strategies, and self-regulation.

ACKNOWLEDGMENTS

We would like to thank the editors of this volume, Dale Schunk and Barry Zimmerman, for their incisive and constructive comments on an earlier draft of this chapter. Our writing of this chapter grows out of the Development of Competence and Commitment Project funded by a

Rackham Research Partnership Grant from the University of Michigan. This project, affectionately known as the "CC Project," involves a number of colleagues, including Eric Anderman, Anastasia Danos Elder, Lynley Hicks, Barbara Hofer, Tim Urdan, Chris Wolters, and Shirley Yu. We would like to thank all of them for their constructive feedback on this chapter and their excellent contributions to the conceptualization and implementation of the overall project.

REFERENCES

Alexander, P. A., & Judy, J. E. (1988). The interaction of domain-specific and strategic knowledge in academic performance. *Review of Educational Research, 58,* 375–404.

Alexander, P. A., Schallert, D. L., & Hare, V. C. (1991). Coming to terms: How researchers in learning and literacy talk about knowledge. *Review of Educational Research, 61,* 315–343.

Ames, C. (1992). Classrooms: Goals, structures, and student motivation. *Journal of Educational Psychology, 84,* 261–271.

Asendorpf, J., & Valsiner, J. (1992). Six biases in contemporary developmental psychology. In J. Asendorpf & J. Valsiner (Eds.), *Stability and change in development* (pp. 249–258). Newbury Park, CA: Sage.

Bandura, A. (1982). Self-efficacy mechanism in human agency. *American Psychologist, 37,* 122–147.

Baumeister, R. F., & Scher, S. J. (1988). Self-defeating behavior patterns among normal individuals: Review and analysis of common self-destructive tendencies. *Psychological Bulletin, 104,* 3–22.

Bereiter, C. (1990). Aspects of an educational learning theory. *Review of Educational Research, 60,* 603–624.

Berglas, S. (1985). Self-handicapping and self-handicappers: A cognitive/attributional model of interpersonal self-protective behavior. In R. Hogan & W. H. Jones (Eds.), *Perspectives in personality: Theory, measurement, and interpersonal dynamics* (pp. 235–270). Greenwich, CT: JAI Press.

Blumenfeld, P. C., Mergendoller, J., & Puro, P. (1992). Translating motivation into thoughtfulness. In H. Marshall (Ed.), *Redefining student learning* (pp. 207–239). Norwood, NJ: Ablex.

Blumenfeld, P. C., Pintrich, P. R., & Hamilton, V. L. (1987). Teacher talk and students' reasoning about morals, conventions, and achievement. *Child Development, 58,* 1389–1401.

Borkowski, J. G., Carr, M., Rellinger, E., & Pressley, M. (1990). Self-regulated cognition: Interdependence of metacognition, attributions, and self-esteem. In B. F. Jones & L. Idol (Eds.), *Dimensions of thinking and cognitive instruction* (pp. 53–92). Hillsdale, NJ: Lawrence Erlbaum Associates.

Brophy, J. (1987). On motivating students. In D. Berliner & B. Rosenshine (Eds.), *Talks to teachers* (pp. 201–245). New York: Random House.

Brown, A. L., Bransford, J. D., Ferrara, R. A., & Campione, J. C. (1983). Learning, remembering, and understanding. In J. H. Flavell & E. M. Markman (Eds.), *Handbook of child psychology: Cognitive development* (Vol. 3, pp. 77–166). New York: Wiley.

Cantor, N., & Fleeson, W. W. (1991). Life tasks and self-regulatory processes. In M. L. Maehr & P. R. Pintrich (Eds.), *Advances in motivation and achievement* (Vol. 7, pp. 327–369). Greenwich, CT: JAI Press.

Cantor, N., & Kihlstrom, J. F. (1987). *Personality and social intelligence.* Englewood Cliffs, NJ: Prentice-Hall.

Corno, L. (1986). The metacognitive control components of self-regulated learning. *Contemporary Educational Psychology, 11,* 333–346.

Covington, M. V. (1992). *Making the grade: A self-worth perspective on motivation and school reform.* Cambridge, MA: Cambridge University Press.

Covington, M. V., & Beery, R. G. (1976). *Self-worth and school learning.* New York: Holt, Rinehart & Winston.

Cross, S., & Markus, H. (1991). Possible selves across the life span. *Human Development, 34,* 230–255.

Deci, E. L., & Ryan, R. M. (1985). *Intrinsic motivation and self-determination in human behavior.* New York: Plenum.

Doyle, W. (1983). Academic work. *Review of Educational Research, 53,* 159–199.

Dweck, C. S., & Leggett, E. L. (1988). A social-cognitive approach to motivation and personality. *Psychological Review, 95,* 256–273.

Eccles, J. S. (1983). Expectancies, values, and academic behaviors. In J. T. Spence (Ed.), *Achievement and achievement motives* (pp. 75–146). San Francisco: W. H. Freeman.

Eccles, J. S., Midgley, C., Wigfield, A., Buchanan, C., Reuman, D., Flanagan, C., & MacIver, D. (1993). Development during adolescence: The impact of stage-environment fit on young adolescents' experiences in schools and families. *American Psychologist, 48,* 90–101.

Elliott, E. S., & Dweck, C. S. (1988). Goals: An approach to motivation and achievement. *Journal of Personality and Social Psychology, 54,* 5–12.

Entwistle, N., & Marton, F. (1984). Changing conceptions of learning and research. In F. Marton, D. Hounsell, & N. Entwistle (Eds.), *The experience of learning* (pp. 211–236). Edinburgh, Scotland: Scottish Academic Press.

Feather, N. T. (1982). Human values and the prediction of action: An expectancy-valence analysis. In N. T. Feather (Ed.), *Expectations and actions: Expectancy-value models in psychology* (pp. 263–289). Hillsdale, NJ: Lawrence Erlbaum Associates.

Flavell, J. H. (1979). Metacognition and cognitive monitoring: A new area of cognitive-developmental inquiry. *American Psychologist, 34,* 906–911.

Fordham, S., & Ogbu, J. U. (1986). Black students' school success: Coping with the "burden of acting White." *Urban Review, 18,* 176–206.

Garcia, T., & Pintrich, P. R. (1993, April). *Self-schemas, motivational strategies, and self-regulated learning.* Paper presented at the annual meeting of the American Educational Research Association, Atlanta, GA.

Garner, R., & Alexander, P. A. (1989). Metacognition: Answered and unanswered questions. *Educational Psychologist, 24,* 143–158.

Graham, S. (1992). "Most of the subjects were White and middle class": Trends in published research on African Americans in selected APA journals, 1970–1989. *American Psychologist, 47,* 629–639.

Graham, S., & Golan, S. (1991). Motivational influences on cognition: Task involvement, ego involvement, and depth of information processing. *Journal of Educational Psychology, 83,* 187–194.

Hare, B. R. (1985). Stability and change in self-perception and achievement among Black adolescents: A longitudinal study. *Journal of Black Psychology, 11,* 29–42.

James, W. (1890). *The principles of psychology.* New York: Holt.

Kindermann, T., & Skinner, E. (1992). Modeling environmental development: Individual and contextual trajectories. In J. Asendorpf & J. Valsiner (Eds.), *Stability and change in development* (pp. 155–190). Newbury Park, CA: Sage.

Kuhl, J. (1992). A theory of self-regulation: Action versus state orientation, self-discrimination, and some applications. *Applied Psychology: An International Review, 41,* 97–129.

Malone, T., & Lepper, M. (1987). Making learning fun: A taxonomy of intrinsic motivations for learning. In R. Snow & M. Farr (Eds.), *Aptitude, learning, and instruction. Vol. 3: Conative and affective process analysis* (pp. 223–253). Hillsdale, NJ: Lawrence Erlbaum Associates.

Markus, H., & Nurius, P. (1986). Possible selves. *American Psychologist, 41*, 954–969.

Markus, H., & Wurf, E. (1987). The dynamic self-concept: A social-psychological perspective. *Annual Review of Psychology, 38*, 299–337.

Marsh, H. (1990). The structure of academic self-concept: The Marsh/Shavelson model. *Journal of Educational Psychology, 82*, 623–636.

McCombs, B. L. (1989). Self-regulated learning and academic achievement: A phenomenological view. In B. J. Zimmerman & D. H. Schunk (Eds.), *Self-regulated learning and academic achievement: Theory, research, and practice* (pp. 51–82). New York: Springer-Verlag.

McKeachie, W. J., Pintrich, P. R., & Lin, Y. G. (1985). Teaching learning strategies. *Educational Psychologist, 20*, 153–160.

Neisser, U. (1976). *Cognition and reality.* San Francisco: W. H. Freeman.

Norem, J. K., & Cantor, N. (1986). Defensive pessimism: Harnessing anxiety as motivation. *Journal of Personality and Social Psychology, 51*, 1208–1217.

Paris, S. G., Lipson, M. Y., & Wixson, K. K. (1983). Becoming a strategic reader. *Contemporary Educational Psychology, 8*, 293–316.

Paris, S. G., & Winograd, P. (1990). How metacognition can promote academic learning and instruction. In B. F. Jones & L. Idol (Eds.), *Dimensions of thinking and cognitive instruction* (pp. 15–51). Hillsdale, NJ: Lawrence Erlbaum Associates.

Peterson, C., & Seligman, M. E. P. (1984). Causal explanations as a risk factor for depression: Theory and evidence. *Psychological Review, 91*, 347–374.

Peterson, C., Semmel, A., von Baeyer, C., Abramson, L. Y., Metalsky, G. I., & Seligman, M. E. P. (1982). The attributional style questionnaire. *Cognitive Therapy and Research, 6*, 287–300.

Pintrich, P. R. (1989). The dynamic interplay of student motivation and cognition in the college classroom. In C. Ames & M. L. Maehr (Eds.), *Advances in motivation and achievement: Motivation-enhancing environments* (Vol. 6, pp. 117–160). Greenwich, CT: JAI Press.

Pintrich, P. R., Cross, D. R., Kozma, R. B., & McKeachie, W. J. (1986). Instructional psychology. *Annual Review of Psychology, 37*, 611–651.

Pintrich, P. R., & De Groot, E. V. (1990). Motivational and self-regulated learning components of classroom academic performance. *Journal of Educational Psychology, 82*, 33–40.

Pintrich, P. R., & Garcia, T. (1991). Student goal orientation and self-regulation in the college classroom. In M. L. Maehr & P. R. Pintrich (Eds.), *Advances in motivation and achievement: Goals and self-regulatory processes* (Vol. 7, pp. 371–402). Greenwich, CT: JAI Press.

Pintrich, P. R., & Schrauben, B. (1992). Students' motivational beliefs and their cognitive engagement in classroom tasks. In D. Schunk & J. Meece (Eds.), *Student perceptions in the classroom: Causes and consequences* (pp. 149–183). Hillsdale, NJ: Lawrence Erlbaum Associates.

Pintrich, P. R., Smith, D. A. F., Garcia, T., & McKeachie, W. J. (in press). Predictive validity and reliability of the Motivated Strategies for Learning Questionnaire (MSLQ). *Educational and Psychological Measurement.*

Pressley, M. (1986). The relevance of the good strategy user model to the teaching of mathematics. *Educational Psychologist, 21*, 139–161.

Renninger, K. A. (1992). Individual interest and development: Implications for theory and practice. In K. A. Renninger, S. Hidi, & A. Krapp (Eds.), *The role of interest in learning and development* (pp. 361–395). Hillsdale, NJ: Lawrence Erlbaum Associates.

Rosenberg, M., & Simmons, R. (1972). *Black and white self-esteem: The urban school child.* Arnold M. and Caroline Rose Monograph Series. Washington, DC: American Sociological Association.

Schiefele, U. (1991). Interest, learning, and motivation. *Educational Psychologist, 26,* 299–323.
Schneider, W., & Pressley, M. (1989). *Memory development between 2 and 20.* New York: Springer-Verlag.
Schommer, M. (1990). Effects of beliefs about the nature of knowledge on comprehension. *Journal of Educational Psychology, 82,* 498–504.
Schunk, D. H. (1989). Social cognitive theory and self-regulated learning. In B. J. Zimmerman & D. H. Schunk (Eds.), *Self-regulated learning and academic achievement: Theory, research, and practice* (pp. 83–110). New York: Springer-Verlag.
Schunk, D. H. (1991). Self-efficacy and academic motivation. *Educational Psychologist, 26,* 207–231.
Steele, C. M. (1988). The psychology of self-affirmation: Sustaining the integrity of the self. *Advances in Experimental Social Psychology, 21,* 261–302.
Steele, C. M. (1992, April). *Addressing the challenges of increasing and varied minority populations.* Paper presented at the annual meeting of the American Educational Research Association, San Francisco, CA.
Steele, C. M., & Liu, T. J. (1983). Dissonance processes as self-affirmation. *Journal of Personality and Social Psychology, 45,* 5–19.
Swing, S., & Peterson, P. (1988). Elaborative and integrative thought processes in mathematics learning. *Journal of Educational Psychology, 80,* 54–66.
Weiner, B. (1986). *An attributional theory of motivation and emotion.* New York: Springer-Verlag.
Weinstein, C. E., & Mayer, R. (1986). The teaching of learning strategies. In M. Wittrock (Ed.), *Handbook of research on teaching and learning* (pp. 315–327). New York: Macmillan.
Weinstein, C. E., & Underwood, V. L. (1984). Learning strategies: The how of learning. In J. Segal, S. Chipman, & R. Glaser (Eds.), *Thinking and learning skills: Relating instruction to research* (Vol. 1, pp. 241–258). Hillsdale, NJ: Lawrence Erlbaum Associates.
Weinstein, C. E., Zimmerman, S. A., & Palmer, D. (1988). Assessing learning strategies: The design and development of the LASSI. In C. E. Weinstein, E. T. Goetz, & P. A. Alexander (Eds.), *Learning and study strategies: Issues in assessment, instruction, and evaluation* (pp. 25–40). San Diego: Academic Press.
Wentzel, K. (1989). Adolescent classroom goals, standards for performance, and academic achievement: An interactionist perspective. *Journal of Educational Psychology, 81,* 131–142.
Wigfield, A., & Karpathian, M. (1991). Who am I and what can I do? Children's self-concepts and motivation in achievement situations. *Educational Psychologist, 26,* 233–262.
Zimmerman, B. J. (1990). Self-regulated learning and academic achievement: An overview. *Educational Psychologist, 25,* 3–17.
Zimmerman, B. J., & Martinez-Pons, M. (1986). Development of a structured interview for assessing student use of self-regulated learning strategies. *American Educational Research Journal, 23,* 614–628.

7

Self-Regulated Reading and Getting Meaning From Text: The Transactional Strategies Instruction Model and Its Ongoing Validation

Rachel Brown
SUNY at Buffalo

Michael Pressley
SUNY at Albany

Since the late 1970s, cognitive psychologists have analyzed in detail the nature of expertise (e.g., Chi, Glaser, & Farr, 1988). One of the most salient properties of any form of expertise is that the expert self-regulates his or her thinking and performances in his or her domain of competence, proceeding reflectively, coordinating a variety of decisions fluidly. Thus, the expert airline pilot monitors a number of systems while navigating through stormy weather on a challenging approach for landing. Adjustments are made as needed, and although the co-pilot might provide some prompting, there is no doubt the captain could land the plane safely on his or her own if it was necessary to do so. The expert surgeon facing a complication in mid-surgery reflects, plans, and carries out the plan. Although the skilled surgeon works in cooperation with other physicians and nurses, he or she is the executive, making decisions that keep the operation on course, responsibly seeing the surgery through to the end.

Capable academic thinkers self-regulate their reading, problem solving, writing, and general navigation of the world. They coordinate reading, problem solving, and writing as part of accomplishing ambitious goals. Educational psychologists interested in such skilled self-regulation have specified it in terms of components, with four prominent in the model of effective thinking we most favor (e.g., Pressley, Borkowski, & Schneider, 1989), a model informed by a great deal of basic, experimental research on memory, problem solving, and reading (for reviews, see Pressley, Bork-

155

owski, & O'Sullivan, 1984, 1985; Pressley, Borkowski, & Schneider, 1987, 1989):

- Good thinkers use cognitive *strategies*, which are coordinated with one another as part of complex thinking. For example, the skilled writer executes planning strategies before any attempt is made to write a first draft. As the draft is executed, more planning may occur as gaps in the written argument or narrative become obvious. Once a first draft is completed, revision strategies are carried out, with shortcomings in the manuscript detected during revision, prompting more planning and rewriting.
- The situationally appropriate application of strategies is permitted by two types of *metacognition*: One is long-term knowledge that good thinkers have acquired about where and when to use the procedures they know. Such knowledge can be developed during explicit instruction of strategies. Thus, as children are taught to plan, draft, and revise, they are provided instruction about when these various strategies that comprise skilled writing can be used (e.g., planning is the first step; revision generally follows drafting; once writing begins, however, more planning may be required; once revision begins, more planning may be needed, and more writing definitely will be required). A second form of metacognition is generated as the cognitive task is carried out. Good thinkers monitor their progress, shifting strategies when they sense problems and moving forward when subgoals are accomplished. Thus, once the good writer senses that sufficient planning has occurred so that good progress can be made in drafting a manuscript, writing begins. When the writer senses an impasse due to conceptual gaps, the skilled writer plans and researches some more.
- Use of strategies is coordinated with other *knowledge* possessed by the skilled thinker. For example, part of planning for writing is searching prior knowledge for what is known about the topic already. Part of writing is translating what one knows into text and coordinating one's own ideas with information discovered during other aspects of planning, such as library research activities. Until one has knowledge, either built up in the long term or acquired in the short term through search and inquiry involving external sources, there is nothing to write about. Of course, knowledge expands as a function of effective self-regulated cognition: Self-regulated readers learn more from the texts they read than do less skilled students. Effective problem solvers incidentally learn a lot of information related to the problem situations they are addressing, but they also invent new solutions and learn more about old solutions (e.g., a

trusted old algorithm is not as efficient as a new one invented to solve a current problem). One of the by-products of composing a new argument is gaining both new knowledge required to construct the argument and new ways of viewing old knowledge. Knowledge is dynamically related to self-regulated cognition, both permitting it and expanded by it.

• Good thinkers possess *motivational beliefs* that support their coordination of strategies, metacognitive knowledge, and other knowledge. Such motivation is required because good, strategic thinking is effortful. Motivational beliefs include confidence in one's ability to succeed by exerting strategic effort and recognition that success often comes only after some frustration. Good thinkers possess self-efficacy with respect to the academic tasks they tackle (e.g., Schunk, 1989, 1990, 1991; Zimmerman, 1989a, 1989b, 1990a, 1990b): Years of success through reflective coordination of strategies and knowledge have produced appropriate self-confidence about academic abilities, which in turn motivates future academic efforts and thus, self-regulated cognition is dynamically related to motivational beliefs, both fueled by such beliefs and fueling them.

Self-regulated cognition is simply too large an entity to study in its entirety—and certainly too ambitious in scope to discuss completely given the space of a single chapter. Thus, in this chapter, we focus on self-regulated reading: As part of our overall scholarly effort to understand self-regulated reading, we and our associates have conducted research and reviewed the studies aimed at illuminating the nature of self-regulated reading. That is, we have asked what reading is like at its very best—when skilled readers are reading content in a domain of high expertise in pursuit of a goal that is important to them. In these investigations, skilled readers typically have been asked to think aloud as they read. If strategies, metacognition, knowledge, and motivation are important in regulating reading, their effects should come through in such analyses. We cover this line of research briefly in the next section.

After that we take up instruction that was designed to foster better reading comprehension. Not all attempts to do so have produced self-regulated reading. Part of understanding what works is to understand what does not work and thus, there is a section on the reading comprehension instructional research of the 1970s and 1980s that set the stage for the instruction (and research on instruction) that is our main concern here. The second half of this chapter is dedicated to describing strategy instructional research that seems to stimulate the strategic, metacognitive, knowledge, and motivational components that comprise skilled reading, including discussion of both qualitative, descriptive studies and quantitative, hypothesis-testing efforts. Although our research on the nature of instruction that stimulates self-regulated reading continues, it is possible at this time to make some claims about such teaching with considerable confidence, and we do so. Before that, however, we consider further the type of active reading that we want to foster: Such reading involves coordination of strategies, prior knowledge, and metacognition to construct meaning, activity motivated in part by years of success in gaining knowledge through highly strategic reading.

THE NATURE OF SKILLED READING

Approximately 40 studies (reviewed by Afflerbach & Pressley, in preparation) were published in the last 15 years in which skilled readers were asked to think aloud as they processed text. What was observed typically in these studies was that good readers coordinated a number of strategies as they came to understand text. Good readers also monitored their use of strategies, for example, initiating new strategic efforts or changing strategies when they sensed miscomprehension. Good readers also are extremely evaluative about what they read, filtering the ideas presented in the text through their prior knowledge and beliefs. Thus, good readers sometimes reject information in texts if it is not in synchrony with prior knowledge; on other occasions, they recognize the value of a perspective offered in a reading because they can relate it to prior knowledge. Skilled reading is exceptionally active, reflecting use of diverse strategies for making sense of text, with strategies efforts coordinated with and empowered by content domain knowledge (i.e., many strategies, such as "relating new information in text" to prior knowledge only work if there is high prior knowledge.

The complexity that is skilled, self-regulated reading can be appreciated by considering a think-aloud study in which great efforts were made to code all activities reported by readers. Wyatt, Pressley, El-Dinary, Stein, Evans, and Brown (1993) asked accomplished social scientists to select an article in their discipline that they very much wanted to read, one directly relevant to some ongoing professional activity. As these 15 professors read, they thought aloud. Their reading was extremely strategic, with most of the readers displaying all of the following strategies, intermingling their use in reaction to demands of the text at the moment:

- Anticipating, predicting information that would be presented in text, as well as testing predictions

- Looking for information relevant to personal and/or professional goals, including their own research, writing, or teaching
- Jumping forward, looking for particular information in text, and then returning to continue reading
- Jumping back, looking for particular information in text, and then returning to continue reading
- Rapidly moving back and forth in text (e.g., to go to a table or figure in the article, integrating across parts of text)
- Backtracking (rereading what was just read for clarification)
- Attending closely to figures or tables
- Varying reading style according to the relevance of the text to reading goals
- Constructing paraphrases/explanations of what is in the text and/or giving examples
- Constructing conclusions or summary interpretations beyond information provided in the article

Metacognitive processing was apparent as well, with the readers monitoring their reading in several different ways, with these various forms of monitoring leading in some cases to shifts in strategies:

- Explicitly noting how difficult the text is to read, whether the text is understood or the meaning of it puzzling
- Explicitly noting when information in text is known previously
- Evaluating the relevance of what is being read to the reader's goals in reading the text

The most salient aspect of text processing, however, was readers' evaluations of what they read, with all 15 readers providing multiple reactions to the text in light of prior knowledge possessed by the readers. These reactions, which often included either negative affective reactions (e.g., anger, weariness) or expressions of interest, specifically included the following:

- Reacting on the basis of extremely personal prior knowledge, such as own theories, own writing, and personal knowledge of the text's author
- Evaluating the quality of literature reviewed and cited, theoretical perspectives offered, methods used, analyses conducted, novelty of

findings, conclusions, discussion, writing and editing, and styles and biases of the author

In short, the evidence in Wyatt et al. (1993) was overwhelming that the social scientists engaged in reflective, self-regulated reading. Moreover, when Afflerbach and Pressley (in preparation) collapsed the self-report data from all 40 of the think-aloud studies of skilled reading, they found that the reported processes in those studies could be grouped into the same three large categories identified by Wyatt et al. (1993)— strategies, monitoring, and evaluative reactions. Across those studies, there were many indications of motivated readers whose knowledge of when and where to deploy particular strategies was obvious from their precise adjustments of strategies to particular types of information and problems in text. Even though the reading in the 40 studies can be reduced to strategies, monitoring, and evaluations and explained in terms of strategies, metacognition, knowledge, and motivation, skilled reading is very complex: Ten and a half single-spaced, typed pages were required to list in telegraphic fashion the strategies reported across the 40 studies; seven and a half pages were required to summarize the monitoring processes; and three pages were needed to capture the types of evaluations generated.

One reason that we conducted the Wyatt et al. (1993) study, and Afflerbach and Pressley (in preparation) reviewed the literature on skilled reading, was to determine what to aim for in designing comprehension instruction for children. Just what should children be taught to do in order to stimulate their development as self-regulated readers? We concluded that they should be taught to use strategic processes, monitor text and their understanding of it, and relate what they are reading to prior knowledge. Students should be taught that affective, evaluative reactions are a natural part of reading and reflect deep processing with respect to prior knowledge. Although this conception of what should be taught in order to stimulate self-regulated reading seems natural in light of the analyses of the think-aloud data, in fact, what was offered as comprehension instruction to students in the 1970s and 1980s fell far short of teaching strategies, extensive and flexible monitoring of reading and text, and evaluative processing with respect to prior knowledge.

READING COMPREHENSION INSTRUCTION
IN THE 1970s AND 1980s

A number of investigators in the 1970s and 1980s advanced hypotheses that particular individual comprehension strategies could be taught to students profitably. Prominent among these were summarization (i.e., construct a summary of what was just read), imagery (i.e., create an image corresponding to the meaning just processed), question generation (i.e., construct integrative test questions over the reading), and text structure analysis (e.g., story grammar strategies, involving analysis of the setting, characters, problems, and resolutions in a story) strategies. The typical research tactic taken in studies of individual strategies was to teach one group of students to use a particular cognitive strategy while reading— one consistent with the cognitive theory or analysis favored by the researcher, with control students left to their own devices to understand text as best they could. Thus, cognitive scientists believing that good comprehension entails the development of macropropositions, as van Dijk and Kintsch (1983) described them, taught students to summarize. Researchers interested in the implications of dual-coding theory (e.g., Paivio, 1971) for reading comprehension taught students to construct mental images as they read (e.g., Gambrell & Bales, 1986; Pressley, 1976). Self-questioning strategies were favored by those who felt that good thinking involves internalized dialogue (e.g., Elliott-Faust & Pressley, 1986) in the tradition of Soviet theorists such as Vygotsky (e.g., 1978) or Americans such as Meichenbaum (e.g., 1977). In general, teaching elementary grade children to use such approaches improved their comprehension and memory of what they read (for reviews, see Dole, Duffy, Roehler, & Pearson, 1991; Pressley, Johnson, Symons, McGoldrick, & Kurita, 1989). What also became apparent, however, was that students seldom continued using single strategies that they learned after strategy instruction ended.

The understanding that skilled readers coordinate a number of strategies in coming to terms with text—an understanding imparted by some of the early think-aloud studies reviewed by Afflerbach & Pressley (in preparation)—in part motivated efforts to develop instructional interventions that involve teaching articulated use of multiple comprehension strategies. Without a doubt, the most famous of these efforts was Palincsar and Brown's (e.g., 1984) reciprocal teaching. Palincsar and Brown taught students to apply four strategies to expository text as they read, including (a) prediction of upcoming content, (b) asking questions about text content when reading, (c) seeking clarification when confused about meaning, and (d) summarizing what has been read. The students carried out these strategies in order in reading groups, with the adult teacher releasing control of the strategic processing as much as possible by ceding control to a designated student leader in the reading group. Palincsar and Brown's hypothesis, consistent with Vygotsky's (e.g., 1978) theory about the development of skilled reasoning through social interaction, was that participation in reading group discussions that involves prediction, questioning, seeking clarification, and summarization would lead to internalization of these processes by group members. In general, a month or two of reciprocal teaching produced some improvement in use of the strategies taught and reading comprehension, although the cognitive gains often were not large when assessed using standardized measures of comprehension (see Rosenshine & Meister, 1992).

In addition to reciprocal teaching, there were other attempts to teach multiple comprehension strategies. Some, those involving teaching a large number of strategies quickly, failed to produce compelling evidence of gains (e.g., Paris & Oka, 1986). Others offering more intensive direct explanation and modeling of the coordinated use of fewer strategies were more successful in affecting comprehension and other aspects of reading (e.g., Bereiter & Bird, 1985; Collins, 1991; Duffy et al., 1987).

Many educators became aware of the strategies instructional successes, largely because the scientists doing the work were sending the message to the field (e.g., through publications in journals dedicated to practice, such as *Reading Teacher* and *Journal of Reading*) that great improvements in comprehension could be realized by teaching students strategies. What became apparent, however, was that when strategies instruction was successfully deployed in schools, it involved much more than the operations studied in the well-controlled experiments (Pressley, Goodchild, Fleet, Zajchowski, & Evans, 1989). Pressley and his associates concluded that the scientific analyses of strategies instruction would not be complete until it was understood how educators taught students strategies so that the students used them in a self-regulated fashion. They believed from the outset that such work had great potential for informing the larger educator community as well as stimulating new theoretical models of strategy instruction, ones that might be more realistic about the development of self-regulation through instruction than previous efforts. They also recognized, however, that the research tactics needed to understand that field-based instructional programs would necessarily be different from the research tactics used in the theory-testing exercises that had been completed up until that point in time.

DESCRIPTIVE, QUALITATIVE STUDIES OF INSTRUCTION DESIGNED TO INCREASE SELF-REGULATED USE OF COMPREHENSION STRATEGIES BY ELEMENTARY-LEVEL STUDENTS: TRANSACTIONAL STRATEGIES INSTRUCTION

Beginning in 1989, Pressley and his colleagues set out to study real-school strategies instruction that seemed to be working. Their first studies were conducted at Benchmark School (Media, Pennsylvania), an institution dedicated to helping elementary-age children overcome reading problems

(Gaskins, Anderson, Pressley, Cunicelli, & Satlow, 1993; Pressley, Gaskins, Cunicelli et al., 1991; Pressley, Gaskins, Wile, Cunicelli, & Sheridan, 1991). A focus of the intensive Benchmark curriculum is strategies instruction for decoding, comprehension, and composition, delivered across subject areas and grades beginning for most Benchmark students at age 8. That Benchmark instruction works is a credible hypothesis based on the school's track record: After 4 to 7 years, most Benchmark students, who entered the school at great risk for long-term school failure, emerge well within the normal range of academic achievement. Pressley's Benchmark investigations were followed by studies in one Maryland public school system's elementary-level programs dedicated to increasing the use of strategies for reading comprehension. Their Strategies for Achieving Independent Learning program (SAIL) and Summer Institute for Achievement (SIA) both had proven potent relative to other county programs, especially in improving the reading comprehension of economically disadvantaged students (i.e., Chapter 1 students). Students in these programs were taught to coordinate use of a few comprehension strategies (e.g., predicting, questioning, seeking clarification, constructing mental images, summarizing, and using fix-up strategies when a word or its meaning is unclear). As the studies in the Maryland schools continued (Brown & Coy-Ogan, 1993; El-Dinary, Pressley, & Schuder, 1992; Pressley, El-Dinary, Gaskins et al., 1992; Pressley, El-Dinary, Marks, Brown, & Stein, 1992; Pressley, Schuder, SAIL Faculty and Administration, Bergman, & El-Dinary, 1992), new investigations of comprehension strategies instruction were launched in Carroll County, Maryland Public School programs. The starting point for the Carroll County instructional program was Palincsar and Brown's reciprocal teaching model, although the Carroll County educators substantially adapted and elaborated the original Palincsar and Brown model (see Coley, DePinto, Craig, & Gardner, 1993; Marks et al., 1993).

A variety of qualitative methods were used to study the instruction at Benchmark School and in Carroll County, Maryland and the other Maryland county (one wishing anonymity as a condition for research participation). These included ethnographies; interviews involving questions emanating from Pressley, Goodchild et al.'s (1989) tentative description of strategies instruction, interviews constructed to illuminate observations made in program classrooms, long-term case studies, and analyses of classroom discourse. Although the programs differed in their particulars, a number of conclusions seemed reasonable across programs. That there has been converging evidence using various methodologies to study diverse programs has reassured us about the conclusions we have reached. In 1993, we are confident that we know a great deal about how strategies instruction is deployed in schools where there is some evidence that the instruction is improving self-regulated reading.

Collapsing across the settings and studies, the following conclusions about classroom instruction of comprehension strategies seem justified:

- Strategy instruction is a long-term affair, with effective strategies instructors offering it in their classroom throughout the school year; the ideal is for high-quality process instruction to occur over a number of years, as it does at Benchmark and for some SAIL students. Teachers recognize that the younger the children, the more that is required for them to understand the individual strategies; the younger the children as well, the more that is required for them to learn how to coordinate the use of the individual strategies they are learning.
- Teachers explain and model effective comprehension strategies. Typically, a few powerful strategies are emphasized. For example, the SAIL program involves prediction of upcoming information in a text, relating text content to prior knowledge, constructing internal mental images of relations described in text, use of problem-solving strategies such as rereading and analyzing context clues when meaning is unclear, and summarizing. The Carroll County program retains the four reciprocal teaching strategies at its heart, so as students dialogue about stories, they make predictions about subsequent content, ask questions, seek clarifications, and construct summaries. As part of generating questions, students analyze text for meaningful relationships, resulting in cause-and-effect questions, inquiries about temporal sequences in text, comparison-and-contrast probes, as well as other types of questions.
- The teachers coach students to use strategies, on an as-needed basis, providing hints to students about potential strategic choices they might make. There are many mini-lessons about when it is appropriate to use particular strategies.
- Both teachers and students model use of strategies for one another, thinking aloud as they read. They also model monitoring of progress in understanding text and detection of difficulties in understanding text.
- Throughout instruction, the usefulness of strategies is emphasized, with students reminded frequently about the comprehension gains that accompany strategy use. Information about when and where various strategies can be applied is commonly discussed. Teachers consistently model flexible use of strategies; students explain to one another how they use strategies to process text. Much of instruction is aimed at instilling the belief that achievement is possible by exerting the effort required to carry out effective strategies. This part

of the instruction is critical from our perspective (see Pressley & Ghatala, 1990), for children often use effective strategies and do not recognize that their performances improve, or if they do recognize strategy-induced benefits, the children do not use this understanding of strategy efficacy in deciding whether to use a strategy in the future (e.g., Pressley, Ross, Levin, & Ghatala, 1984). Instruction often must be quite explicit, with the instructional situation arranged so that strategy gains are salient, if children are to understand the benefits strategies confer and effectively use that information in making strategy deployment decisions (e.g., Ghatala, Levin, Pressley, & Goodwin, 1986).

- The strategies are used as a vehicle for coordinating dialogue about text. Thus, at the Benchmark School, a great deal of discussion of content occurs as teachers interact with students, reacting to students' use of strategies and prompting additional strategic processing (see especially Gaskins et al., 1993). In particular, when students relate text to their prior knowledge, construct summaries of text meaning, visualize relations covered in a text, and predict what might transpire in a story, they engage in personal interpretation of text, with these personal interpretations varying from child to child and reading group to reading group (Brown & Coy-Ogan, 1993).

- Variegated practice with strategies permits many opportunities for students to experience occasions when strategies facilitate performance. As part of group instruction, teachers think aloud as they make strategic choices, often explaining why they are choosing the strategies they use—and so do students. In short, the instruction Pressley and his associates studied promotes metacognitive knowledge about when and where to use strategies through multiple opportunities for students to acquire metacognitive knowledge about the appropriate use and utility of the strategies they are learning.

Pressley and his associates have begun to refer to the instruction they have been studying as *transactional strategies instruction*, for three reasons related to alternative theoretical definitions of transaction. First, long-term strategies instruction emphasizes that getting meaning from text involves an active thinker using the text as a starting point for construction of meaning, and thus, the strategies instruction we have been observing encourages transactions with text in the sense of the term used by Rosenblatt (1978). Second, the interpretations of stories that emerge as groups of children apply strategies to stories are different than the interpretations of those stories that would occur if children read the stories by themselves, so that the meaning construction that occurs in reading groups practicing strategies is transactional in the sense of the term employed by organizational psychologists (e.g., Hutchins, 1991). Third, a teacher's actions and reactions cannot be anticipated when the reading group uses strategies to construct an interpretation of text. Rather, the teacher's reactions and interpretations are determined in part by the interpretations and reactions of the students in the group, and thus, real-classroom strategies instruction is transactional in a sense identified by developmental psychologists (e.g., Bell, 1968): Teachers and students co-determine each other's reactions and behaviors.

What we have observed in all of the settings studied is that transactional instruction of reading strategies is an integral part of the regular school curriculum, with teaching often focused in the context of reading group. Even so, strategies instruction usually continues throughout the day and across the curriculum to some extent, with teachers reminding students throughout the day about how the strategies they have learned can be used to learn diverse content. Teacher explanations and modeling is followed by guided practice of the strategies, with teacher assistance provided on an as-needed basis (i.e., strategy instruction is "scaffolded"; Wood, Bruner, & Ross, 1976). What occurs as students practice strategies in reading groups are lively interpretive discussions, with students exposed to diverse reactions to text.

Just as we have learned that it takes some time for students to be able to coordinate their use of strategies, we have also learned that it takes time for teachers to be able to teach strategies comfortably. We have not encountered a single teacher who felt that the first year with strategies instruction was especially easy (see El-Dinary et al., 1992; Pressley, Gaskins, Cunicelli et al., 1991). Many teachers give up, frustrated by the demands of explaining and modeling strategies as well as by the great efforts required to monitor student progress in learning strategies.

More positively, however, many teachers come to believe that it was definitely worthwhile to learn how to teach strategies. Accomplished strategies instruction teachers are comfortable and professionally pleased with the teaching they are offering their students. Strategies instruction teachers come to understand the advantages when students learn to use the comprehension strategies employed by excellent readers. To date, the comparative data we have generated are consistent with the hypothesis that there are measurable differences in students provided transactional strategies instruction compared to other types of high quality language arts instruction. In the next section we take up some outcomes that are supportive of the conclusion that transactional strategies instruction can lead to long-term differences in cognitive processing during reading.

Before doing so, however, we want to emphasize that the new model of strategy instruction that emerged from the qualitative analyses shared many features with the old model of instruction that emerged from basic research. We are struck that strategies, knowledge, metacognition, and motivation all are prominent in the classroom strategies instruction we have observed in the past 4 years—just as they were prominent in the strategies instructional models derived directly from the basic research findings (see Schneider & Pressley, 1989). Cynics might argue that our qualitative lenses were distorted to discover in the teachers' behavior the theory that was in our heads all along. Our response to them is that at every stage of our qualitative enterprise, we took the conclusions back to the practitioners for their reactions and suggested corrections. We trust that if our lenses might have been fogged, theirs were not. Many sets of eyes (and the minds behind them) were involved in sifting through the qualitative data we collected and coming to the conclusions we made. All of us kept seeing strategies being taught in interaction with other knowledge, with the use of strategies depending on metacognition and instruction aimed at motivating active analysis during reading as a means of coming to understand text.

THE NATURE OF READING FOLLOWING LONG-TERM INSTRUCTION AIMED AT INCREASING SELF-REGULATED USE OF COMPREHENSION STRATEGIES

During the 1991–1992 school year, we conducted a year-long, quasi-experimental investigation of the effects of transactional strategies instruction on Grade 2 children's reading. Five Grade 2 classrooms receiving SAIL instruction were matched with Grade 2 classrooms taught by teachers who were well regarded as language arts teachers, but who were not using the SAIL approach. (The control teachers could be characterized as good "whole-language" teachers, which is the language arts tradition embraced in general by teachers in the participating school system at present.)

In each classroom in the study, a group of readers who were low achieving at the beginning of Grade 2 were identified, because our specific interest was in whether a year of SAIL instruction would improve the reading comprehension of the weaker readers compared to matched controls receiving excellent conventional instruction: SAIL was originally devised for Chapter 1 students and hence, it seemed appropriate that the first well-controlled investigation of its effects would focus on a disadvantaged population. Because the previous comparisons developed by the school district that suggested SAIL was effective involved socioeconomically disadvantaged populations, the decision to focus on at-risk students increased the continuity between the school-based research and the investigations we were conducting.

In the fall of 1991, the SAIL and non-SAIL participants in our study did not differ on standardized measures of reading comprehension and word attack skills. By the spring of 1992, there were clear, significant differences on these measures favoring the SAIL classrooms. (If within-classroom variability is accepted as the standard for determining an effect size, the end of the year effect in favor of SAIL was 0.7 SD. If between-class variability in classroom means is taken as the standard for determining effect size, then a 1.8 SD effect size was observed at the end of the year.) Such end-of-the-year differences favoring SAIL are important in that previous researchers evaluating classroom reading strategies programs have set greater improvements on standardized tests in strategies-trained compared to control classrooms as a benchmark that a strategies instructional intervention is effective (see Rosenshine & Meister, 1992).

Even so, standardized tests are only very inexact measures of process, and our view is that a successful strategies instructional program must unambiguously affect processing of text if it is to be considered successful. Thus, in addition to standardized measures, the students in the 1991–1992 study were asked questions targeting their knowledge of strategies, with the same strategic awareness items administered in fall 1991 and spring 1992. In addition, both SAIL and non-SAIL students participated in a think-aloud exercise in spring 1991; they read a passage and were required to report their thinking as they went through the text. Both the strategic awareness measure and the think-aloud exercise provided substantial data supporting the conclusion that the SAIL instruction increased knowledge and self-regulated use of strategies.

Strategic Awareness Interview

Reading researchers have observed clear, positive relationships between awareness of comprehension strategies and reading performance (e.g., Forrest-Pressley & Waller, 1984), which is sensible from a self-regulation perspective. Awareness of strategies, when they can be applied, and how they affect reading is essential if readers are to elect to use strategies appropriately. It especially makes sense that there should be clear differences between students who experience a comprehension strategies instructional program and those who do not, because much of the emphasis in such a program is increased awareness of strategies and their effects on reading (e.g., Duffy et al., 1986; Jacobs & Paris, 1987). The strategic awareness interviews administered individually to students in our 1991–1992 study were inspired by and informed by the previous metacognitive investigations of Forrest-Pressley and Waller (1984), Paris and his colleagues (e.g., Paris & Oka, 1986), and Duffy et al. (1986).

We posed the following questions in our interviews: What do good readers do when they read? What do you do before you start to read a new story? What do you think about before you read a story? What do you do when you come to a word you don't know? What do you do when you read something that just doesn't make sense? This interview resulted in identification of clear differences in strategic awareness between the SAIL and non-SAIL students at the end of Grade 2, even though the two groups were similarly aware of strategies at the beginning of their Grade 2 years. We present here the most important outcomes obtained in this interview portion of the 1991–1992 investigation.

In fall 1991, the SAIL and non-SAIL students did not differ in the number of comprehension strategies identified or described during their interviews. By the spring, however, there were clear differences between the groups. For example, only the SAIL students talked about setting reading goals, visualizing, looking back, using text clues to clarify confusions, using picture clues to aid comprehension, relating current text to prior knowledge, summarizing, or browsing. Although non-SAIL students mentioned the strategies of predicting, verifying, asking someone for help when text is confusing, skipping over difficult parts of text, and rereading, SAIL students mentioned these strategies more often. The responses to these interview questions made clear that the SAIL students had learned much more about comprehension strategies during their second-grade year than did the non-SAIL students.

In particular, the SAIL students emerged from second grade with a burgeoning conception of what good readers do when they read. By spring 1992, SAIL students were more likely than their non-SAIL counterparts to mention that good readers think; use comprehension strategies such as predicting, summarizing, and visualizing; and employ fix-it strategies (e.g., rereading, guessing, skipping, or using picture clues) when reading comprehension goes awry. Of course, these responses reflect the SAIL curriculum and the strategies taught in it, as we hoped the SAIL students' responses might by the end of the year. In contrast, the non-SAIL students offered many more general claims about processes that good readers use, for example, indicating that good readers behave, listen, and pay attention. Although some SAIL students also provided such general responses, when they did so, SAIL participants typically elaborated their responses to indicate more completely how behaving, listening, and paying attention mediate good reading.

When asked at the beginning of the year about what good readers do before they start a story, both SAIL and non-SAIL students provided answers such as, "I open my book," "I get ready to read," or "I read the title." Even prompts to elaborate these answers did not result in more extensive commentary in the fall. By the end of the year, both SAIL and non-SAIL students were talking about predicting, although the two groups differed substantially in their descriptions about what they meant by predicting. SAIL students generally indicated looking at the title or illustrations to predict what was going to happen in the story. In contrast, non-SAIL students use the title and illustrations to predict whether they would like the book or find it difficult.

In summary, there was little to differentiate the SAIL and non-SAIL students during the fall interview. By the spring, however, the SAIL students provided much more elaborated answers than non-SAIL students. By year's end, SAIL students were facile in using the names of the strategies they had learned in SAIL and defining the strategies with respect to the questions posed during the strategic awareness interview. During the spring interview, the SAIL students provided responses reflecting their understanding of the usefulness of the strategies they had learned during the year as well as their awareness of when and where the strategies could be applied. The SAIL students perceived that skilled reading is thinking and problem solving. In short, after a year of SAIL, students had much of the knowledge required to be self-regulated readers.

Think-Aloud Analysis

A persistent concern in interpreting metacognitive interview data is that such data reflect more whether students can talk about cognitive processes rather than whether they can and do use them. Our purpose in the 1991–1992 study was to capture as broadly as possible the differences in reading produced by a school year of SAIL instruction and thus, such awareness data seemed essential. We were much more interested, however, in whether SAIL instruction increased self-regulated use of strategies. A think-aloud analysis conducted in the spring established clearly that SAIL students more certainly employed strategies as they read than did non-SAIL students.

During the think-aloud exercise, we asked both SAIL and non-SAIL students to read an Aesop's fable, "The Dog and His Reflection." In this tale, the dog steals a piece of meat from his owner's table and rushes into the woods with it. When he comes to a bridge, he looks down and sees his reflection. Wanting the other piece of meat, he growls at the reflection and in the process the meat he is holding in his mouth drops in the water, with the moral of the tale being the consequences of excessive greed. This story was chosen in part because there were four natural break points in it, so that students could stop at those points and think aloud without disrupting ongoing reading.

Each child read individually. After reading the title, the investigator asked the students to "think aloud" about the title. Then, after each story segment, students were asked three questions: "What are you thinking?" "What do you think happened on this page?" and "Is there anything else you could say or do before reading on?"

The SAIL students were more strategic during this think-aloud task than were non-SAIL students. SAIL students used a variety of strategies more frequently than did non-SAIL students, including setting a reading goal, predicting, verifying, relating facilitative background knowledge to text content, summarizing, questioning for clarification, visualizing, using picture clues to resolve a point of confusion, and looking back in the text when confused. It was not that non-SAIL students were entirely lacking in strategies. (We did not expect them to be because the very competent control teachers in our study taught comprehension strategies consistent with many contemporary Grade 2 curricular packages.) Non-SAIL students, however, manifested a smaller repertoire of strategies than SAIL students, typically relying heavily on predicting, verifying, using background knowledge, and analysis of picture clues.

One negative possibility raised by critics of comprehension strategies instruction is that use of strategies might reduce interpretive responses. This, in fact, did not occur in this study. In fact, SAIL students were more likely than non-SAIL students to report interpretations of and reactions to text based on their prior knowledge. For example, consider some of the comments provided after students read the following text:

As he carried the chop over a bridge, the dog looked down into the stream. There he saw his own reflection in the clear water, but he thought he was looking at another dog with another bigger looking lambchop. Being greedy, he wanted to have that, too.

One prior knowledge-based interpretation offered by a SAIL student, ". . . Um . . . he's getting angry at his reflection 'cause he thinks the other steak is bigger but its actually not. . . . [he wants it] . . . so he'll grow up to be a strong dog . . . so when he grows up a cop will get him and will let him be like a crime fighting dog. . . . That's the dog I want to get." Another SAIL student offered the following evaluative interpretation in response to the text: "I think he was a little bit stupid to let his out to get another one and then when he went to get the other, it wasn't there . . . I think he shouldn't have opened his mouth to try and get the other one." In contrast, three of the non-SAIL classrooms were notable in that the students attempts at interpretations were much more retellings than interpretations reflecting the application of prior knowledge as part of trying to understand text. For example, in reacting to the bit of text presented earlier, one non-SAIL student said, "He's looking at his reflection . . . he thinks its another dog . . . and he wants to have another piece of meat . . . he was running to the forest and went over the bridge and looked down on the water while he was running and he stopped and saw his reflection . . ." Such rephrasings were much more common in the non-SAIL than in the SAIL classrooms.

Although critics of comprehension strategies instruction might find it surprising that strategies-instructed students would relate text to prior knowledge, we do not. Transactional strategies instruction encourages students to use strategies as tools to relate text to prior knowledge (Gaskins et al., 1993; Pressley, Gaskins, Cunicelli et al., 1991). Hence, it is perfectly sensible that students applying transactional strategies instruction would in fact produce many reactions to text in terms of their prior knowledge. Thus, the strategies instruction we favor not only improves performance on standardized measures of performance, it also increases the likelihood that students will go well beyond the text in finding an interpretation, consistent with the perspective of many literary critical theorists that sophisticated interpretations reflect both reader knowledge and text content, not simply literal text content and inferences that logically follow from premises included in text (Rosenblatt, 1978). Such reader-based interpretations were yet one more indication of more extensive cognitive processing following a year of Grade 2 SAIL instruction compared to a year of conventional, albeit high quality, language arts instruction.

Summary

After a year of SAIL, students not only talk a good game with respect to reading, they read better than otherwise comparable students who have not experienced SAIL. SAIL students can answer more comprehension questions on text they have read than can non-SAIL students; SAIL students' processing reflects greater use of strategies and more sophisticated inferences than does the processing of non-SAIL students. Even disadvantaged students in the early elementary grades can understand the concept of a repertoire of strategies and use such a repertoire productively if they are given long-term instruction that requires extensive practice self-regulating use of strategies—as transactional strategies instruction does.

Our optimism that SAIL had a long-term impact on reading achievement is fueled by some more recent data that we have been collecting. During 1992–1993, we decided to ask some SAIL students who participated in the 1991–1992 study (now in Grade 3) to think aloud as they read another story. This testing is being conducted without the students knowing of its connection with last year's instruction or study, with testing carried out by an individual not connected to last year's study as far as the students know.

We are also asking some control Grade 3 students, who did not experience SAIL during Grade 2, to read the same story, thinking aloud as they do so. Although not all of the data are collected at the time of this writing, and the data that are collected are only partially analyzed, it is clear that the majority of SAIL students are manifesting the SAIL strategies 6 to 9 months after their SAIL instruction concluded. We expect that these data are going to bolster the case that transactional strategies instruction can lead to long-term increases in self-regulated use of comprehension strategies.

Our long-term interest, however, is not in SAIL per se but in comprehension strategies instruction. Thus, other evaluations of comprehension packages are in the works even as the SAIL quasi-experimental outcomes are being analyzed. In particular, after documenting the nature of the classroom-adapted form of reciprocal teaching developed in Carroll County, Maryland (Coley et al., 1993; Marks et al., 1993), Thommie Depinto and Michael Pressley are carrying out a study of such teaching using a design very similar to the one used to evaluate the SAIL program. The transactional version of reciprocal teaching is being studied in Grade 5 classrooms, however, with a few new dependent variables added to the investigation. Most critically, we believe that transactional strategies instruction may be much more motivating and enjoyable for students than conventional language arts. Thus, the ongoing investigation of revised reciprocal teaching includes affective measures that were not included in the quasi-experimental evaluation of the SAIL program. The addition of such information will round out what is becoming a fairly full portrait of real-school comprehension strategies instruction that increases children's use of sophisticated text-processing strategies in a self-regulated fashion.

A RECAP OF COMPREHENSION STRATEGIES INSTRUCTIONAL RESEARCH: FROM RESEARCH EVALUATING SINGLE COMPREHENSION STRATEGIES TO PROMOTION OF SELF-REGULATED COMPREHENSION PROCESSING THROUGH TRANSACTIONAL STRATEGIES INSTRUCTION

The strategies instructional investigations published in the 1970s and 1980s were decidedly positivist: Various researchers tested strategies that they felt might promote reading comprehension, with two main sources of hypotheses about strategies to teach: (a) representational theories (e.g., dual-coding theory, with its assumption that combined imagery and verbal codings are better than either code alone) and (b) think-aloud protocols of skilled reading (e.g., good readers in Bereiter & Bird, 1985,

Study 1, noted portions of text not understood, set up "lookers" for information related to the difficult point, backtracked, and restated difficult sections of text; Bereiter & Bird, 1985, Study 2, thus, trained junior high school students to react to problems in text in the same ways). This strategies instructional literature of the 1970s and 1980s did much to validate the models of effective processing emerging from representational theories and protocol analyses: When students carried out the instructed processes, their comprehension tended to improve.

Because many of the scientists doing this work were legitimately interested in the implications of cognitive psychology for education, there was ready communication of the results of these studies to the educator community. Pressley and his co-workers noted in 1989, however, that comprehension strategies instruction in schools that seemed effective differed greatly from the laboratory versions of strategies instruction that had been carefully studied by educational psychologists. Pressley and his associates concluded that a much more complete understanding of effective strategies instruction might be possible by studying educators who had adapted strategies instruction effectively to school settings.

Through use of qualitative methods, Pressley and his colleagues developed a theory about the nature of strategies instruction that can increase self-regulated use of comprehension strategies (Pressley, Gaskins, Cunicelli et al., 1992; Pressley et al., in preparation; also Pressley et al., in press). This theory is grounded in data (e.g., Strauss & Corbin, 1990), and it is more complex than alternative theories. For example, transactional strategies instruction differs from reciprocal teaching, which is simpler, in the following ways:

- Transactional strategies instruction is intended to extend over multiple years, with no expectation of meaningful gains in a month or two of instruction, which has been the period of instruction in the most visible evaluations of reciprocal teaching to date. The developmental implications of Vygotsky's (1962, 1978) model are taken seriously in transactional strategies instruction, with development of reading comprehension skills occurring over a matter of years of interactions rather than over a matter of weeks or days.

- Teacher modeling and explanation is more salient and continues for the duration of transactional strategies instruction. As is the case with all mature apprenticeship models, the burgeoning reader interacts with a skilled reader for a long period of time, with the skilled reader ever upping the ante as students become more proficient in using strategies to read ever more complex texts.

- Student choice of strategies is emphasized, rather than rigid adherence to cycles of questioning, seeking clarification, summarizing, and predicting. There are no rigid sequences in the transactional approach, with the emphasis on students evaluating the text situation to determine which process is appropriate to use in a particular situation. The flexible application of strategies encouraged in transactional strategies instruction is consistent with the flexible use of strategies observed when highly skilled readers process texts in domains of expertise.

- Interpretive processes are encouraged more, with transactional teachers favoring evaluations that reflect deep comprehension rather than literal comprehension. Thinking aloud in transactional strategies instruction reflects a commitment to encourage students to interpret text with respect to prior knowledge continuously.

- More strategies are taught as part of transactional strategies instruction. Important interpretive processes, such as generation of images, which are never taught as part of reciprocal teaching, are key processes in transactional strategies instruction.

Despite the theoretical gains in understanding classroom strategies instruction that occurred because we abandoned hypothesis testing for a few years in favor of hypothesis discovery, our colleagues continually asked how we knew that the instruction we were studying worked. Although there were anecdotal and correlational data, we certainly did not know that these interventions were effective in anything like the sense that an intervention can be known to be effective following a true experiment. We could not, however, return to true experimentation: It takes a great deal of time and effort for teachers to become facile in instruction of a repertoire of comprehension strategies (e.g., El-Dinary et al., 1992; Pressley, Gaskins, Cunicelli et al., 1991; Pressley, Schuder et al., 1992), and once a teacher becomes a strategies instruction teacher, there is commitment to the approach. It is not realistic to suppose that such strategies-instruction-committed teachers could ever be randomly assigned to strategies instructional treatment and control conditions. The best that can be hoped for are quasi-experimental investigations that control for as many between-condition variables as possible, and that is the methodological tactic we took in both the SAIL study and the Carroll County reformed reciprocal teaching investigation that are underway at the time of this writing.

We might add, however, that as we moved toward more controlled study of complex strategies instruction, we were not abandoning the qualitative approach entirely. We are good and getting better at collaborative interviewing as part of our investigations (e.g., Pressley, Schuder et al., 1992). This entails spending a great deal of time watching instruction and formulating questions about the teaching during these observations. Along the way, the investigator interacts with the teachers to refine the questions and identify aspects of the instruction that might not have been noticed by an outsider. This approach has produced important insights about difficulties in implementing strategies instruction, many potential effects of such teaching, and possible modifications of strategy instruction in order to improve its compatibility with classroom constraints. Such qualitative data are enriching our understanding of the interventions far beyond the understandings that would emerge from the quasi-experiments alone.

We have come full circle as we close this chapter. Although we have certainly learned much about strategies instruction not apparent in the basic research studies conducted in the 1970s and 1980s, the basic research of that era (see Schneider & Pressley, 1989; Schunk, 1989, 1990, 1991; Zimmerman, 1990a, 1990b) and the more recent qualitative and quasi-experimental work (Pressley, Gaskins, Cunicelli et al., 1991) converge on two conclusions: (a) To understand self-regulated use of strategies, it is important to understand how strategies interact with prior knowledge, depend on metacognitive knowledge, and are affected by motivational variables. (b) To promote long-term use of strategies, it is necessary to build metacognitive understandings about strategies, a coherent network of knowledge about the world, and motivational beliefs supportive of active cognition.

ACKNOWLEDGMENTS

The original research reported in the latter half of this chapter was supported in part by contractual support to Michael Pressley as a principal investigator, National Reading Research Center at Universities of Maryland and Georgia, funded by the Office of Educational Research and Improvement (OERI), U. S. Department of Education. The views expressed here are those of the authors, and no endorsement by either the U. S. Department of Education or the National Reading Research Center should be inferred. We are deeply indebted both to our school-based collaborators, including Ted Schuder and Irene Gaskins, and to our Maryland-based associates, in particular, Pamela Beard El-Dinary and Marilyn Marks.

REFERENCES

Afflerbach, P., & Pressley, M. (in preparation). *Portrayals of engaged reading through verbal reports: Cognition and reader response.*
Bell, R. Q. (1968). A reinterpretation of the direction of effects in studies of socialization. *Psychological Review, 75,* 81–95.

Bereiter, C., & Bird, M. (1985). Use of thinking aloud in identification and teaching of reading comprehension strategies. *Cognition and Instruction, 2,* 131–156.

Brown, R., & Coy-Ogan, L. (1993). The evaluation of transactional strategies instruction in one teacher's classroom. *Elementary School Journal, 94,* 221–233.

Chi, M. T. H., Glaser, R., & Farr, M. J. (Eds.). (1988). *The nature of expertise.* Hillsdale, NJ: Lawrence Erlbaum Associates.

Coley, J., DePinto, T., Craig, S., & Gardner, R. (1993). Teachers adapting reciprocal teaching. *Elementary School Journal, 94,* 255–266.

Collins, C. (1991). Reading instruction that increases thinking abilities. *Journal of Reading, 34,* 510–516.

Dole, J. A., Duffy, G. G., Roehler, L. R., & Pearson, P. D. (1991). Moving from the old to the new: Research on reading comprehension instruction. *Review of Educational Research, 61,* 239–264.

Duffy, G. G., Roehler, L. R., Meloth, M., Vavrus, L., Book, C., Putnam, J., & Wesselman, R. (1986). The relationship between explicit verbal explanation during reading skill instruction and student awareness and achievement: A study of reading teacher effects. *Reading Research Quarterly, 21,* 237–252.

Duffy, G. G., Roehler, L. R., Sivan, E., Rackliffe, G., Book, C., Meloth, M., Vavrus, L., Wesselman, R., Putnam, J., & Bassiri, D. (1987). Effects of explaining the reasoning associated with using reading strategies. *Reading Research Quarterly, 22,* 347–368.

El-Dinary, P. B., Pressley, M., & Schuder, T. (1992). Becoming a strategies teacher: An observational and interview study of three teachers learning transactional strategies instruction. In C. Kinzer & D. Leu (Eds.), *Forty-first Yearbook of the National Reading Conference* (pp. 453–462). Chicago: National Reading Conference.

Elliott-Faust, D. J., & Pressley, M. (1986). How to teach comparison processing to increase children's short- and long-term listening comprehension monitoring. *Journal of Educational Psychology, 78,* 27–33.

Forrest-Pressley, D. L., & Waller, T. G. (1984). *Metacognition, cognition, and reading.* New York: Springer-Verlag.

Gambrell, L. B., & Bales, R. J. (1986). Mental imagery and the comprehension-monitoring performance of fourth- and fifth-grade poor readers. *Reading Research Quarterly, 21,* 454–464.

Gaskins, I. W., Anderson, R. C., Pressley, M., Cunicelli, E. A., & Satlow, E. (1993). Six teachers' dialogue during cognitive process instruction. *Elementary School Journal, 93,* 277–304.

Ghatala, E. S., Levin, J. R., Pressley, M., & Goodwin, D. (1986). A componential analysis of the effects of derived and supplied strategy-utility information on children's strategy selections. *Journal of Experimental Child Psychology, 41,* 76–92.

Hutchins, E. (1991). The social organization of distributed cognition. In L. Resnick, J. M. Levine, & S. D. Teasley (Eds.), *Perspectives on socially shared cognition* (pp. 283–307). Washington, DC: American Psychological Association.

Jacobs, J. E., & Paris, S. G. (1987). Children's metacognition about reading: Issues in definition, measurement, and instruction. *Educational Psychologist, 22,* 255–278.

Marks, M., Pressley, M., in collaboration with Coley, J. D., Craig, S., Gardner, R., Rose, W., & DePinto, T. (1993). Teachers' adaptations of reciprocal teaching: Progress toward a classroom-compatible version of reciprocal teaching. *Elementary School Journal, 94,* 267–283.

Meichenbaum, D. (1977). *Cognitive behavior modification.* New York: Plenum.

Paivio, A. (1971). *Imagery and verbal processes.* New York: Holt, Rinehart & Winston.

Palincsar, A. S., & Brown, A. L. (1984). Reciprocal teaching of comprehension-fostering and monitoring activities. *Cognition and Instruction, 1,* 117–175.

Paris, S. G., & Oka, E. R. (1986). Children's reading strategies, metacognition, and motivation. *Developmental Review, 6,* 25–56.

Pressley, G. M. (1976). Mental imagery helps eight-year-olds remember what they read. *Journal of Educational Psychology, 68,* 355–359.

Pressley, M., Borkowski, J. G., & O'Sullivan, J. T. (1984). Memory strategy instruction is made of this: Metamemory and durable strategy use. *Educational Psychologist, 19,* 94–107.

Pressley, M., Borkowski, J. G., & O'Sullivan, J. T. (1985). Children's metamemory and the teaching of memory strategies. In D. L. Forrest-Pressley, G. E. MacKinnon, & T. G. Waller (Eds.), *Metacognition, cognition, and human performance* (pp. 111–153). New York: Academic Press.

Pressley, M., Borkowski, J. G., & Schneider, W. (1987). Cognitive strategies: Good strategy users coordinate metacognition and knowledge. In R. Vasta & G. Whitehurst (Eds.), *Annals of child development* (Vol. 4, pp. 89–129). Greenwich, CT: JAI Press.

Pressley, M., Borkowski, J. G., & Schneider, W. (1989). Good information processing: What it is and what education can do to promote it. *International Journal of Educational Research, 13,* 857–867.

Pressley, M., El-Dinary, P. B., Brown, R., Schuder, T., Bergman, J. L., York, M., & Gaskins, I. W. (in preparation). *A transactional strategies instruction Christmas carol.*

Pressley, M., El-Dinary, P. B., Brown, R., Schuder, T., Pioli, M., Green, K., SAIL Faculty and Administration, Gaskins, I., & Benchmark School Faculty. (1994). Transactional instruction of reading comprehension strategies. In J. Mangieri & C. C. Block (Eds.), *Mindfulness: Increasing thinking abilities.* Fort Worth, TX: Harcourt, Brace, Jovanovich.

Pressley, M., El-Dinary, P. B., Gaskins, I., Schuder, T., Bergman, J., Almasi, L., & Brown, R. (1992). Beyond direct explanation: Transactional instruction of reading comprehension strategies. *Elementary School Journal, 92,* 511–554.

Pressley, M., El-Dinary, P. B., Marks, M. B., Brown, R., & Stein, S. (1992). Good strategy instruction is motivating and interesting. In K. A. Renninger, S. Hidi, & A. Krapp (Eds.), *The role of interest in learning and development* (pp. 333–358). Hillsdale, NJ: Lawrence Erlbaum Associates.

Pressley, M., Gaskins, I. W., Cunicelli, E. A., Burdick, N. J., Schaub-Matt, M., Lee, D. S., & Powell, N. (1991). Strategy instruction at Benchmark School: A faculty interview study. *Learning Disability Quarterly, 14,* 19–48.

Pressley, M., Gaskins, I. W., Wile, D., Cunicelli, B., & Sheridan, J. (1991). Teaching literacy strategies across the curriculum: A case study at Benchmark School. In J. Zutell & S. McCormick (Eds.), *Learner factors/teacher factors: Issues in literacy research and instruction: Fortieth yearbook of the National Reading Conference* (pp. 219–228). Chicago: National Reading Conference.

Pressley, M., & Ghatala, E. S. (1990). Self-regulated learning: Monitoring learning from text. *Educational Psychologist, 25,* 19–34.

Pressley, M., Goodchild, F., Fleet, J., Zajchowski, R., & Evans, E. D. (1989). The challenges of classroom strategy instruction. *Elementary School Journal, 89,* 301–342.

Pressley, M., Johnson, C. J., Symons, S., McGoldrick, J. A., & Kurita, J. (1989). Strategies that improve memory and comprehension of what is read. *Elementary School Journal, 90,* 3–32.

Pressley, M., Ross, K. A., Levin, J. R., & Ghatala, E. S. (1984). The role of strategy utility knowledge in children's strategy decision making. *Journal of Experimental Child Psychology, 38,* 491–504.

Pressley, M., Schuder, T., SAIL Faculty and Administration, Bergman, J. L., & El-Dinary, P. B. (1992). A researcher-educator collaborative interview study of transactional comprehension strategies instruction. *Journal of Educational Psychology, 84,* 231–246.

Rosenblatt, L. M. (1978). *The reader, the text, the poem: The transactional theory of the literary work.* Carbondale: Southern Illinois University Press.

Rosenshine, B., & Meister, C. (1992). *Reciprocal teaching: A review of nineteen experimental studies*. Manuscript submitted for publication.

Schneider, W., & Pressley, M. (1989). *Memory development between 2 and 20*. New York: Springer-Verlag.

Schunk, D. H. (1989). Social cognitive theory and self-regulated learning. In B. J. Zimmerman & D. H. Schunk (Eds.), *Self-regulated learning and academic achievement* (pp. 83–110). New York: Springer-Verlag.

Schunk, D. H. (1990). Goal setting and self-efficacy during self-regulated learning. *Educational Psychologist, 25*, 71–86.

Schunk, D. H. (1991). Self-efficacy and academic motivation. *Educational Psychologist, 26*, 207–232.

Strauss, A., & Corbin, J. (1990). *Basics of qualitative research: Theory, procedures, and techniques.* Beverly Hills, CA: Sage.

van Dijk, T. A., & Kintsch, W. (1983). *Strategies of discourse comprehension.* New York: Academic Press.

Vygotsky, L. S. (1962). *Thought and language.* Cambridge, MA: MIT Press.

Vygotsky, L. S. (1978). *Mind and society.* Cambridge, MA: Harvard University Press.

Wood, S. S., Bruner, J. S., & Ross, G. (1976). The role of tutoring in problem solving. *Journal of Child Psychology and Psychiatry, 17*, 89–100.

Wyatt, D., Pressley, M., El-Dinary, P. B., Stein, S., Evans, P., & Brown, R. (1993). Comprehension strategies, worth and credibility monitoring, and evaluations: Cold and hot cognition when experts read professional articles that are important to them. *Learning and Individual Differences, 5*, 49–72.

Zimmerman, B. J. (1989a). A social cognitive view of self-regulated academic learning. *Journal of Educational Psychology, 81*, 329–339.

Zimmerman, B. J. (1989b). Models of self-regulated learning and academic achievement. In B. J. Zimmerman & D. H. Schunk (Eds.), *Self-regulated learning and academic achievement* (pp. 1–25). New York: Springer-Verlag.

Zimmerman, B. J. (1990a). Self-regulated learning and academic achievement: An overview. *Educational Psychologist, 25*, 3–18.

Zimmerman, B. J. (1990b). Self-regulating academic learning and achievement: The emergence of a social-cognitive perspective. *Educational Psychology Review, 2*, 173–201.

8

Self-Regulating Academic Study Time: A Strategy Approach

Barry J. Zimmerman
Daphne Greenberg
Graduate School of City University of New York

Claire E. Weinstein
University of Texas

> *Time is one of life's priceless commodities, but, unlike other commodities, we can not save, borrow, or recover lost time. However, we can choose to use it.*
>
> —Delzell (1985, p. 26)

Historically, the issue of how students plan, use, and evaluate their time during learning has been subordinated to conceptions of learning time as an indirect measure of mental ability or personality traits. Study time was not treated initially as a strategically controllable factor in a learner's academic performance but rather was seen as a manifestation of stable underlying individual differences in aptitude or motivation. As a result, time use was defined in seconds, minutes, or days needed to learn a task or complete an assignment, rather than in terms of cognitive or behavioral processes.

Recently a number of investigators have begun to focus on cognitive and behavioral processes that students use to plan and manage their academic learning time. It has been suggested that effective use of one's study time is a product of students' use of learning strategies such as planning and goal setting (Weinstein & Mayer, 1986; Zimmerman & Martinez-Pons, 1986). These anticipatory strategies can, in turn, prompt students to use other self-regulatory processes such as monitoring the speed of their progress and adjusting their efforts accordingly. Thus, time use can also be viewed as an important *performance outcome* that students can use to self-regulate their current and future learning and academic performance.

In this chapter, we discuss various theoretical conceptions of time use during academic learning and performance, ranging from noncognitive views such as trait and operant formulations to cognitive views such as information processing, metacognitive, and social cognitive formulations. Then we survey research on academic study time and focus on the role of key self-regulatory processes including strategic use of planning, goal setting, and self-monitoring. We also focus on the role of students' self-efficacy perceptions regarding time planning and use and academic achievement. This is followed by a discussion of needed research on student use of time during studying. Finally, we present a description of how college students can be taught systematically to improve their use of academic study time.

THEORIES OF ACADEMIC STUDY TIME

Aptitude-Trait Views of Academic Study Time

Carroll (1963) was one of the first theorists to emphasize the concept of time in a model of student learning. In his theory, three of five learning elements are related to students' use of time: their aptitude, opportunity to learn, and perseverance (Carroll, 1963, p. 729, 1989). *Aptitude* was defined as "the amount of time needed to learn the task [to criterion] under optimal instructional conditions"; *perseverance* referred to "the amount of time the learner is willing to engage actively in learning"; and *opportunity to learn* was defined as "time allowed for learning."

Carroll's model sparked much research and aided our understanding of the importance of student use of time during learning. For example, Gettinger and White (1979) found that students' learning time for units in six academic areas was a better predictor of their achievement on standardized tests than IQ. The authors concluded that learning time was an effective personal index of learning aptitude. In addition, persistence on difficult or unsolvable learning tasks was widely used as a measure of individual differences in students' achievement motivation (Atkinson & Feather, 1966). In Carroll's (1963) model, time use was not conceived as a source of self-regulation but rather as a manifestation of underlying personal factors such as aptitudes or motivational traits.

Operant Views of Academic Study Time

A number of operant theorists in the 1960s and 1970s analyzed students' academic behavior in terms of the time required for task completion. These theorists pioneered the use of time series graphs to describe and explain individual student's task performance. These graphs involved plotting (a) the *frequency* of key behaviors, such as completion of task assignments on the vertical axis, and (b) the *time* or date of this behavior on the horizontal axis, in intervals of minutes, hours, or days. Student's level of task completion could be assessed under regular studying conditions as well as after various interventions were introduced, such as earning attractive rewards. The speed of learning or performance could be inferred from the slope of the plotted line over period of time. Operant researchers have studied characteristic differences in response patterns due to the type of reinforcement contingency. Intermittent reinforcement schedules based on time or response ratio have been shown to produce more lasting response changes than continuous schedules.

Operant educators have used time series graphs to analyze individual student's progress during mastery learning programs such as Keller's (1968) Personalized System of Instruction (PSI). In this approach, students are allowed to complete a course of study as rapidly as they want; however, they are required to pass a criterion referenced test for each unit at a mastery level of 80% or 90% accuracy before they can move to the next unit. The students' progress in completing each of 15 to 30 units in a course are plotted using a cumulative graph. According to operant theory, time is an important dimension of behavior that is subject to self-control. If students self-record their progress, they can use this graphic stimulus to manage their use of time more effectively. In contrast to traditional forms of education, the Keller Plan allows students to be more flexible in controlling their study time, a feature called self-paced instruction. When introduced, this plan was unique in that it relaxed time requirements, allowed students to learn at their own pace, and rewarded them for their progress with a pre-specified grade. Studies of the Keller Plan have shown high rates of superiority over traditional group-paced instructional methods and have received positive evaluations by students (Johnson & Rudskin, 1977). Clearly, allowing students to self-regulate task completion time had important advantages.

Information Processing Views of Academic Study Time

Academic study time has been conceived of also from an information processing perspective. For example, Britton and Glynn (1989) theorized that students' time management was composed of three essential processes: a goal manager, a task planner, and a scheduler. A *goal manager* takes into consideration one's desires and constructs a list of goals and subgoals. A *planner* takes this list of goals and produces a sequenced list of tasks and subtasks, and a *scheduler* then converts the list into timed events. All three roles in this model are influenced by such task characteristics as deadlines, degree of concentration required, and length of persistence necessary for completion. The essential feature of information processing views of self-regulation is a negative feedback loop wherein performance is compared and adjusted to meet the time goals or standards. This sequential formulation was useful in describing students' use of time when planning, writing, and revising by computer.

Metacognitive Views of Academic Study Time

According to this perspective, time use is linked to students' use of strategies for planning and organizing one's study time or taking tests (see Weinstein & Meyer, 1991). Time management strategies can be classified (Paris, Lipson, & Wixon, 1983) as a form of procedural knowledge (how time can be used to guide acquisition of information) that, in turn, depends on one's declarative knowledge (information already known about a topic) as well as one's conditional knowledge (knowing when managing study time can be a problem). It is theorized that effective students acquire and use specific strategic methods for managing their academic time, such as scheduling a particular time period each day to study or complete homework.

The key self-regulative variable in the metacognitive approach is the quality of students' cognitive monitoring (Flavell, 1979). If students don't realize when they aren't learning, they will not plan or adjust their time use strategy appropriately (Garner, 1990). There is evidence that students often fail to monitor their learning (Ghatala, Levin, Foorman, & Pressley, 1989) and often fail to self-regulate their use of time (e.g., Gettinger, 1985), even when they are motivated to learn.

Conversely, there is evidence that use of time management strategies can assist academic tasks such as writing. For example, research on graduate students' "thesis blocking" indicates that nonblockers engage in more purposeful and conscious planning of time management strategies than blockers (Rennie & Brewer, 1987). Furthermore, professional writers, academicians, and successful dissertation writers regularly use time criteria such as daily output charts to help them meet deadlines for their writing tasks (Boice, 1982; Harris, 1974; Wallace & Pear, 1977).

Social Cognitive Views of Academic Study Time

According to this perspective, students' management of academic study time involves triadic self-regulatory processes (Bandura, 1986). Time use is assumed to be influenced by *behavioral* and *environmental* influences, as well as by *personal* learning strategy influences (Zimmerman, 1989). Behavioral influences include efforts to self-observe, self-evaluate, and self-react to academic performance outcomes. Environmental influences include the use of planning aides such as wrist watches, alarms, and appointment books to manage time optimally. Social cognitive theorists (Bandura, 1989; Schunk, 1989; Zimmerman, 1989) recognize the role of personal influences, such as goal setting, attributions, and perceptions of self-efficacy, as critical to effective time management during studying. That is, in order to manage time effectively, students should set specific and attainable study goals, must attribute outcomes to strategy use, and must feel efficacious to learn a task within the allotted time (Zimmerman & Martinez-Pons, 1992). There is substantial evidence that strategic efforts to control each of these personal variables play a key role in students' academic self-regulation (e.g., Schunk, 1981; Zimmerman, Bandura, & Martinez-Pons, 1992). Conversely, poor time management may reflect deficiencies in behavioral, environmental, or personal self-regulatory processes.

RESEARCH ON ACADEMIC STUDY TIME

Individual Differences in Use of Academic Study Time

To test Carroll's (1963) model of school learning, Gettinger (1985) studied elementary students' aptitude using a measure of time needed to learn. This concept was defined operationally as the number of trials needed by the subject to achieve a score of 100% on a mastery test in social studies. One group of subjects was presented with a written passage and questions for each of six trials. Another group of subjects was presented with the same task as the first group, but with a limited number of trials. In the third condition, subjects were permitted to self-regulate the number of trials and were allowed to discontinue studying once they felt that they had attained mastery on the test.

Corroborating Carroll's model, results indicated that when the time allocated to learn was reduced by the experimenter, performance was adversely affected on the tests. However, more interestingly, children who were allowed to self-regulate their studying time used only 68% of the time the experimenters predicted that they needed. This failure to study was correlated significantly with lower performance levels on the multiple choice tests. Although the children were permitted to take more trials, they did not exercise this time option. It is unclear whether the self-regulators prematurely ended the task due to boredom, fatigue, misperceptions of their achieved mastery, poor time management skills, or social desirability (the belief that finishing quickly indicates higher ability).

In addition to serving as an index of aptitude, study time has been used as an indicator of student motivation. Morris, Surber, and Bijou (1978) studied student procrastination during self-paced instruction. Subjects who enrolled in a PSI section of a college psychology course were randomly assigned to self-paced or instructor-paced conditions. During a semester, all students were expected to complete 15 units of the curriculum, and upon completion of each unit, students were required to attain 90% mastery on a test. In the self-paced condition, students could complete the course at their own rate during the semester. In the instructor-paced condition, students were required to master at least 1 unit of material each week.

Results indicated no differences between the groups in the final grades: Over 90% of the subjects in both groups achieved an A in the course. There was no difference between the two groups in the number of units covered; however, the pacing of the groups did differ significantly. Instead of completing the units according to a uniform time schedule as the instructor-paced group did, the self-paced group displayed "procrastination patterns" in their completion rate. Because these patterns of delay were not associated with diminished overall achievement, they did not necessarily imply poor time management skills. They may have indicated merely that the "dilatory" students exercised their full time options in meeting the course requirements. Perhaps other courses, which did not allow for such time flexibility, were given priority over this self-paced course. These students may have been skilled in meeting deadlines, and their response pattern merely reflected the type of reward contingency used by the instructor.

Wallace and Pear (1977) discussed characteristic response patterns in people's behavioral progress toward deadlines. The novelist Irving Wallace reported that he often is less productive in the beginning stages of writing a chapter than he is in the final stages. During the last few days on each chapter, he increases his writing time by significantly decreasing other potential distractions. He recounted feeling a growing impulse to complete his work, a learning effect that has been historically termed a *goal gradient phenomenon* (Hilgard & Bower, 1975). Wallace attempted to manage his work time more effectively by keeping daily records of his written output. This graph enabled him to increase his self-observations and judgments of daily progress and provided direct evidence of a fixed ratio reinforcement effect wherein his daily word count increased as he neared the end of each chapter.

Similar effects occur when students are less strict with their management of time a week before a final exam than they are the night before a test. Thus, it appears that goal gradient effects can occur whether an outcome is self-imposed (e.g., the chapter deadlines in the Wallace and

Pear, 1977, study) or imposed by an instructor (e.g., the completion date in the traditional course in the Morris et al., 1978, study).

Self-Monitoring and Academic Study Time

Researchers have shown that successful learners spend more time studying difficult items than easier ones (Le Ny, Denhiere, & Le Taillanter, 1972; Zacks, 1969). Furthermore, Nelson and Leonesio (1988) showed that unsuccessful students fail to allocate enough study time to retain the difficult items over time. The authors speculated that although those students test themselves and find that they have mastered the item immediately after studying it, they neglect to test for long-term recall. During an actual test, students might fail an item due to the lack of storage in long-term memory. If more time were spent studying the material, the student's transfer from short-term to long-term storage might be improved. This conclusion is consistent with Maki and Berry's (1984) finding that effective goal setting involves accurate monitoring of one's comprehension and predicting of how well one will remember the material in the future.

How can students be taught to self-monitor their academic learning more effectively? Mount and Terrill (1977) assigned undergraduate volunteers to various recording conditions in which there were two target behaviors: the amount of time that students studied for class, and the amount of time they experienced "guilt" about studying when they weren't engaged in it. The type of target behavior did not influence the effectiveness of these self-monitoring results differentially. Students who used note cards and graph paper achieved significantly higher final examination grades than those who used either recording form alone. The authors concluded that the superiority of the combined method of self-monitoring was due to its provision of more continuous feedback than either method alone. This study clearly showed that instructions to self-monitor time use on recording forms had an impact on college students' achievement.

There is some evidence that self-monitoring time use may not be as beneficial as student monitoring of other dimensions of academic learning. Morgan (1985) compared the effectiveness of college students' self-monitoring of subgoal attainment with self-monitoring of distal goals, time use, or studying. A course in educational psychology was divided into separate study sessions. Students in the subgoal self-monitoring group were asked to rate their attainment of a number of specific behavioral objectives for the session, whereas students in the distal self-monitoring group rated their meeting of a single comprehensive goal for the study session. Those who were assigned to the time self-monitoring group set time aside for studying and kept a record of actual time spent studying. Some students in each group were asked to turn in their study notes (an extrinsic note-taking condition), and the other students were asked to take notes but were not asked to turn them in (an intrinsic note-taking condition). Students in a control group did not self-monitor except for those in the extrinsic note-taking condition (an activity self-monitoring group).

According to the final examination results, students who self-monitored subgoal attainment outperformed those who self-monitored either distal goal attainment, study time, or their study activities. Interestingly, the group that self-monitored time use actually studied significantly longer; however, their examination performance was not improved significantly. In addition to the benefits on learning, self-monitoring of subgoals enhanced the students' intrinsic interest in the course according to a semantic differential scale. The requirement that students turn in their notes did not affect their examination performance significantly, but it did combine with self-monitoring of subgoals to improve their intrinsic interest in the course. These results suggest that self-monitoring of time use may divert a learner's attention from other more essential process dimensions of learning if it is not integrated as just one component of a strategic approach to studying and learning.

Planning, Goal Setting, and Self-Efficacy to Regulate Time

Schunk and Swartz (in press) reported somewhat similar findings regarding students' goal setting. It has been theorized that goals help individuals to direct their attention to tasks, and to increase their effort, persistence, and self-monitoring (Locke, Shaw, Saari, & Latham, 1981). Schunk and Swartz compared the effectiveness of *process* and *product* goals during writing. The process goals focused on using a specific writing strategy, and product goals focused on writing paragraphs. Product goals are similar to time use goals because both involve outcomes of learning. These researchers hypothesized that process goals would focus the students' self-monitoring on their progress in learning the writing strategy, whereas product goals or no goals (control) would not focus attention on key strategy steps during acquisition. In addition, some students in the process goal condition received progress feedback during training. Students with process goals who were given progress feedback displayed the greatest strategy maintenance and transfer. Students with process goals who did not receive feedback did better than subjects with product goals or no goals. In addition, the self-efficacy of the students with process goals was significantly higher than those of students in a control group. These results suggested that when self-monitoring activities are diverted from strategy processes, learning can suffer. From an information processing perspective (e.g., Carver & Scheier, 1981), learners should self-monitor process components until they are mastered fully before shifting to performance outcomes. Outcome monitoring is theorized to be superior once learning goals are reached, and performance execution becomes the primary goal. This dimension of self-monitoring academic study time needs to be specifically investigated in future research.

There is evidence that students' goal setting is closely associated with planning. Britton and Tesser (1991) factor analyzed a questionnaire developed to measure college students' planning of their study time. This analysis revealed three major factors: short-range planning, time attitudes, and long-range planning. Short-range planning covers a time span of a week or less, and long-range planning covers more than this time span. The domain of time attitudes measures whether students feel that their time is used efficiently, whether they feel in control of how this time is spent, and whether time use is self-monitored.

Britton and Tesser were interested in whether the cumulative grade-point average (GPA) of college students was influenced by their time management skills. To control for the possible fact that time management is just an aspect of intelligence, they utilized the Scholastic Aptitude Test (SAT) as a traditional measure of intelligence. They hoped to compare the separate contributions of time management skills and intelligence to the GPA. It was found that only the time aptitude and short-range planning components of their scale were significant predictors of cumulative GPA. Furthermore, the effects of short-range planning and time attitude were shown to be independent of and stronger predictors of GPA than the SAT. Thus, the study provided empirical evidence of the influence of time management on scholastic achievement.

Britton and Tesser noted that their time attitude measure is similar to measures of self-efficacy. According to Bandura (1989), self-efficacy involves an individual's beliefs about one's ability to control events. The time attitude component includes items that directly measure the feeling of being in charge of one's time and being able to say "no" to people, in order to concentrate on homework. Bandura (1989) stated that high efficacy increases perseverance and leads to greater learning. Britton and Tesser suggested that their study of college students provided some support for Bandura's assertion that self-efficacy is related to greater persistence.

There is recent evidence that students' perceptions of efficacy in controlling their time have affective and somatic benefits as well as cognitive benefits. Macan, Shahani, Dipboye, and Phillips (1990) developed a questionnaire to assess time management behaviors and attitudes of college students. Of the four subscales that comprise this instrument, Perceived Control of Time involved judgments of self-efficacy. This subscale, which was similar to Britton and Tesser's (1991) Time Attitude items, was the most predictive of student outcomes. Students who perceived greater control of their time reported significantly higher performance evaluations, greater work and life satisfactions, less role ambiguity and overload, and fewer job-induced and somatic tensions.

Britton and Tesser found that student time management was not only related to planning and self-efficacy, it was also closely linked to goal-setting. It makes intuitive sense that goal setting should have an effect on time management as it does on other self-regulated learning processes. There is also evidence that quantitative level of a goal has an impact on students' use of their time. Laport and Nath (1976) divided students into an experimenter-paced and an unlimited study time condition in a reading experiment. Subjects were further divided into a high goal condition (told to aim for 90% mastery on a test), a low goal condition (told to aim for 25% mastery on a test), and a general condition (to do the best they could). Students given unlimited study time and the high goal were found to spent more time studying, and achieved higher recall than the other groups. It was noteworthy that even the subjects in the experimenter-paced group with high goals exhibited higher retention than the other remaining groups. Thus, the quantitative level of students' goals must be considered along with other self-regulative processes in their management of study time.

The studies reviewed thus far support the notion that time regulation includes the following components: self-monitoring, planning, self-efficacy, and goal setting and use. These processes play a central role in social cognitive views of self-regulation (Bandura, 1989; Schunk, 1989; Zimmerman, 1989).

TIME MANAGEMENT STRATEGY USE
AND TRAINING

There is a growing body of evidence to suggest that students' purposive use of a strategy to manage their academic study time is a vital component of other strategic efforts to achieve in school. Weinstein, Schulte, and Palmer (1987) included time management as one of the domains of the Learning and Study Strategies Inventory (LASSI). The LASSI is a 77-item diagnostic/prescriptive self-report measure of strategic, goal-directed learning for college students that focuses on thoughts, attitudes, beliefs, and behaviors that relate to academic success and can be changed and enhanced through educational interventions. It provides standardized scores and national norms for 10 different scales: Attitude, Motivation, Time Management, Anxiety, Concentration, Information Processing, Selecting Main Ideas, Study Aids, Self-Testing, and Test Strategies.

Students' scores on the Time Management scale consistently relate significantly to their scores on all the other scales included in the LASSI. This is not the case for most of the other scale scores. For example, in a sample of 276 college students participating in an undergraduate learning-to-learn course (Weinstein, Stone, & Hanson, 1993), the correlations with the other LASSI scales were Attitude, $r = .59$; Motivation, $r = .74$; Anxiety, $r = .26$; Concentration, $r = .68$; Information Processing, $r = .41$; Selecting Main Ideas, $r = .32$; Study Aids, $r = .40$; Self Testing, $r = .54$; Test Strategies, $r = .45$. These data indicate that time management is a key component and relates to many other aspects of strategic learning and self-regulation of academic studying.

Zimmerman and Martinez-Pons (1986) developed an interview schedule that assessed students' planning and goal setting as well as their use of 12 other strategies to self-regulate their learning. In a study of 10th grade students, these researchers found that high achievers displayed significantly more goal setting and planning than low achievers. This variable was defined by the authors as "statements indicating student setting of educational goals or subgoals and planning for sequencing, timing, and completing activities related to these goals" (Zimmerman and Martinez-Pons, 1986, p. 619). Use of this strategy made a significant contribution to the overall prediction of the students' achievement track in school.

Wibrowski (1992) conducted structured interviews with high achieving and regular students attending an inner city school. The questions focused on home activities as well as classroom and out-of-class events. Among 18 academic activities that were identified, two were associated with academic study time: time accounting and time budgeting. *Time accounting* referred to statements indicating awareness of the specific time when activities take place, and *time budgeting* statements referred to the amount of time allotted to an activity. Both of these time-related activities were predictive of the students' degree of academic self-regulation according to their teachers. Even more interesting was the correlation of these two activities with other academic activities. These academic time activities, which fell in the personal domain according to social cognitive theory, correlated with more activities in the other two triadic domains (i.e., behavioral and environmental) than any other activity. For example, student reports of time accounting were associated with their keeping and reviewing learning records, engagement in homework, using a specific place of study, structuring their environment to learn, engaging in reading, seeking information, and seeking social assistance. Time budgeting was highly correlated not only with time accounting but also with engagement in homework, keeping learning records, using a specific place to study, and structuring their environment to learn. The author concluded that self-regulated students rely heavily on time cues when they engage in other learning activities.

The ultimate pedagogical question is whether students can be taught to more effectively manage their own study time, particularly those who are underachieving. There is evidence that adults' time management skills can be improved. Judd, McCombs, and Dobrovolny (1979) interviewed U.S. Air Force recruits who finished a self-paced computer based course and found that many were unable to manage their time effectively. A software program called Student Progress Management (SPM) was implemented that gave a target course completion date and daily feedback on progress toward the deadline. In addition to their computerized instruction, one group of students plotted their progress daily toward the target completion date and discussed these graphs with their respective instructors. Results indicated that students who received both the SPM and the additional training displayed a significant decrease in completion time compared to the recruits who received only the SPM training. Judd et al. concluded that although the recruits were helped by the time management software, those who plotted and discussed their progress exhibited the most improvement. This finding substantiated the importance of teaching students to monitor their time progress.

There is other research that indicates time management skills can be taught. Woolfolk and Woolfolk (1986) gave preservice teachers didactic training and 2 weeks of supervised practice in time management skills. Didactic training included reading a book, watching a film, and attending a lecture on the need for time management skills. Upon completion of this training, the teachers completed standardized daily planning and time monitoring logs under supervision. Other teachers were given didactic instruction without supervised practice.

Results indicated didactic management training was effective for increasing both groups' promptness of submission of the intermediate deadline reports (although this training did not seem to have a promptness effect on the delayed deadline reports). Teachers who were given supervised practice submitted more reports than their unsupervised counterparts. The former group also did not display a significant decrease in self-perceived ability to manage time after subsequent student teaching experience, whereas the latter group did show declines.

The studies of Judd et al. (1979) and Woolfolk and Woolfolk (1986) indicated that time management skills can be taught and that optimal outcomes occur when traditional didactic instruction is combined with actual practice of new skills. Most importantly, both studies addressed the problem that often students who learn self-regulating techniques in a training program fail to internalize and transfer these skills (McKeachie, Pintrich, & Lin, 1985). Both investigations revealed that for training to be effective, students need to be taught what the strategy is, and how and when to use it. Students also need to be taught why a specific strategy is important so that they will be motivated to use it. These ideas are congruent with what is recommended in the literature for general strategy training (Borkowski, Carr, & Pressley, 1987; Paris et al., 1983).

PROGRAM TO IMPROVE STUDENT
SELF-REGULATION OF ACADEMIC STUDY TIME

Using a model of strategic learning that incorporates skill, will, and self-regulation components, a course has been developed at the University of Texas to help students develop greater expertise as learners (Weinstein, in press). The formal title of this course is EDP 310 Introduction to Educational Psychology: Individual Learning Skills. It is an academic course taken for one semester (approximately 15 weeks) for a grade. The students meet in classes of 25–28. The course content focuses on helping students to become more strategic and effective learners. Specific topics include becoming a strategic learner; the role of goal setting, analysis, and using; the role of self-management in strategic learning; management plans for learning; time management; applications of the model for various academic tasks such as note taking, listening, making presentations, preparing for and taking tests, studying in different content areas, and using feedback; and coping with academic stress and frustration.

Learning about time management strategies is an integral part of the curriculum. Initially, time management was taught as a separate topic in the course, but increases in students' use of time management strategies were not maintained well across the semester or into following semesters (based on homework) assignments, student interview data, and LASSI scores). Currently, time management is introduced early in the semester and is integrated into the rest of the curriculum so that students have numerous opportunities to test out and receive feedback about their use of time management strategies from their own self-monitoring and evaluations, as well as the instructor's feedback. Direct conceptual relations and practical applications of the interaction of time management strategies and other topics in the course are also explicitly made. For example, time management strategies are presented as part of the self-control strategies taught, and they are related to beliefs about self-efficacy and positive affect toward learning.

One problem consistently encountered is students' lack of awareness about how they spend their time. One of the first assignments in this area before the topic is ever discussed in class is to have the students keep a log of their activities at 30-min intervals for an entire week. Students often express shock at the data they generate. These individual logs are also used to identify personal time wasted and sources of procrastination, as well as the degree to which these are potentially under the student's control. Time management principles and strategies are then discussed in the context of strategic learning as both a reflection and a cause. Strategies for managing time as well as for reducing or eliminating time wasters are presented, and students practice using them in their classes. Students are also required to monitor their success with these techniques and self-analyze their successes and failures. They also receive feedback from the instructors.

Another common problem students experience is a poor sense of how long it takes to complete academic tasks and assignments. Even when they learn to set goals for their study activities, these goals are often unrealistic due to a lack of understanding of the steps involved and the time required. A series of exercises is used to address this problem. For example, students are often required to fill out a brief form before working on an academic task at their desk or in the library. They have to estimate the amount of time the task will take and what is involved in reaching their study goal. At the end of the time period they have allowed, they must analyze their progress—did they have enough time to complete the task? Was there too much time allotted? Was the task more complex than they thought? How would they approach a similar task or assignment in the future? Exercises such as these not only help students' use of time management strategies, but they also help students' understanding of the interrelatedness of the components of self-regulated learning.

The effectiveness of this instructional program has been evaluated with the sample of 276 college students (Weinstein et al., 1993). Using students' entry-level scores on the Time Management Scale of the LASSI, they were divided into three groups: students with low time-management scores (Low-TM, n = 99); middle time-management scores (Middle-TM, n = 90); and high time-management scores (High-TM, n = 87). Students in the Low-TM group received 56.10% of the D and F grades in the course. Students in the High-TM group received 68.97% of the A and B grades in the course. Finally, a follow-up study, conducted at the end of the semester after they participated in the learning-to-learn course, revealed that the overall grade-point averages (on a 4-point scale) of the students in the Low-TM group went from 1.68 to 2.10, the students in the Middle-TM group went from 1.88 to 2.35, and the students in the High-TM group went from 1.90 to 2.49. These results not only highlight the relationship of time management to college students' academic achievement, but they also highlight the potential success of instructional interventions in self-regulated learning. In another study just completed, gains in grade-point averages were maintained over the course of four semesters.

FUTURE RESEARCH ON SELF-REGULATION OF ACADEMIC STUDY TIME

There are many unanswered questions regarding students' use of their academic study time. For example, relatively little is known about adapting learning strategy instruction to developmental differences in students' ability to use their study time. There is some evidence of developmental differences in children's ability to use their study time effectively (Masur, McIntyre, & Flavell, 1973). Future research should examine whether elementary school children can profit from strategy instruction in time planning and management.

In addition to developmental considerations, researchers should investigate the role of individual differences in cognitive ability (Swing, Stoiber, & Peterson, 1988) and in motivation orientation (Meece & Courtney, 1992; Pintrich & Schrauben, 1992) in using study time information. Different levels of initial time management ability or motivation might require alternative modes of strategy instruction. There is some evidence that student differences in motivation may affect their responsiveness to different forms of instruction. Gettinger (1989) found that elementary school students who self-initiated study of material for the sake of mastery did not benefit from incentives to increase their perseverance. However, students who did not self-initiate did benefit from the offer of incentives. Clearly, the topic of individual differences in study time management and strategy instruction merits further research.

CONCLUSIONS

The resident philosopher of baseball, Yogi Berra, once remarked about the afternoon shadows in left field at Yankee Stadium during the fall, "It gets late early out there" (Pepi, 1988, p. 153). Students who fail to plan their academic study time ahead, who fail to set specific goals for themselves, and who fail to monitor their progress are also at a disadvantage in classes with implicit and explicit deadlines. Time runs out early for them as it does for Yankee left fielders, and these students inevitably arrive in class only partially prepared, turn in papers that aren't carefully revised, and take tests after only last-minute cramming. There is now clear evidence that students' awareness of and strategic efforts to manage their study time does make a difference in their academic achievement. Time management strategies are not only academically helpful; they enhance students' personal perceptions of self-efficacy and intrinsic interest. Both of these constructs have been found to be highly associated with students' academic motivation. These findings indicate that academic study time can be described and analyzed in terms of general models of self-regulation.

However, this review of the literature reveals there may be drawbacks if students focus too narrowly on time criteria: Self-monitoring time outcomes may detract from task-related learning processes, and this in turn can diminish achievement. In general, it is logical to classify students' time-management strategies as supportive rather than primary, because time use is usually secondary to task mastery outcomes during the learning. Nevertheless, as Dansereau et al. (1979) noted, time regulation strategies are vital for successful academic outcomes. Clearly, more attention must be given to this issue in future research.

Ultimately, the importance of time use during learning is undoubtedly context dependent: Some tasks have no time constraints, but in other cases (such as a timed test or an assignment with a short deadline), speed of performance and efficiency in time use are essential. However, even in the case of professional writing, which is typically self-paced, most successful writers employ a wide variety of time management procedures, such as setting aside a regular writing period during each day, keeping word counts of each day's output, and using the clock as a guide to shift from one activity to another. Therefore, the ultimate goal of time management strategies is to use them in a self-regulated way—such that students can systematically plan, self-monitor, and self-adjust their effectiveness.

ACKNOWLEDGMENT

We would like to express our appreciation to Dale H. Schunk for his helpful comments on an earlier draft of this chapter.

REFERENCES

Atkinson, J. W., & Feather, N. H. (Eds.). (1966). *A theory of achievement motivation.* New York: Wiley.

Bandura, A. (1986). *Social foundations of thought and action: A social cognitive theory.* Englewood Cliffs, NJ: Prentice-Hall.

Bandura, A. (1989). Human agency in social cognitive theory. *American Psychologist, 44,* 1175–1184.

Boice, R. (1982). Increasing the writing productivity of "blocked" academicians. *Behavior Research and Therapy, 20,* 197–207.

Borkowski, J. G., Carr, M., & Pressley, M. (1987). Spontaneous strategy use: Perspectives from metacognitive theory. *Intelligence, 11*, 61–75.

Britton, B. K., & Glynn, S. (1989). Mental management and creativity. In J. Glover, R. Ronning, & C. Reynolds (Eds.), *Handbook of creativity* (pp. 429–440). New York: Plenum.

Britton, B. K., & Tesser, A. (1991). Effects of time management practices on college grades. *Educational Psychology, 83*, 405–410.

Carroll, J. B. (1963). A mode of school learning. *Teachers College Record, 64*, 723–733.

Carroll, J. B. (1989). The Carroll Model: A 25-year retrospective and prospective view. *Educational Researcher, 18*, 26–31.

Carver, C. S., & Scheier, M. F. (1981). *Attention and self-regulation: A control theory approach to human behavior.* New York: Springer-Verlag.

Dansereau, D. F., McDonald, B. A., Collins, K. W., Garland, J., Holley, C. D., Diekhoff, G. M., & Evans, S. H. (1979). Evaluation of a learning strategy system. In H. F. O'Neil & C. D. Spielberger (Eds.), *Cognitive and affective learning strategies* (pp. 3–43). New York: Academic Press.

Delzell, J. K. (1985, September). Outwitting the time thieves. *Music Educator's Journal*, 26–29.

Flavell, J. (1979). Metacognition and cognitive monitoring: A new era in cognitive-developmental inquiry. *American Psychologist, 34*, 906–911.

Garner, R. (1990). When children and adults do not use learning strategies: Toward a theory of settings. *Review of Educational Research, 60*, 517–529.

Gettinger, M. (1985). Time allocated and time spent relative to time needed for learning as determinants of achievement. *Journal of Educational Psychology, 77*, 3–11.

Gettinger, M. (1989). Effects of maximizing time spent and minimizing time needed for learning on pupil achievement. *American Educational Research Journal, 26*, 73–91.

Gettinger, M., & White, M. A. (1979). Which is the stronger correlate of school learning? Time to learn or measured intelligence? *Journal of Educational Psychology, 71*, 405–412.

Ghatala, E. S., Levin, J. R., Foorman, B. R., & Pressley, M. (1989). Improving children's regulation of their reading time. *Contemporary Educational Psychology, 14*, 49–66.

Harris, M. B. (1974). Accelerating dissertation writing: A case study. *Psychology Reports, 34*, 984–986.

Hilgard, E., & Bower, G. H. (1975). *Theories of learning* (4th ed.). New York: Appleton-Century-Crofts.

Johnson, K. R., & Rudskin, R. S. (1977). *Behavioral instruction: An evaluative review.* Washington, DC: American Psychological Association.

Judd, W. A., McCombs, B. L., & Dobrovolny, J. L. (1979). Time management as a learning strategy for individualized instruction. In H. F. O'Neil & C. D. Spielberger (Eds.), *Cognitive and affective learning strategies* (pp. 133–175). New York: Academic Press.

Keller, F. S. (1968). Good-bye teacher! *Journal of Applied Behavioral Analysis, 1*, 79–84.

Laport, R. E., & Nath, R. (1976). Role of performance goals in prose learning. *Journal of Educational Psychology, 68*, 260–289.

Le Ny, J. F., Denhiere, G., & Le Taillanter, D. (1972). Regulation of study-time and interstimulus similarity in self-paced learning conditions. *Acta Psychologica, 36*, 280–289.

Locke, E. A., Shaw, K. N., Saari, L. M., & Latham, G. P. (1981). Goal setting and task performance: 1969–1980. *Psychological Bulletin, 90*, 125–152.

Macan, T., Shahani, C., Dipboye, R. L., & Phillips, A. P. (1990). College students' time management: Correlations with academic performance and stress. *Journal of Educational Psychology, 82*, 760–768.

Maki, R. H., & Berry, S. L. (1984). Metacomprehension of text material. *Journal of Experimental Psychology: Learning, Memory, and Cognition, 10*, 663–679.

Masur, E. F., McIntyre, C. W., & Flavell, J. H. (1973). Developmental changes in apportionment of study time among items in a multitrial free recall task. *Journal of Experimental Psychology, 15*, 237–246.

McKeachie, W. J., Pintrich, P. R., & Lin, Y. G. (1985). Teaching learning strategies. *Educational Psychologist, 20*, 153–160.

Meece, J., & Courtney, D. P. (1992). Gender differences in students' perceptions: Consequences for achievement-related choices. In D. H. Schunk & J. Meece (Eds.), *Student perceptions in the classrooms* (pp. 209–227). Hillsdale, NJ: Lawrence Erlbaum Associates.

Morgan, M. (1985). Self-monitoring of attained subgoals in private study. *Journal of Educational Psychology, 77*, 623–630.

Morris, E. K., Surber, C. F., & Bijou, S. W. (1978). Self pacing versus instructor pacing: Achievement, evaluations, and retention. *Journal of Educational Psychology, 70*, 224–230.

Mount, M. K., & Terrill, F. J. (1977). Improving examination scores through self-monitoring. *Journal of Educational Research, 71*, 70–73.

Nelson, T. O., & Leonesio, R. J. (1988). Allocation of self-paced study time and the labor in vain effect. *Journal of Experimental Psychology, Learning, Memory, and Cognition, 14*, 676–686.

Paris, S. G., Lipson, M. Y., & Wixson, K. K. (1983). Becoming a strategic reader. *Contemporary Educational Psychology, 8*, 293–316.

Pepi, P. (1988). *The wit and wisdom of Yogi Berra.* New York: St. Martin's Press.

Pintrich, P. R., & Schrauben, B. (1992). Students' motivational beliefs and their cognitive engagement in classroom academic tasks. In D. H. Schunk & J. Meece (Eds.), *Student perceptions in the classroom* (pp. 149–183). Hillsdale, NJ: Lawrence Erlbaum Associates.

Rennie, D. L., & Brewer, L. (1987). A grounded theory of thesis blocking. *Teaching of Psychology, 48*, 83–92.

Schunk, D. H. (1981). Modeling and attributional effects on children's achievement: A self-efficacy analysis. *Journal of Educational Psychology, 73*, 93–105.

Schunk, D. H. (1989). Social cognitive theory and self-regulated learning. In B. J. Zimmerman & D. H. Schunk (Eds.), *Self-regulated learning and academic achievement: Theory, research, and practice* (pp. 83–110). New York: Academic Press.

Schunk, D. H., & Swartz, C. (1993). Goals and progress feedback: Effects on self-efficacy and writing achievement. *Contemporary Educational Psychology, 18*, 337–354.

Swing, S. R., Stoiber, K. C., & Peterson, P. L. (1988). Effects of alternative classroom-based interventions on students' mathematical problem solving. *Cognition and Instruction, 5*, 123–191.

Wallace, I., & Pear, J. (1977). Self-control techniques of famous novelists. *Journal of Applied Behavioral Analysis, 10*, 515–525.

Weinstein, C. E. (in press). Students at-risk for academic failure: Learning to learn classes. In K. Pritchard & R. M. Sawyer (Eds.), *Handbook of college teaching: Theory and applications.* Westport, CT: Greenwood.

Weinstein, C. E., & Mayer, R. E. (1986). The teaching of learning strategies. In M. C. Wittrock (Ed.), *Handbook of research on teaching* (pp. 315–327). New York: Macmillan.

Weinstein, C. E., & Meyer, D. K. (1991). Cognitive learning strategies and college teaching. *New Directions for Teaching and Learning, 45*, 15–26.

Weinstein, C. E., Schulte, A. C., & Palmer, D. R. (1987). *LASSI: Learning and study strategies inventory.* Clearwater, FL: H & H Publishing.

Weinstein, C. E., Stone, G., & Hanson, G. H. (1993). *The long-term effects of a strategic learning course for college students.* Unpublished manuscript, University of Texas, Austin.

Wibrowski, C. R. (1992). Self-regulated learning processes among inner city students. Unpublished dissertation, Graduate School, City University of New York.

Woolfolk, A. E., & Woolfolk, R. L. (1986). Time management: An experimental investigation. *Journal of School Psychology, 24*, 267–275.

Zacks, R. T. (1969). Invariance of total learning time under different conditions of practice. *Journal of Experimental Psychology, 82*, 441–447.

Zimmerman, B. J. (1989). A social cognitive view of self-regulated academic learning. *Journal of Educational Psychology, 81*, 329–339.

Zimmerman, B. J., Bandura, A., & Martinez-Pons, M. (1992). Self-motivation for academic attainment: The role of self-efficacy beliefs and personal goal setting. *American Educational Research Journal, 29,* 663–676.

Zimmerman, B. J., & Martinez-Pons, M. (1986). Development of a structured interview for assessing student use of self regulated learning strategies. *American Educational Research Journal, 23,* 614–628.

Zimmerman, B. J., & Martinez-Pons, M. (1992). Perceptions of efficacy and strategy use in the self-regulation of learning. In D. H. Schunk & J. Meece (Eds.), *Student perceptions in the classroom: Causes and consequences* (pp. 185–207). Hillsdale, NJ: Lawrence Erlbaum Associates.

IV

Self-Regulation of Performance Outcomes

9

The Role and Development of Self-Regulation in the Writing Process

Steve Graham
Karen R. Harris
University of Maryland

In describing his writing habits, Irving Wallace, a famous contemporary novelist, noted that he often kept a detailed chart of his progress when writing a book, recording the number of pages written by the end of each working day (Wallace & Pear, 1977). According to Wallace (1971), the practice of monitoring his literary output helped him establish discipline over his writing: "A chart on the wall served as such a discipline, its figures scolding me or encouraging me" (p. 65).

Wallace also used a variety of strategies to help him develop and manage the writing of his novels (Wallace, 1971; Wallace & Pear, 1977). These included making outlines, developing scenes and characters, working out the sequence of the story in his head and then roughly on paper, and underlining story problems needing additional work. As he began to write each novel, he carefully monitored the process, making many revisions in his plans and outlines. Once a first draft was completed, he returned to it again and again, rereading the entire manuscript and revising it as he went along.

Wallace illustrated some of the self-regulatory processes skilled writers use when composing. When preparing and writing his novels, he was constantly managing the writing process by checking, planning, monitoring, evaluating, and revising. In this chapter, we explore how students can learn to use these same mechanisms for regulating what and how they write. We begin by taking a more detailed look at the role of self-regulation in the composing process, emphasizing how important theoretical constructs in self-regulated learning apply to writing.

WRITING AND SELF-REGULATION

Self-regulation holds a prominent position in current models of the writing process. Theorists have used constructs such as the writing "monitor" (Flower & Hayes, 1980) or executive control (Scardamalia & Bereiter, 1983) to describe self-regulation and volitional processes that occur during writing.

In the influential model of writing developed by Hayes and Flower (1986), for example, skilled writing is viewed as a goal-directed activity. The writer directs the process of composing by identifying and organizing goals and subgoals for what to do and say. Writers accomplish these intentions or goals by deftly bringing into play cognitive processes involving planning, sentence generation, and revising. Hayes and Flower posited the existence of a control structure, the monitor, to coordinate these processes. The *monitor* is "a strategist which determines when one moves from one process to the next" (Flower & Hayes, 1981, p. 374). The "strategist's" decisions are determined by the writer's goals and habits, allowing for a variety of complex interactions among components. To illustrate, a writer can select to initiate the process of revising at any point during the composing process, interrupting other writing processes if necessary. A writing goal or plan might be revised or reformulated while planning, or a sentence might be erased and restructured as the writer is in the act of putting words on paper.

Hayes and Flower noted that "a great part of skill in writing is the ability to monitor and direct one's own composing process" (Flower & Hayes, 1980, p. 39). When composing, writers must bring into play various processes and subprocesses for accomplishing their goals and completing the writing task; activate different levels of processing, ranging from the unconscious and automatic to the highly intentional and conscious; and deploy processing capability to a variety of functions enabling the act of writing to proceed (Bereiter, 1980). Processes such as planning, sentence generation, and revising must be orchestrated so that the writer can switch attention between these functions and a host of mechanical and substantive concerns (Scardamalia & Bereiter, 1986). "A writer caught in the act looks . . . like a very busy switchboard operator trying to juggle a number of demands on her attention and constraints on what she can do" (Flower & Hayes, 1980, p. 33).

The Hayes and Flower model illustrates that writing is intentional and resourceful. Although the degree of control that individual writers exert depends on factors such as experience, level of knowledge, and metacognitive skills, as well as the writing task and the accompanying social and physical context (Zimmerman, 1989), composing is not a passive activity. It happens by writers, not to them. The theoretical constructs underlying prominent models of self-regulated learning possess considerable potential for describing and explaining the actions of writers.

A Self-Regulation View of Writing

Zimmerman (1989) proposed that self-regulation occurs when one uses personal (or self-) processes to strategically regulate behavior and the environment. He indicated that there are three general classes of strategies that an individual uses to exert control: strategies for controlling behavior, the environment, or covert processes. To illustrate, when working on his seminal work *On the Origin of Species by Natural Selection*, Charles Darwin stabilized the amount of work he completed each day by using a behavioral strategy involving self-evaluation (Stone, 1978). Each time he proved a point and provided a footnote to buttress it, he kicked a pebble away from a daily self-defined pile of pebbles. Similarly, Victor Hugo forced himself to write regularly by manipulating his working environment—he confined himself to his study by removing his clothes and telling his servant not to return them until an appointed hour (Wallace & Pear, 1977). Likewise, Rudyard Kipling set a personal goal to rewrite his own work multiple times on the grounds that it could always be improved (White, 1982).

Zimmerman (1989) further postulated that the use of personal, behavioral, and environmental strategies is regulated by an enactive feedback loop. This involves learning from the consequence of one's actions. Strategies that are successful tend to be retained, whereas those that are not are abandoned (Schunk, 1989). For example, system and record keeping were the hallmarks of Anthony Trollope's writing. The author of more than 50 novels, including *Barchester Towers*, he arose early every morning; spent 30 minutes reading the previous day's work; and then with watch before him, wrote 250 words every 15 minutes, counting each word to record how much was written each day (Adams, 1991). Although Trollope was told that appliances like these were "beneath the notice of a man of genius" (Trollope, 1946, p. 117), he used them because they helped him write regularly, day in and day out.

The proposed feedback loop also provides information that enables one regulative process to influence another. Or in other words, self-regulation involves reciprocal interactions among behaviors, environmental events, and covert processes (Bandura, 1986). For instance, students who use writing criteria in the form of questions to evaluate their own or other's writing appear to eventually internalize at least some of these criteria, resulting in improvements in their own writing (Hillocks, 1986). Thus, use of this strategy enabled students to augment their knowledge base about writing (personal process) and, in turn, this new knowledge served as a guide (personal or covert strategy) for their own writing (a behavioral response).

Three strategies that are hypothesized to play a key role in the enactive feedback loop are self-observation, self-judgment, and self-reaction (Zimmerman & Schunk, 1989). *Self-observation* refers to systematically monitoring one's performance; *self-judgment* involves systematically comparing one's performance to a standard or goal; and *self-reaction* includes responses to one's performance. An anecdote concerning Ernest Hemingway provides an example of these three strategies in operation (Plimpton, 1965). Hemingway recorded his daily output of words (self-observation) on a chart mounted under a gazelle head. If he did not write as much as planned (self-judgment), he curtailed his fishing (self-reaction).

Finally, theorists have identified a variety of different self-regulation strategies for controlling behavioral, environmental, and covert processes (cf. Corno, 1992; Schunk, 1989; Zimmerman, 1989). The use of many of these strategies in writing can be illustrated by examining how the current chapter was developed. In preparing this chapter we used self-regulation strategies to establish a sense of ownership, manage the writing process, and maintain and reenergize our commitment to the project. As we describe these processes in the following pages, individual self-regulation strategies are identified in parentheses, using the categories established by Zimmerman (1989): self-evaluating, organizing and transforming, goal setting and planning, seeking information, keeping records and monitoring, environmental structuring, self-consequating, rehearsing and memorizing, seeking social assistance, and reviewing records.

Writing the Chapter.   When we were first asked to prepare this chapter, it was requested that we write about the self-regulation of outcomes in terms of self-instructions. Because we were more interested in writing about self-regulation in the area of composition, a topic covering a wider range of self-regulation processes but applied to a specific academic discipline, we immediately called the editors. By lobbying and seeking additional clarification, we were able to more directly establish ownership over the requested material. By personalizing the overall goals for the chapter (goal setting and planning), we increased our motivation to write it.

Once we had made a commitment to do the chapter and established a broad, overall goal for what it would address, the hard work of actually writing it became our next challenge. We began the process by developing a rudimentary outline for the structure of the chapter, establishing several writing goals (e.g., illustrate concepts via writing habits of well-known writers), and dividing up the writing task (goal setting and planning).

Next, we located and organized information on the topic. An ERIC search was completed, the table of contents of journals and books were surveyed, interesting references in articles were tracked down, and previously acquired material on the topic was gathered together (seeking information). Before starting to write, this material was read and reread, with important concepts and information underlined and written as notes (keeping records and monitoring). The notes and underlined materials, along with our own knowledge of the topic, were examined several times (*reviewing records*) as we refined our chapter outline (*organizing and transforming*). Throughout this process, we continually assessed the quality of our plans (*self-evaluating*).

Once we started writing the chapter, many of the self-regulating activities that occurred during planning continued. Although the overall plan for writing the chapter did not change dramatically, our goals grew and changed as we more carefully explored our ideas through writing (goal setting and planning). Thus, it became necessary to consult additional resources as we established a clearer idea of what the chapter would accomplish (seeking information). We were also constantly evaluating and changing what we wrote so that it matched our intentions and would be sensitive to the needs of our eventual audience (self-evaluating, and organizing and transforming).

As each of us wrote our assigned sections, we sought each other's help in phrasing ideas or exploring the relevance of a particular concept (seeking social assistance). We also found that we had to rearrange our physical environment more than once so that writing could proceed uninterrupted (environmental structuring). For example, the rest of the family might be asked to take a trip to the "Fun Zone" so "Daddy" could concentrate. The chapter even influenced our public behavior on several occasions. The first author was seen muttering to himself at the movies as he tried to memorize an idea he had for the paper (rehearsing and memorizing). Finally, it became necessary on occasion to reenergize our commitment for finishing the project. To bolster motivation, we sometimes admonished ourselves to keep working or imagined how good it would feel when the chapter was done (self-consequating).

Self-Regulation in Novice and Expert Writers

Writing is not always this neatly organized or self-regulated. For instance, more experienced writers are better able to self-regulate during writing than beginning or poor writers (cf. Graham & Harris, 1989a; Scardamalia

& Bereiter, 1985). Many children, including some college students, approach writing by using a reduced version of the Hayes and Flower (1986) model. They convert the writing task into simply telling whatever one knows—that is, writing-as-remembering or writing-by-pattern (Scardamalia & Bereiter, 1986). Text is generated as ideas come to mind, with each preceding word or sentence stimulating the development of the succeeding text. Little attention is directed at rhetorical goals, whole-text organization, the needs of the reader, or the constraints imposed by the topic.

This approach to writing appears to be especially pronounced among poor writers. In a study by Graham (1990), for instance, fourth- and sixth-grade students with learning disabilities began their essays with a simple "yes" or "no" in response to the assigned topic. This was followed by the generation of a few reasons and elaborations. On the average, the whole process took no more than 6 minutes. These students simply converted the writing assignment into a question and answer task, quickly telling whatever came to mind.

An important goal in composition instruction, therefore, is to foster the development of self-regulation in students' writing. With this goal in mind, we first examine research on explicitly teaching students self-regulatory processes or strategies for writing, including our own research on self-regulated strategy development. Then six principles for creating a writing environment in which self-regulation can flourish are presented.

OBSERVATION, JUDGMENT, AND REACTION

Instructional research designed to prompt self-regulation during writing has relied heavily on the use of self-observations, self-judgments, self-reactions, or a combination of these processes. These procedures are often used in conjunction with goal setting; consequently, research involving all of these self-regulation procedures is examined in this section.

Personal observations, judgments, and reactions, as well as goal setting, contribute to writing in three important ways. First, these strategies play an important role in the writer's regulation and management of the composing process. Self-observation activities such as referring back to one's plans or rereading text, for example, help writers maintain an awareness of their thinking and control the development of ideas (Durst, 1989). Second, these strategies help writers realize their intentions. Self-regulation not only shapes the process of composing, but also shapes the outcomes of writing as well. For instance, monitoring the quality and quantity of text helps writers determine when a paper is finished, identify weaknesses and gaps in their paper, confirm that writing goals were met, and so forth. Similarly, text is commonly revised when writers identify a discrepancy between what they intended and what they produced (Fitzgerald & Markham, 1987). Planning or listing specific topics of ideas to include will also affect how a paper is structured and what is emphasized. Third, these strategies can contribute to students' long-term development as writers (Scardamalia & Bereiter, 1985). When self-regulation strategies like self-observation or self-judgment are used during writing, they provide information that can lead to changes in what writers know and do.

Productivity

In addition to the low quality of their writing, many poor writers, especially students with learning or behavioral problems, are not especially productive (Graham & Harris, 1989a). The papers they produce are often impoverished in their detail and inordinately short. They may further have difficulty completing writing assignments and may resist well-intentioned efforts to get them to write regularly. The same types of self-regulation strategies that Ernest Hemingway and Anthony Trollope used to control their writing output, however, can be successfully used with poor writers such as these.

Hopman and Glynn (1989), for example, found that 13-year-old boys with academic difficulties were able to increase the length of their essays through goal setting and self-monitoring. Prior to writing, each student set a goal concerning the length of his paper. After writing, students counted the number of words written and the instructor noted if the criterion was met, socially reinforcing students when it was. Use of the self-regulation procedures not only increased how many words students wrote, but had a positive effect on writing quality as well.

The effects of self-observation and self-judgment on the writing fluency of 9- to 11-year-old students with behavioral difficulties and low writing productivity were examined in a study by Rumsey and Ballard (1985). During the writing period, students recorded and graphed how many words they wrote and whether they were on-task when a tone sounded at variable intervals. Students were further asked to make a general judgment about their efforts during the writing period. The use of these self-regulation procedures resulted in an increase in on-task behavior and story length, while decreasing disruptive behaviors. Removal and then reintroduction of the self-instructional procedures, however, did not result in a return to the same level of performance as when the treatment was first introduced. Consequently, students who exhibited the most variability in performance began meeting individually with the instructor each day before writing. During this time, the instructor presented a list of four desired behaviors ("I will work on my story"; "I will try to write a really good story"; "I will not talk to others"; "I will ignore people who try to interrupt me"), followed by questions designed to encourage the student to verbalize how these goals would be met. Addition of goal setting to the treatment package had a positive impact on story length and on-task behavior, while decreasing disruptive behaviors.

Harris, Graham, Reid, McElroy, and Hamby (1993) compared the effectiveness of the two self-monitoring procedures used in the Rumsey and Ballard (1985) study: recording and graphing the number of words written versus recording and graphing on-task behavior. They found that the self-monitoring procedures had a positive effect on the on-task behavior and length and quality of stories written by fifth- and sixth-grade students with learning disabilities. Although neither of the self-monitoring interventions was clearly or consistently superior to the other, attention monitoring was a more obtrusive intervention, requiring the use of special equipment.

The studies reviewed so far concentrated on increasing children's output when writing stories and essays. In contrast, two studies by Hull (1981) focused on helping college students establish the habit of writing on a regular basis outside of class. In the first study, general and remedial writers were given a personal goal for how many lines should be written in their journal each day. The graphed their daily output and received weekly feedback from their instructor on their success in meeting the assigned goals. During the second study, remedial writers used the same procedures except half of the students were assigned writing goals, while the rest set their own goals. In both studies, the self-regulation procedures increased the amount of journal writing students did outside of class. Students' output, though, was not differentially affected by who set the goal. Furthermore, when the self-regulation procedures were not in effect, student performance returned to baseline levels.

Finally, in a study by Seabaugh and Schumaker (1981), secondary students with learning disabilities and a history of noncompliance set goals for completing academic work in writing, reading, and math. Students also learned how to devise plans for completing their goals, observing and evaluating progress, and reinforcing themselves for obtaining their objectives. These procedures resulted in an increase in the number of writing assignments completed by the participating students.

These studies demonstrate that the amount that students who have difficulty in school write can be increased by asking them to observe their working behavior or monitor their productivity (Harris et al., 1993). Likewise, setting goals and monitoring performance, combined with external feedback, can increase their writing output both in and out of class (Hopman & Glynn, 1989; Hull, 1981). Writing assignments are also more likely to be completed when they monitor, evaluate, and reward their progress in pursuit of this objective (Seabaugh & Schumaker, 1981). Based on the limited evidence available, however, it does not appear that use of these procedures results in underlying or permanent changes in students' cognitions, writing behaviors, or performance.

Qualities and Features of the Writing Product

According to Hillocks (1986), the evaluation of one's own writing (or the writing of others) using specific criteria can help students acquire declarative and procedural knowledge that is used to regulate what they write. This supposition was based on a meta-analysis of six studies involving either secondary or college-age students. The students in these studies were asked to judge their writing or the writing of others to determine if certain criteria were present (cf. Wright, 1976). Specific scales or questions were used to facilitate this process. In some studies, students were further asked to react to their evaluations by suggesting ways to improve or revise the piece of writing under examination (Benson, 1979; Clifford, 1981; Farrell, 1977). In other studies, the scales or questions were used to help students generate ideas as well as evaluate writing (Kemp, 1979; Rosen, 1974).

Hillocks (1986) found evaluating one's own or others' writing using specific criteria to be more effective than other traditional writing procedures such as studying models of good writing, grammar instruction, and free writing. In explaining these results, he indicated that students internalized at least some of the criteria embodied in the scales or questions as a result of actively applying them to pieces of writing. This new knowledge was then used to guide their production of future compositions. Hillocks further suggested that the internalized criteria should affect what students write by leading them to use means–ends strategies instead of what-next strategies. This explanation should be viewed as working hypothesis, however, since it is not clear what was actually internalized as a result of instruction. Furthermore, it is difficult to isolate the variables responsible for changes in students' writing, because these studies included multiple treatment components. Although Hillocks' thesis is provocative and implies that self-judgments can affect more than the process of revising, additional research is needed to verify his extrapolation.

The value of having younger students assess whether specific qualities or features are present in their writing has been addressed in only two studies. Ballard and Glynn (1975) asked third-grade students to record the number of sentences and number of different action and describing words present in their stories. Assessment of these features, however, had no effect on students' writing until observations were paired with self-reinforcement—students earned a minute of free time for each instance of the desired feature.

In contrast, Graves, Montague, and Wong (1990) found that the quality of stories written by fifth- and sixth-grade students with learning disabilities improved as a result of monitoring the inclusion of common story parts (i.e., setting, characters, problem and plan, and ending). Because the intervention was limited to one writing session and students did not receive any instruction on these elements or the characteristics of good stories, it appears that the self-monitoring procedure served to prompt students to more fully use their available resources.

A final study by Voth and Graham (1993) used goal setting to influence the construction of essays written by seventh- and eighth-grade students with learning disabilities. The procedure was similar to the one used by Charles Darwin when writing *On the Origin of Species by Natural Selection.* Students set goals to explore a specific number of reasons to support their paper's premise and/or to refute a specific number of reasons that ran counter to this premise. Setting goals had a positive effect on students' writing. Their essays became longer and qualitatively better. In addition, when setting a goal to refute reasons that ran counter to their premise— something that was not typically included in these students' papers—they benefited from using a strategy that guided them through the process. The strategy was not needed, however, for the easier task of setting a goal to include supporting reasons.

As Scardamalia and Bereiter (1986) noted, students who are aware of what they are striving for in their writing products and how successful they are in obtaining it are more likely to develop the cognitive processes necessary for competent performance. The Voth and Graham (1993) study demonstrated that setting product goals can improve what is written by students with learning disabilities. Additional research is needed to replicate this finding and to determine if product goal setting is beneficial for other writers as well.

Revising

Although revising is commonly regarded as an important and central part of composing, it appears to have little impact on what most students write (Fitzgerald, 1987; Scardamalia & Bereiter, 1986). Many students, especially younger ones, do little revision without teacher or peer support, and the revisions that students make usually do not improve the communicative quality of their text. Instead, students tend to concentrate their revising efforts on proofreading.

One reason why students may make so few revisions or focus on proofreading is that they assume that their text is clear and readers will have no trouble understanding it. For instance, Beal (1989) argued that revision is hampered by students' limited skills in detecting problems in the communicative quality of their text. She found that third-grade students revised more problematic messages than younger children, but differences in performance were primarily due to the older children's skills in locating the problem (Beal, 1987). Once a problem was detected, younger and older children were equally likely to revise it appropriately.

There are a variety of self-observation and self-judgment strategies that writers use to help them better evaluate their work. These include setting the text aside for a few days, reading it backward, printing the paper in a new font so that it has a different appearance, and reading the paper out loud (Beal, 1989). Espin and Sindelar (1988) evaluated whether reading prepared text aloud helped students with and without learning disabilities to correct textual errors of grammar and syntax. For both groups of students, they found that more errors were corrected when text was read aloud versus silently. This advantage occurred because reading aloud helped students detect more errors. Similar to the Beal (1987) study, once an error was identified, it was equally likely to be corrected in either of the reading conditions.

A different approach to helping children detect message problems has been investigated by Beal, Garrod, and Bonitatibus (1990). They helped elementary-age students evaluate prepared text by teaching them to ask a series of questions about specific events in the stories they were to revise. Students who were taught to use the self-questioning strategy located and revised more text problems than children in a control group. Learning the self-questioning strategy without experience in detecting problems, however, was not especially helpful. Children were better able to locate and revise the target problems when they practiced using the strategy with problematic versus clear stories.

We believe that one of the reasons the self-questioning strategy in the Beal et al. (1990) study worked so well is because students were provided with information about the criteria for successful revising. This information was supplied in the questions students used and the modeling and feedback provided by the instructor. As Hilgers (1986) noted, revised writing may be better writing, insofar as it is guided by appropriate evaluations.

In a number of studies, revising has been facilitated by asking students to judge their own writing or the writing of others to determine if specific criteria were met or present. For instance, use of a self-evaluation form to think about goals and problems in achieving goals influenced college students' judgment of text problems (Beach & Eaton, 1984). Specific criteria have also been used in some peer revising studies where students were asked to give each other feedback on their papers using specific questions to guide the process. In one study, for example, students gave each other feedback on where additional text needed to be added or what parts of the paper were unclear (MacArthur, Schwartz, & Graham, 1991). In studies where peer feedback was facilitated by using self-questions to guide the evaluative process, students revised more often and the quality of their text improved (cf. Benson, 1979; MacArthur et al., 1991; Stoddard & MacArthur, in press).

One of the important findings from the peer revising studies conducted by MacArthur and his colleagues (MacArthur et al., 1991; Stoddard & MacArthur, in press) was that the pattern of students' revisions changed as a result of the intervention—the number of changes affecting the substance of what was written increased dramatically. Although part of this change was undoubtedly a result of the types of questions students asked about text, we believe that a great deal of incidental learning took place as well. By sharing their papers with a peer, students may have developed a sharper sense of audience and purpose that contributed to shaping what they revised.

We have found that many students are capable of making more substantive changes when revising, but fail to do so because they overemphasize the importance of form in writing and revising. Interviews with students with learning disabilities, for instance, suggest that they are more likely than normally achieving students to attribute success and failure in writing to mechanical factors (Graham, Schwartz, & MacArthur, 1993). However, when taught a strategy that included a series of self-directed questions and prompts focusing attention on textual problems of both form and substance, these students were able to change their approach to revising—significantly increasing the number and proportion of revisions that affected the substance of their text, resulting in improved writing (Graham & MacArthur, 1988).

Similarly, Matsuhashi and Gordon (1985) have demonstrated that students' preoccupation with form during revising can be moderated through goal setting. In their study, the mean percentage of substantive changes made by college students increased as a result of asking them to simply add five things to improve their paper. Because goal-setting procedures such as this one are relatively easy for students or teachers to implement, more attention needs to be given to their development, application, and evaluation.

Finally, Bereiter and Scardamalia (1982) argued that children's limitations in revising may be a problem of executive control. Students may be capable of making appropriate evaluations and revisions, but have trouble organizing and integrating the elements of revising into the larger composition process, masking their ability to evaluate and revise. To determine if underlying competence was being "hobbled" by difficulties with executive control, Scardamalia and Bereiter (1983) provided fourth-through eighth-grade children support in carrying out the revising process by having them stop after every sentence and execute a routine of evaluating, diagnosing, choosing a revising tactic, and carrying out the tactic. Students used cards containing either evaluative or diagnostic statements to evaluate each sentence and choose a subsequent revising tactic.

At the conclusion of their experiment, students indicated that the procedure got them to change their normal approach to revising. They were effective in using the evaluation cards to spot a problem and, more often than not, individual revisions were rated as making a positive change in text. Nonetheless, they had problems choosing an appropriate revising tactic, and use of the procedure did not result in an overall improvement in writing quality. Thus, executive control was not the only thing that limited how well the participating children revised.

In a replication of Scardamalia and Bereiter's (1983) study, we also found that students' difficulties with revising represent more than just a problem with organizing and directing cognitive resources. The use of the procedure employed in their study did not result in the appearance of an underlying or latent competence in the revising of fifth- and sixth-grade students with learning disabilities (Graham, 1993). Although the participating students made more revisions when using the procedure, the quality of their text and the types of revisions they made did not change.

As the studies reviewed in this section show, a variety of factors—including executive control, intentions, detecting problems in text, and choosing an effective revising tactic—help to explain why students make so few revisions and tend to place more emphasis on form than substance when revising. The studies reviewed also show that self-regulation strategies involving self-observation, judgment, and reaction as well as goal setting can be used to address these factors. Unfortunately, the amount of research in this area is limited, providing an incomplete picture of how instruction in self-regulation can help students develop more mature revising behaviors.

SELF-REGULATED STRATEGY DEVELOPMENT

A recent emphasis in writing instruction, particularly with students with writing problems, is the explicit, context-based teaching of writing strategies (Graham & Harris, 1989a). A variety of strategies, for instance, have been successfully taught to students with learning and writing problems, including strategies for writing paragraphs (Moran, Schumaker, & Vetter, 1981), framing text (Englert et al., 1991), and editing (Schumaker et al., 1982). Likewise, the writing performance of college students has been improved by encouraging them to use common strategies like outlining (Kellogg, 1987). Strategies such as these help students regulate the writing process by providing structure that organizes and sequences behavior.

Since 1980 we have been involved in evaluating a theoretically and empirically based instructional model for developing writing and self-regulation strategies among students, especially children with learning and writing problems (cf. Harris & Graham, 1992a). We refer to this approach as self-regulated strategy development (SRSD). With SRSD, students are explicitly taught strategies for planning and revising in combination with procedures for regulating these strategies and the writing process.

Development of SRSD was influenced by multiple sources, including Meichenbaum's (1977) model of cognitive behavior modification; the work of Soviet theorists and researchers, especially Vygotsky, Luria, and Sokolov on verbal self-regulation and the social origins of self-control; the concept of self-control instruction presented by Brown, Campione, and Day (1981); and the development of the learning strategies model by Deshler and associates (see Deshler & Schumaker, 1986). Whereas our discussion focuses on the application of the model to the area of writing, SRSD has been used to promote strategic thinking in other academic areas such as reading, mathematics, and spelling.

Characteristics and Goals of SRSD

The SRSD model emphasizes interactive learning between teachers and students, consistent with the dialectical constructivist viewpoint (Pressley, Harris, & Marks, 1992). Students are active collaborators as they work with each other and their teachers to determine the goals of instruction, complete the task, and implement, evaluate, and modify the strategy and strategy-acquisition procedures. Metacognitive information about the strategies being taught is emphasized throughout instruction, providing both impetus for goal setting and a form of attributional training (Harris & Pressley, 1991). Instructors are enthusiastic and responsive to each child, providing individually tailored feedback and support. Finally, we have long noted the importance of embedding writing strategy instruction within a meaningful environment for writing, such as that created in the process approach (Harris & Graham, 1992a, 1992b).

Self-regulated strategy development is designed to help students master the higher level cognitive processes involved in composing; develop autonomous, reflective, self-regulated use of effective writing strategies; increase knowledge about the characteristics of good writing; and form positive attitudes about writing and themselves as writers. Various forms of instructional support for achieving these goals are integrated throughout the model.

One form of support is inherent in the planning and revising strategies students are taught. As noted earlier, a strategy provides structure that helps one organize and sequence behavior. A second form of support involves helping students acquire the self-regulation skills needed to use planning and revising strategies deftly and to manage the writing process. This includes teaching students to:

1. Self-monitor changes in their writing performance or behavior (including strategy use).

2. Set goals for improving specific aspects of their writing or to use the target strategies.

3. Develop an internal dialogue for directing strategy use as well as the writing process.

In developing an internal dialogue, the instructor helps students generate their own self-instructions for defining the problem (What do I have to do?), planning (How should I change the strategy for this assignment?), evaluating (Did I do this right?), reinforcing (I did a great job), and so forth. Students may also be encouraged to develop self-statements for promoting desirable behaviors (I can do this by working hard) or controlling maladaptive behaviors such as impulsivity (Take my time).

Additional support is provided through the methods used to teach the target writing and self-regulation strategies. Initially, the teacher provides students with considerable aid in implementing and regulating strategies by modeling, explaining, reexplaining, and assisting whenever necessary. This scaffolding is gradually withdrawn as students become increasingly able to use writing and self-regulation strategies independently.

Another form of support involves the use of instructional procedures to increase students' knowledge about themselves, writing, and the writing process. Model compositions may be used to illustrate the characteristics of good writing, whereas self-monitoring and goal setting procedures along with teacher feedback help students acquire knowledge of their writing capabilities and how to regulate the composing process.

Stages of Instruction

Seven flexible and recursive stages provide the structural framework for SRSD; the stages can be reordered, combined, or modified to meet student and teacher needs (see Table 9.1 for an example using a specific strategy). These stages represent a "metascript," providing a general format and guidelines (Harris & Graham, 1992b; Harris & Pressley, 1991).

1. The teacher helps students develop those preskills, including knowledge of the criteria for good writing, important to understanding, acquiring, or executing the target strategy (preskill development).

2. Teacher and students examine and discuss prior writing performance and the strategies students presently use to accomplish specific composing assignments (initial conference: instructional goals and significance). The potential benefits and significance of strategy instruction are also discussed, and students are asked to make a commitment to learn the strategy and act as a collaborative partner in this endeavor. Negative or ineffective self-statements or beliefs may also be considered at this time.

3. The strategy, its purposes, and how and when to use it are discussed (discussion of the strategy).

4. The teacher models how to use the strategy along with appropriate self-instructions (modeling of the strategy and self-instructions). The self-instructions can include any combination of problem definition, planning, strategy use, self-evaluation, coping and error correction, and self-reinforcement statements. After analyzing the model's performance, teacher and students may collaborate on how to change the strategy to make it more effective or efficient. Each student then develops and records personal self-statements the student plans to use.

5. The strategy and any accompanying mnemonic as well as the personalized self-statements are memorized; paraphrasing is allowed as long as the original meaning is maintained (memorization of the strategy).

6. Students and teachers use the strategy and self-instructions collaboratively (collaborative practice). Self-regulation procedures, including self-assessment, self-recording, or goal setting, may be introduced at this point.

7. Students are encouraged to use the strategy and self-instructions independently and covertly (independent practice). If self-regulation procedures are in use, students and the instructor may decide to start fading them out.

TABLE 9.1
Teaching a Story Grammar Strategy Using Self-Regulated
Strategy Development

Initial Conference: Instructional Goals and Significance: Instruction began with a conference in which the purpose of instruction was explained. The teacher and students discussed the common parts of a story, the goal for learning the story grammar strategy (to write better stories: ones that are more fun for you to write and more fun for others to read), and how including and expanding story parts can improve a story. The procedures for learning the strategy, students' roles as collaborators, and the importance of effort in strategy mastery were also examined.

Preskill Development: Knowledge of common story parts was an essential prerequisite to using the story grammar strategy and accompanying self-regulation procedures. First, the teacher defined the common parts of a story, specifically the elements included in the setting (characters, place, and time) and a story's episodes (precipitating event, characters' goals, action to achieve goals, resolution, and characters' reactions). Students then identified examples of these elements in the literature they were currently reading, highlighting the different ways writers develop story parts. They also generated ideas for story parts, using differing story origins. Finally, each student examined two or three stories written previously, and determined which story elements were present in each story. At this point, the teacher showed the students how to graph the number of story parts they included in their stories, while at the same time explaining the purpose of graphing (to monitor the completeness of their stories and the effects of learning the strategy).

Discussion of the Strategy: The teacher described the story grammar strategy; each student had a small chart listing the strategy steps and a mnemonic (or reminder) for remembering the questions for the parts of a story. The strategy included five steps: (1) Think of a story you would like to share with others; (2) let your mind be free; (3) write down the story part reminder (W-W-W; What = 2; How = 2); (4) make notes of your ideas for each part; and (5) write your story—use good parts; add, elaborate, or revise as you go; make sense. The mnemonic reminded students to ask themselves the following questions: (1) Who is the main character; who else is in the story? (2) When does the story take place? (3) Where does the story take place? (4) What does the main character do or want to do; what do other characters do? (5) What happens when the main character does or tries to do it? (6) What happens with other characters? (7) How does the story end? (8) How does the main character feel; how do other characters feel? The teacher and students examined the rationale for each step of the strategy as well as how and when to use the strategy, making linkages to reading and writing book reports and other compositions. The teacher further illustrated the types of things she says to herself to free up her mind and think of good ideas and parts when writing. After discussing how these self-statements were helpful, students generated their own preferred self-statements, recorded them on paper, and practiced using them.

Modeling of the Strategy and Self-Instructions: The teacher shared a story idea that she had been thinking about, and modeled (while "thinking out loud") how to use the story grammar strategy to further develop the idea. The students helped her plan, write, and revise the story. While composing, the teacher modeled different types of self-instructions, including problem definition, planning, self-evaluation, self-reinforcement, and coping. Once the story was finished, the types of self-statements used by the teacher were examined. Students then generated and recorded their own self-statements to use while writing. At this point, the teacher asked for recommendations on how the strategy steps and mnemonic might be made more effective.

(Continued)

TABLE 9.1
(Continued)

Memorization of the Strategy: Students memorized the story grammar strategy, the mnemonic, and one of each type of self statement from their list alone or with a partner.
Collaborative Practice: Students now began to use the story grammar strategy to write their own stories, receiving assistance from the teacher as needed. The teacher encouraged students to set goals to include all of the basic parts in their stories and to monitor and graph their success in meeting this objective. Students were also encouraged to use self-statements to guide their writing and strategy use. As students became more adept at using the strategy, reliance on the teacher and instructional materials (charts and self-statement lists) was faded, and the teacher encouraged students to use their self-statements covertly.
Independent Performance: Students independently planned and wrote stories, using the story grammar strategy and accompanying self-regulation procedures. The teacher provided positive and constructive feedback only if needed. At the conclusion of this stage students evaluated the strategy and instruction, discussed opportunities for using the strategy in the near future, and considered how the strategy and self-regulation procedures should be adapted for use in reading and on specific writing assignments.

Note. Stage 1 (Preskill Development) and Stage 2 (Initial Conference) were reordered in this example.

Procedures for promoting maintenance and generalization are integrated throughout the model. These include discussing opportunities to use, and results of using, the strategy and self-instructions with other tasks and in other settings; asking other teachers or parents to comment on the student's success in using the strategy; and working with other teachers to prompt the use of the strategy in their classrooms.

Findings

Most of our research has examined the effectiveness of SRSD in teaching writing and self-regulation strategies to students with learning disabilities in Grades 4–6. Composing strategies taught to these students include brainstorming (Harris & Graham, 1985), semantic webbing (MacArthur, Schwartz, Graham, Molloy, & Harris, 1993), generating and organizing writing content using text structure (Danoff, Harris, & Graham, in press; Graham & Harris, 1989b, 1989c; Sawyer, Graham, & Harris, 1992), goal setting (Graham, MacArthur, Schwartz, & Voth, 1992), revising using peer feedback (MacArthur et al., 1991), and revising for both mechanics and substance (Graham & MacArthur, 1988). In each of the studies conducted to date, SRSD has proven to be an effective means for teaching writing and self-regulation strategies.

We have repeatedly found that the quality and usually the length and structure of students' compositions improved after teaching them either a planning or revising strategy and accompanying self-regulation procedures via SRSD. Effect sizes typically exceed 1.0 (Graham & Harris, in press). In addition, we have found that changes in what students write are accompanied by changes in how they go about the process of composing. For instance, students who initially did no planning in advance consistently developed plans and ideas prior to writing after learning a prewriting strategy using SRSD (Graham & Harris, 1989c). Concurrent changes have also been observed in students' metacognitive knowledge and self-efficacy (i.e., perceptions about one's capabilities to perform specific writing tasks). In a study where a strategy for setting writing goals was taught, for example, students' perceptions of their writing competence became more accurate and their understanding of what good writers do shifted from a focus on mechanical factors to an emphasis on substance (Graham et al., 1992). Furthermore, students' and teachers' evaluations of SRSD have been uniformly positive.

Equally promising have been findings that the effects of instruction were maintained over time and that generalization across settings and persons occurred (Graham & Harris, in press). Students' skills in adapting particular strategies to different writing genres (from expository to narrative writing for example), though, have been more variable. As a result, we recommend that direct and assisted practice in making such transfers be provided as a routine part of instruction.

Other Research Involving Self-Regulated Strategy Development

Several other researchers have combined strategy and self-regulation instruction to help writers better execute and regulate some aspect of the writing task. Glomb and West (1990) observed that high school students with behavioral disorders were able to reduce mechanical errors and increase the length and neatness of their creative writing by using a writing management strategy in conjunction with self-instructions, goal setting, and self-evaluation. Schunk and Swartz (in press-a, in press-b) found that both regularly achieving fifth-grade students and gifted fourth-grade students learned to better use a writing strategy as a result of a goal to master the use of the strategy and positive feedback on their efforts to obtain this objective. Danoff et al. (in press) also found that SRSD improved the writing of regularly achieving fourth- and fifth-grade students. These investigations along with the studies involving students with learning disabilities demonstrate that conjointly teaching writing strategies and self-regulation procedures can benefit a wide range of students.

CREATING A SUPPORTIVE LEARNING
ENVIRONMENT

The instructional research reviewed in the previous sections addressed the development of self-regulation head on by directly telling or showing students how to use specific self-regulation strategies within meaningful writing contexts. The following describes a series of principles for creating a writing environment in which students skills in self-regulation can prosper and grow. This list is by no means exhaustive; it is simply meant to clarify some of the conditions that can foster the development of self-regulation in writing.

Make Writing an Enjoyable and Interesting Activity. Students are less likely to engage in the types of mental activities that epitomize skilled writing if assignments are boring or confusing or the classroom is viewed as an unfriendly or punitive place. Although it is true that some students are able to reduce the tedium or confusion accompanying poorly conceived assignments by seeking clarification or developing unique interpretations of assignments, other students evidence a mental withdrawal or evasion of productive work (Hansen, 1989). Similarly, overemphasizing students' errors in writing may be viewed as punitive, making students less willing to write (Graham, 1982).

What can teachers do to make writing an enjoyable and interesting activity? First, students' writing should be designed to serve a real purpose and aimed at a real audience. By using legitimate writing tasks and encouraging students to share their work with others, teachers increase the likelihood that students will be actively involved and responsible for their own work. Second, teachers need to accept and encourage students' efforts. Students are more likely to enjoy writing and take the risks necessary to refine and expand their self-regulation skills if the classroom environment is supportive, pleasant, and nonthreatening (Graham & Harris, 1988).

Provide Opportunities to Self-Regulate. An important maxim in self-regulated learning is that people learn by doing (Zimmerman & Schunk, 1989). Development of self-regulation in writing will undoubtedly be inhibited if the environment and writing assignments are so tightly structured that students have little room for initiating and directing their own efforts. Students need to have opportunities to exert strategic control over personal, behavioral, and environmental influences (Zimmerman, 1989). For instance, it is important for students to have a voice in what they write, including choosing their own writing topics and developing unique interpretations or personal opinions about teacher assigned topics (Spaulding, 1989). Such control allows them to develop their own goals and purposes for writing and should produce a higher level of task engagement.

Use Writing Tasks That Lead Students to Self-Regulate. Not all writing engenders the same level or even type of self-regulation. Durst (1989), for instance, found differences in students' self-monitoring behavior on analytic and summary writing tasks. Similarly, writing about a personal experience may make fewer demands on cognitive processes because the content is readily available and organized in one's memory (Scardamalia & Bereiter, 1986).

One way of helping students develop self-regulation strategies in writing is to use writing tasks that require students to employ such processes. For example, cooperative writing tasks allow children to learn to accommodate each other's suggestions and writing style, paving the way for each writer to incorporate new influences into their approach to composing (McCutchen, 1988). Likewise, teachers can use highly structured problem-solving writing assignments to evoke self-regulation during writing (cf. Hillocks, 1986). An example includes trying to produce a composition that leads to a prespecified ending (Scardamalia & Bereiter, 1985).

Model the Writing Process and Strategic Thinking. Another common tenet of self-regulated learning is that people acquire knowledge through their social interactions with others (Corno, 1992; Schunk, 1989). Thus, one way in which children learn to regulate the writing process is by observing others, both adults and children, grappling with writing. Surprisingly, there is very little evidence that teachers model or talk about the self-regulation or problem-solving processes involved in writing (Anthony & Anderson, 1987). By modeling effective, self-regulated writing strategies, teachers gain a powerful tool for helping children acquire these skills. We believe that it is particularly important that such modeling make visible the teachers' thinking as they recruit and apply self-regulation strategies and that students see the natural consequences of these efforts. In addition, temporary and adjusted guidance and assistance in using the strategies modeled is often critical in helping students learn to apply complex cognitive processes like self-regulation (Harris & Graham, 1992a).

Encourage Students to Use Self-Regulation Processes. Other important tools for facilitating the development of self-regulation during writing include procedural supports for using specific self-regulation processes. Procedural support can take a variety of forms, including procedural guidance during writing conferences (cf. Fitzgerald & Stamm, 1990), procedural prompts incorporated in computer-based writing programs (cf. Zellerman, Saloman, Globerson, & Givon, 1991), or predictable routines in which self-regulation activities such as revision are expected and reinforced (cf. Atwell, 1987). With procedural support, students are helped or induced to carry out specific writing processes, with the eventual goal being the internalization and self-control of these processes. Although we believe that procedural support is an important ingredient in helping students develop as self-regulated writers, it must be used with care. For example, Hilgers (1986) found that students used their own evaluative criteria for writing less frequently if they expected their teachers to help them with their evaluations.

Continually Help Students Clarify and Enlarge Their Internal Vision of Writing. Students' knowledge of their writing, their approach to writing, and their writing competence contribute to how well they regulate the composing process (Zimmerman, 1989). As a result, we need to help them examine, refine, and extend this knowledge. Their knowledge of writing can be increased via direct instruction on the characteristics of good writing (cf. Fitzgerald & Teasley, 1986), examination and discussion of the literary devices used by professional writers (cf. Bos, 1991), application of questions and scales to evaluate writing (cf. Clifford, 1981), and encouragement to imitate a particular style or technique embodied in a selected writing sample (Hillocks, 1986). Students' knowledge of their approach to writing can be improved by encouraging them to think about and share with others the types of things they do as they compose. This is commonly done during writing conferences and author's chair in the popular process approach to composition instruction (cf. Atwell, 1987). Finally, knowledge of their growth and competence as writers can be increased by asking them to assess the strength and weaknesses of selected compositions as well as monitor their progress over time by keeping a portfolio.

CONCLUDING REMARKS

Self-regulation is a key ingredient in skilled writing. The research reviewed in this chapter shows that considerable progress has been made in our understanding of how to facilitate the development of self-regulation in writing. Much remains to be done, however. Most of the work completed to date has involved students with writing and/or other school-based problems, especially students with learning disabilities. Whereas research with these populations needs to continue, intervention research involving self-regulation in writing needs to move more firmly into the mainstream of schools and educational research.

REFERENCES

Adams, R. (1991, December 15). The writing machine. *Washington Post*, p. 5.

Anthony, H., & Anderson, L. (1987, April). *The nature of writing instruction in regular and special education classrooms.* Paper presented at the annual meeting of the American educational Research Association, Chicago.

Atwell, N. (1987). *In the middle: Reading, writing, and learning from adolescents.* Portsmouth, NH: Heinmann.

Ballard, K., & Glynn, T. (1975). Behavioral self-management in story writing with elementary school children. *Journal of Applied Behavioral Analysis, 8,* 387–398.

Bandura, A. (1986). *Social foundations of thought and action: A social cognitive theory.* Englewood Cliffs, NJ: Prentice-Hall.

Beach, R., & Eaton, S. (1984). Factors influencing self-assessing and revising by college freshman. In R. Beach & L. Bridwell (Eds.), *New directions in composition research* (pp. 149–170). New York: Guilford Press.

Beal, C. (1987). Repairing the message: Children's monitoring and revision skills. *Child Development, 58,* 401–408.

Beal, C. (1989). Children's communication skills: Implications for the development of writing strategies. In C. McCormick, G. Miller, & M. Pressley (Eds.), *Cognitive strategy research: From basic research to educational applications* (pp. 191–214). New York: Springer-Verlag.

Beal, C., Garrod, A., & Bonitatibus, G. (1990). Fostering children's revision through training in comprehension monitoring. *Journal of Educational Psychology, 82,* 275–280.

Benson, N. (1979). The effects of peer feedback during the writing process on writing performance, revision behavior, and attitude toward writing. *Dissertation Abstracts, 40,* 1987a.

Bereiter, C. (1980). Development in writing. In T. Gregg & E. Steinberg (Eds.), *Cognitive processes in writing* (pp. 73–93). Hillsdale, NJ: Lawrence Erlbaum Associates.

Bereiter, C., & Scardamalia, M. (1982). From conversation to composition: The role of instruction in a developmental process. In R. Glaser (Ed.), *Advances in instructional psychology* (Vol. 2, pp. 1–64). Hillsdale, NJ: Lawrence Erlbaum Associates.

Bos, C. (1991). Reading-writing connection: Using literature as a zone of proximal development for writing. *Learning Disabilities Research and Practice, 6,* 251–256.

Brown, A. L., Campione, J. C., & Day, J. D. (1981). Learning to learn: On training students to learn from tests. *Educational Researcher, 10,* 14–21.

Clifford, J. (1981). Composing in stages: The effects of a collaborative pedagogy. *Research in the Teaching of English, 15,* 37–53.

Corno, L. (1992). Encouraging students to take responsibility for learning and performance. *Elementary School Journal, 93,* 69–83.

Danoff, B., Harris, K. R., & Graham, S. (in press). Incorporating strategy instruction within the writing process in the regular classroom: Effects on normally achieving and learning disabled students' writing. *Journal of Reading Behavior.*

Deshler, D. D., & Schumaker, J. B. (1986). Learning strategies: An instructional alternative for low-achieving adolescents. *Exceptional Children, 52,* 583–590.

Durst, R. (1989). Monitoring processes in analytic and summary writing. *Written Communication, 6,* 340–363.

Englert, C., Raphael, T., Anderson, L., Anthony, H., Stevens, D., & Fear, K. (1991). Making writing strategies and self-talk visible: Cognitive strategy instruction in writing in regular and special education classrooms. *American Educational Research Journal, 28,* 337–373.

Espin, C., & Sindelar, P. (1988). Auditory feedback and writing: Learning disabled and nondisabled students. *Exceptional Children, 55*, 45–51.

Farrell, K. (1977). A comparison of three instructional approaches for teaching written composition to high school juniors: Teacher lecture, peer evaluation, and group tutoring. *Dissertation Abstracts, 38*, 1849a.

Fitzgerald, J. (1987). Research on revision in writing. *Review of Educational Research, 57*, 481–506.

Fitzgerald, J., & Markham, L. (1987). Teaching children about revision in writing. *Cognition and Instruction, 4*, 3–24.

Fitzgerald, J., & Stamm, C. (1990). Effects of group conferences on first graders' revision in writing. *Written Communication, 7*, 96–135.

Fitzgerald, J., & Teasley, A. (1986). Effects of instruction in narrative structure on children's writing. *Journal of Educational Psychology, 78*, 424–432.

Flower, L., & Hayes, J. (1980). The dynamics of composing: Making plans and juggling constraints. In L. Gregg & E. Steinberg (Eds.), *Cognitive processes in writing* (pp. 31–50). Hillsdale, NJ: Lawrence Erlbaum Associates.

Flower, L., & Hayes, J. (1981). Plans that guide the composing process: Making plans and juggling constraints. In C. Frederikson & J. Dominic (Eds.), *Writing: Process, development, and communication* (pp. 39–58). Hillsdale, NJ: Lawrence Erlbaum Associates.

Glomb, N., & West, R. (1990). Teaching behaviorally disordered adolescents to use self-management skills for improving the completeness, accuracy, and neatness of creative writing homework assignments. *Behavioral Disorders, 15*, 233–242.

Graham, S. (1982). Composition research and practice. A unified approach. *Focus on Exceptional Children, 14*, 1–16.

Graham, S. (1990). The role of production factors in learning disabled students' compositions. *Journal of Educational Psychology, 82*, 781–791.

Graham, S. (1993). [Procedural facilitation: The effectiveness of the compare-diagnosis-operate revision procedure with students with learning disabilities]. Unpublished raw data.

Graham, S., & Harris, K. R. (1988). Instructional recommendations for teaching writing to exceptional students. *Exceptional Children, 54*, 506–512.

Graham, S., & Harris, K. R. (1989a). Cognitive training: Implications for written language. In J. Hughes & R. Hall (Eds.) *Cognitive behavioral psychology in the schools: A comprehensive handbook* (pp. 247–279). New York: Guilford Press.

Graham, S., & Harris, K. R. (1989b). A components analysis of cognitive strategy instruction: Effects on learning disabled students' compositions and self-efficacy. *Journal of Educational Psychology, 81*, 353–361.

Graham, S., & Harris, K. R. (1989c). Improving learning disabled students' skills at composing essays: Self-instructional strategy training. *Exceptional Children, 56*, 201–214.

Graham, S., & Harris, K. R. (in press). Self-regulated strategy development: Helping students with learning problems develop as writers. *Elementary School Journal*.

Graham, S., & MacArthur, C. (1988). Improving learning disabled students' skills at revising essays produced on a word processor: Self-instructional strategy training. *Journal of Special Education, 22*, 133–152.

Graham, S., MacArthur, C., Schwartz, S., & Voth, T. (1992). Improving the compositions of students with learning disabilities using a strategy involving product and process goal-setting. *Exceptional Children, 58*, 322–334.

Graham, S., Schwartz, S., & MacArthur, C. (1993). Learning disabled and normally achieving students' knowledge of the writing and the composing process, attitude toward writing, and self-efficacy. *Journal of Learning Disabilities, 26*, 237–249.

Graves, A., Montague, M., & Wong, Y. (1990). The effects of procedural facilitation on story composition of learning disabled students. *Learning Disabilities Research, 5*, 88–93.

Hansen, D. (1989). Lesson evading and lesson dissembling: Ego strategies in the classroom. *American Journal of Education, 97,* 184–208.

Harris, K. R., & Graham, S. (1992a). *Helping young writers master the craft: Strategy instruction and self-regulation in the writing process.* Cambridge, MA: Brookline.

Harris, K. R., & Graham, S. (1992b). Self-regulated strategy development: A part of the writing process. In M. Pressley, K. R. Harris, & J. T. Guthrie (Eds.), *Promoting academic competence and literacy in school* (pp. 277–309). New York: Academic Press.

Harris, K. R., & Graham, S. (1985). Improving learning disabled students' composition skills: Self-control strategy training. *Learning Disability Quarterly, 8,* 27–36.

Harris, K. R., Graham, Reid, R., McElroy, K., & Hamby, R. (1993). *Self-monitoring of attention versus self-monitoring of performance: Replication and cross-task comparison studies.* Manuscript submitted for publication.

Harris, K. R., & Pressley, M. (1991). The nature of cognitive strategy instruction: Interactive strategy construction. *Exceptional Children, 57,* 392–405.

Hayes, J., & Flower, L. (1986). Writing research and the writer. *American Psychologist, 41,* 1106–1113.

Hilgers, T. (1986). How children change as critical evaluators of writing: Four three-year case studies. *Research in the Teaching of English, 20,* 36–55.

Hillocks, G. (1986). *Research on written composition: New directions for teaching.* Urbana, IL: National Conference on Research in English.

Hopman, M., & Glynn, T. (1989). The effect of correspondence training on the rate and quality of written expression of four low achieving boys. *Educational Psychology, 9,* 197–213.

Hull, G. (1981). Effects of self-management strategies on journal writing by college freshman. *Research in the Teaching of English, 15,* 135–148.

Kellogg, R. (1987). Writing performance: Effects of cognitive strategies. *Written Communication, 4,* 269–298.

Kemp, J. (1979). A comparison of two procedures for improving the writing of developmental writers. *Dissertation Abstracts, 40,* 1928a.

MacArthur, C., Schwartz, S., & Graham, S. (1991). Effects of a reciprocal peer revision strategy in special education classrooms. *Learning Disabilities Research and Practice, 6,* 201–210.

MacArthur, C., Schwartz, S., Graham, S., Molloy, D., & Harris, K. (1993). [Case studies of classroom instruction in a semantic webbing strategy]. Unpublished raw data.

Matsuhashi, A., & Gordon, E. (1985). Revision, addition, and the power of the unseen text. In S. Freedman (Ed.), *The acquisition of written language: Response and revision* (pp. 226–249). Norwood, NJ: Ablex.

McCutchen, D. (1988). "Functional automaticity" in children's writing: A problem of metacognitive control. *Written Communication, 5,* 306–324.

Meichenbaum, D. (1977). *Cognitive behavior modification: An integrative approach.* New York: Plenum Press.

Moran, M., Schumaker, J., & Vetter, A. (1981). *Teaching a paragraph organization strategy to learning disabled adolescents* (Research Rep. No. 54). Lawrence: University of Kansas Institute for Research in Learning Disabilities.

Plimpton, G. (1965). Ernest Hemingway. In G. Plimpton (Ed.), *Writers at work: The Paris Review interviews, second series* (pp. 215–239). New York: Viking Press.

Pressley, M., Harris, K. R., & Marks, M. B. (1992). But good strategy instructors are constructivists!! *Educational Psychology Review, 4,* 3–31.

Rosen, M. (1974). A structured classroom writing method: An experiment in teaching rhetoric to remedial English college students. *Dissertation Abstracts, 34,* 7524a.

Rumsey, I., & Ballard, K. (1985). Teaching self-management strategies for independent story writing to children with classroom behavior difficulties. *Educational Psychology, 5,* 147–157.

Sawyer, R., Graham, S., & Harris, K. R. (1992). Direct teaching, strategy instruction, and strategy instruction with explicit self-regulation: Effects on learning disabled students' compositions and self-efficacy. *Journal of Educational Psychology, 84,* 340–352.

Scardamalia, M., & Bereiter, C. (1983). The development of evaluative, diagnostic and remedial capabilities in children's composing. In M. Martlew (Ed.), *The psychology of written language: Development and educational perspectives* (pp. 67–95). London: Wiley.

Scardamalia, M., & Bereiter, C. (1985). Fostering the development of self-regulation in children's knowledge processing. In S. Chipman, J. Segal, & R. Glaser (Eds.), *Thinking and learning skills: Current research and open questions* (Vol. 2, pp. 563–577). Hillsdale, NJ: Lawrence Erlbaum Associates.

Scardamalia, M., & Bereiter, C. (1986). Written composition. In M. Wittrock (Ed.), *Handbook of research on teaching* (3rd ed., pp. 778–803). New York: Macmillan.

Schumaker, J., Deshler, D., Alley, G., Warner, M., Clark, F., & Nolan, S. (1982). Error monitoring: A learning strategy for improving adolescent performance. In W. M. Cruickshank & J. Lerner (Eds.), *Best of ACLD* (Vol. 3, pp. 179–183). Syracuse, NY: Syracuse University Press.

Schunk, D. (1989). Social cognitive theory and self-regulated learning. In B. Zimmerman & D. Schunk (Eds.), *Self-regulated learning and academic achievement: Theory, research, and practice* (pp. 83–110). New York: Springer-Verlag.

Schunk, D., & Swartz, C. (in press-a). Goals and progress feedback: Effects on self-efficacy and writing achievement. *Contemporary Educational Psychology.*

\Schunk, D., & Swartz, C. (in press-b). Writing strategy instruction with gifted students: Effects of goals and feedback on self-efficacy and skills. *Roeper Review.*

Seabaugh, G., & Schumaker, J. (1981). *The effects of self-regulation training on the academic productivity of LD and NLD adolescents* (Research Report No. 37). Lawrence: University of Kansas Institute for Research in Learning Disabilities.

Spaulding, C. (1989). The effects of ownership opportunities and instructional suppost on high school students' writing task engagement. *Research in the Teaching of English, 23,* 139–162.

Stoddard, B., & MacArthur, C. (in press). A peer editor strategy: Guiding learning disabled students in response and revision. *Research in the Teaching of English.*

Stone, I. (1978). *The origin.* New York: Doubleday.

Trollope, A. (1946). *An autobiography.* London: Williams & Norgate.

Voth, T., & Graham, S. (1993). [The effects of goal setting and strategy facilitation on the expository writing performance of junior high students with learning disabilities]. Unpublished raw data.

Wallace, I. (1971). *The writing of one novel.* Richmond Hill, Ontario: Simon & Schuster.

Wallace, I., & Pear, J. (1977). Self-control techniques of famous novelists. *Journal of Applied Behavioral Analysis, 10,* 515–525.

White, J. (1982). *Rejection.* Reading, MA: Addison-Wesley.

Wright, N. (1976). The effects of role-playing on the improvement of freshman composition. *Dissertation Abstracts, 36,* 5009a.

Zellerman, M., Salomon, G., Globerson, T., & Givon, H. (1991). Enhancing writing-related metacognitions through a computerized writing partner. *American Educational Research Journal, 28,* 373–391.

Zimmerman, B. (1989). A social cognitive view of self-regulated academic learning. *Journal of Educational Psychology, 81,* 329–339.

Zimmerman, B., & Schunk, D. (1989). *Self-regulated learning and academic achievement: Theory, research, and practice.* New York: Springer-Verlag.

10

Student Volition and Education: Outcomes, Influences, and Practices

Lyn Corno
Teachers College, Columbia University

Volition is an old psychological construct with strong ties to modern philosophy and a range of colloquial meanings (Pervin, 1992). In everyday use, the term denotes willfulness, or dogged perseverance in pursuit of difficult goals. Psychologists have defined volition more precisely, as the tendency to maintain focus and effort toward goals despite potential distractions. Research has shown that people differ in efforts to protect their intentions to accomplish goals from competing intentions and surrounding distractions.

Some individuals plan steps to accomplish goals and then take those steps regardless of interruptions and competing goals. Others construct equally elaborate plans, but seem never to follow through. These differences may also be observed in individuals at various points in their lives. I, for example, intend to pursue a career at the same time that I take good care of my family. These two goals compete for my limited attentional resources. Numerous shorter term distractions impede progress toward each of these goals; when it snows or the children get sick, the whole system breaks down. Distractions are nuisances that may or may not be ignored, but competing goals must be prioritized. Time must be managed carefully, and procrastination is something that, for me now, no longer exists.

This class of psychological activity—prioritizing goals, managing effort and time, completing tasks with dispatch—also has much to do with the inherent values and desired outcomes of schooling in modern society. But educational research on volition is just beginning to appear, and there is a fair amount of confusion—even among educational psychologists—about how best to define and study this domain. One view is that volition picks up where motivation leaves off. Motivation denotes commitment, and volition denotes follow-through.

In some research related to education, volition has been cast as a central aspect of student "self-regulated learning." Self-regulated learning reflects students' deliberate use of higher level *strategies* to direct and control their concentration on academic tasks; subsets of these strategies are volitional (Zimmerman, 1990). Two examples are motivation and emotion-control strategies. Both are useful when interest or self-assurance wanes: Promise yourself something nice; or count to 10 and breathe deeply. But the motivation and emotion control strategies are not adequately reflected in research on other (cognitive and metacognitive) strategies in education. Research reported elsewhere in this volume and in a previous volume by Zimmerman and Schunk (1989) suggests that the inclusion of cognitive, motivational, and volitional factors in conceptions of self-regulated learning helps to explain its important role in student academic achievement. (See Mithaug, 1993, and Karoly, 1993, for other theoretical perspectives on self-regulation.)

Accordingly, the following sections of this chapter provide an overview of past conceptions and currently emerging theory of volition, suggest a typology for conceptualizing research on student volition in education, and discuss promising future research directions in relation to the needs of teachers, counselors, and school psychologists.

HISTORICAL OVERVIEW

Historical accounts of volition associate the earliest theory with 19th-century German will psychology, particularly the introspective data of Ach (1910; see, e.g., Kuhl & Beckmann, 1985). Ach's work was highly regarded for its careful, qualitative analyses in the context of controlled experimentation, and for raising central questions about distinctions between motivation and volition. As Kuhl and Beckmann (1985) pointed out, however, these ideas received little attention in the United States when Lewin's (1926) early work on motivation equated the concept of intention with need. Lewin contended that the same underlying tensions that move individuals to persist toward meeting needs also apply to goals, thus subsuming volition within motivation. The aspects of volition that might be distinct from motivation then remained uninvestigated by researchers persuaded to adopt Lewin's point of view.

More pertinent to education are the writings about volition by both John Dewey and William James at the turn of the century. Dewey

(1895/1964) contrasted his ideas about how education should capitalize on student interests to develop self-expression with those on education as discipline-based training of the will. James (1890) defined volition as the ability to attend and focus: "attending to a difficult object and holding it fast before the mind" (p. 561). In keeping with their respective predispositions, Dewey was inclined to pursue arguments about how education might free individual self-expression or will. James gave a psychological accounting of how individuals and institutions differ in efforts to tame the will, or assist individuals in buckling down when necessary.

Elsewhere (see, e.g., Corno, 1989, 1993), I have written about modern process theories of volition as formulated largely by Heckhausen and Kuhl (1985). These theorists established the foundation for a new generation of research on volition—research that overcomes shortcomings of earlier work by emphasizing self-regulation in the context of action control. This foundation has many potential implications for education and educational research.

Action control theory proposes that when individuals move from planning and goal-setting to the implementation of plans, they cross a metaphorical Rubicon (Heckhausen & Gollwitzer, 1987). At that "dynamic point of volition," their goals tend to be protected and fostered by self-regulatory activity, rather than reconsidered or changed (Kuhl & Beckmann, 1985). Effective postdecisional processing or follow-through reinforces the original decision in turn, making it harder to disengage from goals even if it may be desirable to do so.

Thus, volitional striving can be maladaptive, particularly when goals are situationally inappropriate, or when continuing focus on a task enables students to avoid evaluation or avoid more difficult tasks (McCaslin & Good, in press). The desirable aspect of volition is that it can help individuals—students—to focus when necessary; the undesirable aspect is that it can make it harder for students to change goals when they should. In the scramble to focus attention and other resources, feedback may be seen by students as just another intrusion, instead of a useful source of information. And, of course, striving can aid the pursuit of ignoble goals.

Action control theorists Heckhausen and Kuhl (1985) defined volition as "a psychological state characterized by thoughts about the implementation of goals into action; a predisposition to use available resources to manage the maintenance of intentions" (pp. 151, 153). Drawing on theoretical distinctions made by these authors, educational psychologists (e.g., McCaslin & Good, in press; Snow, 1989) have begun to examine measurement and research issues that will bring volition into sharper focus with other critical aspects of human functioning in education, including cognition, motivation, and affection.

EMERGING VIEWS OF VOLITION IN CLASSROOMS

The volitional processing that underlies effective action in school helps to protect and maintain students' intentions to accomplish academic goals in the face of competing (such as socioemotional) goals and other distractions (Corno, 1993). Volitional activity is manifested in tasks assigned for completion both within and outside school (e.g., homework), as well as in tasks students take on themselves, "of their own volition." Certain conditions are more likely than others to call forth volition in students; such conditions include the perceptions that a task is too difficult or too easy or too tedious; or that goals are little valued, vaguely defined, too complex, or too novel. Enactment may also be perceived as difficult because the task or classroom environment is filled with distractions, or because distractions are inevitable when work stretches out over time.

It should be noted that Heckhausen and Kuhl's (1985) definition of volition emphasizes using available resources to pursue goals, whatever their sources. Resource management or allocation by students themselves (Kanfer & Ackerman, 1989) represents a new perspective on the concept of effort. In the attributional literature, effort is interpreted as an internal characteristic of individuals that exists apart from the external environment (Weiner, 1990). In volitional theory, effort is a function of person–situation interaction, and occurs when available external and internal resources combine. Effort is not trying in the absence of resources; it is striving to enlist all available resources to pursue goals. These resources include individual skills and talents, as well as support from the larger sociocultural environment. Volitional effort is "mindfully," not blindly, invested by students (Langer, 1989; Salomon, 1983). Even when students are expected to comply with teachers' goals, mindful effort investment can help students to accomplish their own goals simultaneously.

Students have many resources to call upon in academic pursuits. Some classrooms and schools offer more resources than do others (Kozol, 1991), and some social and community values invite the use of more resources (Williams, 1993). Environmental resources include teachers and materials, of course; they also include (a) time as a variable that can be affected by individuals, (b) peers, and (c) sociocultural networks or subgroups. All of these may help students seeking to accomplish tasks. Even without abundant environmental resources, most students have internal resources to use in accomplishing tasks. They have cognitive and communicative skills and talents, and capacities for self-motivation through creative resource management, attention, and emotion control.

The protective goal-maintenance aspect of this new view of volition has special significance (Corno & Kanfer, 1993). Protectiveness implies noticing the erosion of effort and "nipping it in the bud." Volition involves using whatever resources may be available to make important moments count—even, perhaps, making available some resources not readily there (e.g., through political actions such as petitions).

Limited time explicitly managed provides one means for self-motivation to occur. Effective time management can encourage self-motivation and provide quicker access to priorities that might not be among one's own, but are the priorities of others such as teachers, coaches, or counselors. Time is then available for students to savor more of the moments that provide personal satisfaction.

Creatively modifying tasks to increase the pleasure of engaging in them is highly volitional behavior—mindful investment of effort. This kind of resource management has been observed in children as young as three at work on various tasks (Shoda, Mischel, & Peake, 1990). In one school for gifted preschoolers, Wright (1987) documented a variety of ways children adapted tasks. Some students streamlined tasks the teacher assigned; others embellished the tasks with stories and games. But teacher reinforcement for such creative behavior failed to occur in the classroom observed in this study.

Other research (McCaslin & Good, 1992) suggests that a press for generalized compliance is pervasive in school, even at higher grade levels. Teachers foster student dependency at the expense of self-regulation (Deci & Ryan, 1985). Teachers' press for compliance is often coupled with other situational deterrents to self-regulated classroom learning, such as natural distractions and differing systems of values, management, and reward (Ames, 1992; Blumenfeld, 1992). The question becomes: Where in the classroom is there room for self-regulation?

Some teams of practitioners and researchers are restructuring aspects of school governance, assessment, and other policies, in part to address such concerns (see, e.g., Darling-Hammond & Snyder, 1992). Other research has sought to acquaint teachers and community school boards with alternative patterns of teaching that better afford opportunities for student self-regulated learning (see, e.g., Ames, 1992; Corno, 1992; Williams, 1993). Both these lines of intervention research are new, however, and much remains to be learned about how best to accomplish such goals.

A TYPOLOGY OF RESEARCH ON VOLITION IN EDUCATION

Most related research to date has been piecemeal, addressing specific aspects of the overall volitional domain. There are, for example, studies of self-regulated learning, resource utilization or time management, active learning styles, and metacognitive strategy training. An integrated review of this work regarding volition has been provided by Corno and Kanfer (1993). Also notable is that different measurement procedures are used in each of the various studies. Table 10.1 presents two provisionally defined categories for educational research on volition given more or less attention in recent years (after Corno, 1993).

Studies emphasizing the volitional function labeled *action control* include many investigations of self-regulated learning, resource management, and the protective processes previously described. Often, the aim is to identify potentially modifiable regulatory skills or strategies that might be amenable to some sort of shaping in earlier years. Some studies have focused on meta*cognitive* monitoring (self-observation) and control of cognition. These strategies may be used to consolidate new learning or augment available knowledge (Salomon, 1983). Other volitional strategies, including controlling both motivation and emotion, have been less frequently investigated. *Metamotivation* involves efforts such as self-arranged contingencies and the redesign of tasks. Emotion control

TABLE 10.1
Multiconstruct, Multimethod Matrix for Volition and Examples of
Recent Studies Reflecting Each Category

Methods of Measurement	Volitional Clusters	
	Action Control	Volitional Styles
Questionnaires	Kuhl (1984) Karabenick & Knapp (1988, 1991) McDonough et el. (1991)	Deci & Ryan (1985) Trawick (1991)
Interviews	Benson (1988) Zimmerman & Martinez-Pons (1986, 1990) Trawick (1991)	
Direct Observations	Good et al. (1987) Wright (1987) Caragine (1993)	Willingham (1985) Finn & Cox (1992)
Performance Tasks	Kanfer & Ackerman (1989) Kuhl & Kraska (1989) Kuhl (1993) Mischel et al. (1989)	
Other	ESM: McCaslin & Murdock (1991) Ethnography: McDermott et al. (1984)	Projective: Ryan & Grolnick (1986)

Note. Rows identify the various measurement procedures focal in the studies shown within cells. These studies represent a sampling of recent research of each type, rather than a comprehensive list. Selected studies are grouped to indicate gaps in the larger literature, as well as where the bulk of the work can be found.

involves strategies such as inner self-speech, visualization, and controlled breathing. Environmental resources must also be managed to protect individual goals. Efforts to control the environment through overt behavior such as finding a quiet place to work have a longer research history. Environmental control strategies enhance and support cognition, motivation, and emotion control (Kuhl, 1984).

The second category shown in Table 10.1 is labeled *volitional styles* to distinguish the research emphasis on stable, individual differences in volition from specific skills or strategic processes (i.e., the "state" vs. "dispositional" distinction in the previously quoted definition by Heckhausen & Kuhl, 1985). The specific skills and strategies studied in the action control category of research may underlie measurable dimensions of student personality investigated here—including, for example, impulsiveness, conscientiousness, and dependability (Snow, 1989). Educational research on such constructs often seeks to establish the predictive validity of volitional styles for the learning outcomes of schooling.

Not surprisingly, the bulk of research in both categories has used self- or other-rating scales as data. Some studies anchor rating scales with behavioral indices. An increasing number of efforts involve more labor-intensive interviews; performance tasks, projective measures, and experience-sampling methods are also being developed. The studies listed in Table 10.1 are particularly promising examples of volition-related research clearly relevant to education. Some of them merit consideration in detail.

Predictive Research on Volitional Styles

Willingham (1985) conducted a study of factors that predicted success in nine private liberal arts colleges. The personal quality of "productive follow-through" was found to be a key factor demonstrating predictive validity for several academic success indicators, including university faculty members' judgments of students' leadership and nonacademic accomplishments. Productive follow-through was defined as "a pattern of persistent and successful effort over time, preferably in more than one area of extra-curricular accomplishment, such as student government or sports" (p. 8). Unlike other measures of volitional style, which rely on informal self- or other-observation (Kuhl, 1984; Snow, 1989), this variable was measured by a 5-point rating scale, filled out by school faculty that required reference to publicly verifiable evidence of purposeful, continuous commitment in a few different areas (e.g., government, sports, community outreach), rather than sporadic efforts in diverse areas or continuous effort in one area.

Scores on productive follow-through were uncorrelated (!) with academic indicators (high school GPA plus SAT scores) in this college sample. Nonetheless, students rated highly on follow-through by high school teachers and counselors were reported to be overrepresented by as much as 20% to 30% in each of several categories of success, taking both the high school GPA and SAT into account. Following academic indicators, the productive follow-through variable was the best of several predictors used in analyses. These results suggest that nonacademic measures are valuable for college admissions decisions and as evidence of progress in college; students can succeed in college through nontraditional means.

A similar approach was taken by Finn and Cox (1992), who developed a behaviorally based rating scale for teachers to use in judging student classroom participation in the upper elementary grades. Twenty-five items reflect a range of participatory and "nonparticipatory" (refusing to participate) behavior (e.g., "annoys or interferes with peers' work"). Participatory behavior included minimal adequate effort (e.g., "pays attention in class"), and initiative (e.g., "does more than just the assigned work"). The 5-point scale is anchored by *never* (1) and *always* (5), to pick up stylistic tendencies rather than strategic moves.

Similar to Willigham's (1985) findings, active participation correlated significantly with student achievement in reading and mathematics in this study of more than 1,300 fourth graders. The "active versus passive" contrast was more significant than the "passive versus nonparticipative" (or refusing to participate) contrast, and these correlations increased consistently over Grades 1 to 3. Because gender and ethnic/racial differences were estimated directly, these authors were able to conclude that "the handicap associated with nonparticipation in learning activities is just as debilitating for White as for Black . . . and (for) boys and girls alike" (p. 156).

Teachers in both this study and in Willingham's (1985) reported that they found the rating scales easy to complete. These scales could also be used to obtain self-ratings from students. Current efforts to use portfolio contents for student performance assessment (e.g., Chittenden, 1991) offer the chance to further validate and clarify these volitional constructs of productive follow-through and student initiative (see later). Other correlational research could clarify the volitional versus motivational aspects of these styles.

Predictive studies using global measures of student volitional styles thus make clear contributions. However, they do not reveal the factors that lead students to commit to, and follow through on, schoolwork. The ways in which educators might foster these volitional qualities in students who would most benefit remain unexplained. Hints are offered about how style measures might be used for early diagnosis or as part of ongoing assessments of individual student performance. But until volitional styles such as productive follow-through are indexed in such contexts, the potential of such measures remains unrealized. Can educators develop productive follow-through or initiative through early intervention, rather than just measure its predictive validity later on?

Correlational Research on Volitional Processes

This issue requires considering the factors that lead students to commit to and follow through on goals, including the processes that underlie documentable accomplishments both inside and outside school. Pintrich and Schrauben (1992) and Lepper (1988) reviewed research relating student motivational factors to efforts to learn in school. This work shows a strong association between certain perceptions of self and task (i.e., motivational factors) and timely effort toward learning (i.e., volitional processes). For example, adopting a "learning/mastery goal orientation" promotes higher engagement (Ames, 1992; Dweck, 1975). Learning/mastery goal orientations are judged to be present when students (a) demonstrate an intent to master new skills or knowledge, (b) value learning, and (c) believe that sufficient types of effort can expand intellectual competencies. In contrast to this relationship between goal orientation and cognitive engagement, self-perceptions of high ability (or efficacy for academic achievement), show lower positive correlations with cognitive engagement outcomes (Ames, 1992; Kanfer & Ackerman, 1989). Insubstantial linear correlations suggest the possibility that the relationships are curvilinear. For example, a moderate sense of efficacy might best predict volition; particularly strong volition may be a sense of inadequacy in hiding.

Related to this issue is another approach to the investigation of volition in schooling exemplified by the correlational work of Karabenick and Knapp (1988, 1991). These researchers related college students' reported efforts to seek help on coursework (i.e., volitional behavior) to expected grades and self-reported need for help (i.e., motivational factors). Consistent with emerging volitional theory is their argument that help-seeking behavior is an achievement-related activity, not an indication of dependency or "developmentally inappropriate."

Data from their 1988 study show marked curvilinearity in the relationships between reported help seeking and expected grades and stated needs, respectively ($N = 609$). Students who most needed help were least likely to report seeking it. Few students sought help overall (see also Newman & Goldin, 1990). This pattern has also been observed in studies of students working in cooperative groups, where help seeking can lead to negative peer evaluations of ability (Good, Slavings, Harel, & Emerson, 1987).

In their 1991 study, Karabenick and Knapp again correlated reports of help seeking with other factors—this time with self-reported use of learning strategies (some of which are volitional) and perceived threat of seeking help (another motivational factor). Results showed that students who reportedly used more learning strategies were most likely to seek help when needed; the volitional variables in this study correlated positively, as theory would predict. Among the strategies highly correlated with help seeking when needed were "resource management" and time management, both volitional variables. Students who actively managed their time were more likely to report help seeking, whereas students who perceived a threat were less likely to seek help. These authors also correlated help seeking with rated intentions to engage in other instrumental activities such as trying harder, studying more, and taking better notes. Again, correlations were positive and significant in this sample.

A different research strategy was adopted in a series of studies on self-regulated learning constructed by Zimmerman and Martinez-Pons (1986, 1990; see also Zimmerman, Bandura, & Martinez-Pons, 1992). Scenario-based interviews provided data on student responses that were recorded verbatim. Students were asked about classrooms, home, writing outside class, math outside class, test preparation, and low motivation: the "methods they used to participate in class, to study, and to complete assignments." Concrete examples were provided to encourage students to talk. For example, "Most teachers give tests at the end of marking periods, and these tests greatly determine report card grades. Do you have any particular method for preparing for this type of test in English or history?". Students rated the consistency with which they used each strategy mentioned. (The 4-point scale, from *seldom* [1] to *most of the time* [4], suggested habits rather than infrequently used strategies.) Strategies were coded into several motivational and volitional categories.

The correlational data from these studies showed that the self-regulation interview reliably distinguished high- from low-achieving students. In addition, self-reported strategy use again appeared to be independent of the contribution of other predictors (i.e., self-reported efficacy). Correlations were moderately positive between self-reported efficacy and use of many of the strategies measured in this research. Correlations between self-efficacy and the volitional strategy of seeking assistance from adults were found to be −.14 and −.16 (Zimmerman & Martinez-Pons, 1990). These results lend further support to the validity of distinctions between volition (measured as environmental resource management) and motivation (measured as beliefs in one's efficacy).

In another student volition study, Trawick (1991) used similar interviews with underachieving junior college students. Although interviews are labor intensive, they can be used in the form of group exercises and thus to augment instructional interventions to enhance volitional control. Interviews may also provide more "authentic" measures of the use of self-regulation strategies than group rating scales. The validity of interview data gleaned from diverse samples of students may benefit from pictorial illustrations of contexts that accompany verbal scenarios (Kuhl & Kraska, 1989).

Developmental Studies

Valuing learning, and belief in the importance of strategic or mindful effort investment, probably underlies volitional behavior in school. Such values and attitudes have roots in students' home and more general sociocultural environments (e.g., Clark, 1983; Williams, 1993). As mentioned earlier, evidence of volitional control has been observed in young children (Mischel, Shoda, & Rodriguez, 1989; Wright, 1987), but people presumably refine this capability significantly as they get older.

Kuhl and Kraska (1989), using a Metamotivational Knowledge Test for Children (MKTC), examined developmental trends in self-regulatory capability. Sixth-grade children in Germany and Mexico ($N = 60$ per sample) were shown pictures depicting situations in which maintaining intentions appeared difficult. In one picture, a student works on homework while friends play outside. Children were asked about alternative strategies for maintaining desired intentions and avoiding distractions (e.g., self-instructions, moving away from the window, refocusing on task). Those children who identified more effective strategies were also rated significantly higher by teachers on self-regulatory behavior in the classroom (Kuhl, 1993). In tests of developmental trends across both samples, scores on this measure for motivation, attention-control, and coping-with-failure strategies increased almost linearly from Grades 1 to 4. Scores on emotion control (e.g., avoidance of thoughts about pleasure or pain) remained flat, however—suggesting that emotion control is one aspect of volition that may develop later in childhood.

Concurrent studies of developmental trends need to be supplemented by longitudinal studies to uncover influences on volitional development over time. McCaslin and Murdock (1991) described a variety of contextual factors (in the home and school) that underlie student "adaptive learning"; that is, "the internalization of values and goals, motivation to commit to goals or to challenge and reform them, and competence to enact and evaluate those commitments" (p. 213). The "competence to enact and evaluate those commitments" aspect of this definition reflects student volition.

To construct longitudinal case studies of two working-class sixth graders from the same classroom, these authors interviewed parents as well as students. They obtained data on student thoughts and behavior through experience sampling (ESM) journal entries (Csikszentmihalyi & Larsen, 1984), whereby students were cued by teachers to record the information in journals at various points during class (e.g., seatwork, groupwork).

Qualitative analyses showed that one of the two students lived in a family characterized as "authoritarian-restrictive" (after Baumrind, 1987). The child was kept in a subordinate role within the family throughout several years of development. In contrast, the other child studied was found to have experienced a more "traditional" form of family management. Strong influence was exerted by parents during the child's early years, but coercive tactics became less frequent as the child grew.

McCaslin and Murdock (1991) emphasized that it would be inappropriate to characterize either home environment as "better" than the other. But their research on the school-related perceptions and academic performance of each student indicated that the continued restriction experienced by the first student, associated with early adjustment, resulted in increasing difficulty in school as the child matured. In contrast, the second child's home environment served her better as she progressed through school than it did in earlier grades. The parents' goals for the second child involved "learning the meaning of responsibility, and learning how to organize oneself in ways that afford responsible behavior" (p. 45; see also Clark, 1983). As long as schools continue to value and evaluate students on such dimensions as competence, motivation, and self-sustained action as they mature, this child would be expected to do "better" in that context.

In summary, developmental studies suggest that volitional competence occurs in part through adult interactions with children at early enough ages to benefit their work in school and related contexts. Difficult questions can be raised about whether the apparent "fit" between certain home and school environments, such as those observed by McCaslin and Murdock (1991), is defensible within a democratic society (Williams, 1993). Nonetheless, the question remains: To what extent can planned, systematic interventions with children as they enter school lead to favorable outcomes?

Planned Interventions

One study with first graders yielded some evidence on this question. Using a novel procedure for self-rating, McDonough, Meyer, Stone, and Hamman (1991) taught 46 first graders to reduce their distractibility during reading groupwork. Three classes, each composed of advanced, average, or below average readers, were taught how to set goals "not to distract themselves," and "not to distract others" during reading group time. On the second day, they were also taught to use specially designed goal setting/monitoring forms for rating the extent to which they achieved their goals following group sessions.

Students in each class were observed to reduce their distractibility significantly (even exceeding their goals) over sessions on average. But the reductions were greatest in the class of advanced readers. This raises the question of whether average and below average first-grade readers are developmentally prepared to handle certain aspects of volitional control.

Consistent with the findings of Kuhl and Kraska (1989), another study (Benson, 1988) found even sixth graders' discussions of ways to handle homework distractions to be relatively unsophisticated. Of the 93 students interviewed in this study, few mentioned that they, as individuals, might lack self-discipline, commitment, or motivation when distracted during homework. Rather, most of these students attributed distractions to factors outside themselves (in the home environment) and suggested that parents should monitor the environment to prevent distractions during homework.

What kinds of interventions might clarify the volitional skills and strategies most useful for students as they work at school and at home? Trawick (1991) tested a volitional enhancement intervention with 79 academically underprepared urban junior college students. Results showed that a short-term, intensive instructional program offered by a college counselor could make these students more knowledgeable about appropriate study environments and strategies for handling distractions. But the students seemed to need more extensive, connected experiences when asked to integrate sophisticated strategies into regular study routines. A strategy on the order of "If your interest wanes, change the task to make it more fun, or connect it to something you enjoy," for example, is more sophisticated than "If it's noisy, turn on a hair dryer."

Metacognitive strategies and strategies for handling motivation and emotion control appeared particularly difficult for these underprepared college students to internalize. In their schoolwork, these students may be functioning at developmental levels below their chronological ages. Thus, follow-up instruction with these students—as well as instruction with younger students—would seem to require taking rudimentary applications deliberately to a higher level.

The foregoing selective review illustrates the ways in which educational researchers have approached the study of volitional factors to the present. Although the work is varied, it should be evident that few studies measured volitional factors with more than one procedure or in more than one context. Measurement systems for both aptitudes and outcomes need improvement in future work on volition. More penetrating qualitative or ecological research on volition that will reveal both the pitfalls and possibilities within volitional theory is also needed. A deficit model must be avoided by focusing attention on new ways of organizing educational practice, so that Dewey's vision of education (as promoting self-determination) will be upheld (see Mithaug, 1993). Finally, many researchers use their own specialized language to conceptualize and form conclusions. Few presently use the term *volition* in relation to their work. Multivariate, programmatic research in schools and related contexts seems indicated. Theoretical efforts should generate a common language to better promote understanding of this domain.

FUTURE RESEARCH RELATED TO EDUCATIONAL PRACTICE

Future research in education will also need to reach further into the larger school and community settings in which children learn to be volitional. Educational psychologists have been humbled by the lack of enthusiasm among practitioners for research-based calls for change. The next decades offer new possibilities for community-based educational reform in which practitioners and researchers work collaboratively. In such work, research and practice is intentionally intertwined (Darling-Hammond & Snyder, 1992, on "learner-centered schools"). Change is both planned and examined at once, and research follows several complementary paths.

One evolving program at Teachers College can be used as an example. Two interrelated aspects of this "Volitional Enhancement" program are noteworthy—studies of the sociopsychological dynamics of homework, and efforts on the part of teachers and school counselors *working with researchers* to design curricula for teaching students about the role of volition in schoolwork.

Doing Homework

Jianzhong Xu (in prepration) is conducting qualitative research on homework interactions in urban families with second-grade children. What little other research has been done on students "doing" homework has shown that parents frequently assist children on homework in the early grades, and this assistance often takes the form of modeling volitional strategies (Cooper, 1989; McDermott, Goldman, & Varenne, 1984). The range of strategies parents model varies considerably, however, and parents—

much like teachers—often take over and handle for children those aspects of volitional control that the children could be handling themselves.

Research has, for example, found parents setting up the homework environment by encouraging children to find a quiet place and to gather materials. Parents have also been observed telling children to monitor their time and removing siblings from the room. Some parents encourage self-monitoring—for example, by asking the child, "How do you know that? Let's see what you have" (McDermott et al., 1988, p. 407). Some tell their children not to worry and to feel good about their work. But many parents seem to walk a fine line between taking control themselves and promoting self-control in the child.

Xu's investigation triangulates parent and student interview data with video-based observations during homework interactions. Student interviews incorporate previously mentioned procedures for assessing study habits or self-regulated strategy use (Zimmerman & Martinez-Pons, 1986). Parents are questioned as they view the videotapes in "stimulated recall" interviews.

Cases being developed describe family context and academic history for six ethnically diverse students from the same Manhattan public school. Data illustrate what homework means to both parent and child and the manner in which homework is typically carried out. Documented are various student- and parent-regulation strategies in preparation for and during homework, including methods for handling distractions, along with any environmental "press" for the child to assume the volitional burden over the sessions observed.

One stimulated-recall interview entry from the first case study suggests the potential of this kind of analysis. In commenting on the tape segment at a point when the student's mother left the room, she was quoted as saying "Now it's time for him to do the actual homework. We have discussed the article at length, and he understands, and I am separating myself from him." As was the case for McCaslin and Murdock (1991), it is expected that the psychosocial dynamics will be different across the six separate cases. The management of affect (or emotion control) for children and parents in particular appears frequently throughout the currently available transcripts.

Ultimately, this line of research should have implications for educators who work with parents on how to manage their children's homework. Models can be made available for parents, and emphasis can be placed on efforts to shift volitional control from parent to child over time. Research-based guidelines and hints can be provided to parents as well—about ways to prevent potentially negative emotional responses from children as they experience homework, and ways to handle the inevitable disruptions that arise.

Volition in the School Curriculum

Teaching Students About Volition in School. Parent programs mesh
naturally with programs teachers provide to ehnance students' knowledge and skill related to volitional control. Accordingly, a concurrent
research effort aims to observe students closely during classroom
instruction to broaden student understanding of volitional functions in
academic pursuits. This work appropriately follows much of the developmental and descriptive work just reviewed; it is being conducted in
the context of strategy instruction in subject areas as well (Caragine, 1993).

A working group of researchers, teachers, and school psychologists at
Teachers College have designed a series of interactive activities for
teachers and counselors to use with their students to convey the logic of
volitional functioning and assess volitional control as early as the third
grade. The logic follows an argument made by a curriculum theorist,
Sockett (1988), who defended the development of school and curricular
goals around certain "aspects of personal capability," including "deter-
mination, carefulness, conscientiousness, self-restraint, and endurance"
(p. 195). Sockett noted that evidence of these qualities in students has
long been regarded, at least by U.S. schools, as objects of formal
evaluation. At the same time, these qualities are rarely considered explicit
objectives for teaching. Ethics would dictate that the objects of student
evaluation—whatever they are—be part of the explicit rather than the
"hidden" agenda of schooling.

Homework usually begins and external pressure on students to take
responsibility for learning escalates around the third grade (Cooper, 1989).
Unlike the majority of McDonough et al.'s (1991) first graders, many
third-grade students appear "developmentally ready" for strategy instruction. They ask about how to handle distractions and how to protect
their work, yet the strategies that most 8-year-olds themselves use are
less sophisticated than those discussed by older students (Benson, 1988;
Kuhl & Kraska, 1989; Mischel et al., 1989).

Two teacher–researcher teams at Teachers College are working
independently toward the same goals, with very different plans of attack.
One team is proceeding systematically—establishing knowledge and
skill-based instructional objectives for volitional enhancement teaching
sessions and preparing a set of coordinating sample activities/tasks.
Tables 10.2 and 10.3 present the currently available output of this team
(see also Trawick, 1991).

The second team, in contrast, has worked more fluidly to develop
topics or "themes" to be taught to students about the value of volitional
functions, both in and out of school. These lessons are literature based,
and the goals emphasize broadened understanding, meaningful dialogue,

TABLE 10.2
Objectives of the Volitional Teaching Sessions

---

1. Students will describe examples of strategies they might use to protect their concentration in a variety of actual school and extracurricular tasks. Following teacher demonstrations and stories about good students, students will identify strategies as more or less useful or effective and discuss why. They will be able to distinguish strategies that "set the mind" from strategies that "control the environment." (LESSON CONTENT OVERVIEW)
2. Students will demonstrate their knowledge of various effective and ineffective strategies by analyzing prepared scenarios in which hypothetical students respond in various ways. (KNOWLEDGE/COMPREHENSION QUIZ)
3. Students will role play more effective strategic responses to distracting or difficult work conditions, and peers observing the role play will record and evaluate the actors' choice of strategies. (DIRECTED APPLICATION/EVALUATION)
4. Students will be observed by teachers as they complete work assignments in class to determine improvement in task efficiency and resource management by individuals and small groups. Students will also evaluate their own task efficiency and resource management in these observed tasks. Teachers and students will discuss observed improvement. (RETENTION/EVALUATION/FEEDBACK)

---

and challenging assumptions more than volitional skill. Students will engage in discussions of selected children's literature conveying designated themes, such as "follow-through," "persistence," and "resiliency."[1] Written assignments and "culminating projects" will display their learning. Some of the lessons developed by this team were based on the model provided by Calfee's Project READ—Plus/Inquiring School model (Calfee Projects, 1992).

All teaching sessions videotaped for research can be analyzed for both student and teacher response; eventually, field experiments should be conducted. An important part of the data base for each team's efforts consists of portfolio contents for indexing volitional processes and styles. These include samples of student writing on designated themes, evidence of progress through and completion of assigned projects, formal and informal teacher, self-, and peer judgments of performance, and records of longer term, extracurricular accomplishments (e.g., Caragine, 1993).

Students will be asked to write down any school-related incidents that demanded volition and how they handled them, for example. Such records permit consideration of circumstantial subtleties at the same time they alert students (and teachers) to behavior patterns (e.g., frequent lack of follow-through) that may suggest a need for instruction in this area.

---

[1]Examples include classical myths and folk tales of "quests," which often carry themes of follow-through or persistence (*Sysiphus; John Henry*), as well as classic and contemporary children's fiction (e.g., Hardie Gramarky's *Little Toot*, or Florence Heine's *The Day of Ahmed's Secret*). One book (Cecil & Roberts, 1992) presents more than 200 selections from children's literature featuring characters who display "positive coping behaviors."

TABLE 10.3
Sample Class Activities for Volitional Enhancement
Teaching Program (Team 1)

1. Teacher and students list and discuss prominent disturbances to working and studying at home and in class.
2. Working with student lists, teacher makes a master list of "most frequent" disturbances on board and categorizes them according to their origins (i.e., the setting or the student's mind).
3. Teacher and students discuss ways to handle the distractions, beginning with those students "typically use." Responses are recorded next to distractions, and each is considered on the basis of "how well it works." Teacher defines more and less "effective" strategies as those that draw on inner or environmental resources to refocus on task versus those that escalate distractions or siphon off resources, respectively.
4. Teacher models/demonstrates both effective and ineffective responses to a distracting situation that students suggest, relates personal experiences with such situations.
(Items 1–4 Coordinate with Student Objective 1)

5. Teacher leads students through 20-item quiz requiring identification and classification of more effective strategies in various distracting work scenarios; provides supportive feedback.
(Coordinates with Student Objective 2) [First Session Ends Here]

6. Using written scenarios, small groups of students role play more effective strategies for handling distractions. Peer audiences identify and evaluate (rate) actors' choice of strategies. Group discusses results of role play before rotating roles to other members of the group.
(Coordinates with Student Objective 3] [Second Session Ends Here]

7. Teacher reminds students that he or she will be looking for evidence that they are using their strategies for handling distractions and doing their work. Several tasks are targeted for teacher observations over a three-week period. Teacher records the amount of time to complete tasks by individuals and groups, as well as efforts by students to creatively manage workloads using newly acquired strategy knowledge. Students evaluate their own resource management in these same targeted tasks and provide the results to the teacher. Teacher and students discuss results at a designated later date.
(Coordinates with Student Objective 4) [Third Session Ends Here]

A previously validated, behaviorally anchored "distractibility" rating scale for teachers can be used to provide complementary data on volition, measured in a different way (Lambert, Bower, & Hartsough, 1979). It will be important to document the various intended and unintended consequences of such volitional enhancement programs in the educational settings where they are used.

Counseling Programs for Individual Students. In conjunction with classroom curricular initiatives, the Teachers College volitional enhancement research is attending to the needs of special education teachers, counselors, and school psychologists who work regularly with individual students and their families to address areas of particular concern

(Mithaug, 1993). School psychologists are beginning to investigate the use of practical techniques for teaching special students about commitment and follow-through.

One teacher who works with hearing-impaired students has planned a project to evaluate their responses to an article entitled "Get Motivated!," which appeared in a recent issue of a magazine for adolescents: *Scholastic Choices*. Gaskins (1992) interviewed several motivation/volition researchers to aid in preparing the article's content. She also described personal experiences ("motivation hurdles") shared by interviewed teenagers. Exercises are included for students to complete as they read. Characteristics of a "good goal" (i.e., realistic, challenging, clear, measurable) are discussed, and students are asked to identify examples of goals with these characteristics. Students are also asked to write their own goals and how they might measure progress. Students may practice creating proximal subgoals, using the resource network for support, and handling distractions that arise. Their practice can be observed by the teacher, who will then provide feedback. Motivational slogans and pictures add to the article's appeal for students in the middle and secondary grades. The participating special education teacher believes this article may be helpful in her work with those mainstreamed hearing-impaired students who have difficulty with goal setting and follow-through—difficulty stemming from the heavy emphasis on oral instruction in school.

Finally, school psychologists have long used available products and tools to help children learn self-control. Many of these products are games addressing particular cognitive-behavioral difficulties related to volition, such as failure to complete tasks, distractibility, daydreaming, or inability to follow rules. Cards, dice, and directions are similar to those in other board games for children, and the games often include inventories designed to assess accomplishment of therapeutic objectives as well (see, e.g., "The Self-Control Game," Center for Applied Psychology, King of Prussia, PA).

The effectiveness of such products in improving long-range volitional behavior and the validity of the inventories they contain are rarely evaluated, however. Among other things,[2] the Volitional Enhancement program at Teachers College seeks to identify the range as well as the common and distinctive properties of self-control products used by

---

[2]Another effort involves parents in teaching science lessons to kindergarteners. In addition to lessons in simple chemical reactions, these classes are learning about child psychology by recreating the "delay experiment" attributed to Mischel and others (see Mischel et al., 1989). The students help to conduct the experiment using the delay paradigm at the same time that they learn the value of various self-control strategies. Students are permitted to keep the toys they earn by delaying.

practicing school psychologists. The relative effectiveness of these products should be examined—in the light of valid indicators of self-control and other volitional factors—before advice concerning their use is offered to practitioners.

CONCLUSION

The world is replete with enchanting distractions for even the most eager of students. Schools are complex social networks as well as places of work. Homes provide children with television, computer games, and compact discs. After-school clubs engulf what little spare time children have. To succeed academically, students must learn to cope with the competition between their social and intellectual goals and to manage and control the range of other distractions that arise. Volitional strategies have a promising role to play in achieving these goals.

The case for educational research on volition has been made, but critical issues for future work remain. What evidence can be considered most valid for judging skills of self-management and dispositions toward self-responsibility—for judging volition—in students? And what can be done with students who display difficulty in these areas early on? The foregoing examination of past, previous, and ongoing educational research on volition is intended to suggest some directions for practitioners and researchers working together to respond to these persistent concerns.

ACKNOWLEDGMENTS

Portions of this chapter were presented at the annual meeting of the American Psychological Association, August 1993, Toronto, Canada. Other parts were discussed in a seminar at Educational Testing Service in February 1993. Special thanks to N. L. Gage, Liz Sullivan, and Richard Hooley for comments on an earlier draft, and to Carol Nichols who found many children's books related to volition.

REFERENCES

Ach, N. (1910). *Uber den willensakt und das temperament*. Leipzig, Germany: Quelle & Meyer.
Ames, C. (1992). Classrooms: Goals, structures, and student motivation. *Journal of Educational Psychology, 84*, 261–271.
Baumrind, D. (1987). A developmental perspective on adolescent risk taking in contemporary America. In C. Irwin, Jr. (Ed.), *Adolescent social behavior and health*. San Francisco: Jossey-Bass.

Benson, R. (1988). Helping pupils overcome homework distractions. *The Clearing House, 61,* 370–372.

Blumenfeld, P. (1992). Classroom learning and motivation: Clarifying and expanding goal theory. *Journal of Educational Psychology, 84,* 272–281.

Calfee Projects. (1992). *READ Plus/Inquiring School Project News and Commentary.* Stanford, CA: School of Education, Stanford University.

Caragine, C. A. (1993). *Inferencing strategies in context: Supporting four Chapter 1 students in sixth grade reading.* Unpublished doctoral dissertation, Teachers College, Columbia University, New York.

Cecil, N. L., & Roberts, P. L. (1992). *Developing resiliency through children's literature.* Jefferson, NC: McFarland.

Chittenden, E. (1991). Authentic assessment, evaluation, and documentation of student work. In V. Peronne (Ed.), *Expanding student assessment* (pp. 22–31). Alexandria, VA: Association for Supervision and Curriculum Development.

Clark, R. (1983). *Family life and school achievement.* Chicago: University of Chicago Press.

Cooper, H. (1989). *Homework.* New York: Longman.

Corno, L. (1989). Self-regulated learning: A volitional analysis. In B. Zimmerman & D. Schunk (Eds.), *Self-regulated learning and academic achievement* (pp. 111–142). New York: Springer-Verlag.

Corno, L. (1992). Encouraging students to take responsibility for learning and performance. *Elementary School Journal, 93,* 69–84.

Corno, L. (1993). The best-laid plans: Modern conceptions of volition and educational research. *Educational Researcher, 22,* 14–22.

Corno, L., & Kanfer, R. (1993). The role of volition in learning and performance. In L. Darling-Hammond (Ed.), *Review of research in education* (Vol. 19, pp. 3–43). Washington, DC: American Educational Research Association.

Csikszentmihalyi, M., & Larsen, R. (1984). *Being adolescent.* New York: Basic Books.

Darling-Hammond, L., & Snyder, J. (1992). Reframing accountability: Creating learner-centered schools. In A. Lieberman (Ed.), *The changing contexts of teaching. Ninety-first yearbook of the National Society for the Study of Education* (pp. 11–35). Chicago: University of Chicago Press.

Deci, E. L., & Ryan, R. (1985). *Intrinsic motivation and self-determination in human behavior.* New York: Plenum.

Dewey, J. (1964). Interest in relation to training of the will. In R. D. Archambault (Ed.), *John Dewey on education* (pp. 260–285). Chicago: University of Chicago Press. (Original work published 1895)

Dweck, C. S. (1975). The role of expectations and attributions in the alleviation of learned helplessness. *Journal of Personality and Social Psychology, 31,* 674–685.

Finn, J. D., & Cox, D. (1992). Participation and withdrawal among fourth-grade pupils. *American Educational Research Journal, 29,* 141–162.

Gaskins, P. (1992). Get motivated! *Scholastic Choices, 7,* 7–12.

Good, T., Slavings, R., Harel, D., & Emerson, H. (1987). Student passivity: A study of question asking in K-12 classrooms. *Sociology of Education, 60,* 181–199.

Heckhausen, H., & Gollwitzer, P. (1987). Thought contents and cognitive functioning in motivational vs. volitional states of mind. *Motivation and Emotion, 11,* 101–120.

Heckhausen, H., & Kuhl, J. (1985). From wishes to action: The dead ends and short cuts on the long way to action. In M. Frese & J. Sabini (Eds.), *Goal directed behavior: The concept of action in psychology* (pp. 134–160). Hillsdale, NJ: Lawrence Erlbaum Associates.

James, W. (1890). *The principles of psychology.* New York: Holt.

Kanfer, R., & Ackerman, P. L. (1989). Motivation and cognitive abilities: An integrative/aptitude-treatment interaction approach to skill acquisition. *Journal of Applied Psychology—Monograph, 74,* 657–690.

Karabenick, S. A., & Knapp, J. R. (1988). Help seeking and the need for academic assistance. *Journal of Educational Psychology, 80*, 406–408.

Karabenick, S. A., & Knapp, J. R. (1991). Relationship of academic help seeking to the use of learning strategies and other instrumental achievement behavior in college students. *Journal of Educational Psychology, 83*, 221–230.

Karoly, P. (1993). Mechanisms of self-regulation: A systems view. *Annual Review of Psychology, 44*, 23–52.

Kozol, J. (1991). *Savage inequalities*. New York: Crown.

Kuhl, J. (1984). Volitional aspects of achievement motivation and learned helplessness: Toward a comprehensive theory of action control. In B. A. Maher (Ed.), *Progress in experimental personality research* (Vol. 13, pp. 99–171). New York: Academic Press.

Kuhl, J. (1993). The self-regulation-test-for-children (SRTC). In F. E. Weinert & W. Schneider (Eds.), *The Munich Longitudinal Study on the Genesis of Individual Competencies (LOGIC)* (pp. 12–19). (Report No. 9). Munich, Germany: Max-Planck-Institute for Psychological Research.

Kuhl, J., & Beckmann, J. (1985). Historical perspectives in the study of action control. In J. Kuhl & J. Beckmann (Eds.), *Action control: From cognition to behavior* (pp. 89–100). New York: Springer-Verlag.

Kuhl, J., & Kraska, K. (1989). Self-regulation and metamotivation: Computational mechanisms, development, and assessment. In R. Kanfer, P. L. Ackerman, & R. Cudeck (Eds.), *Abilities, motivation, and methodology: The Minnesota Symposium on Individual Differences* (pp. 343–374). Hillsdale, NJ: Lawrence Erlbaum Associates.

Langer, E. J. (1989). *Mindfulness*. Reading, MA: Addison-Wesley.

Lambert, N. M., Bower, E. M., & Hartsough, C. S. (1979). *Pupil Behavior Rating Scale*. Monterey, CA: McGraw-Hill.

Lepper, M. R. (1988). Motivational considerations in the study of instruction. *Cognition and Instruction, 5*, 289–310.

Lewin, K. (1926). Untersuchungen zur handlungs- und affekt-psychologie. II: Vorsatz, wille und bedurfnis. *Psychologische Forschung, 7*, 330–385.

McCaslin, M., & Good, T. L. (1992). Compliant cognition: The misalliance of management and instructional goals in current school reform. *Educational Researcher, 21*, 4–17.

McCaslin, M., & Good, T. L. (in press). The informal curriculum. In D. Berliner & R. Calfee (Eds.), *Handbook of educational psychology*. New York: Macmillan.

McCaslin, M., & Murdock, T. (1991). The emergent interaction of home and school in the development of students' adaptive learning. In M. Maehr & P. Pintrich (Eds.), *Advances in motivation and achievement* (Vol. 7, pp. 213–259). Greenwich, CT: JAI.

McDermott, R., Goldman, S., & Varenne, H. (1984). When school goes home: Some problems in the organization of homework. *Teachers College Record, 85*, 381–409.

McDonough, M. L., Meyer, D. K., Stone, G. V. M., & Hamman, D. (1991, March). *Goal-setting and monitoring among first grade readers during seatwork: Process and differences in process among reading ability groups*. Paper presented at the annual meeting of the National Association of School Psychologists, Dallas, TX.

Mischel, W., Shoda, Y., & Rodriguez, M. (1989). Delay of gratification in children. *Science, 244*, 933–938.

Mithaug, D. (1993). *Self-regulation theory: How optimal adjustment maximizes gain*. New York: Praeger.

Newman, R. S., & Goldin, L. (1990). Children's reluctance to seek help with schoolwork. *Journal of Educational Psychology, 82*, 92–100.

Pervin, L. A. (1992). The rational mind and the problem of volition. *Psychological Science, 3*, 162–164.

Pintrich, P. R., & Schrauben, B. (1992). Students' motivational beliefs and their cognitive engagement in academic tasks. In D. Schunk & J. Meece (Eds.), *Students' perceptions in the classroom: Causes and consequences* (pp. 149–183). Hillsdale, NJ: Lawrence Erlbaum Associates.

Ryan, R. M., & Grolnick, W. S. (1986). Origins and pawns in the classroom: Self-report and projective assessments of individual differences in children's perceptions. *Journal of Personality and Social Psychology, 50,* 550–558.

Salomon, G. (1983). The differential investment of mental effort in learning from different sources. *Educational Psychologist, 18,* 42–50.

Shoda, Y., Mischel, W., & Peake, P. (1990). Predicting adolescent cognitive and self-regulatory competencies from preschool delay of gratification: Identifying diagnostic conditions. *Developmental Psychology, 26,* 978–986.

Snow, R. E. (1989). Toward assessment of cognitive and conative structures in learning. *Educational Researcher, 18,* 8–15.

Sockett, H. (1988, February). Education and will: Aspects of personal capability. *American Journal of Education,* pp. 195–214.

Trawick, L. (1991). Volitional strategy training in students with a history of academic failure. *Dissertation Abstracts International, 52,* 165A. (University Microfilms No. 91–27, 987).

Weiner, B. (1990). History of motivational research in education. *Journal of Educational Psychology, 82,* 616–623.

Williams, L. R. (1993). Developmentally appropriate practice and cultural values: A case in point. In B. L. Mallory & R. S. New (Eds.), *Diversity and developmentally appropriate practice.* New York: Teachers College Press.

Willingham, W. (1985). *Success in college.* New York: The College Board.

Wright, L. R. (1987). The social and nonsocial behaviors of gifted preschoolers during free play. *Dissertation Abstracts International, 48,* 9A. (University Microfilms No. DEV 87–21, 186)

Xu, J. (in preparation). *Doing homework: A study of possibilities.* Unpublished doctoral dissertation, Teachers College, Columbia University, New York.

Zimmerman, B. J. (1990). Self-regulating academic learning and achievement: The emergence of a social cognitive perspective. *Educational Psychology Review, 2,* 173–201.

Zimmerman, B. J., Bandura, A., & Martinez-Pons, M. (1992). Self-motivation for academic attainment: The role of self-efficacy beliefs and personal goal setting. *American Educational Research Journal, 29,* 663–676.

Zimmerman, B. J., & Martinez-Pons, M. (1986). Development of a structured interview for assessing student use of self-regulated learning strategies. *American Educational Research Journal, 23,* 614–628.

Zimmerman, B. J., & Martinez-Pons, M. (1990). Student differences in self-regulated learning: Relating grade, sex, and giftedness to self-efficacy and strategy use. *Journal of Educational Psychology, 82,* 51–59.

Zimmerman, B. J., & Schunk, D. H. (Eds.). (1989). *Self-regulated learning and academic achievement: Theory and research.* New York: Springer-Verlag.

V

Self-Regulation of Environmental Resources

11

Creating Interactive Sociocultural Environments for Self-Regulated Learning

Ronald W. Henderson
Linda Cunningham
University of California, Santa Cruz

> *What a child can do in cooperation today he can do alone tomorrow. Therefore the only good kind of instruction is that which marches ahead of development and leads it.*
>
> —Vygotsky (1962, p. 104)

THE SOCIOCULTURAL PERSPECTIVE

During the past several years, the sociohistorical perspective formulated by Vygotsky has attracted a growing following both in the United States and Europe. Among U.S. psychologists, interest in Vygotsky's approach has grown, in part, out of dissatisfaction with previously dominant viewpoints that attempted to understand the development of children as the result of processes that were relatively independent of the influences of the social context. In experimental research, learning was decontextualized by controlling all but the relevant manipulated variables. In the case of Piaget's influential theory, the intent was to identify generalized processes and structures without regard to specific learning experiences. Thus, both of these dominant paradigms viewed learning and development in a decontextualized way, and many contemporary educators and psychologists, recognizing the limitations of decontextualized views of development, have looked to sociocultural theory as a promising alternative. Although Vygotsky did not use the term *sociocultural*, he remains the major figure of

255

present-day sociocultural theory—a perspective that holds major implications for developmental studies of self-regulation.

Although Vygotsky referred to his approach as *sociohistorical*, the term *sociocultural* theory is now often used to designate the general perspective originated by Vygotsky and some of his Soviet contemporaries, such as Bakhtin, as elaborated by a host of present day followers. The quotation that opens this chapter was chosen because it communicates the essence of the sociocultural perspective. This perspective asserts that individuals and the social milieus of which they are a part constitute mutual, interacting elements of a single system (Cole, 1985). Thus, it is through culturally constituted interaction with others that individuals develop the higher order mental functions required in the performance of organized, planful actions. Vygotsky used the term *higher mental function* to designate any consciously directed thought process (Smolucha & Smolucha, 1989). Vygotsky's conception of higher mental functions would include self-regulation in a sense that is compatible with Zimmerman's (1989) notion of self-regulation as active participation, at metacognitive, motivational, and behavioral levels, in one's own learning processes.

From a Vygotskian perspective, self-regulation includes the coordinated exercise of several higher mental functions, such as memory, analysis, evaluation, synthesis, and planning, forming a psychological system within the context of interaction. That is, within a social context, individual knowledge is constructed and significantly affected by the ideas and actions of others, and whatever higher psychological functions arise through activity with others are affected by historical development and cultural mediation (Cole, 1985). Just what that means, and what implications it holds for the development of self-regulation, we hope to make clear.

In this chapter we offer first an overview of sociocultural theory. We make no pretense of being comprehensive, but seek to describe those features of the theory that are essential to understanding the sociocultural perspective on the development of higher order thinking skills within which self-regulation is included. It is important at the outset to recognize that, within the sociocultural perspective, the acquisition of self-regulation skills is not distinct from the development of other higher order conceptual knowledge. We then examine the implications of the sociocultural perspective for the design of responsive classroom environments, with special attention to its relevance to instructional design for culturally diverse populations of students. This is followed by consideration of a special form of classroom interaction as the context for development: that of technology-based instruction. We conclude with a discussion of issues for future research.

Thinking and Speech

How exactly did Vygotsky propose that individuals gain command of their own planful actions? The answer lies primarily with two ideas. The first concerns the role of speech in social interaction. The second is a construct that, of all aspects of Vygotsky's ideas, has attracted the attention of educators concerned with the design of instructional environments: the zone of proximal development.

In Vygotsky's (1962) view, "thought is not merely expressed in words, it comes into existence through them" (p. 125). This dynamic relationship between thinking and speech or thought and language plays a key role in the development of self-regulation. Within an activity, speech has both a communicative and a social function. It has the privileged role of being a mediational tool. Language, gestures, and affective tone, for example, are all semiotic signs with which human individuals communicate.

The Ontogenesis of Speech

Vygotsky held a developmental perspective on how the individual achieves self-regulatory capacities through the use of *signs*. The infant, through contact with caretakers and others, gains the idea that words have referential functions. At this, the affective-conative stage, an infant who may say the word *mama* and point to another object in the room may be interpreted by the caretaker as asking, "What is that object?" or perhaps, "I want that object." The word itself may have many different meanings, all dependent upon the context in which the word is spoken and the gestures (that is, the other mediational signs) that accompany it. Vygotsky (1981) identified this referential act as the "original function of speech" (p. 219).

The child gains entry into a mediated social life through the development of word meaning, which constitutes the second stage in the ontogenesis of speech. At this stage the child comes to realize the significance of the sign forms he or she has already been using in social interaction. Semantic word meanings themselves are considered to be dynamic; that is, they cannot be understood without reference to the context and "flow of activity" in which they are engaged (Wertsch, 1979).

Within the sociocultural perspective, self-regulation is seen as a linguistically guided process (Whitman, 1990). Claire Kopp's (1982) description of the development of self-regulation provided a useful perspective on the relationship between speech and thought in the ontogenesis of sign-mediated activity during the third stage, and of how that relationship contributes to the individual's capacity to execute planful behavior. In Kopp's view, the development of self-regulation involves a transition from regulation evidenced by responses to the commands of others, which she calls *self-control*, to that of *self-regulation*, which involves the use of goal-oriented monitoring, appraisal, and coping activities on an instrumental level.

This description is consistent with Vygotsky's formulation that from the preschool age of around 3 years, speech begins to be used as an inner mode of mental organization. As we mentioned earlier, speech is initially restricted to referential acts. Then, with internalization of parent commands and understanding of symbolic representation, children begin to use overt speech to monitor their own behavior. However, this "overt" speech is unlike social speech directed toward another; it appears to be directed to no one in particular and represents the child's attempt to use language as a tool. These utterances are referred to as *private* speech. The child uses this self-directed speech as a tool in planning, guiding, and monitoring problem-solving activities (Frauenglass & Diaz, 1985). Two critical points clarify the nature of private speech and its manifestations in self-regulation. First, private speech emerges from the social interaction with others. Vygotsky (1981) wrote that:

> Any function in the child's cultural development appears twice, or in two planes. First it appears on the social plane, and then on the psychological plane. First it appears between people as an *inter*personal category, and then within the child as an *intra*psychological category. This is equally true with regard to voluntary attention, logical memory, the formation of concepts and the development of volition. We may consider this position as a law in the fullest sense of the word, but it goes without saying that internalization transforms the process itself and changes its structure and functions. Social relation or relations among people genetically underlie all higher functions and their relationships. (p. 163, italics added)

Second, the manifestation of private speech and its function in moving the individual from "other" or interpsychological regulation to that of intrapsychological or "self"-regulation occurs within the zone of proximal development.

The Zone of Proximal Development

From a sociocultural perspective, the development of self-regulation requires an awareness of socially approved behaviors, in addition to the maturation of the thought and speech processes just described. As we have seen, the gestures and referential acts of an infant are given meaning by the adult caretaker, with meaning being construed by the context of the activity in which it emerges. At first, the responsibility for gaining meaning from the child's actions and for helping the child to make progress toward the goal of an activity lies largely with the adult. This has been termed the first stage or transition in the *zone of proximal development*, which Vygotsky (1978) defined as "the distance between actual development as determined by independent problem solving and the level of potential development as determined by problem solving under adult guidance or in collaboration with more capable peers" (p. 86).

This first stage or transition in the process from regulation by others in a social context to self-regulation in a social context highlights the degree of intersubjectivity or "consensual interpretation" that exists between the child and the more competent adult. Wertsch (1979) delineated four stages of intersubjectivity that correspond to the degree of responsibility held by each party in an activity. At first there may be little or no intersubjectivity—the child does not understand the meaning of the adult's words or gestures. Then with the aid of maturation and sensitization of the adult to the child's lack of intersubjectivity (that is, the adult may use speech and situation definitions that are strategic for the child and not the adult (Wertsch, 1979), there is movement to a second phase characterized by shared meaning between the two parties involved in the task. The way in which social relations (with particular reference to instructional settings) can be constructed to facilitate the development of higher mental functions such as self-regulation is aptly captured by the metaphor of "scaffolding" whereby the adult acts as and when needed (Wood, Bruner, & Ross, 1976). The responsibility for regulating behavior and committing planful action still lies with the adult, as often the child has not fully gained the significance of the meaning of an activity. In the third phase, the child gains the connection between speech and activity and takes most of the responsibility for the task. It is in this third phase that private speech manifests itself clearly in the self-regulation of an individual. Often strategic patterns of reasoning that the child has previously been encouraged to follow by a more competent other in an activity can be distinctly observed (Wertsch, 1980). Instead of relying on an adult to provide regulative communication, the child "appropriates" this regulative communication that has previously occurred in social dialogue and carries out the actions in an activity independently using private speech. Through such reciprocal interactions the child "internalizes" these strategies and actions and reenacts them in an *internal symbolic dialogue* when planning and deciding on the next steps to take in accomplishing the goals of the task (Ratner & Stettner, 1991). Research in private speech has indicated that private speech emerges when the individual is involved in a difficult task. Tasks that are within an individual's level of competency do not elicit private speech (Diaz, 1986).

However, neither do tasks that are beyond the individual's ability level. Such tasks only engender frustration and defeat (see, e.g., Behrend, Rosengren, & Perlmutter, 1989). The task must be within the level of the child's zone of proximal development in order to facilitate the development of self-regulation.

Private speech undergoes a subsequent developmental transformation in which it comes to be no longer verbalized externally by the individual. Rather, it is verbalized internally, thus becoming "inner" speech. The individual has achieved maximum intersubjectivity with the more competent other and the situation in which the activity took place. She or he is at an independent level. Self-regulation is achieved through the use of inner speech. The nature of inner speech and the proper methods for its investigation are subjects of disputation, and although difficult methodological issues remain to be resolved, studies such as those by Frauenglass and Diaz (1985), Berk (1986), and Bivens and Berk (1990) have supported Vygotsky's view that private speech follows a developmental sequence from an audible, externalized fashion to an internalized "whispering" that precedes the child's actions. It is through this change in verbal thought that inner speech comes to provide an orienting, guiding function for the regulation of behavior. The existing research has empirically illustrated a developmental shift in the use of inner speech in self-regulation. Three- and 4-year-old children tend to use a form of externalized, audible speech when they are attempting a difficult or novel task. By the time they are 7 or 8 years old, they have shifted, largely, to an internalized form of "talking to oneself," which serves a guiding function.

The zone of proximal development should be thought of as a bandwidth of competence, rather than fixed stages. These phases are recursive: When faced with a difficult or new task we often have to rely on more competent others, or to a lesser extent, if it is a task in which

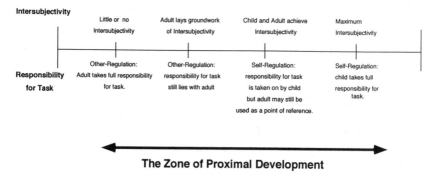

The Zone of Proximal Development

FIG. 11.1. Relationship between task responsibility and intersubjectivity within the zone of proximal development.

we have some definitional knowledge, we rely on the guiding function of private speech to orient our actions. Self-regulation is not a state that, once attained, applies across all content domains or activity settings. Adults may go through something very like this process, in interaction with more competent others, whenever they engage in activities that are in unfamiliar cognitive territory for them.

Vygotsky (1978, p. 86) originally thought of the zone of proximal development idea as an alternative to the traditional ways of thinking about ability, and to the standardized assessment practices associated with those established conceptions. He advocated a holistic, dynamic, interdependent conception of the individual in society—a view that was incompatible with the static "snapshot" embodied in the measurement of intelligence. The following example illustrates the alternative interpretation of ability and its assessment advocated by Vygotsky:

> Imagine that we have examined two children and have determined that the mental age of both is seven years. This means that both children solve tasks accessible to seven year olds. However, when we attempt to push these children further in carrying out the tests, there turns out to be an essential difference between them. With the help of leading questions, examples, and demonstrations, one of them easily solves test items taken from two years above the child's level of [actual] development. The other solves test items that are only half a year above, his or her level of [actual] development. (Vygotsky, 1956, pp. 446–447, cited in Wertsch, 1985, p. 68)

The level of functioning achieved with the aid of prompts and other assistance is thought of as the child's level of potential development (as contrasted with the actual developmental level). Viewed in this way, the zone of proximal development can be thought of as an instructional tool for teachers (see, e.g., Rommetveit, 1985, p. 194). With the assistance of the teacher or other more competent person, the child can participate in accomplishing tasks beyond the already achieved level of competence. Moreover, within such an instructional situation the ideas embodied in the zone of proximal development concept can be used as a guide to track how the child puts externally provided information to use. More fundamentally, as Luis Moll (1990) noted, the very nature of social transactions is central to the zone of proximal development. The zone of proximal development provides a conceptual tool with which to understand the tight connection between the individual, active learning, and social interaction.

Dualistic Versus Interactionist Views on Socialization

Exactly how this internalization or appropriation mechanism works is still being debated. Do children make an exact "copy" of the mediational strategies existing in the dialogue process? Or does the child just "take what's needed" and change or transform this new material to their own purposes?

Wertsch (in press) recently questioned the need for the notion of internalization. He argued that the word *internalization* can often be replaced by the word *master*. This suggests that the outcome of an instructional dialogue is an isomorphic copy of the mediational signs used in the interaction. Historically, this perspective poses a duality between the individual (internal) and society (external). The individual learner is viewed as a passive recipient and the teacher or parent as the active provider of "prepackaged" messages. The consequences of this view for instructional practice take the form most commonly in what Tharp and Gallimore (1988) called the *recitation script*: the dominant classroom protocol of both past and present. Lawrence and Valsiner (in press) recently scrutinized the theoretical roots of the internalization concept and critiqued its applications within sociocultural theory. A disadvantage of the internalization concept is that it implies a unidirectional process of cultural transmission—a connotation that is not consistent with the underlying assumptions of the sociocultural perspective. The appropriate view, they hold, is a bidirectional culture transmission model whereby culturally transmitted input is transformed by the individual in an active process where the materials of semiotic nature are given meaning by the individual, but at the same time there is a reciprocal process whereby "what has become part of the conceptual system is injected back into the environment . . . thus becoming the source of a cyclical influence of the social on the individual domain, and the individual on the social" (Lawrence & Valsiner, 1993).

The term *appropriation* may better represent the sociocultural perspective. Rogoff (1993), who first encountered the appropriation concept in the work of Bakhtin (1981), argued that individuals change through their involvement in an activity by "appropriating" or "taking for one's own use" from a common activity. Their involvement is carried forth to subsequent activities through this intrapersonal change. Mikhail Bakhtin (1981) primarily applied the term *appropriation* to the analysis of literature, but it applies as well to any sociohistorical context in which linguistic interaction is present. Bakhtin said:

> The word in language is half someone else's. It becomes "one's own" only when the speaker populates it with his own intention, his own accent when he appropriates the word, adapting it to his own semantic and expressive intention. (1981, pp. 293–294)

Appropriation, then, does not imply the acquisition of an isomorphic copy. Rather, it implies that understanding may be gained by substituting words of a speaker for our own "counter" words—"the greater their number and weight, the deeper and more substantial our understanding will be" (Voloshinov, 1973, p. 102). Others such as Holquist (1981) have taken the phenomenon of appropriation as one of metaphorically "renting" meaning from a word in a certain context. Wertsch's (1991) metaphor was that of a tool kit, whereby the individual having acquired the tools or mediational means of their culture can choose the most appropriate tool for the job (p. 93). Whichever metaphor one prefers, the idea of internalization or appropriation implies the socialization of not only knowledge, beliefs, and cultural practices, but also executive processes such as self-regulation. As Ratner and Stettner (1991) put it, not only are we taught what to "convey publicly, but we are taught to control what we convey to ourselves."

Bakhtin (1981) called this the *hidden dialogicality*; that is, even after the teacher or caretaker who acted as the regulator of an activity is no longer present, the teacher's regulating influence remains, now in the form of self-regulation by the learner. This takes place by means of private speech, whereby the alternating lines of dialogue that can be heard are often responses to questions that may in fact have been directly asked by other-regulators who are now absent, but the strategic functioning they employed is still present: "The second speaker is present invisibly, his words are not there, but deep traces left by these words have a determining influence on all the present and visible words of the first speaker" (Bakhtin, 1984, p. 197). This hidden dialogicality illustrates the perspective of sociocultural theory on Vygotsky's (1981) claim that mental functioning retains a "quasi-social nature." The social nature and plurality of an individual's experiences must be emphasized. Plurality is reflected in Bakhtin's notion of "dialogism" (Bakhtin, 1981), whereby a word or utterance takes on a different meaning as a function of the context of which it is part. Not only does a word or utterance have a multiplicity of meanings, depending on the varied contexts of an individual's experience, but the individual having been part of these multisocial, multicultural, multihistorical interactions is in fact, "multivocal." In a dynamic social interaction, the individual can both appropriate the suitable voice and word to give meaning in that particular context and through shared interaction develop self-regulation.

EDUCATIONAL IMPLICATIONS

Given the increasingly multicultural and multilingual character of populations served by schools in the United States, perhaps the context where there is greatest potential for plurality of experience and "multivocality" is the classroom. At least there is potential for a plurality of experiences, although genuine opportunities for meaningful interaction among students of different backgrounds occur all too seldom. Considering, from a Vygotskian perspective, that higher mental functions such as self-regulation originate and exist through dynamic social interactions with others, a major task of the teacher is to create classroom interactions that are mindful of this dialogic orientation. In institutions of schooling there has been a history of "privileging" one mediational means over another (Wertsch, 1991). In classrooms, this has typically taken the form of formal discourse, principally initiated and maintained by the teacher. Tharp and Gallimore (1988) characterized the most common engagement genre in the classroom as that of the *recitation script*. This script consists mainly of the teacher lecturing in front of the whole class and asking questions to monitor students' grasp of the material. The students are passive participants in the process. Teachers' questions generally call for low-level factual recall, with over 20% of the questions posed requiring only yes or no answers. The recitation script offers little or no peer-to-peer or teacher-to-student interaction. Rather, it utilizes a "classroom voice" that often differs from that the child experiences elsewhere in the home and natal community.

CONTEXTUALIZATION: BRIDGING THE GAP
BETWEEN THE HOME AND SCHOOL COMMUNITIES

Instructional Conversations

Tharp and Gallimore (1988) identified several avenues teachers may take to contextualize instructional activities so as to minimize sociocultural incongruities that may exist. A fundamental requirement to accomplish this is for the teacher to create a dialogue of shared meaning among participants in a classroom. Tharp and Gallimore called this dialogue the *instructional conversation*. Paradoxically, the instructional conversation is both a social interaction among participants, in that it contains the structure of everyday conversation, as well as the transfer and acquisition of knowledge and skills. It stands in marked contrast to the recitation script, which may be miseducative simply because it does not set up the classroom as a community of discursive inquiry. Employing the instructional conversation instead of the recitation script is one element of instruction based on the sociocultural perspective.

Assisted Performance

Another element in the sociocultural approach proposed by Tharp and Gallimore (1988) is *assisted performance*. Assisted performance reflects the instructional principles suggested by Vygotsky's notion of the zone of proximal development. Through the interactive and reciprocal dialogue that defines the instructional conversation, the teacher scaffolds or assists the child's understanding and responsibility for a task until the child is capable of managing and accomplishing the task independently. Tharp and Gallimore (1988) delineated six means of assisting performance: modeling, contingency management, instructing, cognitive structuring, feeding back, and questioning.

Joint Productive Activities

In order to create instructional conversations and to assist performance, the teacher must create a basis for situationally based definitions (intersubjectivity) that allows performance to be assisted. These acts are what Bruner (1982) called *joint-culture creating*. As we have previously discussed, there may be little or no commonality of meaning and interpretation at the beginning. Children often understand neither the concepts the teacher is trying to relate nor the importance or goal gained by such understanding. But through the use of speech and situational definitions (Wertsch, 1979) the child enters into the reciprocal interaction with the teacher, resulting in a mutual learning system. States of intersubjectivity take shape and meaning from the context in which they transpire (Rommetveit, 1985). Teachers can create tasks or activity settings that involve this kind of mutual or joint participation between teacher and student or among students. In these dyads or small groups there is both shared meaning and shared products. Activity settings should be organized around an implicit goal to be achieved. The creation of a task or joint productive activity and its contextualized setting provides the basis for the development of self-regulation.

Contextualization: Scientific versus Everyday Concepts

Tharp (1989) maintained that, "all instruction should be contextualized in the child's experience, previous knowledge and schemata" (p. 355). Many others have argued along similar lines (e.g., John-Steiner & Smith, 1978; Kirkness, 1986; Tharp & Gallimore, 1988). However, this view is not universal. For example, Zeuli (1986) noted that, in Vygotsky's account of interaction within the zone of proximal development, the teacher's role is to help students understand decontextualized concepts. Vygotsky did not, in Zeuli's view, claim that successful instruction must make connections between schooled concepts and what students already know from their own experiences.

Vygotsky (1962) categorized as *scientific concepts*, those learned in school through formal instruction. Concepts learned "spontaneously" or "nonconsciously" elsewhere he considered to be *everyday concepts*. The term *scientific concepts* is somewhat misleading, for it pertains to a much wider range of abstractions than just those that apply to science. *Schooled concepts* is probably a better term (Tharp & Gallimore, 1988). There is room for legitimate differences of opinion about the practicality, indeed, the possibility, of connecting all schooled concepts to students' personal experiences. The matter becomes especially complex with higher level mathematical constructs that have no physical referents. The important point for present purposes is that, from a sociocultural perspective, it is critically important that teachers engage students in the discussion and use of both schooled and everyday concepts. Through such means, both kinds of concepts are "filled in gradually in the course of further school work and reading. . . . The development of the child's spontaneous concepts proceeds upward, and the development of his scientific concepts downward, to a more elementary and concrete level" (Vygotsky, 1962, p. 108). According to Camperell (1981), self-regulation is possible only after students have come to perceive the relations among concepts. Teachers who provide verbal mediation and guidance to students' own use of the concepts facilitate this understanding.

Computer Learning Environments

The widely heralded advent of technology-based instruction has yet to impact on the nature of instruction as some of its enthusiasts predicted. Computers and associated intelligent technology have not been widely implemented in schools—certainly not in any very meaningful way. Nevertheless, technology does promise an as-yet-unrealized potential to change the nature of the learning environments and the ways in which we design activities to support intellectual development, including the metacognitive activities involved in self-regulation. As noted earlier, Vygotsky insisted that the development of an individual's psychological functioning is embedded in a sociohistorical context and that the ontogeny of cognitive processes can be understood only within the context of the culturally regulated social interactions in which it occurs. Although Vygotsky argued that higher forms of thinking are the result of acculturation into the practices of society, and that those practices include its signs and tools and its technology (Moll, 1990), he could not have foreseen the implications that intelligent technologies hold for educational practice today. To date, much of the research on computers in education has concentrated on outcomes, either in terms of the learning of preset objectives (i.e., those that characterize the standard school curriculum), or on attempts to identify the extent to which skills acquired in interaction with computers transfer to other tasks and settings (e.g., from programming to other kinds of problem solving). That such approaches do not fully take advantage of the potential of the technology is not surprising, because social systems tend not to apply new technologies to reconceived purposes. Rather, social systems generally attempt to use new technologies to accomplish old goals in more efficient ways (Scott, Cole, & Engel, 1992). There are exceptions, of course, as seen in the research of Mehan and his associates (Mehan, Maroules, & Drale, 1985), who reported cognitive and social benefits from using a computer as the stimulus for peer interaction.

Drawing upon the work of Cuban (1986), Scott et al. (1992) argued that technology should be used in the service of reform. Consistent with the sociocultural perspective, their approach would involve "a self-conscious effort to construct a social environment with a new morphology of interpersonal communication" (p. 196). If we follow this counsel, we should examine how computers operate, not as isolated tools installed in classrooms, but as parts of an integrated system of social relations. Although there was fear in the 1970s that computer technology would lead to a deskilling of the work force (Scott et al., 1992), the trend has been in the opposite direction. And although it may be true that adolescents working in fast food restaurants no longer need to be able to compute change, jobs requiring above-average educational attainment have been added to the economy at a much faster rate that jobs for which low levels of educational achievement are adequate (Scott et al., 1992). Typically, these jobs require higher order thinking, including the kinds of skills that constitute self-regulated learning. In fact, many jobs require continuous learning, with those individuals who can direct their own learning effectively enjoying a decided advantage.

Another concern frequently heard is that computers may have a dehumanizing effect: that they will lead to a decline in interpersonal interaction and in failure to develop important social skills. Such an outcome would depend on how computers are used. There is evidence that computers can serve as a medium of communication among teachers and students, resulting in an increase, rather than a decrease, in networks of interaction (Riel & Cole, 1982).

A growing number of theorists and researchers have begun to examine ways in which computers might assume the role of the more knowledgeable peers or adults in the support of learning within the zone of proximal development (Henderson, 1986; Moll, 1990; Pea, 1987). The zone of proximal development concept has received a great deal of attention and some scholars (e.g., Moll, 1990) consider it to be Vygotsky's key theoretical construct. As Moll suggested, this idea captures the very essence of the individual learning and developing within a concrete social situation. Whereas some investigators have employed the zone of proximal development as a useful heuristic device in the design of instructional practices (Henderson, 1986; Meichenbaum, 1985), Moll argued that the zone of proximal development is a key theoretical construct, and not simply a clever instructional heuristic. With this in mind, we first examine an example of an application of instructional technology in which the idea of the zone of proximal development has been applied primarily as an heuristic tool.

The Zone of Proximal Development as an Heuristic Device

Henderson and Landesman (1993) drew upon the Vygotskian perspective to guide the development of an interactive videodisc system designed to teach mathematical concepts and operations, specifically, precalculus. In the original design (Henderson, 1986), Vygotsky's notion of the zone of proximal development was employed as a useful heuristic device. The approach was consistent with the position of Salomon and his associates, who observe that interaction with a computer can be seen as activity within the zone of proximal development, one in which the computer plays a role comparable to that of a more capable peer or coach. In interaction with a computer, a learner may engage in cognitive processes of a higher order than would be possible without that partnership (Salomon, Perkins, & Globerson, 1991).

The advent of multimedia systems has made it possible to expand the potential applications of computer-assisted instruction by linking the flexibility and responsive capability of the microcomputer with the capacity of videodisc players for graphic display of problem-solving processes in real-life situations. Using this technology, it should be possible to facilitate the development of metacognitive skills useful in self-regulated learning, to map new concepts onto familiar situations, and to activate student awareness of the real-world applications of mathematical thinking.

To exploit this potential, *Preparing for Calculus*[1] was designed to provide the kind of interactive learning situation suggested by the zone of proximal development construct. The software was devised to function with the current level of technology most widely available in the schools. The Apple II-based platform (interfaced with a videodisc system) was not capable of functioning as an "intelligent tutor," in the sense of a system operating with artificial intelligence. A true intelligent tutor would be able to perform tasks such as diagnosing the capabilities of the learner and of adjusting instruction accordingly, much as a sensitive teacher or

---

[1] A second generation of this software has been developed to run on both DOS and Apple Macintosh platforms (Landesman & Henderson, 1993).

coach might (Henderson, 1986) if the learning-through-joint-productive-activity premise of the sociocultural perspective were to be fully achieved. Although the interactive videodisc technology described was not capable of learning from the learner and making instructional adjustments accordingly, as might be possible with technology possessed of artificial intelligence, it does manifest other capabilities that are difficult for teachers to attain, even in one-on-one instruction.

A major advantage of interactive videodisc technology is that it provides a powerful means of helping students to map the mathematical concepts and skills they are studying onto relevant, contextually rich, "real-world" situations that connect to their own experience (Henderson & Landesman, 1991, 1992), thus bridging the gap between what Vygotsky called scientific concepts and everyday concepts. The program was also designed to provide metacognitive guidance through talk-aloud modeling of problem solving, providing the opportunity for students to adapt these strategies for their own use through the process of appropriation. In addition, the system was devised to be sensitive to student needs by responding to their self-perceived requirements for assistance while engaged in activities within the zone of proximal development.

Students had a broad range of control over the system. They could govern not only the rate with which they could move through the instructional material, but also the order of presentation and the number of problems they attempted to solve. A student interacting with the system could interrupt the instructor (or instructional segments of any form) at any time, skip instructional segments at will, or review a concept, idea, or demonstration just presented. A student experiencing difficulty with the problems could decide to review previously presented knowledge in order to refresh his or her grasp of prerequisite concepts. The system encourages students to attempt the solution of problems as independently as possible, but at the same time, it is designed to be sensitive to the student's need for support and assistance. The student who does not feel prepared to solve a problem independently can call upon the system for assistance by electing to move to a level of support at which prompts are provided to promote recall and application of information provided during explanation and demonstration segments. If this level of guidance proves inadequate, the student is able to select still another level in which she or he will be guided through the problem, step by step. Thus, the system provides the scaffolding necessary to permit students to solve, in joint activity with the technology, problems they could not accomplish independently. Students regulate their own learning by managing the control options provided by the system.

Data from field testing have demonstrated significant learning outcomes for students using the system, across the eight different instructional modules (Henderson & Landesman, 1993). Interview and survey data documented student enthusiasm for this instructional medium. Overwhelmingly, they indicated that the video presentation of real-world exemplars of mathematical concepts helped them to understand the mathematical ideas encompassed by the materials. The majority also expressed preference for this kind of learning over traditional classroom instruction. Moreover, data on academic motivation demonstrated that student goal orientation was a good predictor of learning. Students with stronger competency-oriented goals accomplished greater learning outcomes than those with performance orientations. But, in general, students did not regulate their use of the system as effectively as they might have. On the basis of self-report data, it appeared that fewer students than expected used the scaffolding opportunities provided by the system to full advantage. A detailed analysis of students' use of the program features over which they had control is in progress, using data from dribble files that recorded all learner keystrokes used in controlling the program (Henderson, Landesman, & Granados, in preparation). Preliminary analyses are generally congruent with the earlier self-report data. Not only did many students fail to make full use of the options available to them, but few persisted to a mastery level by attempting all of the interactive problems. The number of problems actually attempted was the strongest single predictor of learning outcomes.

These observations raise a question concerning the degree of learner control appropriate for an instructional program. In some ways, the situation is analogous to the assignment of tasks in a more traditional instructional context. In the case of the technology-based *Preparing for Calculus* instruction, students who did not elect to take advantage of the help options were free to exit from a problem-solving activity if they were not inclined to persist, even with support from the scaffolding features of the system. Similarly, many students working from textbooks often do not read carefully, follow examples, or engage in additional practice even when they are unsure of concepts and procedures. Good self-regulation skills would be effective in both situations. The *Preparing for Calculus* materials did provide modeling of metacognitive activities, but modeling was limited to thinking processes such as recognizing different classes of problems, deciding on appropriate strategies, and recalling relevant information from previous learning.

Although field trial data do indicate effective learning outcomes from well-designed technology-based systems, it is also clear that not all students take advantage of the opportunities provided by learner control. Students who were sufficiently motivated to attempt larger numbers of problems displayed superior learning. Unless students are sufficiently motivated to apply whatever self-regulatory skills they possess to use the options provided by the system to best advantage, learning outcomes are likely to be less than desired. In this regard it should be noted that, under field trial conditions, the interactive instructional technology was used in isolation from the larger social system of the classroom. Such applications of computers and other instructional technologies are more often the rule than the exception. It is conceivable that better results could be achieved by more fully embedding the use of instructional technology within a social environment in which technology is a partner in joint productive activity within classrooms.

Beyond Heuristic Applications of the Zone of Proximal Development Construct

A goal of the interactive video system described earlier was to assist students in attaining independence in solving precalculus problems. Much of the research on learning within the zone of proximal development has taken a similar view of the purpose of such instruction. That is, that the object is to move the learner from assisted performance to independence. Through social interaction, comprised of sensitive guidance by a more knowledgeable person, students operating within the zone of proximal development would be working at the growing point of their knowledge and toward independence: independence with respect to the skills required for self-regulated problem solving as well as conceptual knowledge and skills. This is not the only way to interpret the zone of proximal development. This view has, in fact, been criticized by some sociohistorical scholars (Engestrom, 1987, cited in Lave & Wenger, 1991; Griffin & Cole, 1984). An alternative interpretation, based on Vygotsky's scientific/everyday concept distinction, defines the zone of proximal development "as the distance between the cultural knowledge provided by the sociohistorical context—usually made accessible through instruction—and the everyday experience of individuals" (Lave & Wenger, 1991, p. 48). A third interpretation, coming from Soviet psychology, considers the zone of proximal development from a collectivist viewpoint. This view emphasizes processes of social transformation and "the conflictual nature of social practice" (Lave & Wenger, 1991, p. 49). Whichever of these interpretations one prefers, they have in common an emphasis on the socially constructed nature of knowledge.

A great deal of human enterprise is carried out, not by individuals acting independently, but in joint activities where the efforts of two or more individuals are combined to accomplish tasks that no constituent member could achieve independently. Although collaborative learning has received a great deal of attention in recent years, in prevailing practice the school classroom may be one of the few contemporary cultural settings in which the emphasis is still on individual rather than joint effort. Schools most often focus on the goal of developing individual ability. Even those educators who employ cooperative groupings in their classes generally construe them as a means to the end of enhanced learning for the individual constituents of the groups, or for the development of social skills and intragroup acceptance among group members. Indeed, when the social organization of the classroom does bring students and teachers together in small-group activities, it is rare for educators to think of the group, rather than the individuals in the group, as having the property of intelligence, the ability to carry out the tasks of the group, the ability to do the learning. Thus, it strains our traditional notions to consider ability as something possessed by the collective. It strains credibility even more to think of ability as a property of a human–machine system, as a partnership with technology (Salomon et al., 1991).

If we consider the coupling of intelligent technologies with the ability of individuals we may need to broaden our conception of self-regulation and intellectual competence to consider the performance of the joint system. As Pea (cited in Salomon et al., 1991) noted, when individuals operate in partnership with intelligent technologies, the system rather than the individual accomplishes the task. Pea referred to this phenomenon as *distributed intelligence*. Intellectual ability, then, might be regarded as the property of a joint system (Salomon et al., 1991). Together, the individual and the technology might be considered to be engaged in what Tharp and Gallimore (1988) called joint productive activity. Within such a system, some of the activities traditionally considered as self-regulatory behaviors of individuals may be accomplished by person–technology partnerships.

If intelligent technology comes to be used more broadly than it is today, forming what Salomon and his associates call partnerships in cognition, our traditional notions of what constitutes the component processes of self-regulatory systems may require some revision. Students might need to become more concerned with managing their own behaviors so as to use the capabilities of the technological partner effectively, rather than with activities such as rehearsal, managing information-encoding strategies to enhance retrieval, or comprehension monitoring. Many of the important but routine acts that require self-regulation by individual students in traditional learning situations may be carried out by the technology, freeing the human partner to concentrate on higher order thinking activities, but at the same time requiring new self-management skills to interact intelligently with the technology. It seems reasonable that different uses of instructional technology in educational settings make different kinds of demands on the self-regulatory skills of learners, and the types of outcomes may differ substantially as well. Salomon and his colleagues' (Salomon et al., 1991) distinction between the effects *of* and *with* technology provides a useful framework for considering these differences.

Effects with and of Technology

We have been using the term *intelligent technologies* as Salomon and his associates (1991) did, to encompass any tool that accomplishes significant cognitive activity for its user. Salomon et al. (1991) made a useful distinction between two different kinds of cognitive effects from partnerships between learners and intelligent technologies. They distinguish between effects *with* and effects *of* intelligent technology. Lasting changes in students' skill, knowledge, and understanding that result from the use of a technology may be considered to be effects of technology, while effects with a technology involve instances in which the tool bears part of the intellectual burden of information processing. The automatization of lower level cognitive processes that support higher order thinking may become unnecessary because the tool assumes that function (Salomon et al., 1991). For example, a system might enable students to solve problems beyond their independent capability by manipulating symbols, thus enabling the learners to engage in higher order thinking.

Even when technology has the capability for joint participation, these outcomes do not occur automatically. Just as many students who used *Preparing for Calculus* failed to take advantage of the opportunity to optimize their learning by fully exercising the options available in the program, observations of students using other well-regarded programs, such as Learning Tools and STELLA, also demonstrate that the students do not automatically take advantage of opportunities for partnership with intelligent technologies (Kozma & Van Roekel, 1986; Perkins, 1985; cited in Salomon et al., 1991). Programs that offer such opportunities must be used in a mindful way, and mindfulness requires effort (Salomon et al., 1991). Students may possess the self-regulatory skills they need to interact with technology in a mindful way but, left to their own volition, fail to expend the effort necessary to put those resources to work.

DIRECTIONS FOR RESEARCH

In the preceding section on the educational implications of the sociocultural perspective, discussions of theory, research, and instructional practice were interwoven. That strategy, rather than one in which research and its educational implications are treated separately, is in some sense dictated by the sociocultural perspective itself. Implicit in the nature of sociocultural theory is the idea that research and practice cannot be separated. Practice is situated within a context, and it is situated practice (not limited, of course, to classroom practice) that is the object of study for sociocultural theory. In the same vein, issues for further study within this framework are not easily separable into tidy studies that refine or fill the gaps in the theory, one chink at a time.

Most of the recent empirical work in sociocultural theory has employed qualitative research methods. There are some notable exceptions, such as the long-term work of the KEEP project (Tharp & Gallimore, 1988), in which a large array of qualitative (e.g., interviews and observations) and quantitative (e.g., analysis of program effects on standardized test scores) methods were combined in a complementary fashion to form an iterative process of feedback and program improvement. More such multiple methods investigations are needed, which integrate both basic inquiry and applied (improvement of academic performance) questions. It should be noted, however, that some scholars who identify themselves with the sociocultural perspective feel that outcomes-oriented studies and the hypothesis testing approach to research are based on a flawed philosophy of science. With these considerations in mind, we recognize that our recommendations for future research directions would not find universal acceptance among sociocultural theorists and researchers.

A broad range of inquiry concerning the relationship of self-regulation to motivation and classroom practice is needed. We have noted that many students, given the occasion to exercise self-regulation in interaction with instructional technology, fail to take advantage of that opportunity. Just because individuals have the opportunity and the ability to self-regulate does not guarantee that those skills will be used. Virtually all theories of self-regulation acknowledge this fact (Zimmerman & Schunk, 1989). How can one optimize the chances that self-regulatory processes will be used, once developed? The sociocultural perspective suggests that students will be motivated when learning activities are embedded in a social system. The issues of motivation and the development of self-regulation are intimately intertwined. For example, joint participation in learning activities may encourage participation for the welfare of the group, especially where there are tangible outcomes of the joint activity. When activities are guided by a knowledgeable adult who provides responsive scaffolding, learners should develop the capacity to independently govern their own participation and learning with similar tasks. One would also expect students to display greater motivation within the context of joint participation activities than with more traditional instructional approaches (e.g., recitation script) oriented to the same desired outcomes. These are reasonable predictions, but there has been far too little research on how general these effects are, under what conditions they are most likely to occur, or how individual characteristics (e.g., social and linguistic skills) interact with outcomes from joint activity versus more traditional approaches. Most conclusions have been based on the analysis of dialogue, with very small samples. Without in any way diminishing the value of those studies, we believe outcomes-oriented investigations are needed to determine the conditions under which self-regulated learning is most likely to develop within the context of joint activity, and to examine the generalizability of effects suggested by qualitative studies.

Do self-regulatory behaviors acquired through social interaction transfer to new activities, or to independent learning tasks outside of the social participation in which they are acquired? This is not really the way to phrase the question for the sociocultural perspective. The appropriate concept for inquiry is *appropriation*, because transfer carries a connotation similar to that of *internalization*, the limitations of which we discussed earlier. It is obvious that students do not appropriate the speech, attitudes, or behaviors of every person with whom they interact. Yet we have little detailed knowledge, in school settings, of the factors that determine what will be appropriated, under what conditions. What determines the extent to which appropriators and appropriatees have a shared understanding of the meanings involved? In other words, as the appropriated word or behavior is reshaped to the appropriator's own use, what conditions govern whether enough shared meaning remains to facilitate communication or joint activity?

We also need greater conceptual clarity regarding the distinctions that are now being made between internalization and appropriation, and between these ideas and arguably similar ideas from other theoretical perspectives. For example, current discussions by sociocultural theorists of the distinctions between internalization and appropriation appear to parallel distinctions between mimicry and rule-governed learning in the observational or imitative learning literature. Research in the social cognitive tradition (Rosenthal & Zimmerman, 1978) demonstrates that individuals acquire new behaviors or cognitions, and modify existing ones, as a consequence of observing the behavior and verbalizations of others. What is acquired is not a carbon copy of the observed behavior. Rather, individuals learn cognitive rules for the production of newly acquired skills and behaviors, which are then called on in appropriate situations and contexts. It is not precisely clear how this phenomenon differs from the concept of appropriation in sociocultural theory. Rogoff (1993) defined appropriation as "the process by which individuals transform their skills and understanding through their participation." In contrast to social cognitive theory where the research paradigm has emphasized behavioral, cognitive, or affective change on the part of the individual, the unit of analysis for sociocultural researchers is more likely to be the activity itself, and cognition is viewed as the active process of solving problems, in contrast to views emphasizing the acquisition of specific capabilities (e.g., skills, schemas, scripts) by individuals. These are important distinctions that should not be dismissed as the result of irreconcilable differences in world views. If modeling and appropriation involve different processes, the nature and consequences of those differences should be documented.

Assuming that appropriation is a positive force in children's learning, what factors influence whose language or other actions are most likely to be appropriated by students? For example, work on relational support (Estrada, 1993) suggests that intersubjectivity is more likely to develop between students and teacher when teachers provide relational support. Relational support refers to instrumental and emotional support provided by a parent, friend, teacher, or other significant person in a student's life. Such support is personalized and depends on a high degree of intersubjectivity between the provider and recipient of the support. For a variety of reasons, students receive less relational support from teachers as they move into the departmentalized programs of middle and junior high schools. Detailed studies are needed to document the association between relational support and intersubjectivity, on the one hand, and between intersubjectivity and the likelihood of appropriation, on the other. The loss of opportunities to cultivate intersubjectivity between teachers and students, which seems especially prevalent at the point of transition to departmentalized school structures, might well contribute to the explanation of problems with motivation and self-regulated engagement with academic tasks in secondary schools.

Of the many other lines of research we could suggest, we conclude with one of special importance as schools in the United States are called on to serve populations that are more and more diverse in language and culture. Questions regarding the effects of culturally compatible instruction on the development of self-regulation afford a fruitful research arena that has barely begun to be explored. The dominant mode of instruction with students from all cultural backgrounds is guided by the mainstream value of individual independence. Most research on self-regulation is based on that same assumption. Yet, in some cultures, children are socialized to value participation in collective, peer-group-oriented activity. Furthermore, whereas instruction is generally intended to teach an analytic approach to problem solving, in which problems are broken into component parts, Tharp (in press) has presented evidence that some cultures, Hawaiian and Navajo, for example, socialize a more holistic view. Both such instances of cultural incompatibility, independent versus group action and analytic versus holistic approaches, hold implications for self-regulation and pose a number of important problems for research.

In either case we must ask, how can instruction be organized to build on the cultural preferences acquired in the natal culture, while also providing a learning environment that facilitates the appropriation of alternative approaches to self-regulation—approaches that will be advantageous when interacting within the dominant culture? The question applies the other way around, as well. Students from the dominant culture need to develop self-regulation skills that facilitate collaborative effort within social organizations that value joint productive activity, thus affording them the flexibility to call upon a repertoire of situationally appropriate competencies. This latter possibility has been given insufficient attention because, although collaborative activity is condoned outside the school context, dominant views of the role of the school still focus on learning for independent action. Work is needed to describe how students develop and apply situationally appropriate self-regulation skills, and on the means by which these ends can be achieved in classrooms comprised of students from a multiplicity of backgrounds.

CONCLUSIONS

In this chapter we have examined the sociocultural view that higher mental functions originate in dynamic social interactions with others. A major task of educators seeking to use sociocultural theory as a guide to instructional design is to create activity settings that enable students to accomplish tasks in partnership with others. Self-regulation skills are included among the higher mental functions that develop through such social interaction. Classroom practices that make effective use of sociocultural principles structure occasions for interactions in which, under the sensitive guidance of a teacher who provides scaffolded instruction, students are able to accomplish tasks beyond their capabilities as individuals. The role of teachers and other agents of socialization is not, in this view, to "transmit" knowledge to the student. Rather, knowledge is assumed to be coconstructed by students and teachers as participants in joint productive activities. The outcomes of coconstruction are assumed to include the ability to guide one's own learning independently.

Small group interaction provides a setting in which participants have the opportunity to appropriate the speech and actions of other members of the social group, modifying those competencies and meanings for their own use. A number of conditions might contribute to effective appropriation. For example, instructionally oriented social interactions might work most effectively when the relations between and among participants support the development of situationally based meanings (intersubjectivity). Positive affect between student and teacher is likely to be a facilitating factor, but these issues require more thorough investigation.

The use of instructional technology presents a unique set of challenges and opportunities for the study of self-regulation. It is clear that many students do not take full advantage of the features of technology-based instructional systems. This is both a self-regulation issue and a motivational issue. In general, the role of motivation has not received sufficient attention within the sociocultural framework, so the issue is not confined to settings involving the use of computers or other intelligent technologies. But with direct reference to instructional technology, a number of specific issues require consideration. If the intelligent technology in student–technology learning partnerships carries out important but routine acts—acts that, in more traditional instructional settings, facilitate the learning of individuals—we may need to begin thinking in new ways about what constitutes effective self-regulation. It will be important to learn what conditions enhance the probability of mindful use of the full range of features afforded by technology and contribute to a willingness by students to expend the necessary effort to put into practice those self-regulatory competencies already possessed. Sociocultural theory suggests that motivation will be heightened when the technology is fully integrated into the social system of the classroom, as contrasted with the more typical situation in which technology stands outside the network of social interaction, as an ancillary tool. It may also be prudent for us to broaden our conception of self-regulation and intellectual competence as qualities of individuals, to consider, in addition, the processes by which joint learner–technology systems function most effectively.

Problems of compatibility between the culture of the school and the natal cultures of students have heretofore not been addressed in research on self-regulation. From a sociocultural perspective, these issues are of vital importance.

REFERENCES

Bakhtin, M. M. (1981). *The dialogic imagination.* Austin: University of Texas Press.
Bakhtin, M. M. (1984). *Problems of Dostoevsky's poetics.* Minneapolis: University of Minnesota Press.
Behrend, D. A., Rosengren, K., & Perlmutter, M. (1989). A new look at children's private speech: The effects of age, task difficulty, and parent presence. *International Journal of Behavioral Development, 12*(3), 305–320.
Berk, L. E. (1986). Relationship of elementary school children's private speech to behavioral accompaniment to task, attention, and task performance. *Developmental Psychology, 22,* 671–680.
Bivens, J. A., & Berk, L. E. (1990). A longitudinal study of the development of elementary school children's private speech. *Merill-Palmer Quarterly, 36,* 4, 443–463.
Bruner, J. (1982). The language of education. *Social Research, 49,* 835–853.

Camperell, K. (1981, December). *Other to self-regulation: Vygotsky's theory of cognitive development and its implications for improving comprehension instruction for unsuccessful students.* Paper presented at the Annual Meeting of the American Reading Forum, Sarasota, FL. (ERIC Document Reproduction Service No. ED 211 968)

Cole, M. (1985). The zone of proximal development: Where culture and cognition create each other. In J. V. Wertsch (Ed.), *Culture, Communication, and Cognition: Vygotskian Perspectives* (pp. 146–161). New York: Cambridge University Press.

Cuban, L. (1986). *Teachers and machines: The classroom use of technology since 1920.* New York: Teachers College Press.

Diaz, R. M. (1986). Issues in the empirical study of private speech: A response to Frawley and Lantolf's commentary. *Developmental Psychology, 22,* 5, 709–711.

Estrada, P. (1993, March). *The importance of creating peer and teacher-student relationships in the service of learning.* Paper presented at the Annual Meeting of the National Association for Bilingual Education, Houston.

Frauenglass, M. H., & Diaz, R. M. (1985). Self-regulatory functions of children's private speech: A critical analysis of recent challenges to Vygotsky's theory. *Developmental Psychology, 21,* 2, 357–364.

Griffin, P., & Cole, M. (1984). Current activity for the future: The ZOPED. In B. Rogoff & J. Wertsch (Eds.), *Children's learning in the zone of proximal development* (pp. 45–64). San Francisco: Jossey-Bass.

Henderson, R. W. (1986). Self-regulated learning: Implications for the design of instructional media. *Contemporary Educational Psychology, 11,* 405–427.

Henderson, R. W., & Landesman, E. M. (1991). Visualizing precalculus concepts: Interactive representation via videodisc technology. *Computers and Education, 17*(3), 195–202.

Henderson, R. W., & Landesman, E. M. (1992). Technology-based developmental instruction in precalculus. *Journal of Educational MultiMedia and HyperMedia, 1,* 65–76.

Henderson, R. W., & Landesman, E. M. (1993). The interactive videodisc system in the zone of proximal development: Academic motivation and learning outcomes in precalculus. *Journal of Educational Computing Research, 9*(1), 29–43.

Henderson, R. W., Landesman, E. M., & Granados, R. (in preparation). *Student self-perceptions and learner control of academic support during videodisc instruction.*

Holquist, M. (1981). The politics of representation. In S. Greenblatt (Ed.), *Allegory in representation: Selected papers from the English Institute* (pp. 163–183). Baltimore: John Hopkins University Press.

John-Steiner, V., & Smith, L. (1978). *The educational promise of cultural pluralism: What do we know about teaching and learning in urban schools?* (Vol. 8). St. Louis, MO: CEMEREL.

Kirkness, V. J. (1986). Native Indian teachers: A key to progress. *Canadian Journal of Native Education,* 47–53.

Kopp, C. B. (1982). Antecedents of self-regulation: A developmental perspective. *Developmental Psychology, 18,* 2, 199–214.

Kozma, R. B., & Van Roekel, J. (1986). *Learning tool.* Ann Arbor, MI: Arboworks.

Landesman, E. M., & Henderson, R. W. (1993). *Preparing for calculus.* New York: McGraw-Hill.

Lawrence, J. A., & Valsiner, J. (1993). Conceptual roots of internalization: From transmission to transformation. *Human Development, 36,* 150–167.

Lave, J. & Wenger, E. (1991). *Situated learning legitimate peripheral participation.* New York: Cambridge University Press.

Mehan, H., Maroules, N., & Drale, C. (1985). Some cognitive and social benefits of peer interaction on computers. In H. Mehan & L. Moll (Eds.), *Computers in classrooms: A quasi-experiment in guided change. Final report.* (ERIC Document Reproduction Service No. ED 292 460)

Meichenbaum, D. (1985). Teaching thinking: A cognitive-behavioral perspective. In S. F. Chipman, J. W. Segal, & R. Glaser (Eds.), *Thinking and learning skills: Vol. 2. Research and open questions* (pp. 407–426). Hillsdale, NJ: Lawrence Erlbaum Associates.

Moll, L. (1990). Introduction. In L. Moll (Ed.), *Vygotsky and education: instructional implications and applications of socio-historical psychology* (pp. 1–27). New York: Cambridge University Press.

Pea, R. D. (1987). Integrating human and computer intelligence. In R. D. Pea & K. Sheingold (Eds.), *Mirror of minds: Patterns of experience in educational computing* (pp. 128–146). Norwood, NJ: Ablex.

Ratner, H. H., & Stettner, L. J. (1991). Thinking and feeling: Putting Humpty Dumpty together again. *Merill-Palmer Quarterly, 37*(1), 1–26.

Riel, M., & Cole, M. (1982). *Mislabeled, but not misidentified.* Final Report to the National Institute of Education. San Diego: Laboratory of Comparative Human Cognition, University of San Diego. (ERIC Document Reproduction Service No. ED 249 740)

Rogoff, B. (1993). Guided participation and appropriation. In R. Wozniak & K. Fischer (Eds.), *Development in context*. Hillsdale, NJ: Lawrence Erlbaum Associates.

Rommetveit, R. (1985). Language acquisition as increasing linguistic structuring of experience and symbolic behavior control. In J. V. Wertsch (Ed.), *Culture, communication, and cognition: Vygotskian perspectives* (pp. 183–204). New York: Cambridge University Press.

Rosenthal, T. L., & Zimmerman, B. J. (1978). *Social learning and cognition*. New York: Academic Press.

Salomon, G., Perkins, D. N., & Globerson, T. (1991, April). Partners in cognition: Extending human intelligence with intelligent technologies. *Educational Researcher, 20*(3), 2–9.

Scott, T., Cole, M., & Engel, M. (1992). Computers and education: A cultural constructivist perspective. In G. Grant (Ed.), *Review of Research in Education* (Vol. 18, pp. 191–251). Washington, DC: American Educational Research Association.

Smolucha, L., & Smolucha, F. (1989, April). *A Vygotskian perspective on critical thinking.* Paper presented at the Conference on Science and Technology for Education in the 1990's: Soviet and American Perspectives. (ERIC Document Reproduction Service No. ED 314 770)

Tharp, R. G. (1989). Psychocultural variables and constants: Effects on teaching and learning in schools. *American Psychologist, 44*(2), 349–359.

Tharp, R. G. (in press). Intergroup differences among Native Americans in socialization and child cognition: An ethnogenetic analysis. In P. Greenfield & R. Cocking (Eds.), *Cross-cultural roots of minority child development*. Hillsdale, NJ: Lawrence Erlbaum Associates.

Tharp, R., & Gallimore, R. (1988). *Rousing minds to life.* Cambridge: Cambridge University Press.

Voloshinov, V. N. (1973). *Marxism and the philosophy of language*. New York: Seminar Press.

Vygotsky, L. S. (1962). *Thought and language* (pp. 125, 141). Cambridge, MA: MIT Press.

Vygotsky, L. S. (1978). *Mind in society.* (M. Cole, V. John-Steiner, S. Scribner, & E. Sabermen, Eds.). Cambridge, MA: Harvard University Press.

Vygotsky, L. S. (1981). The development of higher forms of attention in childhood. In J. V. Wertsch (Ed.), *The concepts of activity in Soviet psychology*. Armonk, NY: Sharpe.

Wertsch, J. V. (1979). From social interaction to higher psychological processes. *Human Development, 22*, 1–22.

Wertsch, J. V. (1985). *Vygotsky and the social formation of the mind.* Cambridge, MA: Harvard University Press.

Wertsch, J. V. (1980). The significance of dialogue in Vygotsky's account of social, egocentric, and inner speech. *Contemporary Educational Psychology, 5*, 150–162.

Wertsch, J. V. (1991). *Voices of the mind: A sociocultural approach to mediated action.* Cambridge, MA: Harvard University Press.

Wertsch, J. V. (in press). Internalization: Do we really need it? *Human Development.*

Whitman, T. L. (1990). Self-regulation and mental retardation. *American Journal on Mental Retardation 94*(4), 347–362.

Wood, D., Bruner, J. S., & Ross, G. (1976). The role of tutoring in problem-solving. *Journal of Child Psychology and Psychiatry, 17,* 89–100.

Zeuli, J. P. (1986, April). *The use of the zone of proximal development in everyday and school contexts: A Vygotskian critique.* Paper presented at the Annual Meeting of the American Educational Research Association, San Francisco. (ERIC Document Reproduction Service No. ED 271 509)

Zimmerman, B. J. (1989). Models of self-regulated learning and academic achievement. In B. J. Zimmerman & D. H. Schunk (Eds.), *Self-regulated learning and academic achievement* (pp. 1–25). New York: Springer-Verlag.

Zimmerman, B. J., & Shunk, D. H. (1989). *Self-regulated learning and academic achievement.* New York: Springer-Verlag.

12

Adaptive Help Seeking:
A Strategy of Self-Regulated Learning

Richard S. Newman
University of California, Riverside

The self-regulated learner has available a repertoire of strategies that he or she spontaneously employs in goal-directed ways. In the classroom, students who are self-regulated blend "personal ingredients" of cognition, metacognition, motivation, and affect with behavior in such a way that the blending flexibly suits the classroom environment. The purpose of this chapter is to examine several ingredients of self-regulated learning by focusing on one particular classroom activity: *help seeking*.

When faced with difficult tasks that require assistance from a more knowledgeable person, the self-regulated learner is expected to seek assistance by asking questions. High achievers—whom I will assume often engage in self-regulated learning—have, in fact, been found to engage in help seeking from their instructor or classmates relatively frequently (Karabenick & Knapp, 1991; Zimmerman & Martinez-Pons, 1986). The strategy of help seeking seems simple and the rationale for including it in a repertoire of self-regulation straightforward. Yet in the reality of classroom life, student questioning is seen infrequently (Dillon, 1988; Good, Slavings, Harel, & Emerson, 1987). The implicit rule perceived by many students is that if one does not know an answer or does not understand the lesson, he or she keeps quiet and perhaps listens but definitely does not raise a hand to ask for help (Morine-Dershimer, 1985). Students often say they are reluctant to seek help because they are afraid of looking "dumb" in the eyes of their classmates (Newman & Goldin, 1990). Adults as well, when faced with health- and job-related decisions, often report that help seeking elicits perceptions of personal inadequacy, incompetence, and threats to their self-esteem (Rosen, 1983; Shapiro, 1983).

Are there ways of changing the situation so as to facilitate help seeking in the classroom? In order to address this question, I first discuss the instrumentality, or *adaptiveness*, of help seeking and how adaptiveness can be represented in a general model. Second, I discuss how adaptiveness in help seeking is influenced by children's academic goals and the affective relationship between help seeker and help giver. Third, I discuss several specific ways of applying what we know about adaptive help seeking in order to help students regulate their own learning in the classroom.

A MODEL OF ADAPTIVE HELP SEEKING

An important way in which individual differences in students' academic help seeking traditionally have been explained is according to the dimension of *dependence* versus *independence*. Help seekers have been characterized as students who are immature or dependent on others, whereas those who can work on their own without needing help have been characterized as mature and autonomous. Indeed, the label *self-regulated learner* conjures up individuals who independently control their own academic outcomes without need for assistance from others. Perhaps especially in Western societies, which tend to emphasize self-reliance and individual competitiveness, help seeking among school-aged children has been perceived as an activity to be avoided because of its negative connotation of incompetence, immaturity, and overdependence on others.

Although there is merit in viewing certain elements of children's social and emotional development in broad terms of a change from dependence to increasing independence (Hartup, 1963), such a characterization is not necessarily appropriate for explaining individual differences in academic help seeking, that is, for identifying which students in a classroom tend to rely on assistance from others and which do not. Only recently have individual differences in help seeking been discussed in a less simplistic and more accurate way (Nelson-Le Gall, 1985). Help seeking is useful and efficacious under certain conditions; the key is the qualifier, "under certain conditions." Simply put, dependence is not the same as overdependence. The help seeker can act purposefully and instrumentally, not only remedying an immediate problem but ensuring long-term autonomy through mastery of a task. Such a view of "instrumental help seeking" is consonant with work of clinical psychologists who have long posited the value of maintaining proximity to and seeking support from others in childhood as well as across the lifespan (e.g., Ainsworth, 1991). It is also consonant with work of motivational theorists who view help seeking as a way of achieving environmental control in the learning process. Help seeking is a volitional strategy that can protect one's intention to learn when one is faced with "competing action tendencies," such as giving in to distractions or giving up (Kuhl, 1985). When stuck, relying on assistance from teachers and classmates is a type of task engagement that is much preferred to dysfunctional perseveration (Rohwer & Thomas, 1989).

Expanding Nelson-Le Gall's (1985) view of "instrumental help seeking," Newman (1991) specified that *adaptive help seeking* in the classroom is defined by a sequence of decisions and actions that:

1. Follows the student's awareness of a lack of understanding.

2. Involves the student considering all pertinent and available information in making the following decisions: (a) necessity of the request: Is it necessary that I ask for help?; (b) content of the request: What should I ask? (or how shall I formulate the particular question?); and (c) target of the request: Whom should I ask? (the teacher or a classmate).

3. Involves the student expressing the request for help in a way that is most suitable to the particular circumstance.

4. Involves the student processing the help that is received in such a way that the probability of success in subsequent help-seeking attempts is optimized.

A general model of adaptive help seeking is proposed in Fig. 12.1. The model illustrates how executive decision making and the involvement in this decision making of the self-system (cf. McCombs, 1986) play an important role in self-regulated learning in general and in help seeking in particular. The term *self-system* is meant to connote all our personal thoughts, beliefs, desires, values, and feelings that help construct our choices and decisions.

In Fig. 12.1, I assume that the student's work on a task, say in text processing or problem solving, proceeds to some point at which the student monitors his or her comprehension with self-questions such as "Do I understand this?" or "Is this answer right?" (e.g., Markman, 1981). If the student's answer is "yes," he or she expresses whatever is in his or her short-term memory store of understanding. If the student's answer is "no," a motivational-affective "filter" of the processing system is accessed. Through the filter, several questions are addressed: (a) Should I proceed?, (b) How should I proceed?, (c) What should I ask?, and (d) Whom should I ask?.

The student first considers perceptions of task difficulty and others' expectations of his or her performance in relation to self-perceptions such

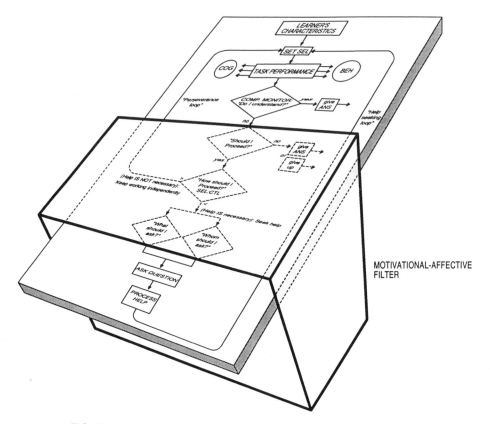

FIG. 12.1. A general model of adaptive help seeking. Learner's characteristics include a confidence tolerance level (CTL). Learner's self-confidence or self-efficacy level is designated by SEL. Cognitive and metacognitive processes are designated by COG, and behaviors by BEH. The
motivational-affective filter, through which all processing passes, includes
the learner's self-system of attitudes, beliefs, goals, values, and feelings in
relation to the classroom environment.

as attributions for the lack of understanding (Why am I having difficulty?),
personal goals (Why should I proceed: in order to learn? to get the right
answer and be seen as smart?), values (What do I get out of all this
effort?), agency (Do I have the ability to go on?), and expectations (Do I
expect to succeed?). The student analyzes the costs and benefits of
proceeding with the task. The student has two options to the question,
Should I proceed? If the answer is "no," he or she either expresses his
or her current understanding or gives up. If the answer is "yes," the
student proceeds to the next self-question.

This next decision, How should I proceed? (i.e., Should I rely on myself
or others?), might be thought of as a comparison between two parameters,

(a) a preset confidence tolerance level (CTL) and (b) a self-confidence or self-efficacy level (SEL) for the particular task and answer at hand. The confidence tolerance level is presumably already set according to one's self-system beliefs, in particular, one's level of intrinsic preference for challenge (Harter, 1981), one's goals of task versus ego involvement (Nicholls, 1979), and one's proclivity to take risks (Clifford, 1991). The confidence tolerance level is traitlike and can be characterized as an individual-difference, or "personal style," variable. The confidence tolerance level is relatively low for children who prefer challenges, are task-involved, and are willing to take risks; it is relatively high for children who do not prefer challenges, are ego-involved, and are not willing to take risks. It represents the tolerance level below which one feels that help from someone else is necessary and beyond which one feels comfortable relying on oneself. The student compares his or her tolerance level with an ever-changing, task- and answer-specific level of self-confidence or self-efficacy (Bandura, 1977; Schunk, 1989).

If the confidence tolerance level is exceeded by the current level of self-efficacy, the student perseveres, working independently under a cognitive executive-monitoring system that directs different activities. Perhaps the student makes no change in activity, or perhaps he or she employs increased attention or effort, a new strategy, some external aid such as a dictionary or a reference book, or self-questions. Self-questions can take many forms, such as How do I do this, What is the main idea of the story, or Do I add or subtract? If the confidence tolerance level is not exceeded by the current level of self-efficacy, the student decides to seek help. At this point, the student further considers all pertinent and available information regarding, for example, task demands, personal resources, and costs and benefits, in making the remaining two decisions: (a) What should I ask, and (b) Whom should I ask? Following these decisions, which were discussed in Newman (1991), the student expresses the request for help and processes the help that is received.

It should be noted that this model of adaptive help seeking, although presented in a flow-chart format for the purpose of specifying component processes and decisions, is not meant to imply that the various processes and decisions necessarily are executed in a sequential way. Graesser and McMahen (1993) made a similar point that their three-component model (i.e., anomaly detection, question articulation, and social editing) of question asking may be executed in a nonsequential, interactive fashion whereby, for instance, the social editing process influences both anomaly detection and question articulation. The motivational and affective "filtering" that is involved in both Graesser and McMahen's social editing of questions and the present model's decision making influences the cognitive and behavioral processing of help seeking in a very fundamental, "constructivist" way. It is impossible to specify precisely the point at which the non-self-regulated learner "goes wrong" in Fig. 12.1 on a given task. All we can say is that the self-regulated learner takes the time and expends the energy to proceed thoughtfully through these various points of decision making. The nonself-regulated learner does not.

THE ROLE OF MOTIVATION AND AFFECT IN ADAPTIVE HELP SEEKING

For the self-regulated learner, the help-seeking process is complex because there are so many decisions that must be made and so many factors having to do with both the person and the classroom environment that are considered in the decision making. Help seeking is different from most other strategies of self-regulated learning because it is a social strategy, involving individuals other than the learner. Because help seeking is not an isolative activity, motivational and affective factors strongly come into play in constructing the stage for, and influencing in an ongoing way, the help-seeking process. In this part of the chapter, I discuss the role of the motivational-affective filter through which the cognitive and behavioral processing of help seeking takes place.

Academic Goals

Numerous self-system beliefs such as causal attributions, expectancies for success and failure, level of interest, academic goals, perceived control, sense of self-worth, and self-perceptions of ability have been discussed in relation to students' level of task engagement in general (Corno, 1986), and students' likelihood of academic help seeking in particular (Newman, 1991; Newman & Schwager, 1992). Of all these motivation-related measures, the most consistent set of research findings regarding help seeking has involved students' academic goals.

Goals can be conceptualized in many different ways, from very specific and discrete classroom goals (e.g., to finish all the problems in the assignment as quickly as possible, to get a good grade on the test, to look smart in front of classmates; see Nicholls, Patashnick, & Nolen, 1985; Wentzel, 1989) to very general orientations that cut across specific contexts and usually are measured in a bipolar way (e.g., intrinsic vs. extrinsic, Harter, 1981; learning vs. performance, Dweck, 1986; and task-involved vs. ego-involved, Nicholls, 1979). The goals that have been demonstrated most clearly to be related to academic help seeking are of the latter, orientational type, namely, intrinsic versus extrinsic orientation and task versus ego involvement.

The role of intrinsic orientation on help seeking is shown in the following two studies, each of which utilized different motivational subscales (i.e., striving for independent mastery, curiosity and interest, and preference for challenge) of Harter's (1981) scale of intrinsic orientation. Nelson-Le Gall and Jones (1990) examined the independent mastery and curiosity/interest dimensions of intrinsic orientation. Third and fifth graders characterized as intrinsic, in particular in their striving for independent mastery, were more likely to seek help by asking for hints than by directly asking for answers on a vocabulary task. Children characterized as extrinsic were just as likely to ask for hints and answers. Hints, more than direct answers, seem to be indicative of an active, inquisitive, and mastery-oriented type of learning. The curiosity/interest dimension of intrinsic orientation was not related to help seeking.

Further evidence of a relationship between intrinsic orientation and help seeking comes from Newman (1990). Findings again suggest differentiation among different dimensions of intrinsic orientation, as well as the existence of different relations according to students' grade level. Two dimensions of intrinsic orientation were measured: striving for independent mastery, and preference for challenge. Children were in elementary school (Grades 3 and 5) and middle school (Grade 7). Across all three grades, the greater the children's preference for challenge, the greater was their self-reported likelihood of seeking help. Striving for independent mastery was related to help seeking in a more complex, grade-related way. At the elementary grades, the weaker the students' striving for independent mastery (i.e., the greater their dependence on the teacher), the greater was the likelihood of seeking help, whereas at middle school the stronger the students' striving for independent mastery, the greater the likelihood. For younger children, then, two seemingly divergent purposes (challenge and dependency) may be important in explaining help seeking; for older children, on the other hand, two seemingly convergent purposes (challenge and independent mastery) may be important.

These two sets of findings provide a reminder that categorizing students' intrinsic orientation is not simple. There can be multiple influences that are not always consonant with one another, that operate simultaneously, and that have varying degrees of personal importance to the individual over the school years. In addition to goals being viewed as an individual-difference variable that characterizes children in a trait-like way, goals can also be viewed as an influence coming from the teacher, that is, an influence that characterizes the classroom.

Newman and Schwager (1991) demonstrated how a goal that simulates a classroom influence can affect students' help seeking. Elementary-aged children were presented math problems and were invited to address questions to an experimenter/tutor. Children were assigned to one of two goal conditions, *task-involved* and *ego-involved*. The children assigned to the task-involved condition were told, "Working on math puzzles like these will probably help you learn new things in math . . . doing these puzzles tends to 'sharpen the mind' and make you think . . . it helps you become more skillful at solving all sorts of problems. . . ." The children assigned to the ego-involved condition were told, "How you do on math problems like these helps us know how smart you are in math and what kind of grade you might get in math class . . . we are interested in how you do compared with other kids at your grade level. . . ."

Students' questioning was recorded and categorized according to type of question. These included requests for process-related information to help solve the problems (e.g., do I add, or how do you do it?), requests for confirmation of an answer, and direct requests for the answer. Because students could ask (and have answered) any number of questions on each problem, within-problem *patterns of questioning* (i.e., sequences of question–answer interactions with the tutor) were also categorized. One particular pattern of questioning that was often seen was noninquisitive behavior (e.g., immediately ask for the answer without first attempting any work; or work on the problem, give a wrong answer, and give up).

The goal condition affected questioning in two ways. First, students with a task-involved goal showed a greater desire to confirm their work to see if they were right than did students with an ego-involved goal. Presumably students in the task-involved condition requested confirmations with the purpose of using the feedback for debugging and self-correcting their work. Second, the ego-involved goal was associated with noninquisitive behavior. The emphasis on students' comparing performance results with others apparently attenuated desire for mastery and reduced perseverance. Incidentally, goal also affected problem-solving performance: Task-involved students solved more problems correctly than did ego-involved students. Sixth graders were more likely than third graders to request process-related help and less likely to both directly ask for the answer and engage in noninquisitive behavior. Findings confirm the importance of children's academic goals in the learning process (e.g., Graham & Golan, 1991) and, furthermore, force us to consider the potential impact of "real-life" classroom factors that can be much more enduring than subtle experimental manipulations. Goal-related expectations, perceptions, and messages—both implicit and explicit—from teachers, parents, and classmates can powerfully affect children's classroom interaction and achievement (Eccles & Wigfield, 1985).

Affective Relationship Between Help Seeker and Help Giver

Of the two components of the motivational-affective filter, the affective is perhaps the more difficult to research and understand. How children feel about seeking assistance in the classroom has not been directly examined. In general, feeling states (or moods or emotional experiences) are difficult if not impossible to measure with reliability and validity in nonindividual, nonclinical settings. However, I think we can learn about the role of affect on academic help seeking in two ways: first, by examining the literature on children's attitudes and beliefs about help seeking, and second, by examining what is known about the social and affective origins of self-regulation.

Attitudes and Beliefs. An important link between the means to achieve a goal and the spontaneous employment of those means is the individual's sense of *instrumentality* concerning the means (Skinner, Chapman, & Baltes, 1988). At least two aspects of instrumentality that are critical in explaining whether children spontaneously use particular strategies are utility and economy (Paris, Newman, & Jacobs, 1985). That is, the individual must understand and personally believe in the effectiveness of the strategy. A sense of utility in employing the strategy is personally constructed by weighing costs (e.g., the amount of effort required or the time taken away from competing activities) versus benefits (e.g., the value of task success).

For adults, typical costs of seeking help for job- or health-related needs are threats to one's self-esteem due to perceived personal inadequacy. Typical benefits are resultant learning or long-term mastery of the problem (Rosen, 1983; Shapiro, 1983). Elementary school children similarly perceive personal costs and benefits of classroom help seeking. Most notably, children commonly feel embarrassed, or "dumb," in the eyes of classmates or the teacher if there is an expectation that help should not be required (van der Meij, 1988). Children as young as 5 and 6 years associate help from the teacher with low ability (Graham & Barker, 1990).

Although there is no evidence of any grade-related change beyond the early elementary years in students' awareness of costs and benefits of help seeking, the relationship between this awareness and the likelihood of acting on the awareness may change (Newman, 1990). Across Grades 3, 5, and 7, children's positive attitudes about help seeking (i.e., about the benefit of learning) are predictive of the children's self-reported intentions of seeking help. In addition, at Grade 7, children's negative attitudes about help seeking (i.e., about the cost of embarrassment) are predictive of their intentions of not seeking help. In other words, starting in middle school, students' help-seeking intentions seem to be impacted in a complex, adultlike way by competing positive and negative attitudes.

Feelings of personal failure, inadequacy, and low self-esteem often make children and adolescents reluctant to reveal their vulnerability by seeking assistance in the classroom. Reluctance to seek help is expected in situations where failure is perceived as indicative of an injured ego. However, when one perceives that failure is due to the lack of a specific skill rather than a global inadequacy—that is, when failure is not necessarily expected in the future and one's ego is not in jeopardy— reluctance to seek help tends to be minimized (Rosen, 1983; Shapiro, 1983).

Social and Affective Origins of Self-Regulation. In the absence of research that has dealt directly with students' feelings about seeking help, it is informative to think about the motivational-affective filter in the help-seeking process in terms of the social and affective origins of the child's capacity to self-regulate. Although the term *self-regulation* in the context of school learning is relatively new, it has been used prominently in Soviet developmental psychology (e.g., Vygotsky, 1978) and child clinical psychology (e.g., Stern, 1985).

According to Vygotsky (1978), a child's cognitive development is integrally connected with social influences, in particular, assistance, coaching, and direct instruction, from an adult caregiver—usually a parent. Tasks, such as reading stories, categorizing objects, and assembling puzzles, are worked on "intersubjectively," that is, with joint participation and shared goal. Assistance is provided in the form of scaffolding, whereby the adult monitors how the child is doing and what the child needs so that just the right amount of help—not too little and not too much—can be given. The adult provides needed assistance, weans the child from unneeded assistance, and inculcates goal-directedness so that executive functioning becomes internalized. At the point when other-regulation becomes self-regulation, the child has not simply internalized the adult's directives, but has taken over the adult's regulating role (for further discussion, see Diaz, Neal, & Amaya-Williams, 1990; Wertsch, 1985).

Importantly, during the socialization process at times of task difficulty, the adult may have to reintroduce assistance to the child. Likewise, once the child is on his or her own, at times of task difficulty, the child may have to seek assistance from someone else. When goals require volitional protection and maintenance, self-regulation may require help seeking. One of the important socializing functions of the parent, then, is to share and practice with the child the knowledge of when, how, and to whom to ask questions. This *conditional knowledge* of strategy use (Paris, Lipson,

& Wixson, 1983), which helps the individual make the three important decisions that define adaptiveness (i.e., necessity, content, and target of the request), is often missing in the repertoire of the nonself-regulated learner.

Although the function of other-regulation can be provided at times by more knowledgeable peers (Azmitia, 1988), teachers and mentors (Lave, 1988; Palinscar & Brown, 1984), and even interactive computer tools (Salomon, Globerson, & Guterman, 1989), the parent–child relationship is the most natural context for the child's transformation from interpsychological to intrapsychological functioning (Rogoff & Gardner, 1984). I believe it is the affective experience inherent in the early parent–child relationship that is so critical for this aspect of development. Exploring this relationship helps explain individual differences in children's self-regulatory capacities (Stern, 1985); it may also inform our efforts at facilitating self-regulated learning in the context of the classroom.

Social origins of self-regulation largely involve sharing. Secure attachment between a mother and her young infant is regulated by the mother through actions such as cuddling each other, holding each other, touching each other, and looking into each other's eyes. Within a context of nurturance and warmth with the mother, the infant engages in a deliberate sharing of experiences about events and things and feels comfortable to explore and seek information from the environment. By the time the infant is 7–9 months old, mother and infant share the focus of attention by joint pointing and gesturing, and they share subjective states such as happiness, fear, and uncertainty. Importantly, these experiences involve an attunement of mother's and infant's affect (Stern, 1985). With the emergence of language, sharing also involves words (Bus & vanIJzendoorn, 1988). From age 2 on, during joint problem solving, speech is commonly used by the child when encountering difficulty, for communicating with the adult his or her frustration, or for asking for help (Luria, 1982). The child comes to understand that verbal expression of a need for help is an instrumental means to solve difficult problems.

Intersubjectivity, affective attunement, joint problem solving, and shared goals are experiences that are most likely to be had in families where parents expect mature and obedient behavior from their children and at the same time provide encouragement and nurturance. Children having these experiences are likely to develop instrumental competence, that is, autonomy, achievement orientation, social responsibility, and, I assume, the capacity for self-regulation. The question at hand is whether the Vygotskian notion of shared activity and the affective component of the parent–child relationship can be extrapolated to educational settings to influence schoolchildren's self-regulation. With what we know about motivational and affective influences on children's help seeking, can classroom activity be designed to facilitate adaptive help seeking?

FACILITATING ADAPTIVE HELP SEEKING IN THE CLASSROOM

In previous papers, I have discussed classroom factors, such as climate, goal orientation, structure of class activity, type of learning task, and interest level in the curriculum material, that can influence children's help seeking (Newman, 1991; Newman & Schwager, 1992). To illustrate the influence of motivation and affect on academic help seeking, I briefly discuss two particular classroom strategies, namely, reciprocal questioning and collaborative teacher–student involvement, that teachers might use to facilitate their students' adaptive help seeking.

Reciprocal Questioning

The structure of class activity is one feature around which teachers organize and carry out rules of classroom communication, feedback, and student–teacher interaction (Berliner, 1983). In general, small-group structure involves students cooperating with one another for a common goal. There is a lack of interindividual competitiveness, and there is a sense that students have control over their own academic outcomes. Small-group structure is explicitly designed to promote students' interacting with one another, in seeking, receiving, and giving help (Cooper, Marquis, & Ayers-Lopez, 1982; Webb, 1982).

According to Vygotskian theory, within the context of small-group activity—but not limited to this particular context—instruction tends to be most effective when it "makes thinking public." Group discussions, dialogues, and shared articulation of problems, frustrations, and fears allow teachers to diagnose students' processes of thinking and decision making and allow students to understand each other and become aware of alternative problem-solving strategies. Positive effects on learning and achievement come from peer and student–teacher interaction in which differing views or understandings arise and are reconciled (Bearison, 1982).

One specific tool for enhancing peer interaction and learning during small-group activity is *reciprocal questioning* (King, 1990). Using a generic set of question stems, students are trained to ask each other questions that elicit explanations and other high-level elaboration responses. Typical question stems are: "How does . . . affect . . .?" "Explain why . . .?" "How are . . . and . . . similar?" Students take turns in small groups asking and answering versions of such questions that are pertinent to the presented material. Students learn to interact—seeking and giving help. The question stems have been shown to affect the quality of questions asked and thereby the quality of responses given. With elaborated responses and explanations given, learning tends to be enhanced (Webb, 1982).

The idea of reciprocal questioning is based on previous attempts at fostering active prose comprehension (e.g., Palinscar & Brown, 1984). The important departure from the earlier work is twofold. First, generic question stems are chosen so as to elicit high-level elaborative responses such as giving a detailed description of how something is done, clarifying a concept, providing a rationale, generating examples, or relating new material to prior knowledge. This type of response is in contrast to low-level responses such as simply giving the answer or providing information without any explanation, rationale, or example. The second reason why King's (1990) strategy seems to be especially effective is the systematic way in which students take turns asking and answering questions of each other. There is an emphasis on joint activity and shared goal, in particular, a shared goal of task-involvement and intrinsic striving for mastery. Importantly, students' striving for mastery is on two embedded levels, involving both mastery of the questioning technique and mastery of the presented material.

Collaborative Teacher–Student Involvement

In whole-class activity, such as the presentation of a new lesson, students' attention generally is directed toward the teacher. In such a context, question asking is rare (Nelson-Le Gall & Glor-Scheib, 1985). This is most likely due to students' fear of being publicly embarrassed in the eyes of their classmates (Newman & Goldin, 1990).

One suggestion for alleviating students' fear of embarrassment and thereby facilitating question asking during whole-class activity involves collaborative activity between the teacher and students. Schoenfeld (1987) described three classroom techniques that emphasize collaborative involvement in the context of teaching college-level mathematical problem solving. The techniques are "ordered" according to the amount of intervention provided by the teacher; they illustrate a systematic approach to scaffolding, in particular, with regard to transferring gradually to students the responsibility of self-regulating their learning through questioning.

First, Schoenfeld (1987) showed students videotapes of other students working on problems. The videotapes were discussed and the problem-solving strategies were critiqued with an emphasis on how the videotaped students might better have planned and monitored their work, for example, through self-questioning. Second, the teacher acted as a role model in front of the class. For Schoenfeld, it was important that students and teacher together face dilemmas in problem solving and that students see the teacher struggling (e.g., with false starts, recoveries from "wild goose chases," insights, self-questions) right along with them at the blackboard. The teacher presented " 'problem resolutions' rather than problem solutions" (p. 200). Third, the teacher acted as a scribe, or orchestrator, as students jointly worked on a problem and publicly discussed their solutions. The teacher moderated the discussion—asking for suggestions and reasons for solutions, suggesting regular monitoring of progress (e.g., "We've been doing this for 5 minutes or so. Do things seem to be going pretty well? If so, we should continue. But if not, we might want to reconsider," p. 202), keeping track of students' options, and carrying out the students' decisions at the board. The students got to concentrate on thinking, suggesting, questioning, and making decisions.

These three techniques are meant to prepare students for sessions of problem solving in which the students help one another in small groups, with the teacher simply moving from group to group and giving advice when called for. The ultimate goal of this program of collaborative activity is self-regulated problem solving. Presumably such a program is effective because the teacher shares with students in the interactive experience of real-world mathematical problem solving:

> We talked about mathematics, explained it to each other, shared the false starts, enjoyed the interaction of personalities. In short, we became mathematical people. It was fun, but it was also natural and felt right. (Schoenfeld, 1987, p. 213)

Although Schoenfeld's work involved college students, it makes sense for younger students as well that if classroom activity were more purposeful, that is, more of an "ordinary" shared activity among people (Lave, 1988), it would be more common for students to engage in adaptive help seeking from their teacher and from one another.

Hiding just beneath these descriptions of collaborative teacher–student involvement is an expectation that the teacher take an affective role in students' learning. Personal relatedness, warmth, and caring are aspects of classroom climate consistently related to academic outcomes in general (Moos, 1979) and to children's stated intentions of seeking help from their teacher in particular (Newman & Schwager, 1993). Newman and Schwager suggested that although these basic, intersubjective factors are important at all grade levels in facilitating help seeking, it may be that for older students, teachers additionally need to demonstrate their caring with specific, task-related techniques or supports for questioning.

FUTURE RESEARCH ON HELP SEEKING

Children most in need of help in regulating their own learning are those with an already existing history of academic failure and accompanying low achievement motivation. For teachers and parents of the many children who are considered learned helpless, "at risk," or just disaffected and passive, it must be very difficult to think of resocializing the children regarding costs and benefits of help seeking.

Future research should target such children and address ways of changing self-system beliefs, attitudes, and feelings that interfere with self-regulated learning in general and adaptive help seeking in particular. Explicit instruction in help-seeking skills, such as regarding necessity, content, and target of questioning, should be attempted in conjunction with providing students personal rationales for their actions. I would like to see ideas such as King's (1990) reciprocal questioning and Schoenfeld's (1987) collaborative teacher–student involvement piloted and evaluated for children with "help-seeking special needs." Especially because of the prevalence of whole-class activity at the elementary and middle school levels, techniques for "making thinking public," such as videotaping, role modeling, and moderating of whole-class discussions, should be adapted and tested across different subject areas and with various student populations.

A final thought about research on help seeking has to do with methodology. Studies would profit from taking a developmental perspective, that is, by taking into account age differences in children's cognitive, metacognitive, and social skills that are ingredients of self-regulated learning, as well as by taking into account grade-level differences in classroom environments. Training studies on help-seeking skills and teaching techniques would additionally profit from taking a developmental perspective in the temporal sense of examining change, including measures of maintenance over time and generalization across tasks and subject areas.

CONCLUSIONS

Self-regulated learners have a variety of ways of effecting the learning process and learning outcomes. This chapter has focused on one specific way in which self-regulated learners can, and often do, exert control of features in the classroom environment to help them learn. The chapter has focused on motivational and affective factors that are related to whether or not students seek needed assistance in the classroom. Self-regulated learners do not simply possess a bag of tricks or techniques to help them learn. They more often than not do have requisite cognitive and behavioral skills to bear on academic problems, but more importantly, they also have the will and the wherewithal to deal with situations in which skills are absent. They possess and employ an executive processing system that allows them to improvise.

Academic goals that students bring to the learning situation as well as goals that are infused in the classroom influence the help-seeking process. Students who desire and value challenge and mastery of material rather than simply getting a good grade appear self-regulative in terms of how they go about seeking assistance. They ask for hints rather than answers. They are likely to try to confirm whether or not their work is right, presumably so they can use that feedback for future mastery attempts. They show evidence of not giving up after failure; they persevere and try to get back on track. Although there is no pertinent research evidence to date, I expect that the mastery-oriented or task-involved student is likely to make thoughtful decisions regarding the necessity, content, and target of his or her help-seeking requests.

Students have personal feelings about their capabilities and about school that they bring to the learning situation. These feelings are encoded in a system of attitudes and beliefs that has been formed over the years. Affective histories as well as dynamic, moment-to-moment feelings experienced as students interact with the teacher and classmates influence whether or not students feel comfortable asking questions in class. Little research evidence exists regarding the role of affect on self-regulated learning in general or help seeking in particular. Yet it is clear that feeling states contribute to the filtering or construction of our memories, thoughts, and actions. In the particular case of help seeking, important decisions—regarding whether to ask, what to ask, and whom to ask—are no doubt controlled to a large extent by affect.

The self-regulated learner, or strategic help seeker, has achieved a mature level of cognitive and social development. For the infant and young child, dependence on parent and then teacher is more often than not adaptive for learning and the fostering of long-term independence. With maturity comes the self-awareness and flexibility to choose between autonomy and assistance from a knowledgeable other. At times of difficulty, self-regulated learners persevere but do not perseverate. Once they have assessed the extent of their difficulty and compared it to their own sense of competency and efficacy, considered reasonable alternative strategies and the social costs and benefits of help seeking, and determined the best way to formulate a request and the best person to approach, then they act.

Although "other-regulation to self-regulation" is a general developmental trend, individual differences on both the level of the child and the level of the family unit account for whether or not particular children develop into self-regulated learners. Variations in the parent–child attachment relationship and parenting style, as well as variations in the teacher–child attachment relationship and teaching style, lead to different developmental trajectories for students.

REFERENCES

Ainsworth, M. D. S. (1991). Attachments and other affectional bonds across the life cycle. In C. M. Parkes, J. Stevenson-Hinde, & P. Marris (Eds.), *Attachment across the life cycle* (pp. 33–51). London: Tavistock/Routledge.

Azmitia, M. (1988). Peer interaction and problem solving: When are two heads better than one? *Child Development, 59,* 87–96.

Bandura, A. (1977). Self-efficacy: Toward a unifying theory of behavioral change. *Psychological Review, 84,* 191–215.

Bearison, D. J. (1982). New directions in studies of social interactions and cognitive growth. In F. C. Serafica (Ed.), *Social-cognitive development in context* (pp. 199–221). New York: Guilford.

Berliner, D. C. (1983). Developing conceptions of classroom environments: Some light on the T in classroom studies of ATI. *Educational Psychologist, 18,* 1–13.

Bus, A. G., & vanIJzendoorn, M. H. (1988). Mother–child interactions, attachment, and emergent literacy: A cross-sectional study. *Child Development, 59,* 1262–1272.

Clifford, M. M. (1991). Risk taking: Theoretical, empirical, and educational considerations. *Educational Psychologist, 26,* 263–297.

Cooper, C. R., Marquis, A., & Ayers-Lopez, S. (1982). Peer learning in the classroom: Tracing developmental patterns and consequences of children's spontaneous interactions. In L. C. Wilkinson (Ed.), *Communicating in the classroom* (pp. 69–84). New York: Academic Press.

Corno, L. (1986). The metacognitive control components of self-regulated learning. *Contemporary Educational Psychology, 11,* 333–346.

Diaz, R. M., Neal, C. J., & Amaya-Williams, M. (1990). The social origins of self-regulation. In L. C. Moll (Ed.), *Vygotsky and education: Instructional implications and applications of socio-historical psychology* (pp. 127–154). New York: Cambridge University Press.

Dillon, J. T. (1988). The remedial status of student questioning. *Journal of Curriculum Studies, 20,* 197–210.

Dweck, C. (1986). Motivational processes affecting learning. *American Psychologist, 41,* 1040–1048.

Eccles, J., & Wigfield, A. (1985). Teacher expectations and student motivation. In J. Dusek (Ed.), *Teacher expectancies* (pp. 185–226). Hillsdale, NJ: Lawrence Erlbaum Associates.

Good, T. L., Slavings, R. L., Harel, K. H., & Emerson, H. (1987). Student passivity: A study of question asking in K–12 classrooms. *Sociology of Education, 60,* 181–199.

Graesser, A. C., & McMahen, C. L. (1993). Anomalous information triggers questions when adults solve quantitative problems and comprehend stories. *Journal of Educational Psychology, 85,* 136–151.

Graham, S., & Barker, G. P. (1990). The down side of help: An attributional-developmental analysis of helping behavior as a low-ability cue. *Journal of Educational Psychology, 82,* 7–14.

Graham, S., & Golan, S. (1991). Motivational influences on cognition: Task involvement, ego involvement, and depth of information processing. *Journal of Educational Psychology, 83,* 187–194.

Harter, S. (1981). A new self-report scale of intrinsic versus extrinsic orientation in the classroom: Motivational and informational components. *Developmental Psychology, 17,* 300–312.

Hartup, W. W. (1963). Dependence and independence. In H. W. Stevenson (Ed.), *Child psychology: The sixty-second yearbook of the National Society for the Study of Education* (pp. 333–363). Chicago: University of Chicago Press.

Karabenick, S. A., & Knapp, J. R. (1991). Relationship of academic help seeking to the use of learning strategies and other instrumental achievement behavior in college students. *Journal of Educational Psychology, 83,* 221–230.

King, A. (1990). Enhancing peer interaction and learning in the classroom through reciprocal questioning. *American Educational Research Journal, 27,* 664–687.

Kuhl, J. (1985). Volitional mediators of cognition-behavior consistency: Self-regulatory processes and action versus state orientation. In J. Kuhl & J. Beckmann (Eds.), *Action control: From cognition to behavior* (pp. 101–128). West Berlin: Springer-Verlag.

Lave, J. (1988). *Cognition in practice.* Boston: Cambridge.

Luria, A. R. (1982). *Language and cognition.* New York: Wiley.

Markman, E. M. (1981). Comprehension monitoring. In W. P. Dickson (Ed.), *Children's oral communication skills* (pp. 61–84). New York: Academic Press.

McCombs, B. L. (1986). The role of the self-system in self-regulated learning. *Contemporary Educational Psychology, 11,* 314–332.

Moos, R. H. (1979). *Evaluating educational environments.* San Francisco: Jossey-Bass.

Morine-Dershimer, G. (1985). *Talking, listening, and learning in elementary classrooms.* New York: Longman.

Nelson-Le Gall, S. (1985). Help-seeking behavior in learning. In W. Gordon (Ed.), *Review of research in education* (Vol. 12, pp. 55–90). Washington, DC: American Educational Research Association.

Nelson-Le Gall, S., & Glor-Scheib, S. (1985). Help seeking in elementary classrooms: An observational study. *Contemporary Educational Psychology, 10,* 58–71.

Nelson-Le Gall, S., & Jones, E. (1990). Cognitive-motivational influences on the task-related help-seeking behavior of Black children. *Child Development, 61,* 581–589.

Newman, R. S. (1990). Children's help-seeking in the classroom: The role of motivational factors and attitudes. *Journal of Educational Psychology, 82,* 71–80.

Newman, R. S. (1991). Goals and self-regulated learning: What motivates children to seek academic help? In M. L. Maehr & P. R. Pintrich (Eds.), *Advances in motivation and achievement: Goals and self-regulatory processes* (pp. 151–183). Greenwich, CT: JAI Press.

Newman, R. S., & Goldin, L. (1990). Children's reluctance to seek help with schoolwork. *Journal of Educational Psychology, 82,* 92–100.

Newman, R. S., & Schwager, M. T. (1991). *Children's help seeking during mathematical problem solving.* Paper presented at the Biennial Meeting of the Society for Research in Child Development, Seattle.

Newman, R. S., & Schwager, M. T. (1992). Student perceptions and academic help-seeking. In D. H. Schunk & J. L. Meece (Eds.), *Student perceptions in the classroom* (pp. 123–146). Hillsdale, NJ: Lawrence Erlbaum Associates.

Newman, R. S., & Schwager, M. T. (1993). Student perceptions of the teacher and classmates in relation to reported help seeking in math class. *Elementary School Journal, 94,* 3–17.

Nicholls, J. G. (1979). Quality and equality in intellectual development: The role of motivation in education. *American Psychologist, 34,* 1071–1084.

Nicholls, J. G., Patashnick, M., & Nolen, S. B. (1985). Adolescents' theories of education. *Journal of Educational Psychology, 77,* 683–692.

Palinscar, A., & Brown, A. L. (1984). Reciprocal teaching of comprehension-fostering and comprehension-monitoring activities. *Cognition and Instruction, 1,* 117–175.

Paris, S. G., Lipson, M. Y., Wixson, K. K. (1983). Becoming a strategic reader. *Contemporary Educational Psychology, 8,* 293–316.

Paris, S. G., Newman, R. S., & Jacobs, J. E. (1985). Social contexts and functions of children's remembering. In M. Pressley & C. J. Brainerd (Eds.), *Cognitive learning and memory in children* (pp. 81–115). New York: Springer-Verlag.

Rogoff, B., & Gardner, W. P. (1984). Adult guidance of cognitive development. In B. Rogoff & J. Lave (Eds.), *Everyday cognition: Its development in social context* (pp. 95–116). Cambridge, MA: Harvard University Press.

Rohwer, W. D., & Thomas, J. W. (1989). The role of autonomous problem-solving activities in learning to program. *Journal of Educational Psychology, 81,* 584–593.

Rosen, S. (1983). Perceived inadequacy and help-seeking. In B. DePaulo, A. Nadler, & J. Fisher (Eds.), *New directions in helping* (Vol. 2, pp. 73–107). New York: Academic Press.

Salomon, G., Globerson, T., & Guterman, E. (1989). The computer as a zone of proximal development: Internalizing reading-related metacognitions from a reading partner. *Journal of Educational Psychology, 81,* 620–627.

Schoenfeld, A. H. (1987). What's all the fuss about metacognition? In A. H. Schoenfeld (Ed.), *Cognitive science and mathematics education* (pp. 189–215). Hillsdale, NJ: Lawrence Erlbaum Associates.

Schunk, D. H. (1989). Self-efficacy and cognitive skill learning. In C. Ames & R. Ames (Eds.), *Research on motivation in education* (Vol. 3, pp. 13–44). New York: Academic Press.

Shapiro, E. G. (1983). Embarrassment and help-seeking. In B. DePaulo, A. Nadler, & J. Fisher (Eds.), *New directions in helping* (Vol. 2, pp. 143–163). New York: Academic Press.

Skinner, E. A., Chapman, M., & Baltes, P. B. (1988). Control, means-ends, and agency beliefs: A new conceptualization and its measurement during childhood. *Journal of Personality and Social Psychology, 54,* 117–133.

Stern, D. N. (1985). *The interpersonal world of the infant: A view from psychoanalysis and developmental psychology.* New York: Basic Books.

van der Meij, H. (1988). Constraints on question asking in classrooms. *Journal of Educational Psychology, 80,* 401–405.

Vygotsky, L. S. (1978). *Mind in society: The development of higher psychological processes* (M. Cole, V. John-Steiner, S. Scribner, & E. Souberman, Eds.). Cambridge, MA: Harvard University Press.

Webb, N. M. (1982). Student interaction and learning in small groups. *Review of Educational Research, 52,* 421–445.

Wentzel, K. R. (1989). Adolescent classroom goals, standards for performance, and academic achievement: An interactionist perspective. *Journal of Educational Psychology, 81,* 131–142.

Wertsch, J. V. (1985). *Vygotsky and the social formation of mind.* Cambridge, MA: Harvard University Press.

Zimmerman, B. J., & Martinez-Pons, M. (1986). Development of a structured interview for assessing student use of self-regulated learning strategies. *American Educational Research Journal, 23,* 614–628.

VI

Conclusion

13

Self-Regulation in Education: Retrospect and Prospect

Dale H. Schunk
Purdue University

Barry J. Zimmerman
City University of New York

It is abundantly evident from these accounts that researchers have begun to look at highly varied forms of student self-regulation in a wide range of educational settings. Although the contributors to this volume diverge in many ways, including theoretical perspective, research focus, and methodology, they share an interest in a core set of issues that Zimmerman (this volume) identifies in a conceptual framework. In this concluding chapter we comment on areas of strength in the field of academic self-regulation and suggest places where further research is needed. As part of this discussion we raise questions about student self-regulation that should be addressed in the future.

SELF-REGULATION RESEARCH: THE PRESENT

Types of Research

In the introductory chapter, Zimmerman notes that research on academic self-regulation generally has reflected two objectives: (a) describing characteristics of students who are highly self-regulated (descriptive studies), and (b) teaching students self-regulatory processes and strategies (intervention studies). To accomplish these divergent objectives, researchers typically have employed different research methodologies.

In descriptive studies researchers identify self-regulated learners and study their attributes. Investigators often compare and contrast these learners' attributes with those of students displaying less self-regulation. A variety of student characteristics may be assessed and correlational findings reported. Zimmerman recaps some of the central attributes of self-regulated learners; we do not reiterate these here. Several examples of descriptive research are found in the chapters in this volume: the Meece, Blumenfeld, and Hoyle (1988) study investigating individual differences in and correlations among students' achievement goals, intrinsic motivation, perceptions of ability, and attitudes toward science (Meece, this volume); the Wibrowski (1992) study exploring the relation of time accounting and budgeting to other study activities (Zimmerman, Greenberg, & Weinstein, this volume); the research by Pintrich and Garcia (1991) on the relations among students' goal orientations, motivational beliefs, and self-regulatory strategy use (Garcia & Pintrich, this volume); the McCaslin and Murdock (1991) study that examines home and school factors underlying learning characterized by internalized goals, motivation, and perceived competence (Corno, this volume); and the Wigfield (1992) study exploring how students' ability beliefs and values predict their mathematics achievement and course enrollment (Wigfield, this volume).

This research approach is analogous to the *novice–expert* methodology used to study cognitive learning (Bruner, 1985). Novice–expert researchers believe that to understand learning within a particular domain, one identifies the skill (e.g., solving mathematical word problems, comprehending text), finds one or more experts who perform the skill well, studies these experts, and compares their actions with those of novices who have minimal competence in the domain. Ultimately, the goal is to move the novices toward the expert level as effectively as possible, but the central research thrust of this approach has been on identifying expert–novice differences.

Researchers conducting intervention studies typically select one or more self-regulatory processes from among those portrayed in Table 1.1 (p. 8), alter them systematically, and study their impact on students' learning and performance. Typically, researchers have taught students learning strategies, provided them with various types of goals, delivered attributional and progress feedback, and allowed them to exert control over their own learning.

Examples of interventions found in the present chapters include the Reid and Borkowski (1987) study exploring the effects of strategy information, self-control processes, and attribution training (Borkowski & Thorpe, this volume); the Schunk and Swartz (1993a, 1993b) studies looking at the role of learning process goals and progress feedback (Schunk, this volume); the Weinstein, Stone, and Hanson (1993) project addressing time management strategies (Zimmerman, Greenberg, & Weinstein, this volume); the Strategies for Achieving Independent

Learning (SAIL) instructional studies involving modeling of text comprehension strategies (Brown & Pressley, this volume); the Trawick (1991)
study investigating strategies for handling distractions (Corno, this
volume); the self-regulated strategy development (SRSD) experiments
assessing the development of writing and self-regulation strategies
(Graham & Harris, this volume); the Henderson and Landesman (1993)
study on the role of student control during interactive videodisk
instruction (Henderson & Cunningham, this volume); and the Newman
and Schwager (1991) experiment examining the effects of motivational
goals on students' questioning strategies (Newman, this volume). We
know from this and other intervention research that self-regulatory
processes can be enhanced and that these processes affect motivation,
learning, and performance. Of particular concern to self-regulation
researchers has been the need to show that these changes are sustained
over time and generalize across settings and tasks.

Major Contributions

The chapters in this volume highlight several important, and in some
cases unusual, findings that we believe help advance our understanding
of the operation of academic self-regulation. For one, a focus by learners
on *strategic processes* is a critical component of self-regulation. A wealth
of research summarized in these chapters attests to the value of such
processes as self-regulated strategy use, goal setting, and help seeking.
These processes significantly raise achievement and motivation compared
with the effects of traditional factors involving instruction and time spent
learning.

Related to this point is the notion that students' *goal orientations* play
a major role in self-regulation. Students who hold a mastery goal
orientation aimed at learning and skill acquisition display more adaptive
learning strategies, higher intrinsic motivation, and a stronger sense of
perceived efficacy for learning, compared with students whose primary
goals involve such other concerns as ego involvement (appearing
competent) and work avoidance. These findings suggest the need to
examine contextual factors of educational settings to determine how they
may be altered to raise students' mastery orientations.

Third, the research strongly supports the theoretical point that
self-evaluation is a critical component of self-regulation. As students
monitor their task performance, effective self-regulation depends on their
evaluating their goal progress. Judgments of acceptable progress result
in continuation of their task approach; self-evaluations of unacceptable
progress may lead them to alter their strategy to one that they believe
has a better likelihood of resulting in goal attainment. These self-evalu-

ative activities also strengthen students' self-efficacy for learning and motivation for goal attainment.

A fourth point is that there is a need for *multiple experiences in live social settings* for self-regulatory processes to be acquired and internalized. Multiple experiences can be provided in various ways—for example, through repeated exposures to models, working repeatedly with interactive computer systems, training in generating self-regulatory self-instructions, and goal setting over sessions. When students receive only brief training in self-regulation they may not internalize the processes and may fail to maintain or generalize their use once training is completed.

Related to this point is the notion that *self-regulation may be acquired in stages*. Self-regulatory processes are not acquired overnight but rather become refined through repeated instruction and practice. This idea is analogous to the notion from cognitive psychology that the acquisition of procedural skills proceeds through the stages of knowledge acquisition, procedural representation, and skill refinement (Anderson, 1990).

Finally, we believe the research highlights the *importance of goal setting* in self-regulation and its dependence on such key processes as self-efficacy, achievement values, and self-schemas. Self-regulated learners set goals and control their thoughts and behaviors to accomplish them. Goals are consistent with their achievement values and self-schemas. Selection of a goal enhances efficacy for goal attainment, and the perception of goal progress maintains high efficacy. This dynamic interaction of goals with other self-regulatory processes is a central feature of self-regulation and one that needs to be considered in the design of instructional interventions.

SELF-REGULATION RESEARCH: THE FUTURE

Although we have learned much about self-regulated learners, the field of academic self-regulation is new and there is much to be done. In this section we present our suggestions for future directions, which we believe will advance our understanding of self-regulated learners and the operation of self-regulatory processes.

Distinctiveness of Self-Regulation

One suggestion for researchers is to be clear about what self-regulation is and how it differs from other phenomena. As in most emerging fields, the distinctions among constructs are not always clear. Zimmerman (this volume) contends that self-regulation must have a clear operational meaning for it to be a useful construct. In the literature there are examples of research studies that purport to study self-regulation but seem strikingly similar to traditional learning research. At a minimum, researchers need to clearly define self-regulation and indicate how it is distinct from such other phenomena as motivation, volition, and intrinsic interest.

We make this recommendation knowing that self-regulation is related to many other phenomena. For example, consider *self-regulation* (the process whereby students activate and sustain cognitions, behaviors, and affects, which are systematically oriented toward attainment of their goals) (Zimmerman, 1989), and *motivation* (the process whereby goal-directed activities are instigated and sustained) (Schunk, 1991). These two constructs are reciprocally related. Students motivated to attain such a goal as making an A on a term paper or saving a wilderness area are apt to engage in self-regulatory activities that they believe will help them reach that goal (e.g., write an outline of the paper, seek more information about the area). In turn, self-regulation promotes learning, and the perception of greater competence sustains motivation and self-regulation to attain new goals. Our point is that researchers need to be sensitive to distinctions among constructs as well as their interdependence and that the field will benefit from greater conceptual clarity.

Intervention Research

Although we see the need for continuing descriptive research, we believe the more urgent need is to systematically explore the development of self-regulatory processes. As noted by Zimmerman (this volume), at present our understanding of self-regulation as an explanatory mechanism is far exceeded by our ability to describe self-regulated learners.

We recommend increased intervention research with students in actual learning settings. In much self-regulation research students complete questionnaires and judge whether and how often they engage in self-regulatory activities. These findings are informative and contribute to our understanding of self-regulated learners, but we need more information on how well students' perceptions translate into actual activities. An important issue is the extent to which students who report that they use particular self-regulatory processes actually engage in them during learning. In this regard, three-phase research designs comprising pretest, training, and self-regulative performance seem useful.

This recommendation may require changes in research designs and increased collaboration with teachers. In most classrooms there typically is little opportunity for self-regulation: Students are told what to do, how to do it, and when and where to accomplish it. Self-regulation cannot be studied when students have no choices in any of the five areas discussed by Zimmerman (see Table 1.1, p. 8). By collaborating with teachers, investigators can use instructional materials that prepare students to make choices and allow them choices in such areas as methods, time, and resources. Naturalistic studies involving only one or a few students with significant self-regulatory problems seem appropriate, in which changes in performance are assessed over time, along with continued use of self-regulatory activities after training is discontinued.

Longitudinal Studies

Another recommendation is for greater emphasis on longitudinal studies. Most self-regulation research is of short duration. Studies that assess maintenance and generalization (Graham & Harris, this volume; Schunk & Swartz, 1993a) typically do so over a few weeks rather than several months. Long-term studies are needed to chart the course of development of self-regulatory skills. For example, simply teaching students strategies does not guarantee that students will continue to use them. Strategy use depends on students' understanding of how to use the strategy in personal contexts and believing that strategy use will raise their performance in those settings (Borkowski, 1985; Pressley et al., 1990). Maintenance and generalization of self-regulatory gains brought about by short-term interventions may require periodic refresher instruction and practice (Brown & Pressley, this volume).

Long-term effects may be especially dependent on effective time management, which requires that individuals break distant goals into a series of subgoals, set deadlines for subgoal attainment, and make decisions about how to effectively attain subgoals (Zimmerman, Greenberg, & Weinstein, this volume). Projects that take several weeks to complete offer fertile ground for studying self-regulation of time. Such projects also allow for studying developmental changes in young learners, whose capacities for rehearsing and organizing information and cognitively representing long-term goals can easily change over the course of a few months.

Interaction of Self-Regulatory Processes

In most intervention studies, researchers select one or a few processes for study and attempt to hold others constant. Thus, researchers have studied such processes as students' goals, self-efficacy, attributions, strategy use, and help seeking. A focus on a few processes is important for purposes of experimental control and explaining how changes in self-regulatory behaviors relate to experimental variables, but it does not fully capture the dynamic nature of self-regulation and the interaction among processes.

For example, consider a student (Amy) who desires to learn to speak French because she is planning a trip to France. It is possible for her to regulate her activities in all areas discussed by Zimmerman (this volume). With respect to *motives*, she sets a goal of learning conversational French and believes that she can attain her goal (self-efficacy) by expending effort and proper studying (attributions). For *methods* she chooses to sign up for a night course and plans to study in her free time at home. She schedules her time so she can attend the class and study, and with her trip six months away she figures she has sufficient time to learn. She sets her own *performance outcome* (basic conversational skill). She uses *environmental resources* (night course, tapes) and social resources (studies with a friend) effectively. During the course she implements what she believes are effective study strategies, and her perceptions of increasing competence help maintain her sense of efficacy and substantiate her attributions. When she masters her initial goal she may set a new one and follow up the course work with self-study.

Although few students may employ all of these self-regulatory processes, we recommend increased research emphasis on exploring their dynamic interplay. Long-term studies may offer an ideal vehicle for studying such interaction, and researchers may need to move out of the classroom and explore self-directed learning at work and home. Some sacrifice of experimental control will occur, but this type of research will provide valuable insights into highly personal forms of self-regulation.

Individual Differences

There is much research documenting between-group differences. For example, Zimmerman and Martinez-Pons (1990) found differences in self-regulatory strategies due to gender, grade, and ability level; however, within each subcategory (e.g., male/female, gifted/average) there was considerable variability. This correlational study could not determine the influences on this variation, although the authors suggested that self-efficacy may be partly responsible. What is needed is more research exploring individual differences in covert processes to determine why students with similar attributes and experiences diverge in self-regulation.

In addition to self-efficacy, there are other processes that may help explain student differences within homogeneous groups. With respect to strategy use, students may differ in their knowledge of strategies, beliefs about strategy usefulness, understanding about the range of tasks to which strategies can be applied, attributions for successful strategy use, and beliefs about what factors potentially limit their effective use of strategies (e.g., time available). To address this issue, investigators may need to interview students and ask them to describe how they accomplish tasks. As they actually work on tasks, students can verbalize aloud what they are doing and why they are doing it (e.g., what strategy they are using and why).

There also are likely to be individual differences in how self-regulation is affected by situational influences. Students are likely to differ in their sensitivity to situational cues. For example, some students may employ the same learning strategies in most situations, whereas others judge the appropriateness of strategies for the situation before applying them. Assuming that students are equally knowledgeable of strategies, we might ask what cues influence the judgments of students who are more selective. A related concern is how self-regulatory skills interact with social influences. Newman (this volume) points out that help seeking has a social cost because many students believe that learners who seek help are not very intelligent. Yet even in situations where help seeking is stigmatized, some students do it unabashedly. Do such qualities of students as perceived value of learning, self-efficacy, and perceived control over learning help overcome social sanctions? We urge increased research addressing the interaction of personal and situational factors in the future.

Integrated Theory

The field of self-regulation has attracted scholars with diverse theoretical views (Zimmerman, this volume). As a consequence there are self-regu-latory principles based on metacognitive, constructivist, social cognitive, phenomenological, attribution, Vygotskian, operant, and volitional theo-ries. To date there has been little theoretical integration. Even when theorists hypothesize that constructs from different theories are related, they often do not clearly specify the nature of the relationship.

We are not calling for the development of an omnibus, integrated theory of self-regulation; such global theorizing brings its own set of problems (Weiner, 1990). Rather, we recommend that investigators pay greater attention to constructs from other theories and to the distinctive-ness of their ideas. Tests for discriminant and convergent validity of constructs are needed. Investigators also would do well to test integrated models in different contexts to determine their usefulness for explaining self-regulatory activities.

CONCLUSION

The field of academic self-regulation stands at a critical point. We have a solid theoretical base and empirical literature, an increasing number of researchers, and high interest among school practitioners in fostering self-regulation among students. We are excited about the promise of more research and greater applicability of principles to educational settings. Our hope is that this volume will be a source of ideas to guide and help encourage study of this important topic.

REFERENCES

Anderson, J. R. (1990). *Cognitive psychology and its implications* (3rd ed.). New York: W. H. Freeman.

Borkowski, J. G. (1985). Signs of intelligence: Strategy generalization and metacognition. In S. Yussen (Ed.), *The growth of reflection in children* (pp. 105–144). New York: Academic Press.

Bruner, J. (1985). Models of the learner. *Educational Researcher, 14*(6), 5–8.

Henderson, R. W., & Landesman, E. M. (1993). The interactive videodisc system in the zone of proximal development: Academic motivation and learning outcomes in precalculus. *Journal of Educational Computing Research, 9*(1), 29–43.

McCaslin, M. M., & Murdock, T. B. (1991). The emergent interaction of home and school in the development of students' adaptive learning. In M. L. Maehr & P. R. Pintrich (Eds.), *Advances in motivation and achievement* (Vol. 7, pp. 213–259). Greenwich, CT: JAI Press.

Meece, J. L., Blumenfeld, P. C., & Hoyle, R. (1988). Students' goal orientations and cognitive engagement in classroom activities. *Journal of Educational Psychology, 80*, 514–523.

Newman, R. S., & Schwager, M. T. (1991, April). *Children's help seeking during mathematical problem solving.* Paper presented at the biennial meeting of the Society for Research in Child Development, Seattle.

Pintrich, P. R., & Garcia, T. (1991). Student goal orientation and self-regulation in the college classroom. In M. L. Maehr & P. R. Pintrich (Eds.), *Advances in motivation and achievement* (Vol. 7, pp. 371–402). Greenwich, CT: JAI Press.

Pressley, M., Woloshyn, V., Lysynchuk, L. M., Martin, V., Wood, E., & Willoughby, T. (1990). A primer of research on cognitive strategy instruction: The important issues and how to address them. *Educational Psychology Review, 2*, 1–58.

Reid, M. K., & Borkowski, J. G. (1987). Causal attributions of hyperactive children: Implications for training strategies and self-control. *Journal of Educational Psychology, 79*, 296–307.

Schunk, D. H. (1991). *Learning theories: An educational perspective.* New York: Merrill.

Schunk, D. H., & Swartz, C. W. (1993a). Goals and progress feedback: Effects on self-efficacy and writing achievement. *Contemporary Educational Psychology, 18*, 337–354.

Schunk, D. H., & Swartz, C. W. (1993b). Writing strategy instruction with gifted students: Effects of goals and feedback on self-efficacy and skills. *Roeper Review, 15*, 225–230.

Trawick, L. (1991). *Volitional strategy training in students with a history of academic failure. Dissertation Abstracts International, 52*, 1645A. (University Microfilms No. 91–27, 987)

Weiner, B. (1990). History of motivational research in education. *Journal of Educational Psychology, 82,* 616–622.

Weinstein, C. E., Stone, G., & Hanson, G. H. (1993). *The long-term effects of a strategic learning course for college students.* Unpublished manuscript, University of Texas, Austin.

Wibrowski, C. R. (1992). *Self-regulated learning processes among inner city students.* Unpublished doctoral dissertation, Graduate School, City University of New York.

Wigfield, A. (1992, March). *Long-term predictors of adolescents' performance and choice in high school mathematics.* Paper presented at the biennial meeting of the Society for Research on Adolescence, Washington, DC.

Zimmerman, B. J. (1989). A social cognitive view of self-regulated academic learning. *Journal of Educational Psychology, 81,* 329–339.

Zimmerman, B. J., & Martinez-Pons, M. (1990). Student differences in self-regulated learning: Relating grade, sex, and giftedness to self-efficacy and strategy use. *Journal of Educational Psychology, 82,* 51–59.

Author Index

Subject Index

V

Value, 13, 16–17
  attainment, 106
  beliefs, 132–133
  interest, 107, 109, 113
  utility, 107, 109
Videodisc instruction, 268
Volition, 6, 15, 18, 113–114
  antecedents of, 239
  in classrooms, 232
  and counseling, 246–247
  in the curriculum, 244
  definition, 231
  educational research on, 233–235
  and enhancement teaching, 244–246
  history, 230–231
  in homework, 242–243
  and interventions, 240–241
  and processes, 237
  and strategies, 234
  student, 230
  and styles, 235–236
  versus motivation, 230, 236, 238

W

Writing, 156
  goals, 204, 207
  learning environment, 222–224
  models, 217, 223
  novice writers, 207
  peer revising, 214
  planning, 203–204, 217
  productivity, 209
  revising, 203–204, 212–215

Z

Zone of proximal development, 257–260,
    267–268, 271

DATE DUE